HANDBOOK OF MANAGEMENT AND CREATIVITY

To Caithi, Oisín, Kate, Laurie and Rob – for the future

Handbook of Management and Creativity

Edited by

Chris Bilton

Director of the Centre for Cultural Policy Studies, University of Warwick, UK

Stephen Cummings

Professor of Strategic Management, Victoria University of Wellington, New Zealand

Edward Elgar
Cheltenham, UK • Northampton, MA, USA

© Chris Bilton and Stephen Cummings 2014

All rights reserved. No part of this publication may be reproduced, stored in a retrieval system or transmitted in any form or by any means, electronic, mechanical or photocopying, recording, or otherwise without the prior permission of the publisher.

Published by
Edward Elgar Publishing Limited
The Lypiatts
15 Lansdown Road
Cheltenham
Glos GL50 2JA
UK

Edward Elgar Publishing, Inc.
William Pratt House
9 Dewey Court
Northampton
Massachusetts 01060
USA

A catalogue record for this book
is available from the British Library

Library of Congress Control Number: 2013944949

This book is available electronically in the ElgarOnline.com
Business Subject Collection, E-ISBN 978 1 78100 097 7

MIX
Paper from
responsible sources
FSC   FSC® C013056
www.fsc.org

ISBN 978 1 78100 089 2 (cased)

Typeset by Servis Filmsetting Ltd, Stockport, Cheshire
Printed and bound in Great Britain by T.J. International Ltd, Padstow

Contents

PART V AROUND THE CREATIVE CYCLE

Contributors

Nic Beech is Dean of the Faculty of Arts at the University of St Andrews, UK and Deputy Chair of the British Academy of Management. His research interests are in management practice, change and the construction of identity. His research has focused on analysis of practice and identity in the music industry, film, health and finance. The most recent of his five books is *Managing Change* (Cambridge University Press, with R. MacIntosh, 2012).

Chris Bilton is Director of the Centre for Cultural Policy Studies at University of Warwick, UK. Previous publications include *Management and Creativity: From creative industries to creative management* (Blackwell 2006) and *Creativity and Cultural Policy* (Routledge 2012). Together with Stephen Cummings he wrote *Creative Strategy: Reconnecting business and innovation* (Wiley 2010).

Ruth Bridgstock is Research Fellow in the Creative Workforce Program of the Australian Research Council Centre of Excellence in Creative Industries and Innovation at Queensland University of Technology in Australia. She researches creative career development and entrepreneurship, the pathways from creative education to work and professional learning in the creative sectors. She is co-editor (with Greg Hearn) of *Creative Work beyond the Creative Industries: Innovation, education and employment* (forthcoming; Edward Elgar).

Stephen Cummings is Professor of Management at Victoria Business School, New Zealand. He has published articles on strategy, innovation and the history of management and his books include *Recreating Strategy* (Sage 2002), *Images of Strategy* (Blackwell 2003), *Strategy Pathfinder* (Wiley 2011), and the forthcoming *Strategy Builder* (Wiley 2014). Together with Chris Bilton he wrote *Creative Strategy: Reconnecting business and innovation* (Wiley 2010).

Doris Ruth Eikhof is Lecturer in Work and Organisation Studies at Stirling Management School, University of Stirling, UK. She researches creative work and enterprise, women's work and work–life boundaries, most recently for the Digital R&D Fund for the Arts and Culture in Scotland (Nesta, AHRC and Creative Scotland). She is co-editor of *Creating Balance? International perspectives on the work-life integration of* *professionals* (Springer 2011) and *Work Less, Live More? Critical analyses of the work-life relationship* (Palgrave 2008).

David Grant is Co-Dean and Professor of Organisational Studies at the University of Sydney Business School, Australia. His current research and teaching interests focus on the application of discourse theory and analysis to organisational change and leadership. He has published in a wide range of peer-reviewed journals including *Academy of Management Review, Human Relations, British Journal of Management, Journal of Management Studies* and *Organization Studies* and is co-editor of the *Sage Handbook of Organizational Discourse* (2004).

Gail Greig is Lecturer in Management at the University of St Andrews, UK. Her research concerns collective learning and knowing in relational practices in arts, cultural and healthcare organisations, most recently with Nic Beech for the Digital R&D Fund for the Arts and Culture in Scotland (NESTA/AHRC). Recent publications include papers in *Social Science and Medicine* and *Management Learning* (with Nic Beech) and a book chapter on improvisational practice (with Holly Patrick) in *The Handbook of Institutional Approaches to International Business* (Edward Elgar 2012).

Elizabeth Gulledge is a Research Fellow in Management at the University of St Andrews, UK. Her research areas are the cultural and creative industries, with particular interest in the nature, operation and maintenance of institutional fields, the role of symbolic, social and cultural capital in the economy for symbolic goods and organising practices and their role in creative outcomes. Her current research investigates these issues in book publishing, film and music.

Richard Hall is Associate Dean, Management Education, and Professor of Work and Organisational Studies at the University of Sydney Business School, Australia. He researches and teaches in the fields of leadership, organisational change and technology. He has published in a variety of international journals and is co-author of *New Technology at Work* (Routledge) and co-editor of a forthcoming major work on leadership development and practice for Sage. He is co-director of the Leadership Practice and Performance Systems Research Network at the University of Sydney.

Greg Hearn is a Research Professor in the Creative Industries Faculty at Queensland University of Technology, Australia. His work focuses on policy development and R&D for new technologies and services in the creative industries. He has authored or co-authored over 20 major research reports and books, including *The Knowledge Economy Handbook* (Edward

Elgar 2005 and 2012); (2013 in press); *Eat Cook Grow: Mixing human-computer interactions with human-food interactions* (Cambridge, MA: MIT Press 2013, in press); and *Creative Work Beyond the Creative Industries: Innovation, education and employment* (forthcoming; Edward Elgar).

Loizos Heracleous is Professor of Strategy and Organisation at Warwick Business School, UK. He earned his PhD from the University of Cambridge. He has published over 60 papers and 6 books on issues related to organisation change and development and organisational discourse. His work has been honoured by three awards from the US Academy of Management and his papers have been published in leading journals, including the *Academy of Management Journal, Academy of Management Review, Strategic Management Journal* and *Harvard Business Review*.

Vikki Heywood CBE has been a leading British arts administrator for over two decades. As CEO of the Royal Court Theatre and Executive Director of the Royal Shakespeare Company, she oversaw the award-winning redevelopment of their theatre complexes. She has been executive producer for over 300 productions including masterminding the multi-million pound *Matilda the Musical* to the West End and Broadway. Now Chairman of the Royal Society of the Arts, she is an expert on leadership and change management.

Claus D. Jacobs is Professor of Strategic Management and Organization Theory at Berne School of Management, Berne University of Applied Sciences, and Adjunct Faculty at University of St. Gallen, Switzerland. His recent research focuses on strategy work in pluralistic settings as well as on identity and legitimacy challenges in social entrepreneurial ventures. He recently published – together with Loizos Heracleous – *Crafting Strategy – Embodied Metaphors in Practice* (Cambridge University Press).

Lucy Küng is a professor, author, speaker and adviser specialising in strategy, innovation and leadership in the media, creative Professor of Strategic Management and Organization Theory at Berne School of Management, Berne University of Applied Sciences, and Adjunct Faculty at University of St. Gallen, Switzerland; of Journalism, at the University of Oxford, UK; Professor of Media Management and Economics at the Media Management and Transformation Centre at the University of Jönköping, Sweden; Executive Board Member of SRG SSR; and author of a prize-winning book on strategy in the media industry. She has worked with the BBC exploring the success of their online and digital television services, is Senior Research Fellow at Ashridge Business School, UK and adjunct faculty member at the University of St Gallen (where she received her PhD and Habilitation). From 2008–10 she was President of the European Media Management Association.

Lorraine Lim is Lecturer in Arts Management at Birkbeck College, University of London. Her research interests focus on cultural strategies utilised by cities in Asia to transform themselves into capitals of culture. She has edited a special issue for the *International Journal of Cultural Policy* on cultural policy in Asia and is currently co-editing a book on the creative industries in East Asia (for Palgrave Macmillan).

Margaret Maile Petty is Head of the School of Design at Victoria University of Wellington, New Zealand. Her research investigates the discourse, production and reception of modern design. After completing her doctoral studies in design history and material culture at the Bard Graduate Center in New York City, Margaret lectured at Pratt Institute and Parsons, the New School for Design in New York City. Recently Margaret has assisted in the development and implementation of the Master of Design Innovation (MDI) and the Design Research Innovation Lab (DRIL) at VUW's School of Design.

Kate Oakley is Professor of Cultural Policy and Director of Research at the Institute of Communications Studies, University of Leeds, UK, a Visiting Professor at the University of the Arts in London, and has worked for many years as an independent policy analyst and writer. Her research interests are in the politics of cultural policy, cultural labour and inequality in cultural production and her articles have appeared in journals such as the *International Journal of Cultural Policy* and *Cultural Trends*.

David Oliver is Associate Professor of Management at HEC Montreal, Canada. He formerly worked as a Research Associate at the Swiss-based Imagination Lab, where he explored the impact of serious play on creativity with a variety of corporate and non-profit entities. His current research focuses on organisational identity, the practice of strategy and stakeholder engagement, and his research has appeared in journals such as *Organization Studies*, *British Journal of Management*, *Human Relations* and the *Journal of Business Ethics*.

Shinji Oyama is Lecturer of Japanese Creative Industries in the Department of Film, Media and Culture Studies at Birkbeck College, University of London, UK. He has published articles on brand and promotional culture, cultural software, media globalisation and Japanese creative industries. He is a former account planner at BBDO, a global advertising agency, in its Tokyo office and was involved in a couple of Internet start-ups in New York and Tokyo.

Sarah Proctor-Thomson is a Lecturer in the School of Management at Victoria University of Wellington, New Zealand. Her research sits at the intersection of work and organisation studies, critical management studies, and feminist theory and aims to understand inequalities at work. Her current research focus is on theorising different forms of 'LoveWork' (or work in which love and passion are said to characterise workers' participation) in diverse domains including the creative industries, science and academia, and community and social services areas.

Giovanni Schiuma is Director of the Innovation Insights Hub at the University of the Arts London, UK and Professor at Università della Basilicata, Italy. Giovanni serves as Chief Editor of the *Journal of Knowledge Management Research and Practice*, and as Co-editor in Chief of the journal *Measuring Business Excellence*. He has published a range of articles on knowledge management, strategic performance management and innovation and his books include *The Value of Arts for Business* (Cambridge University Press 2011) and *Managing Knowledge Assets and Business Value Creation in Organisations* (IGI 2011).

Flemming Sørensen is Associate Professor of Management and Innovation, Department of Communication, Business and Information Technologies, Roskilde University, Denmark. He has published articles on innovation in tourism, services and the experience economy. Recently, together with Jon Sundbo, he has edited the *Handbook on the Experience Economy* (Edward Elgar 2013).

Chris Steyaert is Professor for Organisational Psychology at the University of St Gallen, Switzerland. He has published in international journals and books in the area of organisational theory and entrepreneurship. His current interests concern creativity, multiplicity (diversity) and reflexivity in organising change, intervention and entrepreneurship. His latest books are *The Politics and Aesthetics of Entrepreneurship* (2009, edited with Dr Daniel Hjorth and published by Edward Elgar) and *Relational Practices, Participative Organizing* (Emerald 2010, edited with Dr Bart Van Looy).

Jon Sundbo is Professor of Innovation and Business Administration, Department of Communication, Business and Information Technologies, Roskilde University, Denmark. He has published articles and books on innovation, service and the experience economy. Recently, together with Marja Toivonen, he has edited *User-Based Innovation in Services* (Edward Elgar 2011) and with Flemming Sørensen the *Handbook on the Experience Economy* (Edward Elgar 2013).

Torkild Thanem is Professor of Management and Organization Studies at Stockholm University School of Business, Sweden, where he teaches qualitative research methods and organisational change. His research focuses on the bodily and spatial politics that precede, exceed, disrupt and enable the organisation of work and life, and his empirical research includes studies of urban planners, homeless people, workplace health promoters and transvestites. His publications include articles in journals such as *Organization Studies, Organization* and *Gender, Work and Organization* and his book *The Monstrous Organization* (Edward Elgar 2011).

Sara Winterstorm Värlander, Ph.D, is a Senior Lecturer at the Stockholm University School of Business, Sweden and presently a visiting scholar at the Center for Work, Technology and Organization, Stanford University, USA. In her current research Sara uses an ethnographic approach to study global work and how culture is intertwined with the enactment of work practices, innovation and spatial design in global organisations. Previously, Sara has published papers on how organisational space affects flexibility and creativity, the emergent outcomes of the implementation of new technology in organisations, and the embodied and material dimensions of knowledge work.

Ben Walker is a Master of Commerce and Administration graduate from Victoria University of Wellington, New Zealand. His thesis examined the relationship between organisational identity and the use of alcohol in knowledge-intensive workplaces. Ben currently works as an analyst at the New Zealand Qualifications Authority, and is involved in the monitoring and regulation of New Zealand private tertiary education providers. Ben has also established, and produces music for, his own independent record label, 80HD Records.

Suze Wilson is a Lecturer in Management Studies at Massey University, Palmerston North, New Zealand. She has recently completed her doctoral dissertation applying the approaches of Michel Foucault to rethink what we assume to be the foundations of leadership theory. Her most recent publication is 'Situated Knowledge: A Foucauldian reading of ancient and modern classics of leadership thought' in the journal *Leadership*.

Zhichang Zhu's normal education stopped when he was 16, due to China's 'Cultural Revolution'. Zhichang has been a Maoist Red Guard, farm labourer, lorry driver, enterprise manager, system analyst and business consultant in China, Singapore and England. Zhichang is currently a Reader in Strategy and Management at the University of Hull Business School, UK. Previous publications include *Pragmatic Strategy: Eastern wisdom, global success* (with Ikujiro Nonaka, Cambridge University Press 2012).

Acknowledgements

Thanks to everybody at Edward Elgar for their work on this Handbook – to Francine O'Sullivan for initiating the project and allowing us to tackle it in our way, to Tori Nichols for always having an answer to our questions, to our copy editor Amanda Picken, and to Madhubanti Bhattacharyya, our desk editor, for her painstaking attention to detail and her patience.

Thank you to our former editor Rosemary Nixon for cradling many of the ideas we have developed here and to Professor David Wilson for a truly insightful foreword (well worth the detour to the next page of this book).

This book is intended to be used, both in the classroom and in professional practice. As well as thanking our academic colleagues, we would like to give special thanks to the many students and professional managers whose involvement has helped to inform the development of our ideas and whose engagement we hope will continue to reshape their application.

Finally, Chris and Steve would like to thank Anna and Noelle for their encouragement, forbearance, insight and indulgence.

Foreword

The words creativity and management have been around for a long time (both words arguably have sixteenth-century etymological origins), but it is only relatively recently that the two words have become conjoined in meaning (and very closely allied to studies of innovation and entrepreneurship). A major reason for this focus on creativity and management is because (as the editors of this book make clear) creativity generates lasting value (social and economic) as a result of a process of 'bisociation', which entails the making of unexpected connections between apparently opposing frames of reference to address problems or to take advantage of emerging opportunities (Koestler 1964). This is not a new idea, but it is a good one that has been neglected of late, so it is pleasing to see it utilised so thoroughly in this handbook.

There has been a great deal of debate recently, predominantly from those with an economics background, to argue that, broadly, the world is slowing down both in terms of the generation of innovative products and services and in terms of the contribution to the economy that such innovations provide. Gordon's (2000) test of un-inventiveness, for example, argues that the creation of the toilet transformed the lives of billions and that it would be difficult to find a more modern innovation that had an equivalent impact. Gordon also argues that creativity at the turn of the twentieth century was at something of a peak, producing cars, aeroplanes, radio, telephones and antibiotics. The central argument of this thesis is that the pace of innovation has allegedly slowed down in modern times.

I would disagree, since we can not only view creativity as production, as economists predominantly do, but also as consumption. Creativity is a broad social process and not just the production of new things. It is this dual aspect of creativity as both production and consumption that links creativity into virtually all aspects of organisation (strategy, structure, operations and marketing, to name only a few key areas). This book addresses all of these areas (and more) and that is why it is a timely and useful addition to the literature in this field.

Production (favoured by the economists) focuses on achieving innovation, competitive advantage and social benefits by enhancing the 'level' of creativity in the organisation to produce innovative products and services. This, typically, involves looking at entrepreneurship, for example developing a post-Fordist organisational context in which creativity might be fostered (including flexible production and work, moves to niche production aimed at specific groups, globalisation and the international division of labour). It also focuses on the systemic nature of systems (collectivities of organised efforts coupled with the physical environment) to see how the systemic tendencies that gravitate toward stability might be interrupted to stimulate creative actions which, in turn, produce innovative products and services (Kanter 1999). This approach has prompted some scholars (for example, Sternberg 1999, Weisberg 2006, Sawyer 2006) to argue that creativity should result in something that is new and has value (often described in managerial terminology as fit for purpose, or useful).

The creation and the development of the Swatch watch is a good example of creative production. In the 1970s the Swiss watch-making industry, world renowned for its precision, quality watches, was in crisis. In ten years its export market had dropped by half, with Hong Kong and Japan occupying the top spots. In 1978 the Japanese introduced a watch that was only 2 millimetres thick. Switzerland's largest watch group, ASUAG, rose to the challenge and developed a gold watch that was just 0.98 millimetres thick. This was a success and inspired further research at ASUAG to make a slim affordable watch case entirely of plastic. This meant bringing together different technologies (including display technologies from the computer industry) to make Swatch possible to produce. There are now some 30 different and successful designs (such as Scuba, Irony series, Skin, Beat, Bijoux).

The development of the 'iPod for the heart' is also a good example of creative production. This product (which looks like an iPod) uses iPod technology and design to monitor, screen and diagnose heart functions (your own personal ambulatory heart monitor with instant analysis). The previous 12-lead electro-cardiogram was invented in 1942 and is still used today. The first 'portable' electro-cardiogram was invented in 1928 and weighed 50lb. The iPod for the heart was created by two individuals working in the health service who saw the experiential advantages to the consumer and to healthcare professionals if iPod technology could be adapted to a different end use. Cardionetics was formed as a company with two models launched in 2006 with immediate take-up from healthcare professions recommending this product to patients. New models have subsequently followed with demand outstripping supply.

However, creativity lies not just in what we produce, but also in what – and how – we consume. The societal shift from production to consumption is also reflected in the fields of creativity. Consumerism has created a number of fundamental (creative) changes, including the massive growth of shopping malls: shopping as a major leisure activity in itself and the rapid growth of commodities. We now 'need' and use commodities we could not imagine only a few years ago (e.g. shower gels, foot creams, skin products, computer games and other gadgets). Consumerism has also influenced the attachment of identity to shopping (where we shop matters, especially for youthful consumers) and creative marketing by many retailers appeals directly to this identity. Some social theorists argue that consumerism has enriched life by creating a greater range of goods and services. We have great choice over which goods and services we buy and use (supermarkets sell ingredients and recipes unheard of 20 years ago) and we can now participate to a much greater extent in creative activities such as music, DIY, painting, cooking and a wide range of hobbies.

Not available when the toilet was invented are, of course, information technologies and other computer-based technologies which are used globally. Computers have the power to shape and develop both production and consumption relationships and thus play an important and integral role in both creativity and management. Individuals can make decisions, influence others and make connections worldwide, often without leaving their seat. For example, the extent of online shopping (consumption) was around 10 billion transactions (automated, debit and credit card) in the UK in 2012 and it would be a rare production or service organisation that had no computer-based technologies at all. Computers allow and facilitate creativity previously not possible and the spread of globalisation means that many more clever and inventive individuals from rapidly emerging economies have joined the innovation game. We are likely to see rapid and creative advances as a result in fields as diverse as driverless cars, medical care and three-dimensional printing.

At least two further key issues impinge on creativity and management. One is the question of value and the other is the question of how creativity itself is managed and regulated at macro levels (i.e. by governments). It is important to remember that value is a relative term and creativity may not always be good for all. For example, post-Fordist flexible firms utilising such 'novel' techniques as offshoring, teleworking or crowdsourcing can be seen as a creative solution to organisational and economic problems, but can also be seen as exploitative (particularly of labour), self-serving for the powerful (e.g. Enron) or guilty of poor governance when responsibility and accountability is passed from senior managers to the more junior individual or 'remote' work group.

Similarly, creativity in consumption can be argued to destroy traditional cultures and regional solidarities. The dominance of markets and self-gratification has led to a general 'flattening' (McDonaldisation) of life – destroying differences and communities (Seabrook 1996, Ritzer 1993, 2010). In addition, Veblen's (1899/1925) theory of conspicuous consumption suggested that consumption and its display are not open to all.

You can cook a creative meal (for example) but you need enough money to buy the high-quality ingredients and you need to be able to access the shops. You also need the knowledge of how to buy the ingredients and how to prepare the creative meal. In other words, contemporary consumption allows some individuals and groups to be creative but excludes others.

Finally, government plays an important role in either helping foster or suppressing creativity. Many of the world's leading economies are more heavily regulated than they were a century ago. They may be safer and cleaner places in which to live and work, but when governments imposed less regulation, innovation was arguably easier. Of course, this is a delicate balance. De-regulation rarely happens except in extreme circumstances (such as war), where there have been step changes in innovation from radar, through medicine and the jet engine to drones. De-regulation is furthermore often succeeded by re-regulation (as in the European broadcasting industries). It is also a positive thing that governments regulate drugs and emissions from cars and factories, yet public spending on infrastructure and basic research (the seed corn of many innovations including the development of the computer and the Internet) has dwindled significantly, leading some to claim that the twenty-first century is not as readily open to innovation as the twentieth.

Creativity and management have moved a long way from the days when critics would dismiss creativity as meaningless jargon (or management speak). But we have also moved away from a view that creativity is just about making new products (such as toilets and airplanes) towards one where it may also be about new services, relationships, experiences *and* products (or any permeable combination of these). Consequently, despite, and perhaps enabled by, the new environment I have described above, creativity will have to be managed more creatively. In other words, the old modes of creativity with which we became comfortable in the twentieth century may no longer suffice.

This book provides a framework for thinking through such challenges. Chris Bilton and Steve Cummings show not only how creativity is made up of discrete but closely intertwined elements, but also how the clever management of these elements can contribute to organisational strategies, innovation and global exchange, which will ultimately grow and strengthen both the national and the world economy in ways we may not have yet imagined.

Professor David Wilson
Associate Dean, Research, Open University Business School,
The Open University
May 2013

REFERENCES

Gordon, R.J. (2000), 'Does the "New Economy" measure up to the great inventions of the past?', *Journal of Economic Perspectives*, **14**(4), 49–74.

Kanter, R.M. (1999), 'Change in everyone's job: managing the extended enterprise in a globally extended world', *Organizational Dynamics*, **28**(1), 7–23.

Koestler, A. (1976[1964]), *The act of creation*, London: Hutchinson.

Ritzer, G. (1993), *The McDonaldization of society: an investigation into the changing character of contemporary life*, Thousand Oaks, CA: Pine Forge.

Ritzer, G. (2010), *Globalisation: a basic text*, Oxford: Wiley-Blackwell.

Sawyer, R.K. (2006), *Explaining creativity*, Oxford: Oxford University Press.

Seabrook, J. (1996), *In the Cities of the South*, London: Verso.

Sternberg, R.J., (ed.) (1999), *Handbook of Creativity*, New York: Cambridge University Press.

Veblen, T. (1899/1925), *The Theory of the Leisure Class: an economic study of institutions*, London: Allen Unwin.

Weisberg, R. (2006) *Creativity: understanding innovation in problem-solving, science, invention and the arts*, Hoboken, NJ: Wiley.

1. A framework for creative management and managing creativity
Chris Bilton and Stephen Cummings

The test of a first-rate intelligence is the ability to hold two opposed ideas in mind at the same time and still retain the ability to function. (F. Scott Fitzgerald, *The Crack-up*, 1936)

Arsenal Football Club was recently beaten, very badly, by Bayern Munich in a European Champions' League match. As part of the after-match malaise (a malaise that was deepening during a disappointing 2012/13 season), one Arsenal fan posted a comment on the BBC Sport website. It said, 'Obvious, just look at the two boards . . .' (he then provided links to the club webpages that listed and described the board members).[1] Arsenal's board comprised bigwigs from the world of business and high finance. Bayern's had a few of those too, but their number was matched by a collection of some of Germany's greatest ever footballers. 'Nuff said,' the fan concluded.

Everyday people, if they are optimists, opt for the former of the two contradictory common sayings: 'you should seek the best of both worlds,' rather than 'you can't have your cake and eat it too.' Academics, business and creative people, often operating in silos, have generally defaulted to the latter position. This handbook seeks to develop an approach that takes the best from management and creativity research and put them together, around the same table.

We are not alone in this. Creativity and management are two words whose use has expanded exponentially (see Figure 1.1 below). While they are traditionally considered as opposites, they are increasingly used together and seen as complementary. Management, we are told, needs more creativity (Cox 2005, Lampel et al. 2000, Sutton 2001); the creative industries, and creative pursuits more generally, can be better harnessed and deliver greater social value with better management (Hewison 2004).

And yet, while creativity and innovation in management are now recognised as key assets and management practices in the arts, and cultural industries have become increasingly strategic, promising a twenty-first-century alternative to 'business (or art) as usual', little in the way of holistic (i.e., advice from across the spectrum of creativity and management research) or strategic advice as to how effective creative

1

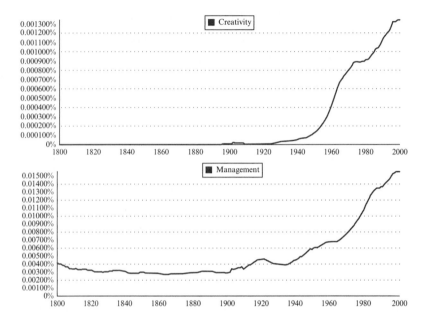

Source: books.google.com/ngrams

Figure 1.1   Google N-Gram viewer showing frequency of words 'creativity' and 'management' in books published 1800–2000

management can be achieved exists. The *Handbook of Management and Creativity* aims to do just this. It seeks to provide a holistic and comprehensively strategic approach to bringing the world of creativity and management together.

In so doing, this handbook's approach may be new, but it builds upon two old but underappreciated ideas at the outset. The first is the only one of eight principles that were said to be followed by excellent organisations that has stood the test of time, in the first popular (and still the best-selling) book on management: Tom Peters' and Robert Waterman's *In Search of Excellence* (1982). This principle is that excellent organisations exhibit 'simultaneously loose and tight characteristics'.

The second old idea is taken from one of the first modern treatises of creation: Arthur Koestler's *Act of Creativity* (1964). This is Koestler's idea that creativity generates lasting value as a result of a process of 'bisociation' – making connections or moving between different frames of reference to address situations or problems in new ways or take advantage of emerging opportunities. In this way, to paraphrase Koestler, the creative act, by connecting or 'shaking together' previously unrelated dimensions of experience, is an act of liberation and defeater of habit, assumption or norm.

These notions of simultaneously loose/tight elements in management and bisociation in creativity are useful to the creation of this handbook. They help us see creativity and management in an unconventional light, one that highlights their similarities in a world where most focus on their differences. Where creativity is categorised as loose, to the point of frivolity, and management seen as tight, to the point of moronic rigidity, or where creativity lives in the right side of a brain while management logic resides in the left (as if the brain consisted of two chambers!), in our experience, examples of good practice in both the worlds of business and the arts, exhibit both looseness and tightness in a bisociative manner.

This handbook consequently builds a more holistic idea of management and creativity by seeing both as requiring oppositional elements traditionally ascribed to the other. But this requires redefining, at the outset, what we mean by 'creativity' and 'management' and the relationship between them.

CREATIVITY

The conventional combination of creativity and management tends to be about injecting or overlaying 'fresh' looser thinking into the tightly wound routines of management practice; or about bringing structure to the wild and zany world of creativity through management best practice. In turn, far too often, 'creatives' and managers are attracted to stereotypical versions of each other, which in the end can reinforce divisions instead of challenging them. Rather than each being dazzled by the other's outward appearance, we argue that both managers and artists can learn from tracing their own reflections as creative managers and self-managing creatives.

In this introduction we aim to provide working definitions which can frame the relation between creativity and management. In particular, what is the alternative to the pop-management stereotypes of 'thinking outside the box' or 'breakthrough thinking' which tend to dominate managerial discourse around creativity?

Most of the academic literature on creativity (Weisberg 2006, Sawyer 2006, Sternberg 1999) emphasises that creativity must meet two criteria. First, creativity must result in something that is new. Second, creativity must produce something that is valuable (or 'useful' or 'fit for purpose').

We can make two observations on this academic attempt at defining creativity. In the first place, novelty and value are relative terms (Novitz

1999). What is new to me may be common knowledge to you. And what is useful in one situation – a way of improving the cornering on a racing car – may be entirely useless in another context (attempts to tackle climate change, for example). Consequently most creativity scholars highlight the importance of context, both in narrow terms of 'fitness for purpose' or 'problem-solving' and more broadly in terms of contributing to a field or domain beyond the immediate subject (Weisberg 1986, Sternberg 1988). Margaret Boden defines these two qualifications as 'P-creativity' (that which is new or valuable to the individual) and 'H-creativity' (that which is new or valuable to the world). Yet the process for both forms of creativity is the same – and the difference between them is unpredictable, even random, like the difference between a successful film or a hit record and another that is adjudged a failure. Boden suggests that the only way of determining 'H-creativity' is a jury of one's peers – but even here, an accurate assessment is easier in hindsight than in predicting future outcomes (Boden 1994: 75–117).

A second observation is that a pursuit of 'novelty' and 'value' may well push the creative process or idea in opposite directions. Something that is entirely new, unprecedented and ground-breaking may well be too novel for its own good. If we are fixated on being new or different, we risk ignoring markets, logistics, organisational capacities, personal strengths. We can put a positive spin on this by defending a failed idea or an eccentric innovator as 'being ahead of one's time'. The reality is that novelty that does not build on and extend existing terms of reference or norms is unlikely to be valued or valuable in our own time; and while future generations may modify this assessment, retrospective recognition is of limited value to the innovator, and could be considered a social phenomenon rather than an intrinsic quality in the artefact or originator (Wolff 1993).

Similarly, an attempt to harness creativity solely to the problem in hand or to a preconceived notion of 'added value' is likely to stifle independent thought and result in predictable outcomes and a failure to innovate. It may also remove the incentive to try new ideas or to take risks, and encourage us to discard a challenging prospect because it (or she/he) does not fit with our agenda at the time. Value and purpose without an injection of newness or originality result in endless repetition and a cycle of ever diminishing returns.

The pursuit of novelty for its own sake is likely to distract us from considerations of value and purpose – and vice versa, focusing only on the immediate solution to a problem is likely to stifle original thought. In management terms, there is a problem here of directing creativity in one way or another, resulting in a perception that creativity is inherently opposed to management or 'unmanageable'.

For the purposes of this book, the contradictory nature of creativity – new *and* valuable – is precisely the point at which creativity resonates with management. Managers too have to deal with seemingly contradictory, but potentially bisociative, processes. They have to manage tensions between product-led and market-led innovation, between entrepreneurial opportunism and strategic purpose, between leading an organisation from the top and encouraging initiative and engagement from below, between providing a coherent and consistent organisational culture and squeezing out organisational diversity and individualism. And good managers seize opportunities therein.

Similarly, the contingent nature of our definition – the fact that creativity always depends on context, that our measure of newness and value are relative terms – is also important to the overall shape of this book. Rather than attempting the impossible – a global definition of creativity which fits all scenarios, cultures and purposes – we will seek to identify different scopes and purposes within which creativity can add value to management. We will highlight the different cultural norms through which creativity can be identified and defined – by individuals, organisations, nations and cultural traditions. Above all we will seek to map the relationship between creativity and management; this is after all not a book about creativity, it is a book about creativity and management and the relation between them.

To summarise, we define creativity as a set of loose and tight processes, personal qualities and product attributes which lead to new and valuable outcomes. We further define creativity as a bisociative, paradoxical concept which requires organisations and individuals to pull in different directions and to reconcile apparently contradictory concepts, purposes and frames of reference. This in turn requires an adroit ability to switch focus between frames of reference, and a tolerance for contradictions both conceptually (in our thought processes and perceptions) and organisationally (in our relationships and interactions with others).

MANAGEMENT

If definitions of creativity can only be understood in relation to a context, we need to turn to the other half of this book's title. In relation to creativity, what exactly do we mean by management?

Again for the purposes of this book we are not seeking a universal definition, but an understanding of management in relation to creativity. Two rhetorical shifts in management theory and practice are worth noting here. First of all, from the late twentieth century it has been recognised in the literature (and long before this by good managers) that predictive, routinised or scientific approaches to management are not very effective in dealing with discontinuous change. And, from the late twentieth century, there has emerged a perception that businesses face increasingly unpredictable markets, processes and behaviours both inside and outside the firm. Management literature has attempted to address this unpredictability by referring to chaos, complexity, narrative sense-making – and creativity. A related shift has seen a growing emphasis on individual potential and the human side of enterprise. Rather than designing perfect systems and models, today's managers are increasingly concerned to adapt collective systems to individual behaviour (from employees, but also from consumers) and applying looser controls geared towards maximum human potential rather than maximum organisational efficiency.

'Creativity', then, has been seen to offer a panacea to some of these management problems because, stereotypically, creativity is considered by many managers to represent individual, unpredictable or spontaneous qualities which challenge old-fashioned, top–down and habitualised approaches to management. Yet as we have seen, this is a narrow stereotype of creativity which misses out some of the dualism and complexity referred to in our discussion of creativity. There is a similar stereotype in assuming that management has switched over from tight to loose, from predictable logic to spontaneous imagination. Surely practical management has always encompassed tensions, compromises, paradoxes and contradictions. Managers every day must face choices between too much control and too little, between favouring the individual or the collective, between certainty and chaos. If creativity has anything in common with management, it is not that it represents a new paradigm of individualistic spontaneity, sweeping away the lumbering juggernaut of scientific management. Rather, good management, like value-adding creativity, requires us to bisociate different capabilities and mindsets. It is this point of similarity, rather than the conventionally assumed differences, which we intend to explore through this book.

So instead of positioning management and creativity as opposites, or indeed defining management itself in terms of opposing terms such as change vs. continuity, individual vs. collective, centralised vs. decentralised, we prefer to describe creative management as a complex process which incorporates all of these elements. Our 'creative' (novel, value-adding) starting point for this handbook then is that 'creative management' is a multifaceted process extending beyond creative and management stereotypes such as the individual genius, 'breakthrough thinking' and the 'seven habits of the highly successful . . .'. *Creative management* is management that develops and promotes, in a process that holds together or connects opposing loose and tight aspects, ideas and other products or services that are at once novel and value-adding over time.

THE IMPORTANCE OF INTEGRATION AND TEMPORALITY: A STRATEGIC VIEW OF CREATIVE MANAGEMENT

The previous paragraphs outlined how this handbook starts from a new and value-adding definition of the subject matter. In addition, it seeks to provide comprehensive and strategic coverage of the field by taking an approach that seeks to *integrate* the elements that contribute to successful creative management and examine how these elements contribute in different ways and at different stages to adding value from creativity over time.

Following from our arguments against one-dimensional views of creativity and management, we take the approach in this book that creative management is not just about innovative products or strategies, risk-taking, charismatic 'creative' leaders or stimulating structures and environments – it is about all these things working together, from innovation and entrepreneurship through to leadership and organisation. We take the view that effective creativity in management (and management in creativity) needs to integrate four elements that have been increasingly treated separately: innovation, entrepreneurship, leadership and organisation (Bilton and Cummings 2010).

Considering these elements in turn, the starting point for the creative enterprise is innovation. Innovation is concerned with change, with new ideas and initiatives. In the next phase, entrepreneurs provide the energy and impetus to launch innovation, connecting potential projects into viable outcomes and linking new ideas to potential markets – without the entrepreneurial push, innovation remains untapped and dissipates into pointless inventiveness or mere tinkering. Organisation and leadership embed the process of change into the ongoing life of the organisation. Leadership steers the enterprise towards a common purpose or direction. Organisation embeds the other three elements – innovative initiative, entrepreneurial energy and leadership purpose and direction – into a sustainable whole, connecting individual elements and behaviours into collective systems, values and cultures. In turn, organisation is continually reanimated by innovative ideas and individuals. And so the cycle (or curve) continues.

Moreover, our research has found that success in each of these arenas often has bisociation at its root. This is made possible because each of these phases of innovation, entrepreneurship, leadership and organisation are themselves 'bisociative', meaning that they each require apparently contradictory or paradoxical elements. This bisociative quality frequently results in a combination of individual and collective processes, with diversified individual competences and inputs framed by collective resources and consequences.

Innovation is primarily concerned with change and with initiating new ideas – but this can be both an active process of making something new *ex nihilo* out of our own capability and will (*creating*) or a more passive process of responding to happy accidents, building on our own and other people's mistakes and allowing space for the unexpected rather than trying to force the pace of change (*discovering*). Bisociative innovation requires managers to connect together different phases of ideation, decision-making and execution, and to mobilise support from different levels of the organisation to release new ideas and energies.

Entrepreneurship too is bisociative. Successful entrepreneurs are alert to new possibilities, ready to take a risk on a new product or market where a more cautious competitor might hold back – they have to be *dilettantes*, moving between different frames of reference without becoming locked into one perspective or project. But on the other hand, they are also *diligent*, latching onto their chosen project and stubbornly (sometimes blindly) refusing to give up until they have seen it through to its conclusion. Entrepreneurs add energy and commitment to the open possibilities of innovation.

Leaders respond to and advance the changes wrought by innovation and entrepreneurship, providing a sustaining vision and purpose to the entrepreneurial launch. Here, too, leaders must combine an ability to look outside and beyond the organisation, while at the same time engaging with colleagues and subordinates. Leaders *envision* the future, whilst they *interact* with the pressing realities of the present. The bisociative nature of leadership may again result in a combination of individual and collective processes, either through the agency of individual leaders, or as a collective capacity distributed through the organisation. Leaders build on entrepreneurial energies and innovative ideas.

In turn, leaders are both dependent on and contributing to an overarching organisational culture and community which embodies the shared vision of leaders and followers. Organisations have to be *loose* enough to allow for new ideas and inputs to be released and thus regenerate them, whilst at the same time being *controlled* enough to draw these diverse inputs into a common direction. Organisation is a collective process and system within which the other elements of creative management can be both sustained and regenerated.

Creative managers move fluently through these phases of innovation, entrepreneurship, leadership and organisation rather than ponderously lurching between them. Because these four phases of creative management are bisociative, comprising tight and loose aspects, and connecting change with sustainability (echoing the 'new' and 'valuable' components of creativity), it is possible to flow between them over time rather than seeing them as opposing tendencies. In other words, we do not need to restrict our view to only one part of the process – seeing managers simply as leaders or organisers, for example. However, it is useful to see how these elements of creative management relate to each over time, relative to the typical growth phases of an enterprise.

Management can, and creative management should, encompass contradictory processes just as in our earlier description of creativity. So, rather than describing a matrix of opposing elements (as is often the case in management – and creativity – textbooks), we represent these overlapping phases of creative management using another idea from the past: the innovation or technology S-curve.

With this simple shape at the heart of our four strategic elements of creative management we can see how, while nothing can happen without a novel and potentially value-adding idea, product, service or experience, entrepreneurship is an equally important partner in getting things 'off the ground'. But even excellence in these two elements may not go very far without astute leadership that develops people and ideas through a combination of skilful interaction and providing a vision for further development. Further on, without a tightly defined organisational culture or structure, scale is difficult to achieve and sustain; but, at the same time, this organisation must also be loose enough in key dimensions to enable the space in which new innovations and entrepreneurs can take root and flight.

Each of these four elements or phases of creative management is connected and interdependent, containing traces of the others. Yet each will require different capabilities in practice and different theoretical frameworks to analyse and understand them. This is the challenge we have asked the contributors to this book to address.

SHAPE OF THE BOOK

The remainder of the handbook follows the definitions and 'shapes' outlined below (Figure 1.2). The book is divided into four main parts: innovation, entrepreneurship, leadership and organisation. Each begins with a brief review of past and current thinking in this area and a scene-setting

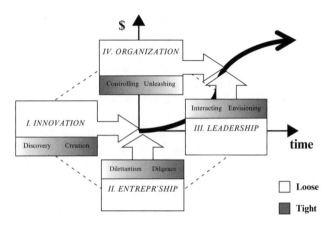

Figure 1.2   How the bisociation across the four strategic elements of creative management can drive the S-curve

case study. Following on from each of these reviews are a number of chapters from leading figures in academia and a wide range of business and creative practices (music, theatre, art, dance, science, fashion, design, multi-media) and cultures, that explore the novel, value-adding, strategic and bisociative nature of the themes that make up that element of success-ful creative management and what their ideas mean for the management of creativity.

As we have already noted, each of these elements – innovation, entre-preneurship, leadership and organisation – are overlapping, both in terms of an overall cycle of cause and effect, and in the switching within each 'stage' of the cycle between opposing competences and mindsets. We, as editors, will seek to draw out the main themes, considerations and links at the beginning and the end of each part before we move on to the next element, showing for example how innovation connects to entrepreneur-ship or how leadership connects to organisation. We have also encouraged our contributors to consider the connections and bisociations within and between each phase of creative management and will attempt to draw together some of their considerations and connections in the final part and chapter of the book.

This connects back to our fundamental argument – that management and creativity represent complementary functions and processes. Each incorporates apparently contradictory elements. Creativity and manage-ment are not confined to two halves of a mental map or to two separate floors in a building; they cut across different categories. From a creativity perspective, innovative ideas only acquire substance and value if they are acted upon and embodied into outcomes and actions, and entrepreneurial behaviours need direction and purpose. From a management perspective, sustaining the strategic vision of leadership requires core aims and processes to be continually reinvigorated by fresh thinking from below; and a collective corporate identity is only sustainable if diversity and difference can be reincorporated into the organisation rather than allowed to dissipate or simply denied. We believe that the key to effective creative management is an ability to tolerate, and even promote, contradictory perspectives, processes and frames of reference; to the extent that managers succeed in this, we believe that 'management' can be considered 'creative'. We can seek to achieve the best of both 'worlds', if we think about it.

In keeping with our arguments above with respect to the effective management of creativity, this book is highly structured and ordered, but, we hope, in a way that will allow the reader to follow it in a linear fashion and/or to move around it in creative combinations. And within this tight structure there is a lot of diversity to combine: Eastern and Western views; writers from the Northern and Southern Hemispheres; practitioners and academics from the public and private sectors, from the so-called creative sector and the otherwise implied non-creative industries; perspectives from management, theatre, science, architecture, sport, gaming and play.

In the words of a writer on creativity who has been very influential to us, Ronald Finke (1990: 27), the most effective strategy may be 'to imagine combining the parts in various interesting ways and then mentally "seeing" if anything meaningful emerges – what Einstein refers to [in the creative process] as "combinative play".' An introduction to the first of our four sections of this *Handbook of Management and Creativity*, on Innovation, follows.

NOTE

1. At the time of going to press, these were http://www.arsenal.com/the-club/corporate-info/the-arsenal-board; http://www.fcbayern.telekom.de/en/company/company/organe/index.php

REFERENCES

Bilton, C. and S. Cummings (2010), *Creative strategy: reconnecting business and innovation*, Chichester: Wiley.
Boden, M. (ed.) (1994), *Dimensions of creativity*, Cambridge, MA: MIT Press.
Cox, G. (2005), *The Cox review of creativity in business: building on the UK's strengths*, London: HMSO.

Finke, R.A. (1990), *Creative imagery: discoveries and inventions in visualisation*, Hillsdale, NJ: Lawrence Erlbaum.

Hewison, R. (2004), 'The crisis of cultural leadership in Britain', *International Journal of Cultural Policy*, **10**(2), July, 157–66.

Koestler, A. (1976[1964]), *The act of creation*, London: Hutchinson.

Lampel, J., T. Lant, and J. Shamsie (2000), 'Balancing act: learning from organization practices in the creative industries', *Organization Science*, **11**(3), May–June, 263–9.

Novitz, D. (1999), 'Creativity and constraint', *Australasian Journal of Philosophy*, **77**(1), 67–82.

Sawyer, R.K. (2006), *Explaining creativity*, Oxford: Oxford University Press.

Seltzer, K. and T. Bentley (1999), *The creative age: knowledge and skills for the new economy*, London: Demos.

Sternberg, R.J. (1988), 'A three-facet model of creativity', in R.J. Sternberg (ed.) *The nature of creativity: contemporary psychological perspectives*, Cambridge: Cambridge University Press, pp. 125–47.

Sternberg, R. (1999), *Handbook of creativity*, Cambridge: Cambridge University Press.

Sutton, R. (2001), 'The weird rules of creativity', *Harvard Business Review*, **79**(8), 86–103.

Weisberg, R. (2006), *Creativity: understanding innovation in problem solving, science, invention and the arts*, Hoboken, NJ: Wiley.

Weisberg, R.W. (1986), 'The myth of divergent thinking', in R.W. Weisberg, *Creativity: genius and other myths*, New York: W.H. Freeman, pp. 51–69.

Wolff, J. (1993), *The social production of art*, Basingstoke: Macmillan.

PART I

CREATIVE INNOVATION

Introduction to Part I: Creative Innovation
Chris Bilton and Stephen Cummings

The final stages of putting this handbook together occurred at the same time as Peter Jackson's first instalment of the *Hobbit* movies hit cinemas. Illustrative of the love (if not the understanding) that the business world has for the 'creative' industries, a number of articles appeared in business magazines that profiled Jackson's approach to the creative process.

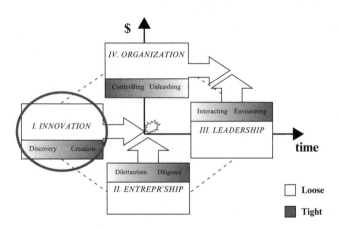

Jackson's words reflect the bisociations that we outlined in our introductory chapter: a tight diligence and focus on the plan, combined with a loose dilettantism that continues to seek new influences; a singular leader's vision, while interacting with and including others in developments; a tightly controlled organisation that at the same time unleashes creative talent. But, mostly, they reflect that eye for innovation with a tight focus on making sure that a product gets created with the open mind that allows for further discovery. For example, Jackson is well known for his intense logistical planning and attention to detail in advance of shooting, but as he noted (*KiaOra* 2012: 27): 'There always has to be spontaneity. You have to be thinking in a flexible way . . . you have to be flexible and craft what you've got.' Even during the shoot things can be changed if one is mindful of the possibilities. According to Jackson (*KiaOra* 2012: 27): 'You can't have an idea that requires a character that hasn't been brought to the set or a particular prop or location that's not in front of you. But so long as you are working with what you have that day, you can be flexible . . .. I always try and have that voice in my head that keeps saying, "Is there anything we can do we haven't thought of that can improve the scene we're shooting?" That includes directing the actors, camera angles, lighting, the way the camera moves.'

It is fitting, then, that the first chapter in this section on creative innovation explores this philosophy further by examining the genre of low-budget horror movies, a world where Jackson first learned his film-making craft. Elizabeth Gulledge, Gail Greig and Nic Beech's contribution, 'Improvisational practice and innovation: shock, horror and confounding expectations in film-making', considers how film-makers manage unpredictability, and how 'ad hoc' and improvised decisions draw on a repertoire of resources and experiences. They develop an approach for planned/ improvised innovation through an 'activity theory' perspective that we believe could be applied to organisations in any industry where creativity is a factor, whether it currently is regarded as a creative industry or not.

Indeed, the next chapter, Greg Hearn and Ruth Bridgstock's 'The curious case of the embedded creative: creative cultural occupations outside the creative industries' questions the very notion of splitting industry into two and dividing it into 'creative' and, therefore by definition, 'non-creative' categories. By examining the activities of what they call 'embedded creatives' (people charged with being creative whether they work for organisations in the so-called creative industries or not), they make a case for this transdisciplinarity, which embedded creatives live every day, as an engine for innovation and growth. In so doing, they broaden out the arguments already advanced in our introduction to the handbook, Peter Jackson's words, and Elizabeth, Gail and Nic's chapter: that being bisociative – discovering and creating; planning and improvising; working with those situated in both the creative and non-creative disciplines – helps innovation and, by association, the management of creativity. Greg and Ruth's thread in this regard (promoting transdisciplinarity and transgressing traditional defined boundaries and outlining how this might be managed) is picked up again towards the end of this book in Doris Eikhof's and Torkild Thanem and Sara Värlander's chapters in Part IV of this handbook – on good organisational practices to support creativity and innovation.

Jon Sundbo and Flemming Sørensen take the idea of bisociation as a driver of innovation further still. Innovation in service firms is usually characterised as unsystematic as it often results from ad hoc encounters with customers. Innovation in manufacturing, on the other hand, has traditionally been more systematic, based on sustained investment in scientific and technological resources. On the other hand, the manufacturing approach is relatively expensive and time-consuming, and may result in innovations which are not well aligned with market needs. In 'The lab is back – towards a new model of innovation', Jon and Flemming seek to achieve the best of both worlds in their model of a 'service laboratory': a more systematic approach to innovation which still retains the strengths of the user-centred service model.

After Jon and Flemming's chapter on how innovation might be operationalised more effectively, Lorraine Lim and Shinji Oyama's challenging chapter looks at a bigger picture. Most that has been written about innovation has been written from a Western perspective. It has even been suggested by some that Eastern cultures are just not as innovative as Western (despite the fact that Japan has for decades topped league tables of patents divided by population among large countries). In 'Beyond conventional Western views of creativity and innovation', Lorraine and Shinji question these attitudes and explore what might be learned by looking at Eastern approaches to innovation. In particular they consider the ways in which innovative content is packaged and branded in the cosmetics and music industries. They show how innovation occurs through global networks of production, distribution and consumption which can no longer be separated out into 'creative' Western firms and 'uncreative' Eastern ones.

One thing that all the chapters in this section of the handbook have in common is that they develop their views from outside of the management mainstream. This is not to say that this mainstream is not an important element to blend with or build upon, only that we expect that there are many other places in which you can find this. If you have not looked at Joe Tidd's books on the subject or John Adair's or other recent Edward Elgar handbooks on innovation, for example, you would benefit from doing so.

And, it is interesting to note that a key aspect that lies beneath the current trend for 'design thinking' (although it is not always recognised) is that it too draws from the kind of bisociative elements that we are describing here. The diagram below (one of the best – certainly one of the simplest – expressions of design thinking that we have seen) shows good design's relationship between the tight focus on user needs, a loosening thinking out or idea generation from this, and then tightening again as ideas are made sense of and refined towards an effective innovation.

While there is much that is good that has been written on innovation before, we have sought to add to these works by encouraging provocative writers to view innovation from a different angle, exploring practices and models of innovation beyond the established methods of R&D laboratories and the familiar 'creative' industries. Innovation highlights a central paradox of management and creativity, the combination of the deliberate and the spontaneous, the so-called 'happy accidents' which spark new

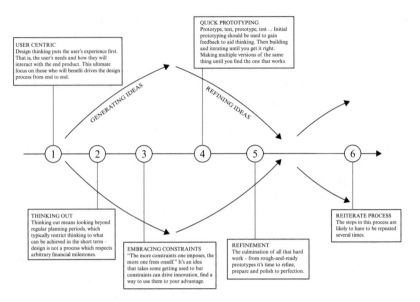

USER CENTRIC
Design thinking puts the user's experience first. That is, the user's needs and how they will interact with the end product. This ultimate focus on those who will benefit drives the design process from end to end.

QUICK PROTOTYPING
Prototype, test, prototype, test ... Initial prototyping should be used to gain feedback to aid thinking. Then building and iterating until you get it right. Making multiple versions of the same thing until you find the one that works.

GENERATING IDEAS

REFINING IDEAS

THINKING OUT
Thinking out means looking beyond regular planning periods, which typically restrict thinking to what can be achieved in the short term – design is not a process which respects arbitrary financial milestones.

EMBRACING CONSTRAINTS
"The more constraints one imposes, the more one frees onself." It's an idea that takes some getting used to but constraints can drive innovation, find a way to use them to your advantage.

REFINEMENT
The culmination of all that hard work – from rough-and-ready prototypes it's time to refine, prepare and polish to perfection.

REITERATE PROCESS
The steps in this process are likely to have to be repeated several times.

Visory's design thinking 'fish'

ideas. We believe this opening collection of chapters in the handbook reflects this paradox and opens up a series of connections which will be revisited in the sections which follow.

REFERENCE

KiaOra (2012), Air New Zealand in-flight magazine, December.

2. Improvisational practice and innovation: shock, horror and confounding expectations in film-making
Elizabeth Gulledge, Gail Greig and Nic Beech

Innovation and creativity are frequently associated with each other and Henry and Walker (1991) provide a useful definitional starting point. Creativity, for Henry and Walker, is having new ideas, whereas innovation is the challenge of making new ideas have a practical result. Innovation, therefore, incorporates individual flashes of inspiration typically accompanied by teamwork to co-produce new outcomes. It entails adaptability and not merely replicating good practice from the past, and relies upon systematic persistence through which surprises, problems and alternatives are regarded not as barriers to action, but as invitations to act (Beech et al. 2004). Bilton and Cummings (2010) propose an understanding of innovation that incorporates both systems (such as innovations throughout the value chain) and practices. The latter is the inspiration for this chapter, in which we use activity theory to analyse innovative practice in film-making.

Bilton and Cummings (2010) argue that copying 'best' practice does not necessarily lead to innovation and they propose an approach to innovation based on learning and engagement with different forms of practice. Innovation is regarded as incorporating both creation and discovery, which operate in a 'bisociative loop' in which there is a building on, or absorbing of, extant ideas and a divergence and initiating of the new. They use the example of the film *The Blair Witch Project*, which was new and unexpected in its own terms but also referenced 'classic movies'. Similarly, Peter Jackson's early work in horror films informed the making of *The Hobbit*. This form of innovation can have an impact on the whole genre and lead to many imitations. However, the imitations can become less and less innovative, as might be evidenced by the diminishing returns of series of films, or what become film 'franchises'. It is a real challenge to be innovative when producing the third film in the trilogy, or yet another thriller/ horror movie. Our focus is precisely in this difficult area of innovation. In well-established genres there is the possibility of picking up on good practices, but the challenge is moving to 'next' and 'promising' practices. Our empirical examples are derived from the production of a 'slasher' movie. Slasher movies constitute a sub-genre of horror films. This type of film is designed for a young adult audience, made to contain explicit deaths with gory, bloody scenes shot in a particular style to build suspense around a serial killer. These films may not create significant disjunctures within the genre, but in order to be successful there is a considerable degree of technical and process innovation. In some cases this revolves around new technologies or new techniques that are introduced into the industry. However, on a day-to-day basis, technical staff are innovative in finding ways to achieve a creative outcome against the odds of limited resources and directors who presume they can fix anything. This type of innovation requires much on-the-spot improvisation, which means adapting, challenging existing practices, developing alternatives and implementing change within very short timescales.

IMPROVISATION AND LOOSE–TIGHT INNOVATION

The conception of creativity and management used in this book is built on two core ideas: simultaneously loose and tight characteristics and bisociation (making unexpected connections). Both of these ideas are brought to practice in improvisation. Improvisation is the taking of spontaneous action, either as a creative act or in order to 'repair' a mistake (Montuouri 2003). It is the practice of creating something new in the moment of performance (Rehn and de Cock 2008), as a process of acting in the moment, and hence can appear to be rule-free and outside social structures. However, in order to be meaningful, improvisation has to have some relation to social structures; in many cases, this involves drawing upon past practices far more than may be thought *prima facie* (Patrick et al. 2012). Hence, improvisation is simultaneously loose and tight: loose in allowing fairly unconstrained and creative action by the organisational member, tight in that the improvised acts have to be of use within social and work structures. Hence, improvisation can be thought of as a mediating practice, in which creativity and structure co-exist, which becomes effectively innovative when something is produced that has value beyond the immediate action – that is, when the improvised practice enables something *more* or *better* to happen.

Improvisation has been seen as a foundation of innovation in organisational strategy. For Brown and Eisenhardt (1998), improvisation is essential to enable 'competing on the edge' as companies operate in novel settings and unknown markets. Hatch (1998) has argued that organisations which have to be highly responsive to changing environments can benefit from loose boundaries and minimal hierarchies that permit organisational members to devise new practices, as they are required in service encounters, or for the development of new products. Vera and Crossan (2004) have argued that many organisational practices require similar skills and concepts to theatrical improvisation. They explore the relationship between scripted and unscripted interaction, highlighting the plurivocal and unpredictable nature of interaction in organisations. Just as in theatrical improvisation, positions (roles) are taken which bring with them expectations (Eikhof 2010), and the expectations that are held of others may require considerable improvisation from them. In the empirical examples below we explore some of the expectations that directors have of technical staff in film-making. These include the ability to correct any problems with sound recorded during shooting (i.e. field sound) and to identify continuity issues so that scenes may be shot non-sequentially. These requirements – to produce perfectly re-mastered audio in post-production sound, and to ensure that scenes may be edited together smoothly – often mean that technical crew members need to develop adaptive and new practices in order to meet such expectations.

In theatre (Frost and Yarrow 1990), as in music (Zack 2000), performances range from the tightly composed and structured to the free and unstructured. The concept of minimal structure (Kamoche and Cunha 2001) has been used to elucidate forms of improvisation that can occur in tighter and looser structures. Three components of minimal structure are identified, including social structure, technical structure and repertoire. The social structure includes the norms, accepted forms of communication and shared understandings of the practising community. These provide a supportive culture for the risk-taking and trust involved in live improvisation. In musical performance the technical structure is the knowledge of music theory, instrumentation and definition of keys, chord progressions and song structures that enable shared understanding and action. In theatrical improvisation, the technical structure can include choices between different idioms of speech, the adoption of character and following or deliberate breaking of narrative form. The repertoire in musical improvisation is the base of songs and riffs that can be used as a basis for improvising. For example, improvisational performance can develop a new version of an old song, use snippets from an existing song in a new improvised composition, or use existing songs and performances as models for improvising a new solo. In theatrical improvisation the repertoire may include well-known plays or stories and established characters, which are often subverted by acting them 'with a twist' or taking them outside their normal context. While the social, technical and repertoire resources provide a basis for performing an improvisation, they do not specify what to do. The improvisation remains a relatively 'open space' (Hatch 1999) in which an indefinite variety of performances is possible (Donald et al.

2010). Thus, minimal structures can be regarded as loose–tight because they enable action but impose the least constraint possible.

Minimal structures are regarded as relevant to management and organisational practices as they relate to the use of resources, in order to achieve hoped-for ends that cannot be firmly predicted, and the need to respond in real time and recognise patterns in action as they unfold. Hence, links can be made to emergent strategising, organisational learning and creative practices (Cunha and Kamoche 1999). Equally, organisational change can be associated with moments 'in between' structure (Beech 2010), as different practices come into close contact and produce competition, synthesis or dialogue (van de Ven and Poole 2005). In film-making, Bechky and Okhuysen (2011) have shown how film crews on horror films draw together resources – what they call organisational bricolage – in order to find ways of dealing with the unexpected, such as equipment breakdowns, damaged sets, the impact of the weather and the need to deal with 'creative leeway' taken on the spur of the moment by the director. The crews had to be able to work together to undo normal routines, take on aspects of each other's roles and restructure their activities in order to achieve required outcomes in unexpected ways. Hence, process innovation was a key outcome of their improvisatory practice. While Bechky and Okhuysen (2011) are concerned with the unexpected, Pitts (2011) explores the increasing expectations associated with new technologies in film. New digital technologies are enabling lower budget film productions to have different narrative structures with longer shots and shots composed of multiple images (Ohanian and Phillips 2000). While these innovations expand the aesthetic choices of directors, they also increase expectations of what can be achieved technically, producing unforetold (and underexplored) impacts on technical roles in all phases of production (Culkin and Randal 2003). For example, Cram (2012) identifies directors' increasing reliance on visual effects supervisors to integrate digital and analogue elements for a homogenised 'look'.

The proliferation of digital technology in film production increases expectations that problems which occur during shooting may be corrected in post-production, and that continuity may be achieved by smoothly editing scenes – shot out of sequence – together. Additionally, increasing audience expectations of film production means that, although there can be considerable suspension of disbelief with regard to plot line and the nature of monsters and heroes, there is little tolerance of special effects that are not sufficiently special. Nor is there tolerance for any slippage in the presentation of the 'everyday' (however constituted in the film genre).

Improvisation is often thought about as a 'front-stage' activity and most studies have considered it in this way. However, in order to make the 'everyday' believable in film-making, there is a considerable degree of unseen improvisation by people doing technical work rather than those acting or directing. This back-stage, unseen, improvisation is the focus of our study. We are interested in better understanding how innovative practices are improvised in such a way that the process of production flows effectively and, consequently, most people involved would be unaware of the innovation – which is, nonetheless, fundamental to the professional groups involved. We do this by exploring how post-production sound editors and script (or continuity) editors work within these expanding demands. We adopt a practice-based analytical approach, cultural historical activity theory (Engestrom et al. 1999, Blackler 1993), in our empirical analysis of improvisation in film production in order to explore its relational nature as an example of innovation. In the next section, we provide a brief overview of this theory.

ANALYSING PRACTICES THROUGH CULTURAL HISTORICAL ACTIVITY THEORY

Practices have increasingly become the focus of research (Schatzki 2001). Although 'practice' is a polysemic and contested term (Gherardi 2009a, Schatzki 2001), it is generally understood to involve 'knowledgeable collective action' which draws upon available resources, within the constraints that apply in a particular situation (Gherardi 2009b: 353). Therefore, practices involve relations between people and artefacts, through which norms and rules are produced, which make practices broadly recognisable through the 'sayings and doings' of those involved (Nicolini 2011: 604). It is through these relations in practice that work – and society – are produced and reproduced (Gherardi 2009b, Chaiklin 2010).

Chaiklin (2010, 2011) proposes three related conceptualisations of practice: a universal conceptualisation of practice (an abstract notion of practice, such as that defined above), a range of specific practices which are broadly recognisable (e.g. teaching, dancing, acting), and concrete practices which involve particular instances of specific practices (e.g. this particular dance). Film-making constitutes a specific social practice which is recognisable to film-makers and audiences, regardless of location. In this chapter, we present data about a concrete example of film-making practice, gathered during the making of a 'slasher' movie.

While film-making is a recognisable specific practice, enacting it involves a range of related practices, including directing, acting, filming, creating sets, lighting and sound. Therefore, as with other types of work, film-making routinely involves a range of practices. These combine in various ways to make the final product (in this case, the film), which meets a range of needs (e.g. the desire to make something creative, to be entertained, to make money, to act, and so on).

(Cultural historical) activity theory focuses on activities which comprise social practices, within which these dynamics unfold (Chaiklin 2010, Lounsbury and Crumley 2007). The concept of activity accommodates the collective, mediated nature of practices (Vygotsky 1978), particularly in complex work settings. Mediation describes what happens when practitioners use available resources (Miettinen and Virkkunen 2005) as they work to produce their contribution to the overall activity. For instance, in our example of film-making, actors use material artefacts such as props (e.g. knives or guns) to mediate their portrayal of what their character is doing in the scripted situation (e.g. killing someone). But in addition to material artefacts, they will also draw upon epistemic artefacts such as their knowledge of the principles (norms and/or 'rules') of the practice of acting, in order to produce a convincing performance (for example, of being a serial killer, even though they have no actual experience of participating in the human activity of serial killing). Similarly, directors will use – through the work of other film-making participants – material artefacts including cameras, lights, scripts, sound recording, and so on, in addition to the epistemic artefact of their knowledge of how to draw all of these elements together, as they work to produce the final version of the film. Here, we can see how the work of others mediates the work of the director, and how the work of the director mediates the work of others (e.g. as direction is given to actors on set).

As multiple actors involved in related practices strive towards a shared aim, they are working collectively to produce what is known as the 'object of activity' (Leont'ev 1974, 1978). The object of activity may be the production of material objects, but this is not necessarily the case. It could equally involve the production of services, performances, ideas or other experiential or psychological 'objects' (for example, meeting healthcare needs or providing advice to social service clients) (Blackler et al. 1999, Blackler and Regan 2009). In our example, the object of activity is making the film.

Objects of activity are partially given and partially created (Engestrom and Blackler 2005, Miettinen and Virkkunen 2005). They are partially given (and constrained) in that they do not occur in a 'social vacuum' but are in the context of part of the attendant traditions, norms and rules of the practices (Chaiklin 2010, Nicolini 2011). However, objects of activity are also partially created through what practitioners do and the way in which their activity is organised in any given situation. From an activity theory perspective, their activities are not predetermined (Axel 1997);

rather, practitioners exercise a degree of interpretation and choice which may reflect the intentions they have for their activity (Blackler and Regan 2009, Nardi 1996). In this way, an activity may be seen to be inherently contextual, simultaneously shaped by the historical and cultural circumstances in which it is conducted, and shaping the way contemporary activity emerges as it is enacted (Nardi 1996, Lave 1993) – that is, in the moment of practising. Therefore activity is both enabling and constraining (Nardi 1996), and is thus simultaneously loose and tight (Bilton and Cummings: this volume, Chapter 1).

As different practices coalesce around the object of activity, some degree of improvisation may well be necessary, in part because of the somewhat contradictory nature of activities. Although they bear practitioners' mutual purposes, objects of activity are typically contested and negotiated (Blackler et al. 1999). Practitioners may interpret the object of activity differently from one another, at least in part due to participating in activity from different practice perspectives (Blackler et al. 1999, Greig et al. 2011, Patrick et al. 2012). Indeed, purposeful work frequently involves what may seem initially to be opposing or contradictory actions, as different practices combine to create the final product.

Sometimes, however, opposing or contradictory actions are foregrounded more strongly, reflecting various pressures and countervailing demands, which emerge through participating in an activity (Engestrom 1987). During these times, bisociation (Bilton and Cummings: this volume, Chapter 1) becomes evident as different practices interact in the course of activity; for example, when there is a requirement to produce something within too short a timescale, or when there is no budget to cover the costs, or when there is inappropriate or a lack of equipment. When such tensions between simultaneously present – but contradictory – aspects of activity become too great, they may give rise to a change in the activity. For example, new ways of mediating particular aspects of activity may be required, new rules or procedures may be introduced, or changes may be made in the overall object of activity itself as overall work practice changes (Blackler and Regan 2006, Engestrom 1999).

Therefore, the way in which practitioners cope with tensions or contradictions becomes a potential source of future learning for practitioners (Engestrom 1987). Managing such challenges may provoke practitioners to improvise, perhaps modifying rules or minimal structures (Kamoche and Cunha 2001) that enable them to manage similar future situations. Such uncertainties in day-to-day working can produce situations where the combination of loose–tight characteristics of relational practices gives rise to tensions or contradictions. In these circumstances practitioners demonstrate instances of bisociation, wherein they can forge innovative relations between practices and situations in mediated activity. Here, improvisation becomes an important aspect of practising (Middleton 1996). Our aim is to develop insights into improvisation in film-making as an example of innovation, which incorporates the loose–tight characteristics of relational practices, and instances of bisociation in everyday working. We base our discussion on data gathered during the making of a 'slasher' movie.

THE PRACTICE OF PRODUCING THE 'SLASHER'

The production process of 'slasher films' involves considerable skill to ensure 'gory' scenes look and sound 'real' to the audience. Script supervisors and post-production sound editors undertake activities which aim to maintain continuity and enhance authenticity in the film.

Script supervisors – also known as 'continuity supervisors' – are responsible for a film's internal continuity, so that scenes follow one another without any sudden breaks or inconsistencies; they also ensure that all the footage captured each day contains essential elements required for a seamless edit. Their work begins with the preparation of the 'continuity synopsis' in pre-production of the film. This is a report on the screenplay that provides basic information on each scene to make sure that filming (when it starts) is in sync with the progression of the story as written in the screenplay and the shooting script. The shooting script is a version of the screenplay that lists the production details and technical direction required for each scene. All departments involved in film-making, from art and production to camera and electrical, refer to these reports or consult the script supervisor to make decisions that are consistent with the story line as well as previous/subsequent scenes. This crucial role is particularly important when scenes are shot out of sequence (i.e. not following the linear narrative of the storyline). In order to ensure continuity, when such discontinuity is a feature of filming, script supervisors keep 'daily logs' that record details including decisions made by the director (e.g. changes to dialogue or action) and technical information (e.g. 'take' number of each scene, camera lens and camera directions or 'axis', sound and action running times). This is passed on to visual and sound editors who use this information to make a continuous flow from the discontinuous parts of the film as it is shot, to compile the film in its entirety. Therefore, the script supervisor liaises between director and editors as the film is made.

Post-production sound editors are responsible for assembling the audio for the final sound mix after shooting is complete. This involves fixing technically inferior sound that has been recorded during shooting by re-recording needed dialogue, creating sound effects, adding music and, finally, precisely 'looping in' (inserting), relinking and synchronising this 're-mastered' audio with the footage. The sound mix therefore includes a combination of three different elements: dialogue, effects and music. The post-production sound team often includes several practitioners, each specialising in one of these areas. In the case of sound effects, editors usually have access to an electronic stock library of sounds. But sometimes other sounds have to be created and recorded especially for the current film. This process is known as 'foleying', when post-production sound staff create sound while watching the footage.

The contribution to film-making of post-production sound editors and script supervisors is sometimes referred to as 'technical' as opposed to 'artistic', and therefore may be considered 'less creative' than the more obvious on-screen roles. But as our data demonstrate, a considerable degree of improvisation and innovation is both expected and required of these practitioners.

In the next section we present two illustrations of improvisation and innovation. The first occurs during the post-production sound edit of 'scenes on the bridge' in the sound studio. The second occurs while shooting 'scenes in the kitchen' on the studio set, with a focus on the activities of the script supervisor.

Illustration 1: 'Scenes on the Bridge'

Three of the post-production sound crew – the supervising sound editor (SSE) who has extensive experience mixing dialogue, effects and music, a junior sound editor (JSE) with experience in effects, and a sound production assistant (SPA), who is a film student at a local college – gather in the recording studio on the production lot. They are 'spotting', which involves watching previously shot footage to identify sounds that need to be augmented, replaced or added. Their pace is frantic because yesterday the director said the sound edit needed to be complete by next week for an early preview of the film. They sit behind the sound mixer watching, on a big screen, footage of scenes shot on a bridge. This includes one scene where an actor limps across the bridge. SSE dictates the effect issues to JSE and SPA, who listen. The actor has a wound on his upper thigh and holds a crow bar in one hand. SSE spots the need to loop in or add three sounds: footsteps with a limp, the sound of crow bar sporadically banging against the metal rails on the bridge, and a coat rustling in the wind (when the actor pauses halfway across the bridge).

JSE searches the stock library of sounds and plays several examples of wind and clothes rustling. SSE nods at one version of 'clothes rustling'.

JSE then plays sounds of clashing metal. SSE decides that none of these works and asks JSE and SPA to use the sound of the bar hitting the rails which was recorded on location, but asks them to enhance it 'in foley'. JSE and SPA go next door to foley stage to create sounds of a 'limping gait' and 'metal clash'. SSE asks them to produce the recordings within an hour. Meanwhile, SSE works in the recording studio on a previous set of scenes, which need a smoother transition between two scenes: the dialogue needs to be clearer and the background production sound eliminated.

Next door, JSE and SPA enter a small walk-in closet filled with 'foley props' (shelves of different shoes, piles of materials such as aluminium cans and chains). JSE grabs a couple of large boots and what looks likes the shaft of a golf club. They go to the foley stage, which includes a large screen with several platforms covered with different surface types. JSE puts on the boots and stands on a small square platform with a cement surface while SPA cues up footage of the limping scene. JSE attempts to drag a 'limping' left foot in sync with the 'limping' actor's movement on the bridge, but the sound isn't right. After a few moments, JSE sends SPA off to find some rocks to put in the boots to create a more 'belaboured'-sounding walk. SPA comes back five minutes later with rocks that seem about the right size, found in the car park outside the foley stage and recording studio. They put the rocks in the boots and try making the sounds again. This time, JSE is satisfied with sound. JSE switches places with SPA, who 'limps' on the foley stage, while JSE works at the mixer, recording the footsteps. It takes 15 minutes and several attempts to record 'limping' footsteps successfully.

JSE rejoins SPA on the foley stage to create the sound of the bar hitting the rails of the bridge. They see a metal pole erected at the corner of the stage. JSE suggests SPA bang the golf club shaft lightly against a metal pole. JSE returns to mixer and plays the 'limping on the bridge' footage while SPA clangs the metal in sync with the actor's movement. JSE records the sound and then spends 20 minutes mixing and overlaying the metal clash that has just been recorded on the foley stage with the clash sounds recorded during the actual 'limping scene' footage.

This illustration demonstrates the improvisational nature of bisociation and loose–tight characteristics associated with post-production sound editing. The contribution of post-production sound editing to film-making activity is to ensure the audience remains unaware that the film is made up of a series of (frequently disconnected) shots by spotting or identifying sounds that need to be deleted, enhanced or replaced in the final film. This involves both tight and loose characteristics: re-mastering the audio captured on the shoot by adding in sounds from a set of pre-recorded material illustrates tight characteristics, while creating new sounds especially for that occasion highlights the necessarily loose aspect of this area of film-making activity. Bisociation arises for post-production sound editors when these additional and replacement pieces of sound must be mixed together, along with audio captured during filming, to produce an authentic sound that enhances the final on-screen action.

Post-production sound editors develop a sense of audiences' abilities to notice or not notice sound, and draw on previous experience and knowledge to identify when this is likely to happen in relation to the on-screen action:

> JSE: We have done a good job in post-production if in the final edit of the film you don't notice the sound to a certain extent. For instance in the bridge scene we worked on today, SSE knew that audience would notice if the sound of the coat rustling wasn't there. When you watch the footage with sound you learn to pick out which sounds the audience is going to expect to hear and what they will notice not hearing. This is not as easy as you think it is. When you are watching a film you don't 'hear' every sound, it would be too much. There is this intuitive way [in post-production] of knowing which particular sounds need to be pronounced and which should be downplayed into background sound. There's a knack to it that you pick up by doing the job for a long time.

This apparent ability, to anticipate the needs of the overall film in terms of sound, may account for the – apparently common – director's assumption that post-production sound can rectify all sound problems that may arise during the course of shooting the film.

> We are the quick-fix for all sound issues . . .. Recording issues are always the first to be overlooked. They just expect that we will 'loop in' afterwards anything and everything that needs it. (JSE)

This reliance on post-production sound to produce perfect sound for the film leads to difficult and innovative work for those involved. JSE and SPA's work on the foley stage, to produce the 'limping' and 'crashing metal' sounds, highlighted the improvisational nature of this everyday – but inherently uncertain – aspect of post-production sound practice. Their need to work with and beyond the 'rules' was clear: although there were materials available to them in the foley stage, and an infinite array of ways in which they could produce a sound, the new sound needed to be authentic to remain 'natural' (and therefore unremarkable) for the audience. In this instance, the usual ways of producing limping sounds were insufficient and SPA improvised by retrieving the right sort of rocks from the car park to create an authentic sound to enhance the drama and suspense of the scene. So although creating new sounds entails space for fabrication and invention, through which innovative solutions to current problems may be discovered, the newly created sounds must perfectly, 'realistically' – and unnoticeably – match with the action on screen and enhance dramatic effect.

The need to fix problems later produces a great deal of tension between production and post-production sound editors. SSE argues that the majority of issues that prevent sound from being properly recorded are predictable and happen repeatedly.

> ... without a doubt, [sound] if properly captured during shooting almost always works better than anything we can come up with in post-production, and this is entirely doable if the production would just take the time to pay attention to ramifications of any choice on sound recording ...

Therefore the most challenging post-production sound issues, which require improvisational and potentially innovative work to rectify problems created during shooting, could perhaps be avoided if film-making colleagues took 'recording' issues into account:

> JSE: A lot of times I can tell that the [production] sound guys weren't given the chance to pick up the room tone [on-set background noise] before shooting and it's probably because the AD (assistant director) didn't give the guys the chance ...

However, before any of this post-production sound improvisation can occur, there is another aspect of film-making where even less visible improvisation and innovation arise, indeed where one might expect no improvisation at all – 'continuity'. In Illustration 2, we focus on the activity of script – or continuity – supervisors.

Illustration 2: 'Scenes in the Kitchen'

SS, a senior script supervisor with over 15 years of experience, and JS, a junior supervisor with limited experience working on small films, arrive on set. Today Scene 82, 'Stab in the Kitchen', and two subsequent scenes, are being shot out of sequence – the preceding scene having been shot four weeks ago. JS has a stop-watch and several reports including the shooting script, continuity synopsis and the daily logs from previously shot scenes. On their way in they confirm a detail about the axis of the scene [camera position/angle] to be shot with a camera operator. JS and SS position themselves in front of a monitor screen, close to the sound stage.

Two actors and the director are working in 'the kitchen'. Seeing SS and JS arrive, one actor asks with which hand he was holding the wine glass in the previous scene. JS responds without consulting notes. As the director changes the placement of the two actors and the direction from which killer enters, JS takes notes, dictated by SS. Shooting begins. JS watches, noting details of the scene, recording timing of actions and associated dialogue. SS looks over JS's shoulder, pointing to the screen if JS misses spotting any continuity issues, which JS then adds to the notes. The director and actors work on the scene through three takes without making additional major changes in action or dialogue, while JS/SS take continuous notes for the daily log.

Between takes 3 and 4, the director encourages the two actors to 'feel' the scene out differently. In take 4, one actor delivers several unscripted lines and unexpectedly lunges towards the other actor. The director likes the improvisation and keeps this in the scene. JS quickly records the changed dialogue and movement details. There are a further 9 takes of the scene. Each time, JS records the director's views and preferences guided by SS, who occasionally speaks directly to the director.

Between takes 7 and 8, a production 'runner' gives SS/JS a message from editing. Scene 75, a previous 'kitchen' scene, is not cutting together easily. An 'insert' is needed of one of the actors colliding into the refrigerator with a bloody stab wound on his shoulder. JS checks the daily log for the details wardrobe and make-up will need to prepare the retake of the 'insert' scene, before they wrap on the 'kitchen set' for the day. While JS is talking to wardrobe, the production assistant for set design asks JS which photos to put on the refrigerator door for the 'insert'. In one previous take of scene 75 there was one photo (the 'wife photo'), but in other takes a different set of three pictures of the whole family were on the refrigerator door. JS says (without consulting the daily log) that the director of photography favoured the three 'family' photos on the right refrigerator door. The set designers prepare the photos for the 'insert' take.

Perhaps the key challenge the script supervisors face is the requirement to cope simultaneously with spontaneity and continuity in their everyday practice, throughout the entire production:

> JS: There is this sort of feeling on the set that the most important thing is to capture the magic of the scene and do whatever needs to be done to make this happen. This means any number of last-minute changes play out, and I've got to do the job of making sure that all those little adjustment details – ones that the audience will see if they aren't consistent – are accounted for . . ..

The script supervisor requires a detailed understanding of what is supposed to happen on the set, while taking notes on what is actually happening (and has already happened and then changed). This calls upon abilities which require some training:

> SS spent an entire weekend showing me how to break down the shooting script and take continuity notes on character, wardrobe and costume. (JS)

The recognised practice of script supervision is achieved through observation, while keeping a running log of every important detail, including deviations from the shooting script and which 'takes' the director and/or director of photography favour. This highlights the tight nature of the job, in that the daily log has to be firmed up each day, in order to provide the basis for making further changes. However, in so doing, it simultaneously constitutes work that enables loose situations in the work of others, such as shooting out of sequence and/or improvising in on-screen action. In addition, although the 'rule' is that the script supervisor should note every detail, in practice this is impossible. The improvisory practice is to decide in the moment which details are sufficiently important, and which are not.

The role of script supervisor embraces a degree of bisociation; playing an enabling *and* constraining role within the overall film-making activity involves observing and retaining large amounts of detailed information which must be produced on demand to meet others' needs. Script supervisors have to improvise as unexpected demands are created through the work of others, like the sudden demand to provide continuity information for Scene 75 which interrupted the recording of Scene 82 between takes 7 and 8, of the 13 takes shot that day.

Being able to do this successfully involves knowing how to quickly pinpoint anomalies in continuity, while recording details of how the action plays out, keeping the scene timings and page counts, monitoring that the actions are in conjunction with the dialogue, and that costume, hair and make-up match the current story line, as well as the subsequent/preceding scenes. Doing this seemingly impossible job therefore involves accommodating the contradictions in ongoing activity. Crucially it involves learning:

> ... the shorthand ways to take the logs every day, and what the editor absolutely *has* to have written about the footage, and [how] this has to be written. (JS)

Therefore, accommodating these contradictions in ongoing activity means being able to know – in the moment – what is/cannot be ignored and improvising to channel relevant details to satisfy others' needs, whether this seems helpful at the time or not:

> They [crew members from other departments] seem so irritated with me when I try to brief them on a detail . . .. But then the same women from wardrobe – who didn't seem to have time for me yesterday – will run up to me at the last minute and check if a character's tie was tied or untied in the last scene. (JS)

While script supervisors have expectations of what the film crew need to know and when they need to know it, other film crew practitioners also have expectations of the script supervisor. Visual and sound editors require high levels of continuity and accurate information to support their parts in overall activity. They need specific details, but exactly which ones are unpredictable and will only emerge in the moment. This means the script supervisor has to improvise in the moment when these demands become evident. Since editing cannot be done successfully without script supervisors' input, they become crucial mediators of editing practice. Therefore script supervisors face a contradictory situation: they need to work very hard to make their work invisible; if they fail, they will have not met others' expectations of them and they will not add to the value of the overall product. Thus their work mediates the whole film, from the initial continuity synopsis to the daily log, such that script supervision has become a 'safety net' in film production.

AN ACTIVITY THEORY PERSPECTIVE ON IMPROVISATION

The illustrations of post-production sound editing and script (or continuity) supervision presented above offer insights into the simultaneously loose and tight and bisociatory characteristic involved in these practices – sometimes regarded as 'technical' rather than 'creative' – in film-making activity (see Chapter 3, Hearn and Bridgstock, this volume, for in-depth discussion of how creative industries are defined and differentiated). Each practice is characterised by a high degree of uncertainty in terms of what the practitioners involved will have to do on any given day. Each of the practitioners copes with the uncertainties, characteristic of their everyday practices, by drawing on past experience and the mediating means they have at hand in the particular situation, to produce improvised solutions (Vygotsky 1978, Leont'ev 1974, Vera and Crossan 2004). The improvisation required to resolve such uncertainties can generate innovation in collective activity (Middleton 1996), as new ways of doing things are discovered and sometimes used to develop a new or modified rule in the minimal structure of practices. Thus through experience, the practitioners are able to meet future needs in different circumstances (Bilton and Cummings: this volume, Chapter 1).

In film-making, such improvisation arises through its relational nature, as work in one aspect of activity creates difficulties that need to be addressed in other aspects. This happens when a series of accidental problems or mistakes are generated in one area of practice, but are not evident

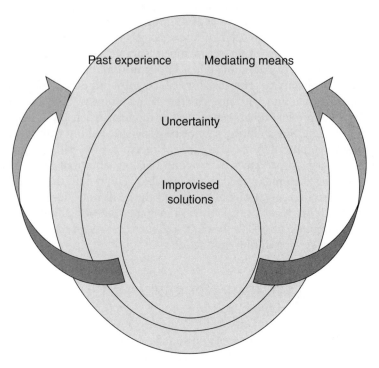

Figure 2.1   A model of improvisational practice

during the original activity (for example, the editing difficulty with Scene 75 was created when the scene was originally shot but only became evident later to practitioners undertaking the different activity of practice). In these circumstances, being able to make the wrong sound – or no sound – sound right, or to make the non-sequential appear sequential, is an essential aspect of film-making practice.

This ability to improvise creates a set of expectations amongst the entire film-making crew which form part of the impetus for this collective activity in order to produce their mutual object of making the film (Chaiklin 2010). Here, an important element of the film is for the audience to be able to suspend their disbelief, in order that the on-screen action creates suspense and tension. But if the 'joins' between scenes (arising through errors in sound or continuity) become discernible, this suspension of (dis) belief would be impossible. The work of post-production sound and script supervision practitioners in making these errors disappear is therefore central to the whole enterprise.

CONCLUSION

The improvisation illustrated in these aspects of film-making allowed on-screen improvisation to occur, which produced innovative practice in making the 'slasher' film. But much of this occurred off-screen. For example, on the foley stage, the post-production sound editors' discovery that they could enhance the suspense of a scene by finding rocks outside and using them to create a limping sound added – by happy accident – to the on-screen acting. Similarly, for the script supervisors, being able to cope with sudden demands for information by creating short-cuts in recording the details of each shot, helped others cope with a series of unplanned changes which impacted on their respective practices (such as the visual editors, in this instance). This required considerable improvisation in the script supervisors' practice which produced innovative ways of practising to enable other practitioners to be more innovative in the way they practised. The minimal structures created by script supervisors (Kamoche and Cunha 2001) allowed them to identify and channel the relevant details appropriately to others on the film crew, as required. Being able to achieve this seemingly confounding requirement of producing work which is simultaneously tight and loose and/or loose and tight, enabled or mediated the overall activity of making the film and thus added value to the final product.

For Bilton and Cummings (Chapter 1, this volume), bisociation is at the root of innovation. The empirical examples discussed here illustrate how instances of bisociation carry both contradiction and paradox, and thus require improvisational practice that can lead to innovation. The concept of loose–tight situations is useful for an examination of innovation because it draws attention to the way in which context is simultaneously enabling and constraining. This theme is further explored in Chapter 4, in which Sundbo and Sørenson consider the different approaches to innovation that involve both systematic and unsystematic practices. Kamoche and Cunha (2001) have emphasised the role of minimal structures in improvisation and we saw evidence of this in our examples. For example, while 'slasher' films may not normally be considered to be innovative, our empirical examples illustrate several areas of innovation. In Chapter 5, Lim and Oyama broaden the discussion of this issue through an exploration of conventional views of creativity and innovation. The production of the genre of slasher films requires a technical side to make the film appear realistic, but at the same time the film is entirely unrealistic. Thus, 'slasher films' involve minimal structures that both impose minor constraints and enable action. This area in which innovation transpires is often neglected, but activity theory helps us to focus on the overlapping practices which create tensions for each other. Escaping from these tensions entails working around, and developing, the minimal structures. Hence, small-scale improvisation can lead to innovation in the practices, and these innovations become socially reinforced, though not in a static way, through membership of the community of practice.

QUESTIONS FOR DISCUSSION

1. Consider other examples of work in the creative industries which incorporate improvisation:
   - How are they similar and/or different to the technical roles described in this chapter?
   - How do the practices create tension and paradox?
   - What are some of the mediating means by which one negotiates these circumstances?

   Thinking more generally:
2. In what other ways might uncertainty and confounding expectations enable improvisation and innovation?
3. Discuss the ways in which context is both enabling and constraining of innovation.

REFERENCES

Axel, E. (1997), 'One developmental line in European activity theories', in M. Cole, Y. Engestrom and O. Vasquez (eds) *Mind, culture and activity: seminal papers from the laboratory of comparative human cognition*, Cambridge: Cambridge University Press.

Bechky, B. and Okhuysen, G. (2011), 'Expecting the unexpected? How SWAT officers and film crews handle surprises', *Academy of Management Journal*, **54**(2), 239–61.

Beech, N. (2010), 'Liminality and the practices of identity reconstruction', *Human Relations*, **64**(2), 285–302.

Beech, N., H. Burns, L. de Caestecker, R. MacIntosh and D. MacLean (2004), 'Paradox as an invitation to act in problematic change situations', *Human Relations*, **57**(10), 1313–32.

Bilton, S. and S. Cummings (2010), *Creative strategy: reconnecting business and innovation*, Oxford and Hoboken, NJ: Wiley.

Blackler, F. (1993), 'Knowledge and the theory of organisations: Organisations as activity systems and the reframing of management', *Journal of Management Studies*, **30**(6), 863–84.

Blackler, F., A. Kennedy and M. Reed (1999), 'Organizing for incompatible priorities', in S. Dopson and A. Mark (eds) *Organisational behaviour in health care: the research agenda*, London: Macmillan.

Blackler, F. and S. Regan (2006), 'Institutional reform and the reorganisation of family support services', *Organisation Studies*, **27**(12), 1843–61.

Blackler, F. and S. Regan (2009), 'Intentionality, agency, change: practice theory and management', *Management Learning*, **40**(2), 161–76.

Brown, S. and K. Eisenhardt (1998), *Competing on the edge: strategy as structured chaos*, Boston, MA: Harvard Business School Press.

Chaiklin, S. (2010), 'The role of "practice" in cultural-historical science', in M. Kontopodis, C. Wulf and B. Fichtner (eds) *Children, culture and education*, New York: Springer.

Chaiklin, S. (2011), 'Social scientific research and societal practice: action research and cultural-historical research in methodological light from Kurt Lewin and Lev S. Vygotsky', *Mind Culture and Activity*, **18**(2), 129–47.

Cram, C. (2012), 'Digital cinema: the role of the visual effects supervisor', *Film History*, **24**(2), 169–78.

Culkin, N. and K. Randal (2003), 'Digital cinema: opportunities and challenges', *Convergence*, **9**, 79–95.

Cunha, M. and K. Kamoche (1999), 'Organisational improvisation: what, when, how and why', *International Journal of Management Reviews*, **1**(3), 299–341.

Donald, J., L. Mitchell and N. Beech (2010), 'Organizing creativity in a music festival', in B. Townley and N. Beech (eds) *Managing creativity: exploring the paradox*, Cambridge: Cambridge University Press.

Engestrom, Y. (1987), 'Learning by expanding: An activity theoretical approach to developmental research', Helsinki: Orienta-Konsultit. [Internet]. (available from http://commu nication.ucsd.edu/MCA/Paper/Engestrom/expanding/toc.htm [Accessed 3 March 2007]).

Engestrom, Y. (1999), 'Innovative learning in work teams: analysing cycles of knowledge creation in work teams', in Y. Engestrom, R. Miettinen and R.L. Punamaki (eds) *Perspectives on activity theory*, Cambridge: Cambridge University Press.

Engestrom, Y. and F. Blackler (2005), 'On the life of the object', *Organisation*, **12**(3), 307–30.

Engestrom, Y., R. Miettinen and R. Punamaki (1999), *Perspectives on activity theory*, Cambridge: Cambridge University Press.

Eikhof, D. (2010), 'The logics of art: analysing theatre as a cultural field', in B. Townley and N. Beech (eds) *Managing creativity: exploring the paradox*, Cambridge: Cambridge University Press.

Frost, A. and R. Yarrow (1990), *Improvization in drama*, New York: St Martin's Press.

Gherardi, S. (2009a), 'Introduction: The critical power of the "practice lens"', *Management Learning*, **40**(1), 115–28.

Gherardi, S. (2009b), 'Knowing and learning in practice-based studies: an introduction', *The Learning Organisation*, **16**(5), 352–9.

Greig, G., N. Beech and V. Entwistle (2011), 'Addressing complex healthcare problems in diverse settings: Insights from activity theory', *Social Science and Medicine*, **74**, 305–12.

Hatch, M. (1998), 'Jazz as a metaphor for organizing in the 21st century', *Organisation Science*, **9**(5), 556–77.

Hatch, M. (1999), 'Exploring the empty spaces of organizing: How improvisational jazz helps redescribe organisational structure', *Organisation Studies*, **20**(1), 75–100.

Henry, J. and D. Walker (1991), *Managing innovation*, London: Sage Publications.

Kamoche, K. and M. Cunha (2001), 'Minimal structures: from jazz improvisation to product innovation', *Organisation Studies*, **22**(5), 733–64.

Lave, J. (1993), 'The practice of learning', in S. Chaiklin and J. Lave (eds) *Understanding practice: perspectives on activity and context*, Cambridge: Cambridge University Press.

Leont'ev, A.N. (1974), 'The problem of activity in psychology', *Soviet Psychology*, **13**(2), 4–33.

Leont'ev, A.N. (1978), *Activity, consciousness and personality*, Englewood Cliffs, NJ: Prentice Hall.

Lounsbury, M. and E. Crumley (2007), 'New practice creation: an institutional perspective on innovation', *Organisation Studies*, **28**(7), 993–1012.

Middleton, D. (1996), 'Talking work: argument, common knowledge and improvisation in teamwork', in Y. Engestrom and D. Middleton (eds) *Cognition and communication at work*, Cambridge: Cambridge University Press.

Miettinen, R. and J. Virkkunen (2005), 'Epistemic objects, artefacts and organisational change', *Organisation*, **12**(3), 437–56.

Montuouri, A. (2003), 'The complexity of improvization and the improvization of complexity: social science, art and creativity', *Human Relations*, **56**(2), 237–55.

Nardi, B. (1996), 'Studying context: a comparison of activity theory, situated action models, and distributed cognition', in B.A. Nardi (ed.) *Context and consciousness: activity theory and human-computer interaction*, Cambridge, MA, London: The MIT Press.

Nicolini, D. (2011), 'Practice as the site of knowing: insights from the field of telemedicine', *Organisation Science*, **22**, 602–20.

Ohanian, T. and M. Phillips (2000), *Digital filmmaking: the changing art and craft of making motion pictures*, Woburn: Butterworth-Heinemann.

Patrick, H., G. Greig and N. Beech (2012), 'Managing improvizational practice: the tension between structure and creative difference', in G. Wood and M. Demirbag (eds) *Handbook of Institutional Approaches to International Business*, Cheltenham: Edward Elgar, pp. 344–62.

Pitts, V. (2011), 'Technologies of culture: digital feature film-making in New Zealand', *New Cinemas Journal of Contemporary Film*, **9**(1), 3–17.

Rehn, A. and C. de Cock (2008), 'Deconstructing creativity', in T. Rickards, M. Runco and S. Moger (eds) *The Routledge companion to creativity*, London: Routledge.

Schatzki, T. (2001), 'Introduction: practice theory', in T. Schatzki, K. Knorr Cetina and E. von Savigny (eds) *The practice turn in contemporary theory*, London: Routledge.

Van de Ven, A.H. and M. Poole (2005), 'Alternative approaches for studying organisational change', *Organisation Studies*, **26**(9), 1377–1404.

Vera, D. and M. Crossan (2004), 'Theatrical improvization: lessons for organisations', *Organisation Studies*, **25**(5), 727–49.

Vygotsky, L.S. (1978), *Mind in society – the development of higher psychological processes.* Cambridge, MA: Harvard University Press.

Zack, M. (2000), 'Jazz improvisation and organising: once more from the top', *Organisation Science*, **11**, 227–34.

3. The curious case of the embedded creative: creative cultural occupations outside the creative industries

Greg Hearn and Ruth Bridgstock

Few managers would dispute that creativity and innovation are important. However, what they mean by those terms would vary widely, and indeed, a survey of researchers and research studies examining creativity and innovation would confirm this diversity. For instance, proponents of the value of innovation laud creativity, but have tended to be biased towards scientific and technical invention and how this can be leveraged in new services and products. On the other hand, artists' works are seen as evidence of creativity that comes through different forms of cultural expression, but here there has been less concern with translation into commercial outcomes (e.g., Smith-Bingham 2006).

Over the last 15 years, the term 'creative industries' has gained currency as a descriptor of sectors that involve the deployment of specialised cultural creativity in industrialised form. For example, the current UK government definition includes the following creative sectors:

- advertising
- architecture
- arts and antique markets
- crafts
- design (including communication design)
- designer fashion
- film, video and photography
- software, computer games and electronic publishing
- music and the visual and performing arts
- publishing
- television.

In effect, creative industries discourse engineered the marriage between innovation discourse and artistic arts and culture. Indeed, the term is now widely used in Europe, East Asia and Australasia (Jones et al. forthcoming).

This chapter is concerned with innovation that involves creative cultural occupations,[1] but not within the creative industries. Rather, we examine the operation of cultural creative occupations that exist *outside* the creative industries – so-called 'embedded creatives' who work across all industry sectors (Cunningham and Higgs 2009). In doing so, we concur with Bilton (2007) that the separation of creative industries from other industries is a 'false step'. All industries must be innovative; however, they also must be able to combine both scientific and artistic creativity, and that creativity comes from the intersection of different thinking styles (Kurtzberg 2005). Moreover, we suggest that there are now detailed empirical studies, as well as a nascent theoretical base, to suggest that the transdisciplinarity which results from embedded cultural creativity is an engine of growth in the broader economy. Thus, it is relevant to both policymakers and managers. Strong growth in creative services revenues and employment (e.g., Freeman 2007) supports this contention, by indicating strong demand for creative input throughout the economy. As Vinodrai (2006: 259) suggests:

> In the contemporary economy, 'creativity' is viewed as a vital input in the production process, both in the cultural industries and across the economy. This situation suggests there is a role for 'creative workers' that extends beyond the boundaries of the cultural industries.

This chapter addresses the following questions: What is the role and significance of the embedded creative? Given a paucity of detailed empirical work in the area to date, what can be deduced from what extant literature there is about the nature of employment and management of these workers? And what are the practical implications of these considerations?

DEFINING AND LOCATING EMBEDDED CREATIVES

A number of empirical studies have confirmed that globally there are as many, if not more, workers in creative cultural occupations employed outside creative industries firms than in creative industries firms (e.g., Andrews et al. 2009, Freeman 2007, Higgs et al. 2008, Higgs et al. 2010). For instance, in 2006, New Zealand – renowned as a country that overperforms on measures of creative export – had 43,000 workers in embedded creative occupations and 36,000 working in the creative industries (Andrews et al. 2009). But what specifically were these occupations? The Australian and New Zealand Standard Classification of Occupations (ANZSCO) recognises two categories of creative occupations:

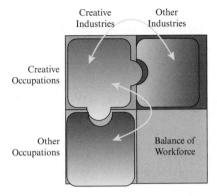

Figure 3.1   Defining creative work outside the creative industries

- 'creative arts', which includes many of the traditional cultural occupations, as well as other occupations that are concerned with creative products of various types
- 'creative services', which denotes a group of occupations that provide specialised creative expertise.

Within these two categories there are a number of creative occupation 'clusters'. These include: advertising and marketing; software and digital content; architecture, design and visual arts; publishing; and film, TV and radio.

In New Zealand, 2.2 per cent of total employment occurred in creative occupations embedded in other industry sectors. Interestingly, the number of creatives employed in different sectors varies quite markedly depending on the sector. It ranges from less than 1 per cent in agriculture, accommodation and transport services, through to over 4 per cent in wholesale trade, financial and insurance services, public administration and utilities. In a related study of Auckland (Higgs and Freebody 2010), a more fine-grained breakdown of the number of each type of embedded creative was undertaken. That analysis showed that 44 per cent of creative arts workers and 59 per cent of creative services workers were embedded in sectors outside the creative industries. The highest number of embedded creatives worked in digital content and software, followed by advertising and marketing specialists, then designers. Publishing occupations also featured strongly. However, the study also found that those in occupations in the performing arts and music were also employed in different industries to a substantial degree. In the New Zealand study, 5 per cent of embedded creatives were in the category of performing and visual arts. Table 3.1

*Table 3.1   The selection of creative occupations by sectors under the
             ANZSCO classification scheme (Andrews et al. 2009)*

Creative occupation ANZSCO	Creative segment
Advertising & public relations manager	Advertising & marketing
Arts administrator or manager	Music & performing arts
Actor	Music & performing arts
Dancer or choreographer	Music & performing arts
Entertainer or variety artist	Music & performing arts
Actors, dancers & other entertainers NEC	Music & performing arts
Musician (instrumental)	Music & performing arts
Singer	Music & performing arts
Photographer	Architecture, design & visual arts
Painter (visual arts)	Architecture, design & visual arts
Media producer (excluding video)	Film, TV & radio
Radio presenter	Film, TV & radio
Television presenter	Film, TV & radio
Author	Publishing
Book or script editor	Publishing
Art director (film, television or stage)	Film, TV & radio
Director (film, television, radio or stage)	Film, TV & radio
Film & video editor	Film, TV & radio
Technical director	Film, TV & radio
Film, television, radio & stage directors NEC	Film, TV & radio
Copywriter	Advertising & marketing
Newspaper or periodical editor	Publishing
Print journalist	Publishing
Technical writer	Publishing
Television journalist	Film, TV & radio
Journalists & other writers NEC	Publishing
Librarian	Publishing
Marketing specialist	Advertising & marketing
Advertising specialist	Advertising & marketing
Architect	Architecture, design & visual arts
Landscape architect	Architecture, design & visual arts
Fashion designer	Architecture, design & visual arts
Industrial designer	Architecture, design & visual arts
Graphic designer	Architecture, design & visual arts
Web designer	Software & digital content
Interior designer	Architecture, design & visual arts

Table 3.1   (continued)

Creative occupation ANZSCO	Creative segment
Urban & regional planner	Architecture, design & visual arts
ICT business analyst	Software & digital content
Systems analyst	Software & digital content
Web developer	Software & digital content
Analyst programmer	Software & digital content
Developer programmer	Software & digital content
Software engineer	Software & digital content
Software & applications programmers NEC	Software & digital content
ICT quality assurance engineer	Software & digital content
ICT systems test engineer	Software & digital content
Architectural draftsperson	Architecture, design & visual arts
Web administrator	Software & digital content
Library technician	Publishing
Jeweller	Architecture, design & visual arts
Camera operator (film, television or video)	Film, TV & radio
Light technician	Music & performing arts
Make-up artist	Music & performing arts
Sound technician	Music & performing arts
Performing arts technicians NEC	Music & performing arts
Library assistant	Publishing
Production assistant (film, television, radio or stage)	Film, TV & radio
Proof reader	Publishing

provides a detailed list of these embedded creative occupations by cluster and category.

Although the phenomenon of the 'embedded creative' has been empirically replicated in statistical studies referred to above, of a number of economies (Australia, United Kingdom, Paris and New Zealand), various questions remain. For example: What exactly is the nature of the work that embedded creatives do? What is it about these workers that leads firms to employ them? Is this work any different from that undertaken in specialist creative firms? How are embedded creatives managed? Are their conditions different from those working in specialist firms? What are the issues for managers seeking to understand how to use embedded creatives effectively?

There is, of course, a very basic answer to the question about the nature of embedded creatives' work. Census statistics for embedded and non-embedded creatives are based on self-reporting of occupations and occupations are categorised based on these descriptions. In other words, embedded creatives would not be categorised as such if they were not doing essentially the same work as those in creative firms. For example, a journalist outside the publishing industry must have described their work in such a way to be categorised as a journalist *per se*.

Unfortunately, there are few, if any, detailed accounts of the work of embedded creatives. One relevant study is that of Vinodrai (2006), who found that 'only 15 per cent of the industrial designers and 37.5 per cent of the graphic designers work in Toronto's design industry; the remainder work throughout other sectors of the economy' (p. 241). This supports the idea that creatives provide 'creative inputs' in a range of other industries. Vinodrai's study found that designers moved between different firms within the design sector, as well as between firms in other industry sectors. These transitions were motivated by a range of factors, including firm downsizing, contract work and upward career mobility.

EXAMINING WHAT THEORY SAYS ABOUT EMBEDDED CREATIVES

Although there is a paucity of descriptive accounts of embedded employment, we can use some theories that relate to the operation of the creative economy and firms within it to get a better understanding of this important category of creative work. For example, there are a number of macro-theoretical perspectives that are relevant to the phenomenon of the embedded creative; these perspectives involve a focus on the so-called 'culturalisation of the economy' and related considerations. After canvassing these ideas, we then explore the resource-based view of the firm as a promising theoretical direction for understanding why firms employ creatives. We also use studies of the evolution of creative services and their organisational and institutional structures (e.g., Bermiss 2009), which enable us to make deductions regarding creative occupational work in non-creative firms. In addition, we examine research that compares creative services with other knowledge-intensive services (e.g., Grabher 2004) and research focused on the outsourcing of creative services (e.g., Horsky 2006) to further develop our framework for understanding embedded creatives. Finally, Bowman and Swart's (2007) notion of embedded capital is explored as a vehicle for understanding the tacit and codified aspects of creative services production and how these play out in the negotiation of employment conditions and other manifestations of power in the organisation of creative workers.

At the macro-theoretical level, there is a considerable amount of work on the ways in which modern corporations have been shaped by the culturisation of economic life (e.g., Lash and Urry 1994). In fact, in most developed economies, most economic activity is driven by consumption (60 to 70 per cent) and increasingly this is directed towards the pursuit of cultural goods or goods with cultural components – the so-called culturisation of the economy (Lash and Urry 1994). The mass media played a role in this process by commodifying identity construction through circulation of the building blocks of identity, namely, images, visual codes and narratives. The integration of familiar social and personal networks into the media sphere, has made this self-construction process even more compelling. The corresponding growth in systems to support delivery and billing for diverse, culturally significant commodities increases cultural commodification.

Of course, there have been numerous political and ethical critiques of the cultural turn of contemporary capitalism, many of which are concerned with the penetration of the market logic into the realm of 'the human' – for example, the commercialisation of identities, intimacies, relationships and values (e.g., Davidson 1992, Harvey 1989, Jameson 1991). However, there is little argument that the aestheticisation of goods and services creates and captures high economic value. At a very broad level, this means it is not surprising that cultural creative jobs are spread throughout all industrial sectors.

Stoneman (2010) provides an operational account of the culturisation of economic life with his idea of 'soft innovation'. He suggests that the high rate of soft innovation found in the creative industries is different from technical research and development (R&D). While most studies of innovation emphasise functional advances through scientific or technical novelty, soft innovation refers to aesthetic changes that are economically important. This might be in purely aesthetic or cultural products such as films and books, but also in clothing or even airlines. Soft innovation is about aesthetic or functional *appeal* rather than functional performance. More could be said about Stoneman's ideas, but of most relevance here is his argument that soft innovation is equally relevant in sectors other than the core creative industries. For example, he refers to the food industry as an example in which the product does not change, but new ways of selling are constantly innovated. He argues that even in the pharmaceutical industry, for instance, aesthetic branding and other soft innovation play a part.

Some studies of designers also provide elaboration of these ideas. For

example, a study by Dell'Era et al. (2011) uses the idea of 'language brokering' to describe the way designers 'capture, recombine and integrate
socio-cultural knowledge and product semantics across social settings'
(p.36). Dell'Era et al. see the work of designers implicated at various
points throughout the product cycle. Designers may be involved in everything from functional redesign to the semantic reframe of a design, to producing different modes of product meaning.

Cunningham (2013) and his collaborators make a stronger claim
for the significance of embedded creative work. In their discussions
about the economic significance of the creative industries, Potts and
Cunningham (2008) and Potts et al. (2008) argue that the creative
economy is a set of economic processes across the economy as a whole,
that invigorate innovation-based growth. These researchers also suggest
that the creative economy needs to be understood as suffused throughout all industries rather than as a sector in its own right. They see creative workers as embedded in all sectors, as well as in the core creative
industries.

The above argument is consistent with that of Mudambi (2008) and
Hearn and Rooney (2008), who both suggest that while R&D activities
(including design) produce high value-capturing knowledge assets at the
beginning of the value chain, other forms of intellectual property (IP)
at the consumption end of the value chain – such as creative copyrights,
brands and sophisticated marketing systems – must also be acknowledged
as knowledge-economy indicators. In addition, Mudambi argues that
the fundamental feature of knowledge-intensive industries is that they

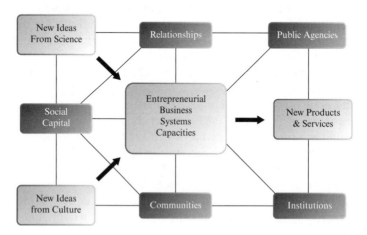

Figure 3.2   Economy is embedded in social networks

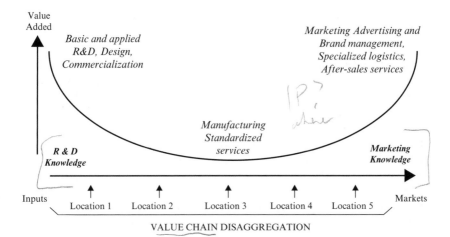

Source: Mudambi 2008

Figure 3.3   The smile of value creation

are built on intangible assets, not only through legally defensible rents (patents, copyrights and brands), but also *through ways of organising these intellectual resources through inimitable organisational structures and inter-organisational relationships.*

The resource-based view of firm competitiveness provides a compatible theoretical account of why firms engage in these knowledge-creating activities. The classical resource-based view argues that firms remain competitive to the extent that they apply the bundle of resources at their disposal (e.g., Barney 1991). Resources can be categorised as: physical; intangible IP; inimitable knowledge due to skill and other barriers; human capital; and organisational, which includes processes, relationships and so on. To maintain competitiveness, resources should be:

- valuable
- rare
- inimitable
- non-substitutable.

There have been a number of studies of the creative industries framed in terms of the resource-based view. For example, Miller and Shamsie (1996) applied the resource-based approach to Hollywood. They found that Hollywood resources included a diverse range of assets: first, physical assets of studios and theatre chains; second, star contracts; and third,

creative skills and ways of organising them. They also found that in turbulent times, the skills and organising processes were better predictors of
firm success.

Abecassis-Moedas et al. (2012) used the resource-based view to study
European design practices that were seeking to internationalise. Their
research paper advances three internationalisation modes: star-based,
process-based and glocality-based. In star-based creative services, the
individual designer operates as a 'brand' after developing a reputation
that attracts customers internationally. In process-based creative KIBS
(knowledge-intensive business services), the reputation of a 'collective creative process' attracts clients (p. 1). In glocality-based creative KIBS, geographical proximity helps to develop two key areas: a close understanding
of the client; and a better knowledge of the client's market.

The idea that specific routines and regimes in the organisation of creative services might be a factor of relevance is taken up by Grabher (2002),
who examines the 'project ecology' of advertising services. Using the
London advertising industry as a case study, Grabher (2002) explores
'the interrelation between projects on the one hand and, on the other, the
agencies, personal ties, localities and corporate networks, which provide
essential resources for project-based organising' (p. 245). In another study,
which compares the project ecology of a software company in Munich and
an advertising agency in London, Grabher (2004) identifies an important
distinction between the *modularisation* and *originality* of knowledge transfer and the processes of learning in the operation of these ecologies. In the
former – characteristic of the software company – knowledge is deployed
in processes of replicable and cumulative learning within the context of
recurring social relationships. In the latter – more characteristic of the
advertising agency – knowledge development and transfer is disruptive
and exploits the process of reconfiguring relationships. This distinction
can be explained by the opposing logics of knowledge creation and sedi-
mentation in the two project ecologies. The imperative for the software
agency, Grabher argues, is the development of repeatable solutions out
of one-off, singular ventures, thus economising on recurrent social ties.
In contrast, the ecology of advertising agencies is driven by the imperative to produce one-off, original solutions to a problem. These opposing
logics suggest, more generally, the value of examining the deployment of
in-house versus outsourced creative services to see the extent to which
embedded creative work is affected by the pressures and imperatives of
the host ecology.

In general, the question of whether firms 'make or buy' (that is, work
in-house or outsource) has received considerable attention in the economics and business strategies literature. In simple terms, this decision offers

a company either the possibility of control through hierarchy, or a choice of service providers through markets. Based on her study of manufacturing firms Parmigiani (2007) argues that even small firms in manufacturing use at least three options: make, buy or use a hybrid of the two. This finding suggests that decisions regarding when to outsource for large firms will be complex. For example, Parmigiani found that 'internal and external sourcing can be synergistic when used concurrently' (p. 306). Overall it is argued by Parmigiani that the decision to outsource or not does not appear to be simple. It is rather a decision requiring case-by-case analysis, of current advantages and disadvantages.

Another study of relevance to understanding in-house versus outsourced services focused on the history of the advertising industry. Bermiss (2009) investigated the emergence of the advertising industry from 1880 to 1920 and from 1924 to 1996. They suggest that the advertising industry's emergence was driven by two factors:

> the development of inter-organisational trust between agencies and advertisers; and the rapid accumulation of advertising knowledge by agencies during this period. These two factors decreased the perceived likelihood of agency opportunism, lowered transaction costs and motivated advertisers to outsource their critical marketing functions. (2009: 3–4)

In the study of the second time period, Bermiss asked whether an advertising company's knowledge assets were embedded within its 'human capital' or within its 'organisational structures and routines'. To answer this question, the research examined how spin-offs affected the survival of parent and progeny firms in the advertising industry between 1924 and 1996. Bermiss found that:

> spin-offs have a significant negative impact on parent firms while they provide a small benefit to the corresponding progeny firms. Furthermore, despite the creative attributes of advertising work product, it is the departure of executives in supporting organizational functions, rather than the loss of creative executives, that drives this effect. (2009: 3–4)

Another relevant study is that of Horsky (2006), who examined how creative media service components can be understood theoretically through bundling. Full-service outsourcing was common in her study; however, firms were willing to 'unbundle' to take advantage of discounts. Furthermore, in-house creative services were found when *either* strong capabilities or weak requirements/low cost and quality were a feature. The decision regarding whether to outsource may also be based on appraisals of risk and intangibility. An empirical study of creative services conducted by Hill and Johnson (2003) into the management of advertising and architectural services indicated that creative services were thought to be more intangible and risky and required different management approaches. This finding is consistent with the general literature on outsourcing (see Parmigiani 2007).

In terms of theorising the organisation of creative service work, Bowman and Swart's (2007) delineation of separable, embodied and embedded forms of capital is also useful. In their study of advertising services – as part of a broader study of professional services – they argue for the importance of recognising the essentially relational nature of knowledge production. In their formulation, all tangible, physical assets (such as plant, equipment and other physical components) and intangible IP (such as computer code, patents and trademarks) are 'separable resources'. In contrast, 'embodied resources', which are primarily explicit and tacit skills and knowledge, cannot exist separately from individuals or teams. So-called human capital takes this embodied form. The third form of capital, 'embedded capital', occurs in the relationship between the two: 'embedded capital exists where there is ambiguity surrounding the rent creating contributions of human capital due to synergistic interactions between separable and embodied capital that are difficult to disentangle' (2007: 494). Bowman and Swart suggest further that embedded capital is critical to knowledge-based, professional service industries in which both value creation and capture processes are driven by this interdependence between separable and embodied forms of capital.

Bowman and Swart (2007: 500) argue that:

> it is likely to be in the interest of managers (acting on behalf of the firm's owners) to reduce the proportion of embedded capital in the capital structure by converting embedded capital to separable capital. This conversion process can be achieved by codifying tacit knowledge, systematising value creation processes to effectively 'de-skill' them, or rotating staff to reduce the firm's dependence on specific relationships formed with clients by individuals or teams. Alternatively, where employees are able to 'convert' embedded capital into embodied capital . . ., their bargaining power increases, and their ability to capture the rents generated is consequently enhanced. They might achieve this by increasing their clients' attachment to themselves as individuals, rather than to them as representatives of the firm, or they might ensure that, over time, the knowledge they have gained through their experiences remains in their heads.

Bowman and Swart's work suggests that human capital cannot be understood simply in terms of individuals with particular skills and competencies. The notion of human capital is also concerned with its relationality: the embedding of human resources within the firm, and in social and cultural capital networks. It is this embeddedness that, we argue, is the defining characteristic of the creative economy. Further to this, Swart and Kinnie (2010) distinguish between three types of knowledge assets of relevance to the work of embedded creatives. First, there is human capital related to domain creativity (e.g., design or digital knowledge), which is the knowledge, skills and experiences of individual creative workers. Second, there is the relational capital that is embedded within social networks either external to the firm (clients or creative service providers) or internal to the firm client (resources, other creatives or other project assets). Third, there is organisational capital that is codified and leveraged through organisational routines. Swart and Kinnie (2010) suggest that the way these knowledge assets combine makes them the foundation for both *exploration* and *exploitation* of knowledge in the innovation process.

PRACTICAL ISSUES FOR MANAGEMENT

Thus, we arrive at what might be called the creative heart of the creative economy, namely, *the social and organisational routines that manage the generation of cultural novelty, both tacit and codified, internal and external, and its combination with other knowledges to produce and capture value.* How then should this creative heart of modern firms be managed? The answer, in many respects, may be to invoke the many principles and prescriptions that have been described regarding both creativity generally and cultural creativity in particular (see, for instance, Bilton 2007, Jeffcut and Pratt 2002). However, by way of conclusion, we want to explore whether the existence and function of the embedded creatives we have drawn attention to might raise any specific issues of relevance to the management of this form of creativity, or might suggest any new insights therein. Based on the arguments and empirical findings reviewed so far in this chapter, we can offer propositions of similarities and differences between the work, employment and career conditions of creative workers inside and outside the creative industries, and canvass some practical suggestions that are likely to be of relevance to the management of embedded creativity.

We know that the creative industries as a sector exhibits a number of distinctive labour market characteristics, which means that there are a number of sectoral-contextual differences between embedded creative workers and specialist creative workers. The creative sector is dominated by networked clusters of small-to-medium enterprises and micro-businesses (Creigh-Tyte and Thomas 2001). Work is often freelance or short-term. Creative businesses constantly change alliances to create new products. By contrast, embedded creative workers are employees of firms in other sectors and thus are more likely to work for firms of

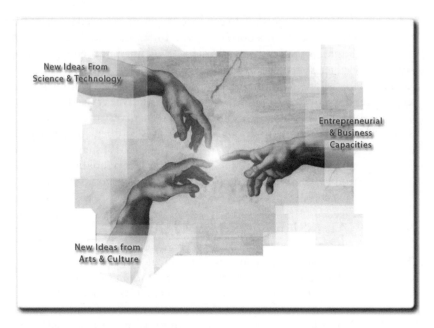

Figure 3.4   The act of creation

medium to large size. Further, creative work is much less likely to be the 'core business' of firms outside the creative industries. Embedded creative workers are likely to provide their skills to contribute aesthetic or creative value-adding to another product or service, for instance, they may develop web interfaces for educational products. Thus, for the embedded creative worker, the 'client' who provides the task brief may often be within the firm, whereas for the specialist creative, the client is always external to the firm.

A number of possible differences between the work and employment of specialist and embedded creatives therefore present themselves, with attendant implications for management:

1.   Both specialist creatives and embedded creatives need expertise in their core creative domain; however, the context of the creative process is different for embedded creatives, primarily in terms of the differences in the organisational culture of the host organisation. For example, embedded creatives may need to create unruly spaces within large bureaucracies, cultural knowledge may not be valued as strongly as within specialist firms, and creative knowledge may be more instrumentalised.

2. Both specialist and embedded creative work is facilitated through the operation of social networks. Embedded creatives may be more likely to have to broker external networks of creative services providers and internal networks of functional specialists from many different disciplines, while specialist creatives are more likely to have to broker external networks of potential clients and, to a lesser extent, potential creative collaborators. For specialist creatives, their internal networks are likely to be fellow creatives.

3. Embedded creatives may primarily need to be intrapreneurs, while specialist creatives are more likely to need to be entrepreneurs. Thus, access to resources may come from different forms of capital institutions (e.g., venture capital versus budget allocations).

4. Embedded creatives and specialist creatives may have different relationships to codified forms of creativity (brands, patents, designs and so on) and the way these can be both an opportunity and constraint in the creative process.

5. Formal professional development for both embedded and specialist creatives may need to be undertaken outside the employing firm. The firm employing the embedded creative may not employ enough creatives to provide the specialised skill development required. The firm employing the specialist creative may not be large enough to have a human resources department. Depending on their creative discipline areas, both specialist and embedded creatives may need to engage in significant informal professional development activities to keep abreast of rapid technological change in the digital creative sphere.

6. Embedded creative careers tend to be more 'traditional' in process and pattern, and embedded creatives are more likely to need to go through standard job application procedures (such as applying for advertised positions by submitting a curriculum vitae, followed by formal shortlisting and interview). On the other hand, specialist creatives are more likely to obtain work informally. Embedded creatives are more likely to work full-time and on an ongoing basis, whereas many specialist creatives exhibit 'portfolio career' patterns characterised by a self-created combination of part-time and casual work, along with self-employment (Bridgstock 2005). Thus, specialist work can be seen to be a more 'risky' career proposition in terms of career continuity and progression.

7. Specialist work can also carry more venture risk than embedded work. For the embedded creative, the risk associated with a creative project or venture is generally carried by the firm. On the other hand, specialist creatives (who are often self-employed or employed

by unincorporated firms) are more likely to carry the risk of ventures personally.

8.   Because the core work of the embedded creative's employer firm is likely to be something other than creative work, and the organisational context is likely to be more formalised and have inflexible teams and networks, there may well be less scope for radical innovation. Opportunity identification is likely to take the form of opportunity recognition or opportunity discovery, which happens when there is a known market and known product or service. In contrast, opportunity creation occurs when both supply and demand are unknown and must be discovered (Sarasvathy et al. 2005).

QUESTIONS FOR DISCUSSION

1.   Can embedded creative capital be controlled by managers?
2.   Which creative professions are most relevant to capturing value at either end of the supply chain?
3.   If you were a human resource manager, what approaches would you take to recruiting and managing creative talent given their career trajectories often alternate between specialist roles in the creative sector and embedded roles in industry verticals?
4.   Creative professions utilise divergent thinking strategies a great deal. How can these be harnessed in cross-functional teams?

NOTE

1.   We do not wish to claim that creativity only exists in these occupations, but seek to define here the domain of work we are concerned with in this chapter. Regardless of the semantic merits of the term 'creative cultural occupations', there are formal occupational codes in national statistics collection that empirically define these occupations and these are made clear later in the chapter.

REFERENCES

Abecassis-Moedas, C., S. Ben Mahmoud-Jouini, C. Dell'Era, D. Manceau and R. Verganti (2012), 'Key resources and internationalization modes of creative knowledge-intensive business services: the case of design consultancies', *Creativity and Innovation Management*, **21**, 315–31.

Andrews, G., J. Yeabsley and P.L. Higgs (2009), *The creative sector in New Zealand: mapping and economic role: Report to New Zealand Trade and Enterprise*. New Zealand Institute of Economic Research.

Barney, J.B. (1991), 'Firm resources and sustained competitive advantage', *Journal of Management*, **17**, 99–120.

Bermiss, Y.S. (2009), *The emergence and evolution of professional service industries*, doctoral dissertation, Northwestern University.

Bilton, C. (2007), *Management and creativity: from creative industries to creative management*. Malden, MA: Blackwell.

Bowman, C. and J. Swart (2007), 'Whose human capital? The challenge of value capture when capital is embedded', *Journal of Management Studies*, **44**, 488–505.

Bridgstock, R. (2005), 'Australian artists, starving and well-nourished: what can we learn from the prototypical protean career?', *Australian Journal of Career Development*, **14**(3), 40–48.

Creigh-Tyte, A. and B. Thomas (2001), 'Employment', in S. Selwood (ed.) *The UK cultural sector: profile and policy issues*, London: Policy Studies Institute.

Cunningham, S. (2013), *Hidden innovation: policy, industry and the creative sector*, St Lucia: University of Queensland Press.

Cunningham, S.D. and P.L. Higgs (2009), 'Measuring creative employment: implications for innovation policy', *Innovation: Management, Policy and Practice*, **11**(2), 190–200.

Davidson, P. (1992), *International money and the real world*, London: Macmillan.

Dell'Era, C., T. Buganza, C. Fecchio and R. Verganti (2011), 'Language brokering: stimulating creativity during the concept development phase', *Creativity and Innovation Management*, **20**(1), 36–48.

Freeman, A. (2007, July), *London's Creative Sector: 2007 update* (Working Paper No. 22), London: Greater London Authority.

Grabher, G. (2002), 'The project ecology of advertising: tasks, talents and teams', *Regional Studies*, **36**(3), 245–62.

Grabher, G. (2004), 'Temporary architectures of learning: knowledge governance in project ecologies', *Organization Studies*, **25**, 1491–1514.

Harvey, D. (1989), *The condition of postmodernity: an enquiry into the origins of cultural change*, Oxford: Blackwell.

Hearn, G. and D. Rooney (eds) (2008), *Knowledge policy: Challenges for the 21st century*, London: Edward Elgar.

Higgs, P., S. Cunningham and H. Bakhshi (2008), *Beyond the creative industries: mapping the creative economy in the United Kingdom*, London: NESTA.

Higgs, P.L. and S.P. Freebody (2010), *Auckland's creative workforce report 2010*, Auckland, NZ: Auckland Tourism, Events and Economic Development Ltd.

Higgs, P.L., S.P. Freebody, P. Anderson and S.D. Cunningham (2010), *What's your other job: A census analysis of arts employment in Australia*, Sydney: Australia Council for the Arts.

Hill, R. and L.W. Johnson (2003), 'When creativity is a must: professional "applied creative" services', *Creativity and Innovation Management*, **12**(4), 221–9.

Horsky, S. (2006), 'The changing architecture of advertising agencies', *Marketing Science*, **25**(4), 367–83.

Jameson, F. (1991), *Postmodernism, or, the cultural logic of late capitalism*, Durham, NC: Duke University Press.

Jeffcutt, P. and A.C. Pratt (2002), 'Managing creativity in the cultural industries', *Creativity and Innovation Management*, **11**(4), 225–33.

Jones, C., M. Lorenzen and J. Sapsed (eds) (forthcoming), *Oxford handbook of creative industries*, Oxford: Oxford University Press.

Kurtzberg, T.R. (2005), 'Feeling creative, being creative: an empirical study of diversity and creativity in teams', *Creativity Research Journal*, **17**, 51–65.

Lash, S. and J. Urry (1994), *Economies of signs and space*, London: Sage.

Miller, D. and J. Shamsie (1996), 'The resource-based view of the firm in two environments: the Hollywood firm studios from 1936 to 1965', *Academy of Management Journal*, **39**(3), 519–43.

Mudambi, R. (2008), 'Location, control, and innovation in knowledge-intensive industries', *Journal of Economic Geography*, **8**, 699–725.

Parmigiani, A. (2007), 'Why do firms both make and buy? An investigation of concurrent sourcing', *Strategic Management Journal*, **28**, 285–311.

Penrose, E.G. (1959), *The theory of the growth of the firm*, New York: Wiley.

Peteraf, M.A. (1993), 'The cornerstones of competitive advantage: a resource-based view', *Strategic Management Journal*, **14**(3), 179–91.

Potts, J.D. and S.D. Cunningham (2008), 'Four models of the creative industries', *International Journal of Cultural Policy*, **14**(3), 233–47.

Potts, J.D., S.D. Cunningham, J. Hartley and P. Ormerod (2008), 'Social network markets: a new definition of the creative industries', *Journal of Cultural Economics*, **32**(3), 166–85.

Rumelt, R.P. (1984), 'Toward a strategic theory of the firm', in R. Lamb (ed.) *Competitive strategic management* (pp. 556–70), Englewood Cliffs, NJ: Prentice-Hall.

Sarasvathy, S.D., N. Dew, S.R. Velamuri and S. Venkataraman (2005), 'Three views of entrepreneurial opportunity', *Handbook of Entrepreneurship Research*, 141–60.

Smith-Bingham, R. (2006), 'Public policy, innovation and the need for creativity', in N. Jackson, M. Oliver, M. Shaw and J. Wisdom (eds) *Developing creativity in higher education: an imaginative curriculum*, London: Routledge.

Stoneman, P. (2010), *Soft innovation: economics, design, and the creative industries*, Oxford: Oxford University Press.

Swart, J. and N. Kinnie (2010), 'Organisational learning, knowledge assets and HR practices in professional service firms', *Human Resource Management Journal*, **20**(1), 64–79.

Vinodrai, T. (2006), 'Reproducing Toronto's design ecology: career paths, intermediaries, and local labor markets', *Economic Geography*, **82**(3), 237–63.

[handwritten margin notes at top of page:]
service laboratories:
structured service lab v. loosely coupled networks
user needs ~ ideas 4 innovation
How IT used in svc. lab.

4. The lab is back – towards a new model of innovation in services

Jon Sundbo and Flemming Sørensen

This chapter considers the 'service laboratory' as a model which bridges two different approaches to innovation in manufacturing and service industries. Innovation processes in service firms are characterised as unsystematic, based on practical experiences of individual customers' needs and on engagement with customers in the service encounter. This approach often involves customers as co-creators of innovation and results in innovations that fit customers' needs. Conversely, it may be limited to incremental innovations that are only used by individual customers. In comparison, manufacturing innovation has traditionally been based on systematic use of natural and technical sciences for which the laboratory is the ultimate ideal (for example, in the pharmaceutical industry and electronics). Combining these two contrasting models relates to the bisociative definition of creativity outlined in the introduction to this handbook. How might service firms develop a more systematic approach to innovation which still retains the strengths of their user-centred model?

In a case study of an insurance company we have observed a potential solution to the lack of systematisation of innovation in service firms. The company has established what they consider to be an innovation laboratory with the purpose of increasing the company's innovativeness through experimentation and systematisation of innovation procedures. We designate this model as a service laboratory, defined as:

> an organisational unit operating as an open and dynamic structure-network, that uses instrumental innovation methods, and that involves internal and external actors in experiments in physical laboratories as well as in real life in order to test and develop new and improved services.

The service laboratory includes some known elements, but also some crucial new ones, which leads to a perception of the service laboratory as an organisational innovation in the service sector. This service laboratory may be a new model for achieving more systematic and research-based ways of organising service innovation activities so as to improve the efficiency of service firms' innovation activities, for example in terms of creating successful services or developing more radical innovations – without losing the advantage of employee and customer involvement that has characterised service innovation.

In order to define the service laboratory concept and relate this to innovation practice, we will begin with an overview of the characteristics of service innovations and the role of the laboratory in service innovation theory. Second, we present in a descriptive manner the service laboratory of the case company. Third, based on various theoretical approaches and the empirical data, we develop a theoretical understanding of the nature and functionality of the service laboratory. Fourth, we present a discussion of the findings and present a definition of the service laboratory. Finally, we summarise the main conclusions of the chapter.

SERVICE INNOVATION THEORY AND THE ROLE OF THE LABORATORY

Innovation in services, unlike in manufacturing, is typically an unsystematic process, based on quick ideas coming from practice, in many cases from the personnel's encounter with customers (Sundbo and Toivonen 2011) – in some cases a creative solution to a specific customer's problem. Theory suggests that service innovation is very market- and pull-oriented (based on demand) and bottom–up-oriented (based on employees acting as corporate entrepreneurs) (Sundbo 1997, Edvardsson et al. 2006). Consequently service innovation activities cannot be measured in the same way as manufacturing innovation activities, for example as investment in R&D or man-hours used on R&D (Djellal and Gallouj 2001, Drejer 2004).

There have been attempts to develop a more systematic or science-based approach to innovation in services, including more engineering-prescriptive models under the name of 'new service design' (Shostack and Kingsmann-Brundage 1991, Voss et al. 1992, Fitzsimmons and Fitzsimmons 2000, Edvardsson et al. 2006) and from the other direction, attempts to develop a more open, consultative approach to the rather closed, internal model of the R&D laboratory in manufacturing (Chesbrough 2006). However, manufacturing innovation theory offers little scope for the involvement of users and employees, and is more oriented to challenging rather than channelling existing user behaviour.

A theoretical explanation of the service laboratory will need to unite open innovation elements (such as involvement of users and employees) with systematic elements (such as systematic methodological work with service innovations). The open innovation approach developed by Chesbrough (2011) applies some principles of service innovation (employee and user involvement) with open manufacturing innovation (see also Bessant 2003, Toivonen 2010, Hasu et al. 2011). Such approaches may provide a theoretical basis for explaining and understanding the service laboratory, but they do not explain its practical operation, to which we now turn.

2 CASE STUDY: THE SERVICE LABORATORY

The following case study is based on a range of qualitative methods including interviews and participant observation as well as documentary analysis. We also draw on actor network theory (Law and Hassard 1999, Latour 2005), strategic reflexivity theory (Tidd et al. 2001, Sundbo and Fuglsang 2002, Sundbo 2003, Bessant 2003) and the new service development (NSD) approach (Fitzsimmons and Fitzsimmons 2000, Edvardsson et al. 2006) to explain and illuminate our findings.

The case company is a Scandinavian insurance company with about 4000 employees and a broad insurance product portfolio and head office in Copenhagen. The top management established a special service laboratory called BusinessLab in 2007. In 2009, the company introduced a new strategy aiming to expand its product portfolio and not simply be an insurance company but also to sell safety and welfare services. A new organisational structure was also introduced. Three departments covering different areas of insurance were established, each of them having three sub-departments: development, sales and marketing. The development sub-departments must co-operate with BusinessLab in their innovation activities.

The top management, particularly the managing director, wanted the company to develop into new market fields because there is little growth potential in traditional insurance fields. Top management therefore defined a new strategy based on a new development vision that emphasised innovation, seeing this as a precondition for realising the strategy. The new strategy has been communicated extensively internally in the organisation to engage all employees in innovation and development so as to realise the strategic goal (as Carlzon (1987) did in the airline company SAS in the 1980s). The top management also wanted more innovation within the traditional insurance fields, but BusinessLab's innovation mandate is much broader.

BusinessLab has a manager, a vice-manager and four employees. This is a low number in comparison with manufacturing laboratories, but is quite large for a services firm, particularly because BusinessLab's innovative function is far away from the production and delivery functions of the rest of the firm in organisational terms. BusinessLab has a board with representatives from the management including the managing director. The managers and employees of BusinessLab can develop their own experiments, but they are supposed to interact with the line departments about ideas that might be developed further.

Physically BusinessLab is composed of office spaces (we term these 'development offices') for its managers and employees and of a physical laboratory, but many activities of BusinessLab also occur outside the company. The heart of the organisational unit called BusinessLab consists of a physical laboratory situated physically in the core of the company. It consists of a large room which can be flexibly arranged in smaller sections where different experiments can be organised. IT projections (also interactive) can be made on the walls or screens. In this physical laboratory BusinessLab works with different and often untraditional means to engage customers and employees in innovation processes. In order to facilitate this BusinessLab has employed people that are not normally found in insurance companies, such as an industrial designer, a set designer and an anthropologist: furthermore, occasionally artists are hired to perform improvisational theatre acts as parts of experiments in the physical laboratory. Scenarios are developed through role-play, games, focus groups, physical design or online resources to explore attitudes and interactions between employees and customers.

The laboratory involves many different persons as participants and audience in its experiments: employees and managers, external company representatives, administrators from public administration, researchers and other external experts, and (not least) ordinary as well as lead users (cf. von Hippel 2005), both existing and potential. In addition to the experiments carried out in the laboratory, anthropological field studies are carried out outside of the company where users are observed and interviewed. Thus a field laboratory is also part of the service laboratory.

BusinessLab also has the task to create entrepreneurship and innovation throughout the entire organisation. It organises training sessions for employees and innovation-awareness campaigns in the organisation. They attempt to create corporate entrepreneurs called 'innovateurs' and rely on them to teach other employees in their departments to be innovative by imitating these 'innovateurs'. The BusinessLab must also follow and assess the innovation activities of all departments and eventually suggest actions to be taken by the management. All innovation must go via BusinessLab, thus its members have to approve the innovative idea, which they do in interaction with the top management. These are perhaps well-known forms of organising service innovation activities (Sundbo 1998, Boden and

Miles 2000, van der Aa and Elfring 2002); however, by being embedded in the service laboratory they acquire new contexts and functions.

BusinessLab has its own budget and can carry out experimental activities within that budget. However, the further development of an innovative idea requires that a specific project is established and that top management approves the project and sets a budget for it. BusinessLab initiates the first idea phase of each innovation project, but as the project moves into the later development phases, the line departments become increasingly involved and take over the project as it nears implementation. BusinessLab's efforts are measured and it must present top management with calculations of the benefits of all its activities. This means that abstract innovative ideas that lie far from the company's actual activities are economically restricted unless a line manager accepts the idea and establishes a development project based on it.

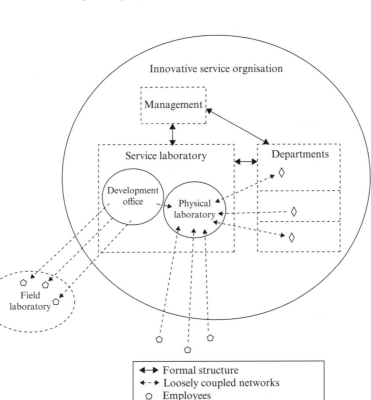

Figure 4.1   Model of the service laboratory

3 PRINCIPLES OF THE SERVICE LABORATORY

In order to develop a theoretical understanding of the service laboratory and of how it functions, we present four aspects: the role of the laboratory's network structure, of its network actors, of its material factors and of the instrumental development of innovations in the laboratory.

The Structure Network of the Laboratory

BusinessLab can be considered a combination of a structure and social processes. On the one hand, the structure is the formal organisational unit which, like technical manufacturing laboratories, has a well-defined place in the hierarchy of the company. It has a budget, it has to perform according to this, and its performance is controlled. This is like an organisational machine.

On the other hand, the social processes of BusinessLab take place in both loosely coupled networks and in more formalised network relationships. The networks are both inside and outside the company. Outside-actors include customers, non-customers, suppliers, competitors, researchers and other experts. Inside-actors are employees and managers. Members of the networks can be involved in BusinessLab on an ad hoc basis. Often external actors are involved only in single experiments, but many of them become involved in several and get longer lasting informal relationships to BusinessLab. The more formalised relationships concern BusinessLab's co-operation with the different departments of the firm and the training that employees from different departments must go through. Thus, the organisation around BusinessLab is a combination of a structured relationship with departments within the firm and loosely coupled – often ad hoc – networks in and outside the firm.

The combination of formal relationships and ad hoc network relations fits with actor network theory (ANT) (Law and Hassard 1999, Latour 2005). Latour (2005) writes that the network metaphor does not really cover the organisational structure that ANT emphasises. The organisational structure is often what ANT calls temporary associations. This is a valid description of the daily work of BusinessLab, but we must add that BusinessLab also has a permanent formal structure. It has a hierarchical relation to other departments because it must decide and develop every innovative idea about innovation, also ideas coming from the departments. We can therefore call the organisation around the service laboratory a structure-network to indicate that it is a combination of a hierarchical structure and a loosely coupled network. The structure secures the proper inclusion in the organisation of the laboratory while the loosely coupled network favours the dynamic and flexible inclusion of different member groups, user groups, experts, etc., so that different experiments involving different actors can be prepared and carried through in a very flexible way.

Roles and Relationships in the Laboratory

While actor network theory can describe the structure-network relationships of the service laboratory, it does not explain how the roles and relationships develop between actors. Such roles may be explained by strategic innovation theory (Mintzberg 1989, Sundbo 1997, 2001, 2003, Tidd et al. 2001, Sundbo and Fuglsang 2002). Strategic innovation theory understands innovation processes as being based on market possibilities. These cannot be discovered by just observing current customers or by asking them. This will rarely produce innovative solutions because customers, unless they are lead users (cf. von Hippel 2005), which very few users are, rarely can express relevant ideas about new solutions that could be the basis for service innovations. Further, since it takes time to develop service innovations, innovations are about future needs. Thus users' needs are often hidden and latent.

In general terms service theory has emphasised how services involve human acts and interactions with the users of the service. But while users and employees both play important roles in development of service innovation, their function differs. Some employees become corporate entrepreneurs (Drucker 1985) that fight to realise their ideas. Users (or customers) are typically given more indirect roles. Sometimes they can be equally active partners in innovation processes but mostly they are objects of user or market studies or they are involved as players in innovation processes with a specific task (for example to assess service prototypes). The users have the ultimate power (to use ANT language) because they are the ones who decide whether to buy a service or not, but during the innovation process they normally play a less influential or more staged role (cf. Pine and Gilmore 1999).

Employees and users play a central role in BusinessLab. These employees and users are the 'chemical substances' of the service laboratory. However, they are not only passive participants, but become active creators of innovations under guidance of the laboratory personnel. In the case of the company's employees these have a double role. They are participants in the laboratory experiments and they are trained to be innovation agents in the organisation. Employees from the company and representatives from BusinessLab state in the interviews that the employees generally find participation in the experiments very interesting and stimulating. The employees also take on the role of innovation agents and some become successful corporate entrepreneurs.

Concerning the users, activities in the physical laboratory are designed to tap into the hidden resources (Kristensson et al. 2002) of the users who participate in the experiments. Thereby they get new roles as active developers of innovations. Users represent the potential buyers of new service products. Our research indicates that users are satisfied with this role because they can influence their future insurance and related product portfolio. They also enjoy participating in the laboratory experiments and have a positive experience of the laboratory.

The managers' role is to create the innovation framework (developing the strategy and an innovation culture), and to control the innovation process (ensuring that the innovations are within the framework of the strategy and deciding for every idea whether it should be developed or not). Managers rarely participate directly in experiments in the physical laboratory. The departmental managers and the top management mostly play the role of general strategic leaders of BusinessLab (in its management board) and make decisions about concrete innovations. BusinessLab has for the managers functioned as a driver for becoming innovative.

Other external actors such as researchers, suppliers and experts participate primarily because they will benefit from it (research results, sale or honorarium). These other actors often become actively engaged in BusinessLab's activities because they are assumed to possess expert knowledge valuable to the company's innovation processes.

Thus, different actors have different roles in the activities of BusinessLab. They provide their own ideas, behave in their own ways and have their own interests, but they also play the laboratory game (e.g., provide knowledge, accept to be trained as innovators, participate in experiments and so forth). Their involvement is facilitated by the loosely coupled network of BusinessLab and their roles are developed and utilised in the experiments in the physical laboratory or by observing and interviewing them outside the company.

Material Factors in the Laboratory

Though services are normally understood as acts, material elements can play an important role, for example in services, where the service is delivered in a physical space such as in a bank or a hotel (Verhoef et al. 2009). Also, IT is increasingly involved in most service production and delivery. New hardware, software and IT systems provide new possibilities for innovating services. The same do other technologies such as physical and chemical cleaning technologies, transport technologies, store and shop technologies, etc. Sometimes IT or other technologies enter in at the later phases of a service innovation process because they are necessary for developing the new service or process.

Material factors are not restricted to technology. The way of thinking in material structures also plays a role in service innovations. This can, for example, be in expressing aspects of services in a physical form such as physical design (as do architects and industrial designers) or having artists to express service elements in painting or music. This can add certain intellectual and creative perspectives to the service function in order to make the innovation more radical and more user-friendly.

Such material factors are of central importance for the function of BusinessLab. The material surroundings of the laboratory enact innovation activities, providing a physical framework for the idea phase of innovation projects (for example using actors or video projections on walls to create a hotel lobby scene) and developing a creative climate. What is distinctive about BusinessLab is that these material factors have been made flexible so that they can be constantly designed and re-designed to fit the particular experiments in the laboratory and create different types of experimental service encounters. The physical laboratory also has symbolic importance for managers and employees of BusinessLab: it gives them an identity and it demonstrates their existence and their importance in the company.

The expression of services in a physical form is central to the activities of BusinessLab, for which reason a technical designer has been employed. She designs IT images that can be projected on the wall of the laboratory room. Further, she designs IT-projected or select material physical objects that can be presented to participants in laboratory experiments to inspire them to think in new insurance, security or welfare products.

Thus, material factors are central to the function of the service laboratory and are determinants of its innovations (cf. the discussion of Latour and Woolgar 1979) in spite of services being essentially immaterial and based on acts. The material and the use of them facilitate both idea generation and the development process related to particular innovations.

Instrumental Development of Innovations in the Laboratory

How are innovative ideas from BusinessLab developed into viable products? New service development (NSD) is a particular branch of service innovation theory which describes systematic, engineering-like methods and instruments for service innovation processes. Johnson et al. (2000) summarise models and instruments developed within NSD. These models emphasise three main aspects: market screening, idea generation and the desk design of the service process by using instruments such as blueprinting.

The models follow the principles of systematically working with theoretical designs of services, which is also the logic of BusinessLab. The most laboratory-like theory is probably the linear stage gate model that Cooper developed in relation to manufacturing innovation processes and applied to service innovation (Cooper and Edget 1999). The stage gate model for services argues that innovations should be developed by systematically assessing their market possibilities and whether the firm has or can procure the necessary technology and competencies. Management is to make decisions at each stage. The development process is carried out in project groups where employees may participate, but the groups have clearly defined tasks and are controlled by management. Though BusinessLab favours open processes, it is also dominated by these characteristics. Furthermore, in the stage gate model the innovation process is guided by strict resource allocation and steering, which also is the case with BusinesssLab.

Another aspect of NSD is its emphasis on customer involvement in the innovation process (Fitzsimmons and Fitzsimmons 2000, Alam 2002, Edvardsson et al. 2006, Prandelli et al. 2008). Various techniques are used including ethnographic studies, brainstorming and co-creation, observation of latent needs and lead user studies (for an overview, see Sanden et al. 2006). BusinessLab utilises users and employees as 'instruments' to test users' reactions to service offers, for example by involving users in acting out a service situation, and thereby to gauge their enthusiasm for and willingness to buy the service. Furthermore, by involving employees BusinessLab can improve the implementation process in the organisation because work procedures, employee attitudes and normal customer relations have been taken into consideration. Furthermore, the laboratory's employees can undertake field work such as sociological or anthropological investigations, or experiments in society at large or at customer locations (for example in business customers' organisation).

Thus NSD can contribute to understanding service laboratories because it emphasises developing toolkits for innovation processes, particularly user-based innovation. Service laboratories, such as BusinessLab, can create and be based on, frameworks that utilise such toolkits and systematised scientific methods in order to instrumentally develop innovation.

THE SERVICE LABORATORY CONCEPT – SUMMARY

Based on the notion of the old natural science laboratory, one can formally define a service laboratory as an organisational unit that a service firm establishes to undertake experiments aimed at making innovations.

However, based on the explorative analysis above, a number of differences between the 'traditional' laboratory and the service laboratory are evident.

In service laboratories experiments focus on developing new forms of behaviour because services can be defined as acts. The methods are often based on human creativity processes, sometimes combined with technology as an auxiliary tool. The service laboratory differs from the traditional technical laboratory used in manufacturing in that it uses more open research and development methods. And while the service laboratory is a physical unit its activities also take place off site, through field work such as sociological or anthropological investigations, or experiments in customer locations. The activities lie somewhere in between the controlled laboratory experiment and the natural field experiment (Sørensen et al. 2010). Thus, the service laboratory is a combination of a more closed research approach and the open innovation that, for example, Chesbrough (2011) describes. The service laboratory can, in theoretical terms, be suggested to be physically more open compared with the traditional perceptions of laboratories and to be more participatory and interdisciplinary.

By involving employees the service laboratory can ensure that implementation processes in the organisation are optimised because work procedures, employee attitudes and normal customer relations have been taken into consideration. This means that the chances that employees will be motivated to innovate and not resist are greater. The involvement of employees also ensures organisational learning about the innovation processes.

By involving users, the service laboratory can undertake market testing and establish whether a new service is financially viable. Employees and users can be involved as actors in the laboratory work. They act as instruments in the experiments such as physical equipment do in the chemical and physical laboratory. However, employees and users are not only passive instruments, but can be active creators of innovations under guidance of the laboratory personnel.

Compared with 'normal' service innovation procedures the innovation activities in the service laboratory are more based on systematic research methods instead of the typical unsystematic creation of quick ideas based on single customer interactions. In the case, BusinessLab has created a new service innovation culture and has implemented new innovation procedures. These have resulted in the development of new service concepts and new insurance products and procedures. These in turn have been further developed in other departments' development sub-departments.

The characteristics and benefits of the service laboratory are related to its structure-network character, the role of actors, the use of material factors and of innovation instruments in the laboratory. These characteristics can be summed up as follows.

1. By being *network*-based the service laboratory can combine innovation push and pull by being based on scientific principles but involving customers, even in their day-to-day situations. It can unite a fixed hierarchical position (*structure*) with a more anarchic networking approach and thereby create a very flexible organisational unit well anchored in the organisation.

2. Actors can take on new *roles*. Employees and managers can become innovation agents in the firm's organisation, and external actors such as users, researchers, suppliers and experts can more easily be involved in a service laboratory because of its scientific and independent character.

3. *Material factors* are central for the activities of the service laboratory. The physical laboratory is important as a framework for creating a creative climate, for example by setting up scenes for experimental service encounters. Technology and design in the physical laboratory support the development and exploration of new behaviour, which forms the basis for new services.

4. New *instruments* for innovation activities can be developed and applied. These instruments can lead to more user- and market-oriented innovations and a more systematic development of innovation in the organisation.

Thus, a more specific definition of the service laboratory which is based on the explorative case study reported in this chapter and which captures the main characteristics of the laboratory is the one that we presented in the introduction.

This definition can be a general definition for service laboratories beyond the case study, capturing relevant characteristics which allow innovation to function and which may be relevant in defining the model as a 'laboratory' and not as something else. The definition also suggests that the service laboratory extends beyond the traditional laboratory. The service laboratory is not simply a room where tests are carried out. Instead, the service laboratory must be perceived as a more open and dynamic organisational unit due to the nature of services.

PROBLEMS IN THE FUNCTION OF SERVICE LABORATORIES

Because BusinessLab operates as a change agent within the organisation (a kind of innovative 'guerrilla' function), it also creates some confusion in the organisation about its role and introduces latent conflicts with existing units that may feel their power and position threatened by this new unit. While most employees and managers we interviewed were positive about BusinessLab's activities, some employees expressed a more negative perception of BusinessLab. Because of the managing director's obvious support for the BusinessLab, they were careful to express criticisms not as conflicts, but in more professional terms such as objective assessments of there being no effect of the laboratory and intimating that the laboratory personnel are deviants in the insurance company's social system. On their side, the employees in BusinessLab indirectly express a distance from the rest of the organisation, not in terms of conflict, but as a kind of missionary statement: the other parts of the organisation are those to convince and make innovative.

There may also be certain limitations to the success of business lab in achieving its goals. For example, it is difficult for certain employees to sustain their role of innovation agents when they return to their job positions. As they, their colleagues and managers explain in the interviews, they become occupied by their daily work and it is difficult to act as an entrepreneur if the rest of the department is not innovation-minded. Furthermore, the formal and independent status of BusinessLab seems in some cases to have impeded managers from becoming innovation-oriented (according to some interviews). Since the laboratory is there, these managers can just repeat the general attitude that the company is innovative and that BusinessLab takes care of it, thus they themselves do not need to act.

Finally, some interviewees question whether or not the innovations coming from the laboratory are more likely to be accepted by the market. If market success is the measure of innovation success, more research and other methods are required to assess the laboratory's accomplishments. However, we believe that there is an even greater potential in the service laboratory than the case illustrates. The employees in BusinessLab are unaware of many instruments that service operations theory and service science have presented (e.g., Cooper and Edget 1999, Johnson et al. 2000, Sanden et al. 2006, Hefley and Murphy 2008), partly because they are not experts in service science or service engineering. Instead, BusinessLab has been manned with industrial designers, set designers and insurance professionals.

CONCLUSION

The service laboratory is a new suggestion for achieving more systematic and research-based ways of organising service innovation activities so

[handwritten margin note: how success measured, innovation]

as to improve service firms' innovation activities, resulting for example in more successful service products or more radical innovations. Service laboratories are particularly interesting for both service firms and service innovation researchers, providing a new practical model and theoretical framework for service innovation.

The service laboratory brings innovation back to the old laboratory; however, it does so in a new form because service innovation is not only about the invention and application of new technology, but mostly about human actions and reactions (including those of customers). Services, unlike manufacturing, involve behaviour of front-line personnel and interaction with the customer. The service laboratory is consequently not a technical laboratory, but an interdisciplinary one. The service laboratory implies more open research and development methods than the traditional manufacturing laboratory (cf. Chesbrough 2006), for example anthropological field studies and systematic involvement of employees in the innovation process.

In the explorative case study reported in this chapter, the service laboratory was advantageous to the service firm: it led to the creation of systematic innovation procedures; it established a clear structure and a clearer budget for innovation activities; it improved the user- and employee-base of innovations; the involvement of users and employees in innovation activities has become more systematic (scientific); and also other external actors (e.g., researchers, experts) were involved. The results suggest that the service laboratory not only results in a more systematic and efficient innovation process in service firms, but it has also wider effects in the organisation. It enhances networking, employee entrepreneurship and organisational change. The service laboratory thus is an important step on the way to creating a more permanent, systematic and push-based innovation organisation. However, it also may create dysfunctional problems that managers should be aware of.

The findings of this chapter cannot be generalised in order to argue that all other service companies will benefit from similar laboratory set-ups as the one in this case company. Other service companies may learn from, and be inspired by, the findings in this chapter, but they must apply the findings to fit their specific needs and contexts. Further research can cast light on how and in which contexts different types of service laboratories can be advantageous. This research is therefore only a first step to investigate and understand the service laboratory and further studies are needed to establish the model's contribution to both the theoretical understanding and practical functioning of innovation in services.

QUESTIONS FOR DISCUSSION

1. In what types of service firms are service laboratories appropriate for organising innovation activities?
2. How can a structured service lab be combined with loosely coupled networks and creativity?
3. How can user-needs and users' ideas for innovation be tapped in service companies?
4. How can IT be used in a service laboratory?

REFERENCES

Alam, I. (2002), 'An exploratory investigation of user involvement in new service development', *Journal of the Academy of Marketing Science*, **30**(3), 250–61.

Bessant, J. (2003), *High-involvement innovation*, Chichester: Wiley.

Boden, M. and I. Miles (eds) (2000), *Services and the knowledge-based economy*, London: Continuum.

Carlzon, J. (1987), *Moments of truth*, New York: Harper Collins.

Chesbrough, H. (2006), *Open innovation*, Boston: Harvard Business School Press.

Chesbrough, H. (2011), *Open service innovation: rethinking your business to growth and compete in a new area*, San Francisco: Jossey-Bass.

Cooper, R.G. and S.J. Edget (1999), *Product development for the service sector*, Massachusetts: Perseus Books.

Djellal, F. and F. Gallouj (2001), 'Innovation in services, patterns of innovation organisation in service firms: postal survey results and theoretical models', *Science and Public Policy*, **28**(1), 57–67.

Drejer, I. (2004), 'Identifying innovation in survey of services: a Schumpeterian perspective', *Research Policy*, **33**(3), 551–62.

Drucker, P. (1985), *Innovation and entrepreneurship*, New York: Harper & Row.

Edvardsson, B., A. Gustafsson, P. Kristensson, P. Magnusson and J. Matthing (eds) (2006), *Involving customers in new service development*, London: Imperial College Press.

Fitzsimmons, J. and M. Fitzsimmons (2000), *New service development*, Thousand Oaks, CA: Sage.

Hasu, M., E. Saari and T. Mattelmäki (2011), 'Bringing the employee back in: integrating user-driven and employee-driven innovation in the public sector', in J. Sundbo and M. Toivonen (eds) *User-base innovation in services*, Cheltenham: Edward Elgar.

Hefley, B. and W. Murphy (eds) (2008), *Service science, management and engineering*, Berlin: Springer.

Johnson, S., L. Menor, A. Roth and R. Chase (2000), 'A critical evaluation of the new service development process', in J. Fitzsimmons and M. Fitzsimmons (eds) *New service development*, Thousand Oaks, CA: Sage.

Kristensson, P., P.R. Magnusson and J. Matthing (2002), 'Users as a hidden resource for creativity: findings from an experimental study on user involvement', *Creativity & Innovation Management*, **11**(1), 55–61.

Latour, B. (2005), *Reassembling the social*, Oxford: Oxford University Press.

Latour, B. and S. Woolgar (1979), *Laboratory life: the social construction of scientific facts*, London: Sage.

Law, J. and J. Hassard (eds) (1999), *Actor network theory and after*, Oxford: Blackwell.

Mintzberg, H. (1989), *Mintzberg on management*. New York: Free Press.

Pine, B.J. and J.H. Gilmore (1999), *The experience economy*, Boston: Harvard Business School Press.

Prandelli, E., M. Sawhney and G. Verona (2008), *Collaborating with customers to innovate*, Cheltenham: Edward Elgar.

Sanden, B., A. Gustafsson and L. Witell (2006), 'The role of the customer in the development process', in B. Edvardsson, A. Gustafsson, P. Kristensson, P. Magnusson and J. Matthing (eds) *Involving customers in new service development*, London: Imperial College Press.

Shostack, G. and J. Kingsmann-Brundage (1991), 'How to design a service', in C. Congram and M. Friedman (eds) *The AMA handbook of marketing for the service industries*, New York: Amacom.

Sørensen, F., J. Mattsson and J. Sundbo (2010), 'Experimental methods in innovation research', *Research Policy*, **39**(3), 313–22.

Sundbo, J. (1997), 'Management of innovation in services', *The Service Industries Journal*, **17**(3), 432–55.

Sundbo, J. (1998), *The organisation of innovation in services*, Copenhagen: Roskilde University Press.

Sundbo, J. (2001), *The strategic management of innovation*, Cheltenham: Edward Elgar.

Sundbo, J. (2003), 'Innovation and strategic reflexivity: an evolutionary approach applied to services', in L. Shavina (ed.) *Handbook of innovation*, Boston: Pergamon.

Sundbo, J. and L. Fuglsang (eds) (2002), *Innovation as strategic reflexivity*, London: Routledge.

Sundbo, J. and M. Toivonen (eds) (2011), *User-base innovation in services*, Cheltenham: Edward Elgar.

Tidd, J., J. Bessant and K. Pavitt (2001), *Managing innovation*, Chichester: Wiley.

Toivonen, M. (2010), 'Different types of innovation processes in services and their organisational implications', in F. Gallouj and F. Djellal (eds) *The handbook of innovation and services*. Cheltenham: Edward Elgar.

Van der Aa, W. and T. Elfring (2002), 'Realizing innovation in services', *Scandinavian Journal of Management*, **18**(2), 155–71.

Verhoef, P.C., K.N. Lemon, A. Parasuraman, A. Roggeveen, M. Tsiros and L.A. Schlesinger (2009), 'Customer experience creation: determinants, dynamics and management strategies', *Journal of Retailing*, **85**(1), 31–41.

von Hippel, E. (2005), *Democratizing innovation*, Cambridge, MA: MIT Press.

Voss, C., R. Johnston, R. Silvestro, L. Fitzgerald and T. Brignall (1992), 'Measurement of innovation and design performance in services', *Design Management Journal*, Winter, 40–46.

5. Beyond conventional Western views of creativity and innovation
Lorraine Lim and Shinji Oyama

There is a long-held assumption that Asians are not creative. Books from scholars based in Asia with titles such as *Why Asians are Less Creative than Westerners* (Ng 2001) and *Can Asians Think?* (Mahbubani 2002) only seem to reinforce the stereotype that Asians are not as creative as their Western counterparts. This notion, however, has not stopped governments in Asia from investing heavily both financially and through myriad policies to support creativity and innovation across a range of industries within their nations. These initiatives range from promoting creativity through design, as exemplified by the newly established Singapore University of Technology and Design, to the Chinese government stimulating creativity in arts and culture by designating certain cities in China as 'creative centres' (Keane 2007). Other schemes include a variety of nation branding plans that are being implemented by the Ministry of Economy, Trade and Industry in Japan and Korea's highly successful support for local popular culture which has resulted in the so-called Korean Wave in East Asian countries (Chua and Iwabuchi 2008).

This drive towards being 'creative' is no doubt due to the belief that creativity is an essential component for any country's economy where the significance of agriculture and manufacturing is in irreversible decline. In today's knowledge economy, creativity has been identified as the 'most potentially successful response for negotiating economic change' and is now credited for everything ranging from 'corporate innovation and technological advancement' to the 'rehabilitation of cities and advancing education and learning' (Banaji et al. 2010: 41, Cherbo et al. 2010: 37). Therefore, creativity is what will allow countries and companies to stay competitive in the knowledge economy in which ideas will spur economic growth. If we are to understand that creativity is playing and will play a large role in driving economic growth, it stands to reason that a perceived lack of creativity in Asia hinders this very growth.

But are Asians really not creative?

This question is all the more urgent as we are beginning to see a rapidly changing power balance between the economies in Europe and America and countries in Asia. In the context of the shifts taking place in the world economy today, this chapter will first begin by highlighting how there is currently an inaccurate assumption that Asians are not creative. In doing so, it will then be possible to highlight a new way of thinking about Asia and its relationship with 'creativity'. We would then argue that what is occurring in reality is not that Asians are not creative but rather that creativity is distributed across national boundaries.

Is it true that Asia is not as creative as the West? One of the main reasons why this perception remains can perhaps be laid at the lack of understanding of what constitutes 'Asia' itself. A vast region, Asia contains countries such as Japan and Singapore, which have transformed themselves into countries with large service economies alongside countries such as Myanmar (or Burma) and Bangladesh, which are still dominated by agricultural industries. As a region, Asia possesses many countries that can be considered far more developed and creative than countries within the European Union (EU). This is borne out with figures from the *Global Innovation Index* (INSEAD and World Intellectual Property Organisation 2012), where Asian countries such as Japan, Taiwan, South Korea and Singapore make up the top 20 countries in the list alongside their North American and European counterparts such as the United States, Switzerland, Finland and Germany. Similarly, if one takes a casual look at the top 20 companies listed in terms of patents filed in the United States in 2011, the list is made up of 10 Japanese and 7 American companies followed by 2 Korean and 1 Taiwanese firm (IFI Claims Patent Services 2012). The first European entry, a German company, comes in at 30th position and there is not a single British company in the top 50. It is clear from these figures here that the current perceptions surrounding the supposed lack of creativity in Asia is not true. This continual belief, contrary to evidence, can best be explained by the concept of Orientalism, which seeks to construct Asia as unchanging, homogeneous and inferior to the West. The slightly updated version of Imperialist Orientalism now constructs Asia as a machine-like factory that is only able to manufacture (or pirate) goods which have been invented by their enlightened and creative Western counterparts. This seems to be a desire embedded in Western consciousness that bears little or no resemblance to the reality today.

The aim of this chapter therefore does not seek to explain why creativity is lacking in Asia (it isn't). Furthermore, there already exist numerous studies that examine the lack of creativity in Asia within a historical and civilisational context. Academic literature that attempts to examine the role of 'innovation' and 'creativity' within the Asian setting often highlights how the continued adherence to 'Confucian' teachings and highly interventionist governments will continue to stymie the development of 'creativity' in Asian countries (see Hutton 2007). Researchers attempting to discover if creativity functions differently within a non-Western context have hypothesised that innovation has a stronger 'orientation towards useful/appropriate solutions in the East and a stronger orientation towards novel/original solutions in the West' (Morris and Leung 2010: 316). This difference, it is argued, comes from the ideas that traits such as conformity and collectivism closely linked to Confucianism result in innovations that are incremental and needs-oriented as these solutions build upon existing practices which allow for the continued maintenance of social bonds within a community. However, the degree of adherence to, and the adaption of, Confucianism varies greatly in countries in Asia and in itself does not explain the vast difference among companies within the same sector in Asia. This line of thinking also does not take into account the multinational investments in creativity and innovation in several research centres all over the world. Instead of speculating whether Asia is as creative as or more creative than the West, this chapter instead will argue that it is increasingly irrelevant to think of creativity and its geographical distribution on the old model of West and non-West or centre versus periphery. By way of two case studies, we would like to argue that creativity is unevenly distributed across the putative line between West and non-West as well as within them and that this distribution is an effect of globalisation.

GLOBALISATION AND CREATIVITY

The term globalisation is used here to highlight a break with the Eurocentric view that is implicit in the discourse on the lack of creativity in Asia. The key symptoms of globalisation as identified by sociologist John Tomlinson highlight key issues surrounding creativity in Asia.

First, cultural products from the West or the presence of Western companies in general no longer dominate the world. The presence of companies from the West in Asia is not as marked as it is believed in the West. Globalisation is a de-centralising process, and there is no longer an absolute centre, a role that the United States undoubtedly played in previous decades. Today the world has a number of sub-centres and regional hubs in the form of Tokyo, Hong Kong and Shanghai in Asia and cities such as Dubai, Cairo and Mexico City in other parts of the world. Not only has the Asian economy as a whole increased its share in global output, the Asian economy is also dependent on the intra-regional markets for capital and consumer goods, which have grown rapidly relative to the EU and North America. While Western tourists and journalists might selectively spot Western brands and cultural goods in Asian cities, it is the case that Asian consumers in particular display a preference for local cultural goods. This can be observed in areas ranging from popular music, magazines and television programmes to consumer brands.

The concepts of 'cultural discount' and 'cultural proximity' might explain these preferences. Cultural goods made for a certain culture usually have little appeal outside that culture because the cultural contents are unique to the culture of origin and often have little relevance to consumers outside the particular cultural sphere. For this reason, significant cultural exports from Asia (mostly Japan) have been limited to products that are best described as 'culturally odourless'. A term coined by Professor Iwabuchi Koichi,[1] 'culturally odourless' products are products that do not contain a cultural presence, thus allowing consumers to remain unaware of the origin of these products (Iwabuchi 2002: 27). He highlights the Sony Walkman as one such example where the 'use of the Walkman does not evoke images or ideas of a Japanese lifestyle, even if consumers know it is made in Japan' (Iwabuchi 2002: 28). This would explain why cultural goods such as video games, comics and cartoons do very well in Western markets. At the same time, companies operating within the creative industries in Asia are also aware that the Western market is one that is mature with many established players, making it difficult to penetrate due to a cultural discount. Therefore, creativity and innovation have been invested in meeting domestic and regional Asian needs and preferences rather than in attempting to break into the sluggish Western market. This makes 'creative' products difficult to spot for Western commentators and scholars. Consequently, most American and European audiences remain oblivious to some of the biggest film or pop stars in Asia.

Second, from a dialectical perspective, globalisation is more accurately characterised as a process of glocalisation (Robertson 1995), a generative process in which the continual interpenetration between global and local cultural and economic forms have created new hybrid structures. The local is always found in global elements and vice versa. Anthropologist Richard Wilk's concept of global 'structures of common difference' (1995) is useful for explicating the key structural features for the geographical distribution of creativity and innovation. Global structures of difference organise and even promote cultural differences along specific dimensions. Thus globalisation is the hegemony of form but not of content, the latter which celebrates particular kinds of diversity while suppressing others. This means that there are small numbers of global forms through which creativity is exercised and innovation takes place. Conceptions of creativity and innovation, which are strongly linked to the romantic notion of originality and individual authorship, must adjust to reflect this change. The fast food chain, an American concept, is one example whereby the global format has been localised and, through this structure, local innovation has flourished.

Using the examples of luxury cosmetics brands and popular culture in Asia, the next section of this chapter will elaborate on how these two effects of globalisation have led to the assumption that there is a lack of creativity in Asia. What must be made clear is that the aim of this chapter is not to show that there is a particular type of non-Western creativity (just as it is not possible to argue for a particular 'Western' creativity) but to broaden the current discourse of what can be considered creative and understand how it is no longer possible to understand the distribution of creativity along the national or civilisational lines of Asia. It is also important here to point out that while the term 'non-Western' is used, this does not imply that this term speaks for Asia as a whole. The two case studies under discussion are drawn from East Asia, which only represent a particular area; they were selected to demonstrate the issues being discussed in this chapter.

It is well known that markets in the West are not as readily receptive as markets in Asia in receiving cultural products from another part of the world. As highlighted earlier, what Western markets embrace in terms of cultural products from Asia are products where their own culture, be it American or European, can be placed onto the products, allowing for a seamless insertion into the local culture. Japanese manga characters are a case in point. While they might look 'Asian', the multi-coloured hairstyles, exaggerated facial features represent a non-race which allow for an easy translation onto Western screens. The examples in this section will illustrate that in order for these products to be popular in the West, the 'creative' origin of these products are usually hidden or masked as many products from East Asia do not translate easily to the West. Consequently, many consumers in the West are often unaware of where these supposedly 'innovative' or 'creative' products come from, thus reinforcing the view that there only seems to be a one-directional flow of creative products from the West in Asia, which then further bolsters the perception that there are no creative products in Asia, leading to the final conclusion that there is a lack of creativity in Asia. The examples here will show that this flow of creativity is actually bi-directional due to globalisation but that the combined issues of market and language form two of the key reasons why this assumption still remains.

HIDDEN ORIGINS OF CREATIVITY

Japan has the second largest cosmetics markets in the world. The impact of cosmetics brands from the West can be seen in luxury department stores in Tokyo today. If we were to map the spaces in terms of brands that are generally perceived to be from Tokyo or London, the following observations can be made. Of the 40 brands on the ground floor of Tokyo's trend-setting Isetan department store in Shinjuku, 24 cosmetic brands originate from the West, with the remaining 11 brands being from Japan. In London's Selfridges department store, the ratio becomes 32 brands from the West to 2 Japanese brands. Both in Tokyo and London, it is clear that the cosmetics industry is dominated by brands from Europe and America. Can this dominance be put down to the superiority of the type of cosmetics sold by Western brands? Can it be argued that the ability of Western brands to market their brands more effectively via their packaging, promotion and advertising to a global audience explains this success as well? Perhaps Japanese cosmetic brands cannot compete on a global market because they're just not 'creative' enough in developing new products as well as packaging and promotion?

Brands are now arguably the most important corporate asset for brand-driven companies, where brand value can account for as much as 70 per cent of a company's market value (Lindemann 2003: 29). Just like other intangible corporate assets, they are now legally protected as intellectual property and are exchanged in a global business-to-business market. Recent decades have seen various forms of brand-driven economic exchange, which has subsumed many Japanese brands. In luxury cosmetics, merger mania has sent most major brands into the hands of a small number of powerful groups, including L'Oréal, Estée Lauder, Louis Vuitton Moet Hennessey (LVMH) or Shiseido, Japan's largest cosmetics manufacturer. The second transformation occurred with the introduction of brand licensing whereby the use of a brand by a brand owner is leased to another company in return for the payment of royalty fees (Perrier 1998: 104–13). All of the large groups take advantage of this more flexible form of brand exploitation to enhance their brand portfolio by forming partnerships with top fashion designers across national boundaries. One such brand that has adopted both these strategies is the world's largest cosmetics maker L'Oréal. Since the 1980s, L'Oréal has acquired the French brand Lancôme, the American brand Maybelline New York, the British brand The Body Shop and Chinese brands Mini Nurse and Yue-Sai, as well as the Japanese make-up brand shu uemura (Jones et al. 2006). In addition, L'Oréal has license agreements with the likes of Italian fashion designer Giorgio Armani and the American fashion brand Ralph Lauren. It now boasts a brand portfolio consisting of more than 20 brands from different continents. Estée Lauder and LVMH have equally large, although somewhat less multinational, portfolios. Likewise, Shiseido has acquired Western brands and developed brands in-house that do not bear the corporate Shiseido brand to bolster its portfolio. These acquired brands include three French brands: Carita, Decléor and Nars Cosmetics, and one American brand, Bare Escentuals. Shiseido also has a license agreement with high-profile French designer Jean-Paul Gaultier, Cuban-American fashion designer Narcisco Rodriguez, and globally renowned Japanese fashion designer Miyake Issey (Jones et al. 2006).

What is key to the discussion about brands is that in any department store in any part of the world, the relationship between different brands within a single group, such as L'Oréal brands or the Shiseido brands, remains invisible to ordinary consumers. A brand portfolio is developed to target different market segments, but it also enables multinational companies to adapt to varying kinds of cultural references in different markets. Multiple markets are particularly relevant to cosmetic brands as the business is directly related to historical constructions of cultural ideas such as beauty, youth, modernity, race and image of its country of origin. Therefore, while Japanese model Ebihara Yuri is the official face of Shiseido MAQuillAGE in most East Asian markets, Shiseido is Japanese only when it wants to be. The rest of the time, it is happy being Chinese, American, French or any other nationality. In East Asian department stores, where Japanese brands go a long way, Shiseido relies more on its corporate Shiseido brands. In contrast, it relies heavily on acquired Western brands in Western markets. In Selfridges London, it deploys Shiseido, but also Nars Cosmetics and Decléor, as well as its licensed fragrance brands Jean-Paul Gaultier and Narcisco Rodriguez. Similarly, Japan's second largest cosmetics maker Kosé and its Japanese subsidiary Albion are taking advantage of their multinational portfolio to a greater degree. While Albion has a number of domestic brands, its expansion in the Asian and Western market has been driven by four Western licensed brands: Anna Sui Cosmetics (licensed from American Chinese fashion designer Anna Sui); Sonia Rykiel Beauté (licensed from French fashion brand Sonia Rykiel); Paul and Joe Beauté (licensed from French fashion designer Paul and Joe); and Ladurée (licensed from French luxury cakes and pastries). What these companies have done is to identify which brands will work within a specific market, tailor their products, packaging and promotion to each market, reaffirming not only cultural assumptions of beauty, race and youth, but at the same time 'masking' where these products are actually from or who they are created by.

This same 'masking' also occurs when it comes to Asian popular culture. Consumers in America are often unaware that some of the most critically and financially successful films made in Hollywood are based on creative ideas that originate from Asia. Filmmakers in the West 'mask' the creative origin of their films, in the same way that their counterparts in cosmetics do as well, to present familiar cultural references to their consumers of which the use of the English language is of paramount importance. American movie audiences are notoriously known for their dislike of subtitled films and the language barrier is a key reason that prevents many films made in Asia from crossing over to the West and Europe. This resistance to watching subtitled films has led to many Asian film rights being bought by American film production companies and transformed into Westernised versions with many audience members unaware of the creative origin of the film. Some notable examples include films such as Korean film *Il Mare*, which would become *The Lake House* starring Sandra Bullock and Keanu Reeves, as well as *The Departed*, directed by Martin Scorsese based on the Hong Kong film *Infernal Affairs*. This is not a trend that has gone unnoticed with Hollywood's industry magazine *Variety*, reporting that Hollywood is 'looking to China more than ever, not just as a place to sell things, but as a source of inspiration' (Jones 2005: 74). What must also be remembered is that this is by no means a new phenomenon, while many American and European audiences might not be familiar with the work of Kurosawa Akira; it is unlikely that they would not recognise the film *The Magnificent Seven*, made in 1960, which is based on Kurosawa's *The Seven Samurai*. This trend in re-making films from Asia into Western versions, erasing any cultural references that reference the creative origin of the films, continues to reinforce the assumption that nothing 'creative' comes from Asia.

One of the consequences of this language barrier is that directors from America and Europe are able to appropriate visual elements from films in Asia, creating iconic images or visual sequences by once again masking the creative origin of the image. These images are then re-translated and presented into these films as if they were 'new'. No one has accused Quentin Tarantino of being unoriginal for dressing Uma Thurman in a yellow tracksuit in *Kill Bill Vol. 1* (see Pang 2006). The Wachowski brothers borrow heavily from Hong Kong action film genres in *The Matrix Trilogy*, by hiring Hong Kong martial arts choreographer Yuen Woo-Ping to choreograph the fight sequences in the film. What these examples listed above have shown is that the perception that Asia is not creative because it does not produce cultural products that are as globally successful as their Western counterparts is one that cannot stand if we examine the bi-directional flow of creativity between the West and Asia more closely. The global success of films such as *The Matrix* would not have been possible without the debt it had to action films from Hong Kong.

MULTIPLE CREATORS, MULTIPLE MARKETS

The flow of creativity can no longer be seen along the lines of West or non-West. What we have now is an increasingly geographical entanglement of creativity that is able to flourish due to a global marketing, production and distribution chain. This chain allows for Paul and Joe's French founder and designer Sophie Albou to work with a team of Japanese creatives in Albion in designing and operating the successful cosmetics line, and for Western directors to increasingly draw inspiration from Asian films and popular culture. What is also possible to demonstrate with the growing bi-directional flow of creativity around the world is that it is no longer possible to think of creativity coming from one person or one 'genius' creator. Rather the creation of a successful product, be it cosmetics or a film, comes about when different people work together, drawing on each other in the form of financial resources, research facilities or being inspired by various elements such as visual iconography or musical styles.

L'Oréal has invested heavily in its research and innovation centre in Japan, making it Asia's biggest research facility. There the company is able to tap into Japan's advanced technologies in biology, environmental and material science, which has resulted in the creation of a type of cosmetic product that does not wear off in the sun. This product is based on a material that is used to maintain a car's exterior in severe weather conditions (Gaishikei 2012). With the following statement, 'I need a rich patron to continue with my creations and L'Oreal is playing the role of my Medici family very nicely,' make-up artist Uemura Shu quips that L'Oréal's financial resources are a reason why he is able to continue to innovate (Uemura in Watson 2008). Once again, this highlights the fact that creation does not come from a singular entity but also requires a mix of resources, be they financial or technological. Currently, companies that possess these financial resources or control the international marketing and distribution chain are largely based, or are seen to be based, in the West, thus reinforcing the image that these products are created in America or Europe. However, companies in Asia are beginning to make their presence felt. This is most keenly seen in today's mobile telecommunications market, where South Korean company Samsung Group as well as HTC, a Chinese company, have managed to establish a significant market share with their mobile phones. Both these companies are challenging the dominance of Apple iPhones in a way that Finnish company Nokia has been unable to do. Samsung Group and HTC might just be the start of a list of Asian companies that could come to dominate the international distribution chain in the near future.

Within the pop music industry in Asia, the exposure to Western influences via films and music from the West have resulted in the incorporation of musical genres from Europe and America such as rhythm and blues (R&B) and hip-hop to create new hybridised musical styles. Jay Chou, a Taiwanese pop star, is one such singer who 'performs in a rhythm and blues style, but within this Western form . . . has inserted Chinese melodies, themes and rhythms' (Fung 2008: 72). With Chou's songs, we can see how the global format of a pop song has been localised to incorporate musical elements familiar to listeners in Asia to create new content within a globally recognised format. Cantonese pop songs, popularly known as Cantopop, have been described as a 'unique and often bewildering mixture of Chinese, other Asian and Western elements' and are another example (Witzleben 1999: 241). Hong Kong Cantopop singer Anita Mui's song *Yuan Jinxiao Yiqi Zuisi* (I Want to Die of Intoxication Together Tonight) is an exemplification of this mix:

> The song is a cover of the Japanese song *Ueo Muite Aruko* (Look up When I Walk), marketed in the West as *Sukiyaki*. Anita Mui's version is performed at a slow tempo similar to a later 1970s English-language version by A Taste of Honey, with the addition of touches of Japonism in the form of synthesised koto (or, more precisely, a Hong Kong iconisation of koto sounds) and a whispered 'sayonara' as the record fades. The song appeared on an album sung in Cantonese and recorded in Hong Kong but entitled, for no obvious reasons, Anita in Brasil (Witzleben 1999: 246).

This one song alone references a variety of musical styles drawn from all over the world, creating a song that can only be described as a musical hybrid, which still functions within a recognisable pop song. What this song also does is highlight the need to start thinking of creativity in a different way, whereby new content is not the result of the work of one person but rather a bringing together of ideas from all over the world, resulting in something new.

We had earlier argued that globalisation is a de-centralising process where there is no longer a fixed centre. Rather, there are now multiple different hubs situated in various cities in the world. We also highlighted that the growth of economies in Asia has resulted in a more affluent society in Asia and many companies in Asia view Asian consumers as a largely untapped potential market, bypassing markets in the West. Japanese products are highly popular in East and Southeast Asia and circulate across the region via numerous legal, illegal, online and offline media channels. In cosmetics, Japan has influenced the region's make-up and skincare trends and regimens and has produced a regional craze for products such as whitening creams and anti-ageing serums that are quite specific to Asian skin types and aspirations (L'Oréal 2012). Japan's cute and girlish aesthetic has become a regional phenomenon and companies are seeking to draw on these ideas in order to understand and adapt their products to the Asian regional markets.

A substantial market also exists in Asia for cultural goods. Even before the economic growth of China, there has always been a local and Asian-wide market for popular music in China as evidenced by Witzleben's article on Anita Mui. He argues that Hong Kong music fans had always preferred their own 'indigenous or domesticated heroines rather than imported ones' (1999: 244). He highlights how in 1995, American rock group R.E.M. played in a smallish venue to an 'overwhelmingly Western' audience leading singer Michael Stipe to dedicate a song during his concert to the 'local people, if there are any of you here' (Witzleben 1999: 245). At the same time, Anita Mui played 14 concerts to 'near-capacity crowds at the 12,500 seat Hong Kong Coliseum' (Witzleben 1999: 244). Within Asia, pop stars from Hong Kong, Taiwan and Japan record their songs in multiple languages because of the availability of the different markets within Asia. Due to this potential, there is little desire for these artists to record in English for the Western market. While their film counterparts seek a foothold in America, 'pop singers have remained seemingly indifferent to internationalism beyond China and Japan' (Witzleben 1999: 252). This is not saying that music from American or European bands are not successful in Asia; however, many Asian pop stars and bands are just as, or even more, popular in Asia.

The growing demand of all sorts for products from the increasingly affluent Chinese in recent years has resulted in a shift in the market for products in the region. This shift can be seen in the career of pop star Faye Wong (who might be more popularly known in the West for starring in many of Hong Kong director Wong Kar Wai's films). Originally from China, her early albums were all sung in Cantonese, as that was where the market was for popular music. It was only after releasing her sixth album that she recorded in Mandarin. She would continue to record both in Cantonese and her native language of Mandarin before going into semi-retirement in 2005. She is not the exception; the popularisation of Japanese pop songs in Asia was due to 'a large number of Chinese' (Mandarin and Cantonese) versions of these songs made by 'Taiwanese and Hong Kong artists' (Ng 2003: 6). In fact, Wong's first successful single was a cover of a Japanese song. The result of this intra-regional market is that Hong Kong pop stars would be famous in Japan, giving successful concerts in Japan or having 'Japanese fans of Hong Kong pop fly to visit their icons or attend concerts' (Ng 2003: 13). This worked for Japanese pop stars and groups as well, with many of them having fan clubs in Taiwan and Singapore. What

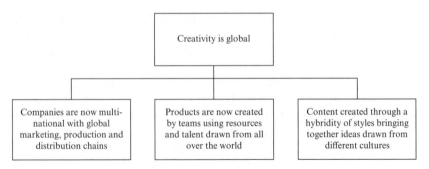

Figure 5.1   Global distribution of 'creativity'

is clear from both these examples is that there is a circulation of creativity manifested in the marketing of cosmetics or in pop music within Asia. However, due to a language barrier and growing market consumption, now boosted with China, there was, and still is, little desire to promote these products or artists beyond Asia. However, just because these products or singers are not well known globally does not indicate that there is no creativity in Asia.

CONCLUSION

This chapter set out to determine if the idea that Asians were not creative was a valid assumption. It raised questions about the ways in which the notion of creativity is discussed within current discourse and highlights that the effects of globalisation coupled with the current shift in the global economy requires a re-thinking of the notion of where creativity comes from. The examples taken from cosmetics and popular culture in Asia sought to highlight that there is now a bi-directional flow of creativity, which is often hidden to consumers in the West due to an unawareness of the creative origin of these products and a language barrier. In short, creativity is distributed across national boundaries.

For many years now, the export of goods and services has largely flowed from the West into Asia, but the growing affluence of countries in Asia such as China and India has seen a change in the global market economy. This shift within Asia and between the West can perhaps be best demonstrated with Hong Kong actor Jackie Chan's film *The Karate Kid*. Having successfully negotiated a shift to America, this film has him firmly back in China. The original film was set in Japan and has now been remade for a Chinese audience, thus demonstrating a significant shift in the importance of China as a growing consumer market for cultural goods. Another change that is taking place within Asia is that not only are firms such as Microsoft, Pfizer and Exxon increasing their investment in research and development in East Asia, but also that companies and governments in Asia are now exploring the potential of developing research and innovation with each other, instead of seeking a European or American partner. Singapore's Agency for Science, Technology and Research (A*STAR) has recently announced a partnership with China's largest search engine Baidu to develop speech recognition technology platforms for use within Southeast Asia (Ho 2012). What the results of this partnership will mean in the future for the development of consumer technologies for Asia, and globally, might not be known in the near future, but this collaboration perhaps demonstrates a confidence within Asia on their ability to create and innovate.

With the examples presented in this chapter, it is no longer possible to state that Asians are not creative due to their culture or government systems. If this assumption rests on the argument that Asia is not creative because the goods that it produces, invents or creates are not well known or consumed globally, this raises a more interesting question about how creative other parts of the world are. What has arisen from this chapter is perhaps the need to question why there has been a continued fascination with or fixation on the perceived lack of creativity in Asia, while inventions and cultural products from many other countries in the world are also not well known globally.

QUESTIONS FOR DISCUSSION

1. The Asian region now accounts for one-third of the world economy and possesses the world's two fastest growing economies, China and India. What do you think the impact of this growth will be on the creation, production and distribution of cultural products in the near future?
2. Are some countries/cultures/civilisations more creative than others? If so, what makes some more creative than others? Is this going to change or stay the same over a period of time? How do these perceptions relate to our definitions of creativity?
3. Does the concept of 'authenticity' have any value in the evaluation or appreciation of creativity in a contemporary globalised world? If it does, what makes something authentic, or inauthentic?
4. Should we use companies rather than nations when we think about creativity in a globalised economy?

NOTE

1. All Japanese and Chinese names in this chapter will be presented with the surname first, followed by their given names. The only exception will be when these names are registered trademarks in their own right, such as the case of cosmetic brands shu uemura.

REFERENCES

Banaji, S., A. Burn and D. Buckingham (2010), *The rhetorics of creativity: a literature review*, 2nd edition. London: Creativity, Culture and Education.
Cherbo, L. and H.L. Vogel (2010), 'Recognition and artistic creativity,' in H. Anheier and Y.R. Isar (eds) *Cultural Expression, Creativity and Innovation*, London: Sage Publications, pp. 37–46.
Chua, B-H. and K. Iwabuchi (2008), *East Asian pop culture: analysing the Korean wave*, Hong Kong: Hong Kong University Press.
Fung, A. (2008), 'Western style, Chinese pop: Jay Chou's rap and hip-hop in China', *Asian Music*, 39(1), Winter/Spring, 69–80.
Gaishikei Kigyō Nihon Ni Kenkyū Kaihatsu Kyoten Wo Shinsetsu Suru Ugoki: Haikei Ni Ajia Sijō No Kakudai in *Mainichi Shinbun*: Japan ['Western companies to develop research facilities in Japan to capitalize growing Asian markets'. Mainichi Newspaper online edition] http://mainichi.jp/select/today/news/20120306k0000m020054000c.html [Accessed 30 May 2012].
Ho, V. (2012), 'Baidu taps A*STAR, researching SE-A languages here', *The Business Times*, 27 July.
Hutton, W. (2007), *The writing on the wall: why we must embrace China as a partner or face it as an enemy*, London: Little Brown.
IFI Claims Patent Services (2012), *IFI claims 2011 top 50 US patent assignees*. Madison, CT: Fairview Research <http://ificlaims.com/index.php?page=misc_Top_50_2011> [Accessed 29 September 2012].
INSEAD and World Intellectual Property Organisation (2012), *Global Innovation Index 2012: stronger innovation linkages for global growth*. Fontainebleau, France: INSEAD.
Iwabuchi, K. (2002), *Recentering globalisation: popular culture and Japanese Transnationalism*. Durham, NC: Duke University Press.
Jones, A. (2005), 'Jumping the Great Wall', *Variety Magazine*, 16–22 May, 74.
Jones, G., D. Kiron, V. Dessain and A. Sioman (2006), 'L'Oréal and the globalization of American beauty', in *Harvard Business School case studies*, Boston: Harvard Business School Publishing.
Keane, M. (2007), *Created in China: the great leap forward*, London: Routledge.
L'Oreal Japan Corporate Communication Department (2012), 'Nihon L'Oreal R&D Wo 25 per cent Kakuju, 3 Bumon Wo Aratani Sousetsu', in *L'Oreal: Japan* <http://prtimes.jp/data/corp/3480/750a57e5992b23c842773e6ff07612d2.pdf> [Accessed 27 July 2012].
Lindemann, J. (2003), 'The financial value of brands', in P. Barwise and R. Clifton (eds) *Brands and branding*, London: The Economist, pp. 27–46.
Mahbubani, K. (2001), *Can Asians think? Understanding the divide between East and West*, South Royalton, VT: Steerforth Press.
Morris, M. and K. Leung (2010), 'Creativity East and West: perspectives and parallels', *Management and Organisation Review*, 6(3), 313–27.
Ng, A.K. (2000), *Why Asians are less creative than westerners*, London: Prentice Hall.
Ng, B.W-M. (2003), 'Japanese popular music in Singapore and the hybridization of Asian music', *Asian Music*, 34(1), Autumn/Winter, 1–18.
Pang, L. (2006), *Cultural control and globalisation in Asia: copyright, piracy and cinema*, London and New York: Routledge.

Perrier, R. (1998), 'Brand licensing', in S. Hart and J. Murphy (eds) *Brands: the new wealth creators*, London: Macmillan.

Robertson, R. (1995), 'Glocalisation: time-space and homogeneity-heterogeneity', in M. Featherstone, S. Lash and R. Robertson (eds) *Global modernities*, London: Sage Publications, pp. 25–44.

Watson, L. (2008), 'Shu Uemura: creator of a global cosmetics brand', *The Independent*, 27 February, 36.

Wilk, R. (1995), 'Learning to be local in Belize: global systems of common difference', in D. Miller (ed.) *Worlds apart: modernity through the prism of the local*, London: Routledge, pp. 110–33.

Witzleben, J.L. (1999), 'Cantopop and Mandapop in pre-postcolonial Hong Kong: identity negotiation in the performances of Anita Mui Yim-Fong', *Popular Music*, **18**(2), May, 241–58.

PART II

CREATIVE ENTREPRENEURSHIP

Introduction to Part II: Creative Entrepreneurship
Chris Bilton and Stephen Cummings

We have divided this handbook and our framework for thinking about management and creativity into four parts. The first part focuses on innovation. The second part focuses on entrepreneurship. In reality, it can be hard to separate innovative and entrepreneurial activity. It has been suggested to us that a strategic innovation framework called 'The Six Degrees of Innovation', which we developed in a book called *Creative Strategy: Reconnecting business and innovation* (Bilton and Cummings 2010), is as much about entrepreneurship as it is about innovation. Indeed, the fourth 'degree' or element of that Six Degrees framework was called 'market innovation', which is quite close to our definition of entrepreneurship. We developed this definition by going back to the etymological roots of the word. From the greater Oxford English Dictionary, 'entrepreneur' is a French word and was originally applied to: 'a. The director or manager of a public musical institution; b. One who 'gets up' entertainments, *esp.* musical performances.' (Recognising the origins of the word caused many Francophiles to criticise the comment made, allegedly, by George W. Bush to Tony Blair during a trade summit that 'The problem with the French is that they don't have a word for entrepreneur.')

That original, simple understanding of the entrepreneur as somebody who successfully brings something, or 'gets something up', to the market is a useful one, indicating the close link between developing an innovation and taking it to prospective users in the context of management and creativity: creating one without managing the other will add little of lasting value.

Looking back, many of the examples that we provided in *Creative Strategy* for market innovation or entrepreneurship came from the music industry. In particular, we focused on how the nature of that industry (and subsequently other industries), and how value was created and paid for, was changed by pioneers such as Radiohead, who, instead of attempting to protect their traditional business from the Internet, embraced it and began to offer music online freely, for whatever people felt like paying for it. They were ahead of their time in recognising that the way innovations were brought to, and paid for by, the market would be changed by advances in technology. Recorded music would increasingly be seen by many as an advertisement for other revenue-generating products that could not be transferred virtually, such as concert tickets, clothes and other associated merchandise. And other companies in other industries have learned from the example of musical artists like Radiohead to think differently about how they bring their products and services to market.

It is interesting to reflect on the fact that those cutting-edge entrepreneurial developments in the music industry happened nearly a decade ago. So what has followed on from them? An excellent recent example is the latest 'album' from Beck, titled *Song Reader*. Released on 11 December 2012, *Song Reader* is not a recorded compilation of tracks. It is a book of sheet music for 20 Beck compositions with an open invitation for people to record their interpretations of the songs. Anyone can submit a song as a YouTube video or in the form of a SoundCloud file. Almost every song submitted appears on Beck's SongReader.net site, which, just a couple of weeks after *Song Reader*'s release, contained hundreds of different versions of the songs. Many exhibited dramatically different interpretations of the same sheet music.

The project is a mix of old and new, it is essentially an old-fashioned sheet music book, but what *Song Reader* has become would not have been technologically possible just a few years ago. According to Jordan Bass, from McSweeney's Books, who worked with Beck on the project and published the book: 'This neat thing happened, as the book was evolving – we were getting farther away from the golden age of song sheets that inspired a lot of the style and tone for this, but we were also getting into this moment of audiences knowing how to engage with something that's asking them to reinvent it' (Berkman 2013). Is it a book, an album, something else or all three? In 'management-speak', Beck's crowdsourcing of his own album via new social media platforms while transgressing traditional industry categories reversed the relationship between producer and consumer, making his fans 'co-producers' of the album. At the same time, crowd-sourcing also works as a traditional marketing strategy, reinforcing brand loyalty (most of the participants will no doubt buy the album as well) and brand image (Beck is a serious artist who writes his own songs).

As Bass concludes: 'The thing that's been neat to me is that [*Song Reader*] was never about running away from the Internet, or from the ways people interact with new music now ... [It] came out of Beck realizing there was room to engage with his audience in all kinds of different ways. To me, it's very cool to see these things coexist – this ink-and-paper, pre-recording medium and the streaming-video world.'

Are Beck and his team innovators or entrepreneurs? Are they explorers seeking new ways of creating value, or exploiters of existing resources, as the strategy literature might put it? They are both, and as such this is a good example to highlight how effective creation often requires the combined focus on creativity and discovery that drives innovation and the diligence and dilettantism that feeds entrepreneurship.

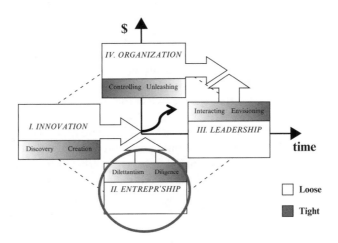

Mindful of this need to connect rather than separate innovation and entrepreneurship as a means of starting something that could create value and last, the first chapter in this Creative Entrepreneurship section of the handbook goes to quite some lengths to demonstrate that thinking that the job of managing creativity is done once good innovations are achieved is a mistake. Stephen Cummings, Margaret Maile Petty and Ben Walker (one business school academic, one design school academic and one practitioner) look again at a study done a few years ago that seemed to show that winning awards for innovative design led to increases in a firm's share price. They raise questions about the validity of this study. Across the four markets that they investigated, only in one (the United States) could anything that could be taken to be an increase in share price be found. And, even here it was almost negligible and skewed by one firm in particular. That firm is Apple, a company that during the period of the study's focus (2001–10) had Steve Jobs – perhaps the best embodiment of an innovator and an entrepreneur in one package. This chapter, 'Innovation is not the only thing', suggests that these findings should make us wary of believing that innovation, in and of itself, or indeed any one 'silver bullet', is all that the management of creativity requires.

Chris Bilton's chapter, 'Learning to fail: lessons from Happenstance', likewise considers entrepreneurship as the motivating force behind innovation. The chapter draws on the Happenstance Project, a case study of technologists in residence in three UK arts organisations, and explores the beliefs and motivations on both sides which drove entrepreneurial behaviour during the residencies. 'Trait-based' theories of entrepreneurship have fallen out of academic fashion, but entrepreneurial businesses continue to be very dependent on the personality and beliefs of the individual entrepreneur. In this case, attitudes to failure and risk were as important as self-belief and commitment. Contrary to the stereotype of the entrepreneur as highly motivated and 'diligent', Happenstance's success depended on a willingness to fail and to learn from failure. Self-doubt and compromise were necessary counterparts to self-belief and determination, and the technologists and arts organisations were able to complement and learn from each other.

Kate Oakley's chapter 'Good work? Rethinking cultural entrepreneurship' builds on this notion of examining entrepreneurship at the micro or individual rather than organisational level and cleverly rethinks the conventional notion of the entrepreneur as an individual who makes a conscious decision to be entrepreneurial. She argues that cultural entrepreneurs are often innovative people who have no choice but to be entrepreneurial; entrepreneurship is a necessary output for their innovative impulse. There is a disconnection here between the political rhetoric of entrepreneurship, which frames creative industries policies in the UK, and the reality of 'forced' or 'adaptive' entrepreneurship in which many young people find themselves. The paradox of forced entrepreneurship is the gap between a dream of autonomy and the reality of self-exploitation. The 'good work' of the chapter's title describes a sub-set of young cultural entrepreneurs who justify their experience of precarious employment and 'voluntary poverty' by setting the ethical, social and aesthetic benefits against the economic costs. While such a lifestyle might be available only to a relatively privileged few, there may be opportunities here for rethinking the purpose of work and the models of organisation in which 'good work' can thrive.

The final chapter in this section considers 'entrepreneuring' as an active process. Chris Steyaert's chapter uses the fictional case of unemployed steel workers in Sheffield from the film *The Full Monty* to show how entrepreneurs move from an initial phase of 'wandering around', immersing themselves in the experiences around them to sense new possibilities, then picking up and working on the new entrepreneurial possibility through an iterative process of hard work and rehearsal. Finally the entrepreneurs take their entrepreneurial venture out into the world again and challenge the old ways of seeing (risking ridicule, but also turning expectations upside down). Chris's framework – summarised as 'AH / AHA / HAHA' – draws on Koestler's *Act of Creation* and expands on Koestler's theory of bisociation which underpins the book as a whole.

REFERENCES

Berkman, F. (2013), 'Beck's new DIY album spawns social media collaboration: a Q&A with McSweeney's editor Jordan Bass', Mashable.com, 13 May 2013, http://mashable.com/2013/01/08/beck-social-media/

Bilton, C. and S. Cummings (2010), *Creative strategy: reconnecting business and innovation*, Chichester, UK: Wiley.

6. Innovation is not the only thing
Stephen Cummings, Margaret Maile Petty and Ben Walker

This *Handbook of Management and Creativity* began with some n-grams looking at the similar rises of the words 'creativity' and 'management'. What was particularly interesting to us in developing this chapter was to look inside the framework developed by the editors of this and track the rise of the use of this framework's four components: innovation, entrepreneurship, leadership and organisation. Plug these four words into a combined n-gram from 1900–2012 (just search 'n-gram' on Google) and you will see that organisation has been a concern since the early 1900s, interest in leadership spiked around the time of the Second World War and has continued to grow since then, innovation has risen steadily since 1965 and jumps a little further from 2000. However, in the general consciousness that the n-gram does quite a nice job of recording, entrepreneurship does not rate. In contrast with the other three, it 'flat-lines'.

This, we believe, is dangerous. Entrepreneurship is a lynchpin. Just being innovative does not mean that anything of lasting value will be created. Innovation must be taken to market in an effective way to gain the beachhead that good leaders can exploit and good organisations can extract value from.

To illustrate the importance of not just relying on innovation as the be all and end all of managed value creation, of 'priming the pump', as it were, but forgetting about delivery, this chapter reports on a study that was done looking at the impact of winning reputable design awards on share price movements in New Zealand, Australian, US and UK listed firms.

In doing this, we recognise that we are dealing in proxies. Winning a design award is not the same as innovation, but given that such awards do seek to determine and recognise effective new design, data on who wins is freely available, and they are awarded on a regular basis, they are a useful simple approximation. Changes in share price are but one measure of business performance and value creation. But while some may argue that it may not even be a particularly good measure, its public availability and relative objectivity make its use far more practical and efficient than seeking and comparing other internally held data.

Moreover, we are inspired in this approach by an earlier study carried out by the UK Design Council in 2005. The Council produced a stock market index of UK firms that had won highly regarded design awards over the past decade and then plotted the share prices of that group of firms against the FTSE all-share index, the FTSE 100 and a portfolio of companies from emerging economies. In their study, a significant separation occurred in the late 1990s, where 'design-index' companies started to streak ahead of the norm. In the ten years to 2004, the 61 companies in the 'design index' rose by 263 per cent, compared with the FTSE 100's 57 per cent. The argument was subsequently made that the best way to outperform the norm and compete with the factor advantages enjoyed by rising companies from emerging economies was to engage superior design or design thinking (Bilton and Cummings 2010).[1]

Despite the inspiring and compelling message conveyed by the Design Council's graph and the assumption that is increasingly becoming an unquestioned convention in business circles that innovative design is a good strategy, the Council has not repeated the study. And nobody else has done this or something similar either. We have sought to replicate this study across four different countries and, unlike the UK Design Council study, we have not found any clear relationship between winning design awards and share price improvement.

Being aware of the limitations of this approach makes it important for us to not read too much into our data here. However, we do think that the seeming lack of a relationship between design/innovation and value/share

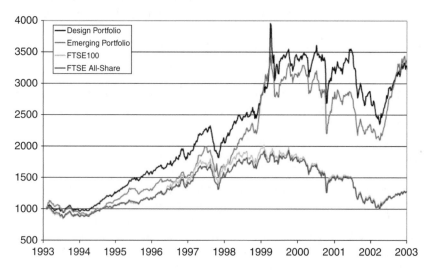

Figure 6.1   Innovative design = good strategy © UK Design Council[2]

price should, at the very least, make us think twice about putting all (or even most) of our eggs in the innovation basket and making sure that we look further at the importance of effective entrepreneurship in managing creativity to add value.

BACKGROUND

Design has become the next big thing. In the decade since 2000 a number of studies from a range of countries have argued that good design is good for business. In 2001 a study of Dutch firms found that integrating a design focus into new product development projects had a significantly positive influence on an organisation's turnover, export sales and profit (Gemser and Leenders 2001). In 2002, a British study found that half of actual export sales made by winners of the UK's Queen's Award for Exports could be attributed to their investment in design (Whyte et al. 2003). In the same year, a survey of 33 European SMEs claimed that design creates a competitive advantage (Mozota 2002). In 2003, the Danish Agency for Enterprise and Housing conducted a wide-ranging survey of Danish companies and found that companies where design was seen to be a core strategic issue performed better on a range of economic measures (Kretzschmar 2003). The 'design focused' group's growth in gross revenues across a period of five years, for example, was 22 per cent higher than the average of all companies. A Swedish study published in 2004 found that companies with 'design maturity' enjoyed very strong growth (Teknikforetagen and SVID 2004). And 2005 was a big year in this regard in the United Kingdom, with large studies published by the Department of Trade and Industry (DTI) and the independent 'Cox review of Creativity in Business' funded by the Government outlining what they saw to be links between design, business success and economic growth (Cox 2005, DTI 2005). Further studies carried out by the UK Design Council in the same year claimed that rapidly growing companies attached greater weight to creative design than average growth companies. They also argued that a much lower percentage of design-intensive firms than the average (just 21 per cent) were driven to compete primarily on price (Bilton and Cummings 2010).

Taking things a step further have been those who have argued that not only is good design good for a business, but thinking like a designer is good for those charged with developing an organisation's strategy. Perhaps the most influential book on strategy over past years, Roger Martin's 2009 book *Design of Business: Why design thinking is the next competitive advantage* does exactly this.

Martin's breakthrough idea may not be that new; a 1984 article by

Kotler and Rath titled 'Design: A powerful but neglected strategic tool' outlined a similar agenda, as have Black and Baker (1987), Bruce and Bessant (2002) and Bolland and Callopy (2004) since. But hot on the heels of the general interest piqued by Martin's work have come a number of bestsellers, such as *Change by Design: How design thinking can transform organisations and inspire innovation* (Brown 2009); *A Fine Line: How design strategies are shaping the future of business* (Esslinger 2009); and *The Designful Company: How to build a culture of nonstop innovation* (Neumeier 2009). A number of conferences have recently been established with the purpose of advancing the design mantra in business, and many existing business conferences have taken a design approach to be their overarching theme (e.g., the European Group for Organization Studies conference theme for 2012 is 'Design!?'). And design thinking is also now coming to be seen as an inspiration for re-inventing the way we teach management (Dunne and Martin 2006, Starkey and Tempest 2009). While there have been pockets of interest in the application of design to business for many years, it is fair to say that over the last five years, these small swells have now become a very large wave advocating innovative design and design thinking as a vital one-size-fits-all solution to the strategic challenges of twenty-first-century business.

Despite this growing mantra, there is little hard evidence to support claims that innovative design is necessarily good business, with partial analysis or anecdotal reference to particular companies generally employed instead to buttress such claims. Indeed, perhaps the item that appeared to be the most compelling piece of 'hard evidence' that good design pays was the graph published in 2005 by the UK Design Council and described at the beginning of this chapter.

In this chapter we set out to test the accuracy of the assumptions described above, and in particular the views advanced in the UK Design Council study, in order to think further about the value of innovative design for organisations (and how innovation more broadly needs to be supplemented) by replicating the Council's study across four different countries: New Zealand, Australia, the United States and the United Kingdom.

METHOD

In order to achieve this chapter's aims, we had to think about how, exactly, we could objectively operationalise national design indices in a manner relatable to that developed by the UK Design Council. This was not straightforward as the UK Design Council had not only included winners of a range of design awards but a number of other listed companies that were identified as design leaders by a panel of experts appointed by the Design Council. Not only was this therefore not a completely objective index, it was difficult to replicate in other countries. Consequently, we went back to the original idea behind the Council's design index – to create a list of companies that demonstrated their design prowess by winning reputable design competitions.

Perhaps the most reputable international design awards are the iF awards sponsored by the *Industrie Forum Design Hannover* and granted since 1953. However, while using winners of these awards over the past decade yields a reasonable sample for a US index, it did not in the other three countries under investigation. In these cases we had to rely on using local awards to create a large enough sample for an index (the specific awards used for each national index are outlined in their respective sections of the chapter). We included all companies who had won an award in the decade surveyed, even though this meant using share price data from before the award was won, taking the view that a reputable award was retrospective in the sense that it would likely come after a long period of work by the company concerned to turn its intent toward design excellence into fruition. In the case of the UK we created an additional index by using the same sample (minus those companies that were no longer operating or listed) as that used by the UK Design Council examining those companies' performance through to 2010.

For each of our five design indices (New Zealand, Australia, United States, United Kingdom and UK Design Council Extended), the historical share price data (period from 1 January 2001 to 1 January 2010) for each company in the Design Index of interest was then collected using a combination of Yahoo and Google Finance in three-monthly intervals for the NZ and Australian Design Indices, and in monthly intervals for the US and UK (new software and more advanced online services for these two markets meant that we were able to collect more regular data for the US and UK Design Indices).

The share price data for the New Zealand and Australian indices was collected manually and entered into Microsoft Excel from Yahoo and Google Finance, while the share price data for the UK and US indices was downloaded automatically from Yahoo and Google Finance using a Microsoft Excel add-in.

The average share price performance for each Index was then calculated by averaging all available share prices of the Design Index companies at each three-monthly or monthly interval (average share price), and finding the percentage increase or decrease relative to the average share price of the Design Index companies at the beginning of the period of interest. So, using NZ Design Index companies as an example, the average share price of the NZ Design Index at April 2001 was 2.59. The average share price of the NZ Design Index at January 2001 was 3.10. Thus, the average share price performance at April 2001 was calculated as follows: (2.59 – 3.10) / 3.10 = –16.45 per cent.[3] This method of calculating average share price performance was used for both Design Indices and Share Indices (e.g. the overall NASDAQ or NZX stock indices).[4]

This average share price performance was then graphed against a comparative share price, such as the total share price performance for the entire New Zealand or Australian stock exchange. Further details on the comparative share price are provided in each of the following sections on the four countries surveyed.

DESIGN INDEX 1: THE NEW ZEALAND DESIGN INDEX

Our New Zealand Design Index (NZDI) comprised the New Zealand-based companies that were listed on the New Zealand Stock Exchange that had won a BeST Design Award between and including January 2001, through to and including January 2010. In total 12 companies from a range of industries met our criteria and were thus included in our index (the NZ Design Index company list can be found in Appendix 1 at the end of the chapter).[5]

Figure 6.2 shows the average share price performance of our New Zealand

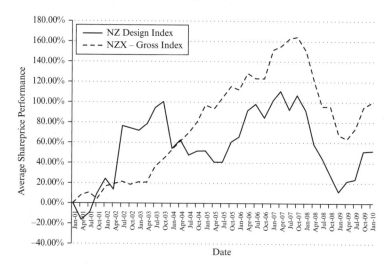

Figure 6.2   Average share price performance of NZ Design Index vs. NZX Gross Index

Design Index against the New Zealand Stock Exchange Gross Index share price performance (all share prices listed on the NZ Stock Exchange, including the NZ Design Index companies, relative to the initial Gross Index share price at January 2001), between and including January 2001, up to and including January 2010. While performance of the NZDI looks promising up until the end of 2003 (coincidentally, the same time as the end of the period analysed by the UK Design Council), from that point on there is little comfort provided to those of us who might expect that winning design awards (as representative of good design) leads to better performance.

DESIGN INDEX 2: AUSTRALIAN DESIGN INDEX

Our Australian Design Index comprised companies that are listed on the Australian Stock Exchange that had won an Australian International Design Award (AIDA) between and including January 2001 through to and including January 2010. In total 18 companies from a wide range of industries met our criteria and were thus included in our Australian Design Index.[6] The company list can be found in Appendix 2 at the end of the chapter, along with the type of AIDA each company won.

Figure 6.3 shows the average share price performance of our Australian Design Index against the Australian Stock Exchange (ASX) Gross Index share price performance (all share prices listed on the AUS Stock Exchange, including the AUS Design Index companies, relative to the

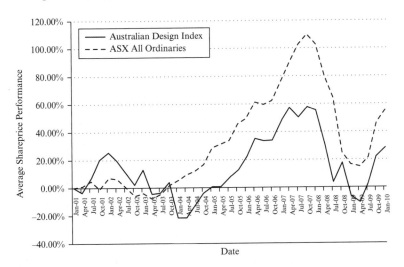

Figure 6.3   Australian Design Index vs. all ASX shares

initial gross share price at January 2001). The time period graphed was between and including January 2001, up to and including January 2010. The performance of the ADI broadly tracks that of the ASX, albeit at a lower level since mid-2003.

DESIGN INDEX 3: US DESIGN INDEX

Our United States Design Index comprised US-based companies that are listed on either the National Association of Securities Dealers Automated Quotations (NASDAQ) Stock Exchange or New York Stock Exchange (NYSE) that had won an iF Design Award between and including January 2001 through to and including January 2010. In total, 38 companies met our criteria and were thus included in our US Design Index.[7] The company list can be found in Appendix 3 at the end of the chapter, along with the type of iF Award each company won.

Figure 6.4 shows the average share price performance of our US Design Index against both the NASDAQ Composite Index and NYSE Composite Index share price performance (all share prices listed on the NASDAQ and NYSE respectively, including the US Design Index companies, relative to the initial gross share price of each stock exchange at January 2001). The period of interest was between and including January 2001, up to and including January 2010. In the case of the US Design

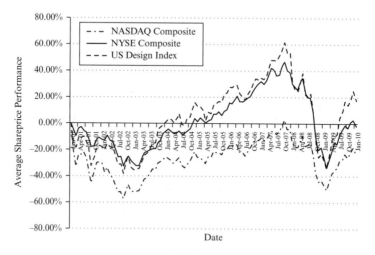

Figure 6.4   US Design Index vs. NASDAQ Composite Index and NYSE Composite Index

Index, it does seem to be the case that good design may indeed outperform the norm. However, it should be noted that this result may be skewed somewhat by the performance of a firm that has blended innovation and entrepreneurship better than any other in recent times: Apple.

DESIGN INDEX 4: THE UK DESIGN INDEX REVISITED

In creating a UK Design Index, a slightly different approach was taken from the previous three indices outlined above. Initially, we tried to adopt a similar approach to the US Design Index, by identifying all those UK-based, publicly listed companies that had won iF Design Awards between 2001 and 2010. However, while there were an extensive number of UK companies that had won the iF award, only two of these companies were publicly listed on the London Stock Exchange – Mothercare plc and Kingspan Renewables Ltd – and they won their awards at the beginning of 2011.

In an attempt to gain a more extensive list, some degree of discretion was used in terms of the award criteria. Using this more relaxed approach, a new UK Design Index was created. In total only seven companies were found for our UK Design Index. Mothercare plc and Kingspan were also included in our UK Design Index, assuming that even though they won their awards post the end of our stock exchange monitoring period, the products that won the awards had been around prior to the end of the period and we might assume that a clear design orientation had been in place prior to those products being launched. These inclusions brought the total number of companies in our UK Index to nine. The company list is shown in Appendix 4 at the end of the chapter, along with the award each company won and a website reference where the award each company won is described.

Figure 6.5 shows the average share price performance of our UK Design Index against the FTSE All Share Index[8] share price performance between and including January 2001, up to and including January 2010 (all share prices listed on the London Stock Exchange, including the UK Design Index companies, relative to the initial gross share price at January 2001). After a decade of ups and downs, the two indices finish very close to one another, showing no significant performance difference.

Given the high degree of discretion that had to be used in generating our UK Design Index, its relatively small size, and the difficulty in comparing this index with the original UK Design Index graph that motivated this study, an additional approach was adopted to gain a more extensive UK Design Index. The criteria used by the UK Design Council to select companies for their original Design Index is shown in Figure 6.6.

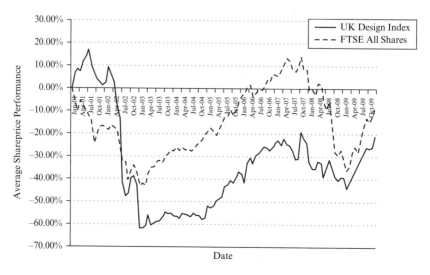

Figure 6.5   Our UK Design Index vs. FTSE All Share Index

The criteria as to what constitutes 'good design' can be seen as very subjective. The study therefore principally used the results of a wide range of design awards as the basis for stock selection, because of their comprehensiveness and relative objectivity. In order to ensure completeness, the study also included nominations from a Design Council panel of experts.

Award and Nomination Schemes

The information used to create the database of selected companies came from five sources and is summarised in Table 3 below.

Table 3: Award and nomination schemes

Name of Scheme	Scheme sponsor	Time period
Design Effectiveness Awards	Design Business Association	1993 to 2003
D&AD Awards	D&AD	1993 to 2003
Interbrand	Interbrand	1999 to 2003
Millennium Products	Design Council	2000
Panel Nominations	Design Council	2000

Figure 6.6   UK Design Council Design Index membership criteria

Subsequently, we sought to extend the Design Council's analysis through to January 2010 (from January 2001) using the new share price data, and eliminating those companies who had been acquired, merged, switched to private ownership or that no longer existed. The final adapted UK Design

1. AEA Technology; **Allied Domecq**; 2. AstraZeneca; **BAA (Taken over by ADI Ltd)**;
3. BAE Systems; 4. Barclays; 5. Barr (A.G.); **Body Shop (Taken over by
L'Oreal); Boots Group**; 6. BP; **British Airways (Taken over by International
Airlines Group)**; 7. British Sky Broadcasting Group; 8. BT Group; **Cadbury
Schweppes (Taken over by Kraft); Cambridge Antibody Technology Group
(Defunct)**; 9. Centrica; 10. Diageo; 11. Easyjet; **Egg (Acquired); Eidos
(Acquired); Emap (Acquired); EMI Group (Acquired); Gallaher Group
(Acquired)**;12. GKN; 13. GlaxoSmithKline; **GUS (Split Up)**; 14. Hilton Group
(Changed to Ladbrokes); 15. HSBC Holdings; **Imperial Chemical Industries
(Defunct)**; 16. Invensys; **Manchester United (Acquired)**; 17. Marks & Spencer
Group; **Matalan (Now Privately Owned); MFI Furniture Group (Defunct)**; 18.
Morrison (WM) Supermarkets; 19. Oxford Instruments; 20. Pearson; 21. Psion;
22. Reckitt Benckiser; 23. Rentokil Initial; **Reuters Group (Merged)**; 24. RM; 25.
Rolls-Royce Group; 26. Royal Bank of Scotland Group; 27. Sainsbury (J); **Scottish
& Newcastle (Acquired)**; 28. Scottish & Southern Energy; 29. Shell Transport &
Trading Co (Royal Dutch Shell); 30. Smith & Nephew; 31. Smith (WH) Group; **SSL
International (Acquired)**; 32. Tesco; **Tomkins (Acquired)**; 33. Ultra
Electronics Holdings; 34. Unilever; 35. Vodafone Group; 36. Wetherspoon (JD);
37. Whitbread; **Woolworths Group (Acquired)**; 38. WPP Group

*Figure 6.7   Updated UK Design Council Index 2010 (companies from the
original 2005 Index no longer on the Index shown in bold)*

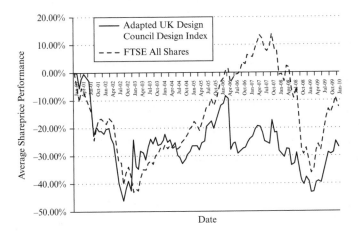

Figure 6.8   Updated original UK Design Index vs. FTSE All Share Index

Council Design Index is shown in Figure 6.7. Companies that were on the
original Design Index list but for which data are no longer available are
also noted in bold. In total, our adapted UK Design Council Design Index
contained 38 companies.

Figure 6.8 shows the average share price performance of our updated

UK Design Council Design Index against the FTSE All Share Index share price performance for the period between and including January 2001, up to and including January 2010 (all share prices listed on the London Stock Exchange, including the UK Design Index companies, relative to the initial gross share price at January 2001). Here performance is similar to that of our own UK Design Index.

DISCUSSION

In summary, of the four national design indices, we found there to be either no significant difference or indeed lower than average performance for design award winners across the decade 2001–10 in all except the US Index. Here the Design Index clearly outperformed the NASDAQ Composite across the period, it kept pace with the NYSE Composite through to 2007, and then pulled out of the global financial crisis and an increasingly globalising competitive international market significantly stronger than the NYSE.

We may reflect on the differences between our US Design Index to develop reasons for this. First, it may well be a measure of the quality or commercial orientation of the iF awards relative to the 'local' design awards used to generate large enough samples in our other three constituent nations. It could be a measure of the international quality or reputation of the US stock market that attracts the world's best companies to list there. It could be that the US Design Index's size (38 companies) was large enough to smooth out the negative influence of a few rogue companies which may have affected the NZ, UK and Australian indices (although we could see no obvious evidence of these indices being brought low by a small number of outliers). Indeed, even if we remove the entrepreneurially minded Apple and its stellar share price performance across the surveyed period, there is still some evidence of an innovative 'design effect'.

Determining the exact causes (if these could in fact be discerned) was beyond the scope of this study, but the positive performance of the US Index led us to look a little further at other means of linking design orientation to share market performance in countries where the number of 'world class' design winners was small and the variables influencing share market performance large. Taking the New Zealand situation, which we were closer to, we first looked at a group of listed companies that had undertaken a design orientation course sponsored by a government agency. Such courses are sponsored in many OECD countries. This course was run by an agency called Better by Design.

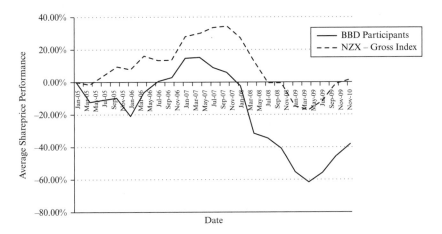

Figure 6.9   BBD Participants Index vs. all NZ shares

Second, instead of comparing the NZ Design Index with the whole of the New Zealand share market, we selected the two most similar or comparable listed companies to each of our Design Index companies and then compared the Index's performance with that of those comparable companies. We describe the findings from these two additional indices below.

Design Index 1a: 'Better by Design' Design Integration Programme Participants Index ('BBD Participants Index')

The 'BBD Participants Index' was created by identifying those companies that had participated in New Zealand Trade and Enterprise's 'Better by Design' Design Integration Programme and who were also listed on the New Zealand Stock Exchange. Seven companies met these criteria and were thus included in our BBD Participants Index.[9]

Figure 6.9 shows the average share price performance of our BBD Participants Index against the New Zealand Stock Exchange Gross Index share price performance for the period between and including January 2005 (the date when the BBD Design Integration Programme was first started), up to and including January 2010 (all share prices listed on the NZ Stock Exchange, including the NZ Design Index companies, relative to the initial gross share price at January 2005). As Figure 6.9 shows, this index may not be the best indication of how design orientation enhances business performance.

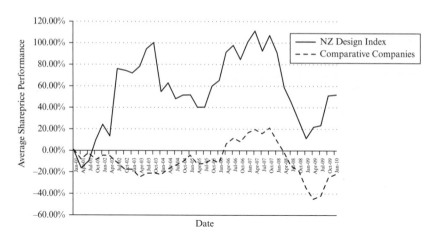

Figure 6.10   NZ Design Index vs. comparable companies

Design Index 1b: NZ Design Index vs. Comparative Companies Index

In order to generate this alternative design index graph, we created a new 'Comparative Companies Index'. This Comparative Index was created by finding two non-BeST Award-winning 'comparative companies' for each of the companies in our NZ Design Index. Comparative companies were found by identifying two companies that were listed in the same 'sector' for each company in our NZ Design Index by the New Zealand Stock Exchange, and which seemed to be a similar company in terms of size and business activities. The list of comparative companies can be found in Appendix 5 at the end of the chapter.

As with the other indices, the average share price performance of the Comparative Companies Index between and including January 2001, up to and including January 2010 was calculated and then graphed against the NZ Design Index average share price performance. The results indicate a far more positive relationship between design orientation and business performance and are shown in Figure 6.10. They add weight to the view that good design may enhance business performance (using share price as a proxy for business performance), if one undertakes a more sensitive analysis than simply taking a group of companies that have won a range of design awards with varying criterion plus some others suspected of design excellence against the whole of a nation's listed companies.

FINDINGS

Any summary of findings from our study must be considered in the light of its strength and weaknesses. Design awards and share price performance of publicly listed companies may not be the best measures of design orientation and business performance respectively. Design awards are based on particular criteria that many might disagree with. A great deal of good design will be happening in companies that are not listed. Share price is based at least partly on sentiment and predictions. Many of our sample sizes are small because not many listed companies win good design awards. However, share price is, to some extent, an objective and unmediated measure of performance that can be relatively easier worked with and one that can be used comparatively and quantitatively in meaningful ways. Design awards are at least a third party assessment of a firm's design orientation as opposed to surveying firms themselves, or their stakeholders, to comment on their own design prowess or orientation. Responses from interested parties such as these will likely be biased.

Mindful of these limitations and strengths, however, we can say with confidence that an orientation toward and achievement of innovative design in a firm's products and services may make a difference to business performance, but the link may not be as simple, universal and all-conquering as has come to be assumed in the last decade. Going on a design thinking course, applying some of the ideas from a book on design or design thinking, or winning a local design award will not necessarily improve business performance.

While graphs like that produced by the UK Design Council in 2005 appeal to an intuitive view that innovative design *should* be a good strategy, they can be misleading if viewed uncritically. Indeed, the subjective collation of a group of so-called leaders in design at a particular point in time, which cannot help but be influenced by performance in the first, may in fact do design a disservice – particularly if the performance of such a group may turn out to only be good in the 'fair-weather' that influenced its selection in the first place. Assuming, or trying too hard to prove, that innovative design, or innovation in general, is a universal panacea for business is in our opinion dangerous in that exaggerating expectations in this way may ultimately lead to disenchantment with, and a subsequent tossing aside of, design onto the scrap-heap of other one-best ways to achieve business success borrowed from other disciplines – such as the notion that a strong culture will improve business performance (anthropology/sociology), or that wiping the slate clean and using business process reengineering to reorganise your business (engineering) is *the* answer we've been searching for. Generally speaking, business is more complex than that.

However, there appears to be enough evidence to suggest (from our US Design Index and from out NZ Design Index versus Comparable Companies) that really innovative design can make a significant difference: if it is backed up with other elements. However, what remains to be done is more research and the gathering of more evidence on how, when and with what exactly an innovative orientation can lead to improved business performance. We hope that this chapter will encourage further research on these important issues. As a good first step, the three chapters in the remainder of this section will provide useful rationales and advice as to how innovation can be effectively married with entrepreneurial activity to ensure that you get greater value from innovative activity.

QUESTIONS FOR DISCUSSION

1. Why might many people like to believe that there is a clear link between award-winning design and business performance?
2. What is the danger in thinking that achievement in one particular creative dimension will lead to success overall?
3. What additional management processes would you seek to put in place to ensure that good design has the best chance of helping an organisation to achieve its performance objectives?

NOTES

1. There may be some irony in the fact that the editors of this book made use of the UK Design Council study in their previous book *Creative Strategy: Reconnection business and innovation*, 2010.
2. UK Design Council (2005), *Design Index: the impact of design on stock market performance*. London: UK Design Council. Retrieved 4 January 2012 from http://www.design-council.org.uk/publications/.
3. Note that because some companies were first listed on their respective stock exchange after the beginning of the period (1 January 2001), not all companies' share prices were included in the calculation of the average share price at every period.
4. Share prices for each period were taken from as close to the beginning of the period as possible. Generally, this was the share price around 1 to 7 days into the period.
5. All data as to what companies had won BeST Awards was obtained from http://www.bestawards.co.nz/.
6. All data as to what companies had won AIDAs was obtained from http://www.designawards.com.au/past_entries.jsp.
7. All data as to what companies had won iF Awards was obtained from http://www.ifdesign.de/exhibition_index_e.
8. 'The FTSE All-Share is a market-capitalization weighted index representing the per-

formance of all eligible companies listed on the London Stock Exchange's main market, which pass screening for size and liquidity. Today the FTSE All-Share Index covers 630 constituents with a combined value of nearly £1.8 trillion* – approximately 98 per cent of the UK's market capitalization. The FTSE All-Share Index is considered to be the best performance measure of the overall London equity market with the vast majority of UK-focused money invested in funds which track it. The FTSE All-Share Index also accounts for 10 per cent of the world's equity market capitalization. The index is suitable as the basis for investment products, such as funds and exchange-traded funds (ETFs). FTSE All-Share Index constituents are traded on the London Stock Exchange's SETS and SETSmm trading systems' (FTSE Group 2011: 1).

9. These companies were Comvita, Methven, Skellerup, Scott Technology, Wellington Drive Technologies, Tourism Holdings, and New Image Group.

REFERENCES

Bilton, C. and S. Cummings (2010), *Creative strategy: reconnecting business and innovation*, Chichester, UK: Wiley.

Black, C.D. and M.J. Baker (1987), 'Success through design', *Design Studies*, **8**(4), 207–16.

Bolland, R.J. and F. Callopy (eds) (2004), *Managing as designing*, Stanford, CA: Stanford University Press.

Brown, T. (2009), *Change by design: how design thinking can transform organizations and inspire innovation*, London: Collins Business.

Bruce, M. and J. Bessant (2002), *Design in business: strategic innovation through design*, New York: Financial Times/Prentice Hall.

Cox, G. (2005), *The Cox review: enhancing the role of creativity in driving the productivity performance of SMEs in the UK*. London: Department for Trade and Industry.

DTI (2005), *DTI Economics Paper Number 15: Creativity, Design and Business Performance*, London: Department for Trade and Industry.

Dunne, D. and R. Martin (2006), 'Design thinking and how it will change management education', *Academy of Management Learning and Education*, **5**(4), 512–23.

Esslinger, H. (2009), *A fine line: how design strategies are shaping the future of business*, New York: Jossey Bass.

FTSE Group (2011), 'FTSE All-Share Index Factsheet', London: FTSE Group. Retrieved 4 January 2012 from http://www.ftse.com/Indices/UK_Indices/Downloads/FTSE_All-Share_Index_Factsheet.pdf.

Gemser, G. and M.A.A. Leenders (2001), 'How integrating industrial design in the product development process impacts on company performance', *Journal of Product Innovation Management*, **18**(1), 28–38.

Hertenstein, J.H., M.B. Platt and D.R. Brown (2001), 'Valuing design: enhancing corporate performance through design effectiveness', *Design Management Journal*, **12**(3), 10–19.

Kotler, P. and A. Rath (1984), 'Design: a powerful but neglected strategic tool', *Journal of Business Strategy*, **5**(2), 16.

Kretzschmar, A. (2003), *The economic effects of design*, Copenhagen: National Agency for Enterprise and Housing. http://www.ebst.dk/file/1924/the_economic_effects_of_design.pdf.

Martin, R.L. (2009), *Design of business: why design thinking is the next competitive advantage*, Boston, MA: Harvard Business School Press.

Mozota, B.B. (2002), 'Design and competitive edge: a model for design management excellence in European SMEs', *Design Management Journal*, **2**(1), 88–104.

Neumeier, M. (2009), *The designful company: how to build a culture of nonstop innovation*, New York: Peachpit Press.

Starkey, K. and S. Tempest (2009), 'The winter of our discontent: the design challenge for business schools', *Academy of Management Learning and Education*, **8**, 576–86.

Teknikforetagen and SVID (2004), *10 points – attitudes, profitability and design maturity in Swedish companies*, Sweden: The Association of Swedish Engineering Industries Design and Swedish Industrial Design Foundation.

Whyte, J.K., A. Davies, A.J. Salter and D.M. Gann (2003), 'Designing to compete: lessons from Millennium Product winners', *Design Studies*, **24**(5), 395–409.

APPENDIX 1 – THE NEW ZEALAND DESIGN INDEX LIST

Company	NZX Code	BeST Award Won
1. Air New Zealand	AIR	BeST Awards 2003 – FINALIST Interior (Hospitality); BeST Awards 2006 – WINNER Identity Development (Large Scale); Design In Business Awards 2006 – Highly Commended; BeST Awards 2007 – BRONZE Corporate Communication; BeST Awards 2007 – SILVER Identity Development (Small Scale); BeST Awards 2007 – SILVER Spatial (Hospitality); BeST Awards 2008 – SILVER Identity Development (Large Scale); BeST Awards 2009 – BRONZE Environmental Graphics; BeST Awards 2009 – BRONZE Spacial (Public & Institutional Spaces)
2. Auckland Airport	AIA	BeST Awards 2008 – BRONZE Environmental Graphics; BeST Awards 2008 – GOLD Identity Development (Large Scale); BeST Awards 2009 – SILVER Spatial (Public & Institutional Spaces)
3. Comvita Ltd (First listed on NZX in October 2003)	CVT	BeST Awards 2008 – GOLD Packaging; BeST Awards 2007 – SILVER Identity Development (Small Scale)
4. Fisher & Paykel Appliances (First listed on NZX in October 2001)	FPA	BeST Awards 2008 – BRONZE Visual Communication; BeST Awards 2008 – GOLD Consumer Product; BeST Awards 2008 – SILVER Consumer Product; BeST Awards 2008 – STRINGER Product Award; Finalist in 2005 Design in Business Awards; DESIGN MARK Australian International Design Award – Consumer 2009; WINNER Australian International Design Award – Consumer 2009; GOOD Design Award 2009 (Chicago) – Kitchen & Appliances (Two awards); GOOD Design Award 2009 (Chicago) – Tabletop 2010
5. Fletcher Building	FBU	BeST Awards 2009 – GOLD Broadcast Graphic Design

Company	NZX Code	BeST Award Won
6. Kathmandu Holdings Ltd (First listed on NZX in November 2009)	KMD	DESIGN MARK Australian International Design Award – Sport & Leisure 2009
7. Methven Ltd (First listed on NZX in November 2004)	MVN	DESIGN MARK Australian International Design Award – Consumer 2005; GOOD Design Award 2005 (Chicago) – Kitchen & Bathroom; GOOD Design Award 2008 (Chicago) – Bath & Accessories; WINNER Australian International Design Award – Housing & Building 2008; WINNER Australian International Design Award – Housing & Building 2009; DESIGN MARK Australian International Design Award – Housing & Building 2010; BeST Awards 2003 – FINALIST Consumer Product; BeST Awards 2003 – FINALIST Furniture; BeST Awards 2003 – FINALIST Furniture; BeST Awards 2005 – HIGHLY COMMENDED Consumer Product; BeST Awards 2005 – HIGHLY COMMENDED Consumer Product; BeST Awards 2007 – SILVER Concept / Experimental; BeST Awards 2007 – SILVER Consumer Product; BeST Awards 2008 – SILVER Concept / Experimental; BeST Awards 2008 – SILVER Consumer Product; BeST Awards 2008 – SILVER Consumer Product; BeST Awards 2008 – SILVER Sustainable Product Award; BeST Awards 2008 – BRONZE Sustainable Product Award; WINNER 2008 Design in Business Awards; BeST Awards 2008 – BRONZE Graphic Design Arts; BeST Awards 2008 – GOLD Corporate Communication; BeST Awards 2009 – BRONZE Identity Development (Large Scale); BeST Awards 2009 – BRONZE Packaging; BeST Awards 2009 – GOLD Consumer Product; BeST Awards 2009 – SILVER Consumer Product; Winner of a New Zealand Plastic Industry Design Award 2010

Company	NZX Code	BeST Award Won
8. Pumpkin Patch Ltd (First listed on NZX in June 2004)	PPL	New Zealand International Business Awards 2009 – Best Use of Design
9. Skellerup Holdings Ltd (First listed on NZX in June 2002)	SKL	BeST Awards 2009 – SILVER Consumer Product
10. SkyCity Entertainment Ltd	SKC	BeST Awards 2005 – STRINGER AWARD Interior; BeST Awards 2005 – WINNER Interior (Restaurants, Bars & Nightclubs)
11. Westpac Banking Corporation (Share price info only available from July 2002)	WBC	BeST Awards 2003 – FINALIST Interior (Commercial); BeST Awards 2004 – HIGHLY COMMENDED Corporate Communication; BeST Awards 2006 – WINNER Graphic Stringer Award (In conjuction with New Zealand Business Council For Sustainable Development); BeST Awards 2006 – WINNER Graphic Design Arts; BeST Awards 2006 – WINNER Corporate Communication (In conjunction with New Zealand Business Council For Sustainable Development); BeST Awards 2006 – HIGHLY COMMENDED Editorial & Books (In conjunction with New Zealand Business Council For Sustainable Development); BeST Awards 2009 – SILVER Spatial (Workplace & Office Environments); Retail Design Awards 2010 – Westpac, Plaza Mall, Riccarton
12. Xero Limited (First listed on NZX in June 2007)	XRO	Design In Business Awards 2008 – Finalist; ONYA Web Awards 2010 – Best User Experience, Best Web Application, Most Outstanding Website

APPENDIX 2 – THE AUSTRALIAN DESIGN INDEX LIST

Company	ASX Code	ASX Sector	AIDA Won
1. Breville Group Ltd	BRG	Retailing	Good Design 2010 (Consumer)
			Design Award 2010 (Consumer)
			Good Design 2008 (Consumer)
			Good Design 2007 (Consumer)
			Design Award 2007 (Consumer)
			Good Design 2006 (Consumer)
			Design Award 2006 (Consumer)
			Good Design 2005 (Consumer)
			Design Award 2005 (Consumer)
			Good Design 2004 (Consumer)
			Design Award 2004 (Consumer)
			Good Design 2003 (Consumer)
			Good Design 2001 (Consumer)
			Design Award 2001
2. Cochlear Ltd	COH	Healthcare Equipment & Services	Design Award 2010 (Medical & Scientific)
			Design Award 2009 (Medical & Scientific)
			Design Award 2006 (Medical & Scientific)
			Good Design 2004 (Medical & Scientific)
			Good Design 2003 (Medical & Scientific)
			Design Award 2001 (Medical & Scientific)
3. Pacific Brands Ltd	PBG	Retailing	Good Design 2010 (Sport & Leisure)
4. Billabong International Ltd	BBG	Consumer Durables & Apparel	Good Design 2010 (Sport & Leisure)
5. Aristocrat Leisure Ltd	ALL	Consumer Services	Good Design 2009 (Business & Technology)
6. Mobilarm ltd	MBO	Technology Hardware & Equipment	Design Award 2009 (Business & Technology)
			Design Award 2006 (Sports & Leisure)
7. Nanosonics Ltd	MVN	Healthcare Equipment & Services	Good Design 2009 (Medical & Scientific)

Company	ASX Code	ASX Sector	AIDA Won
8. Compumedics Ltd	CMP	Healthcare Equipment & Services	Good Design 2009 (Medical & Scientific)
			Good Design 2007 (Medical & Scientific)
			Good Design 2004 (Medical & Scientific)
			Good Design 2001 (Medical & Scientific)
9. ResMed Inc	RMD	Healthcare Equipment & Services	Good Design 2009 (Medical & Scientific)
			Good Design 2008 (Medical & Scientific)
			Design Award of The Year 2006 – Overall Winner
			Good Design 2005 (Medical & Scientific)
			Good Design 2004 (Medical & Scientific)
			Design Award 2003 (Medical & Scientific)
10. Qantas Airways Ltd	QAN	Transportation	Design Award of The Year 2009 – Overall Winner
			Design Award 2008 (Public Spaces)
			Design Award 2004 (Automotive & Transport)
11. Orica Ltd	ORI	Materials	Design Award 2008 (Automotive & Transport)
13. Funtastic Ltd	MXI	Consumer Durables & Apparel	Good Design 2008 (Sports & Leisure)
			Good Design 2007 (Consumer)
			Good Design 2006 (Sports & Leisure)
14. Freshtel Holdings Ltd	FRE	Telecommunication Service	Good Design 2006 (Business & Technology)
15. MediVac Ltd	MDV	Healthcare Equipment & Services	Good Design 2005 (Medical & Scientific)
16. MediGard Ltd	MGZ	Healthcare Equipment & Services	Design Award 2005 (Medical & Scientific)
17. Uscom Ltd	UCM	Healthcare Equipment & Services	Good Design 2003 (Medical & Scientific)
18. Traffic Technologies Ltd	TTI	Transportation	Good Design 2002 (Business & Technology)

APPENDIX 3 – THE US DESIGN INDEX LIST

Company	Design award won	US Stock Code
1. Tiffany & Co	2011 iF Communication Award	NYSE:TIF
2. Dell Inc	2009 iF Communication Award, 2011 iF Product Design Award, 2010 iF Product Design Award, 2009 iF Product Design Award, 2008 iF Product Design Award	NASDAQ:DELL
3. Yahoo Inc	2008 iF Communication Award	NASDAQ:YHOO
4. Hewlett Packard	2007 iF Communication Award, 2010 iF Material Award, 2008 iF Packaging Award, 2011 iF Product Design Award, 2010 iF Product Design Award, 2009 iF Product Design Award, 2008 iF Product Design Award, 2007 iF Product Design Award, 2006 iF Product Design Award, 2003 iF Product Design Award, 2002 iF Product Design Award	NYSE:HPQ
5. Eastman Kodak Company	2006 iF Communication Award, 2010 iF Product Design Award, 2007 iF Product Design Award, 2006 iF Product Design Award, 2001 iF Product Design Award	NYSE:EK
6. Oxo (Parent company is listed – Helen of Troy Limited (NASDAQ: HELE))	2008 iF Material Award, 2010 iF Product Design Award, 2009 iF Product Design Award, 2007 iF Product Design Award, 2008 Universal Design Award	
7. Sony	2008 iF Packaging Award	NYSE:SNE
8. Nike	2011 iF Product Design Award, 2003 iF Product Design Award	NYSE:NKE
9. Apple	2011 iF Product Design Award, 2010 iF Product Design Award, 2009 iF Product Design Award, 2008 iF Product Design Award, 2007 iF Product Design Award, 2006 iF Product Design Award, 2002 iF Product Design Award, 2001 iF Product Design Award, 2008 Universal Design Award	NASDAQ:AAPL, NYSE:AAPL

Company	Design award won	US Stock Code
10. Harman Consumer Group International	2011 iF Product Design Award, 2010 iF Product Design Award, 2009 iF Product Design Award, 2006 iF Product Design Award	NYSE:HAR
11. Motorola	2011 iF Product Design Award, 2010 iF Product Design Award, 2009 iF Product Design Award	NYSE:MMI, NYSE:MSI
12. Logitech Audio	2011 iF Product Design Award, 2010 iF Product Design Award, 2008 iF Product Design Award, 2007 iF Product Design Award, 2006 iF Product Design Award, 2002 iF Product Design Award	NASDAQ:LOGI
13. IBM	2011 iF Product Design Award, 2010 iF Product Design Award, 2009 iF Product Design Award, 2008 iF Product Design Award, 2007 iF Product Design Award, 2006 iF Product Design Award, 2002 iF Product Design Award, 2001 iF Product Design Award	NYSE:IBM
14. Steelcase	2011 iF Product Design Award	NYSE:SCS
15. Cardinal Health	2011 iF Product Design Award	NYSE:CAH
16. Masimo	2011 iF Product Design Award	NASDAQ:MASI
17. Trimble	2011 iF Product Design Award	NASDAQ:TRMB
18. Briggs & Stratton	2011 iF Product Design Award	NYSE:BGG
19. Rockwell Collins	2010 iF Product Design Award	NYSE:COL
20. Plantronics	2010 iF Product Design Award, 2009 iF Product Design Award, 2006 iF Product Design Award	NYSE:PLT
21. Nokia	2010 iF Product Design Award	NYSE:NOK
22. Intel Corporation	2010 iF Product Design Award	NASDAQ:INTC
23. Seagate Technology	2009 iF Product Design Award	NASDAQ: STX
24. Western Digital	2009 iF Product Design Award	NYSE:WDC
25. Tupperware	2009 iF Product Design Award, 2007 iF Product Design Award, 2002 iF Product Design Award	NYSE:TUP
26. Ethicon (Owned by Johnson & Johnson – NYSE:J&J)	2009 iF Product Design Award	
27. Microsoft	2008 iF Product Design Award	NASDAQ:MSFT
28. SanDisk	2008 iF Product Design Award, 2007 iF Product Design Award	NASDAQ:SNDK
29. Avaya Inc	2007 iF Product Design Award	NYSE:AV

Company	Design award won	US Stock Code
30. Lexar Media (Parent company Micron Technology – NASDAQ:MU)	2007 iF Product Design Award	
31. Office Max	2007 iF Product Design Award	NYSE:OMX
32. Abaxis	2007 iF Product Design Award	NASDAQ:ABAX
33. John Deere	2007 iF Product Design Award, 2006 iF Product Design Award, 2002 iF Product Design Award	NYSE:DE
34. Pitney Bowes	2006 iF Product Design Award, 2002 iF Product Design Award	NYSE:PBI
35. 3M Healthcare	2006 iF Product Design Award	NYSE:MMM
36. Estee Lauder	2002 iF Product Design Award	NYSE:EL
37. Garmin International	2007 Outdoor Industry Award	NASDAQ:GRMN
38. Timberland	2007, 2006 Outdoor Industry Award	NYSE:TBL

APPENDIX 4 – OUR UK DESIGN INDEX

Company Name	LSE Code	Design Award Won
1. AstraZeneca	AZN.L	Good Design Award 2010 http://www.g-mark.org/award/detail. html?id=36687&lang=en
2. Barclays	BARC.L	Brit Insurance Designs of the Year 2011 http://group.barclays.com/News/Barclays- news/NewsArticle/1231786513454.html

3. Burberry Group	BRBY.L	British Fashion Awards 2009
		http://www.guardian.co.uk/lifeandstyle/
		  2009/dec/09/burberry-british-designer-
		  2009

4. GlaxoSmithKline	GSK.L	Reddot Communication Award 2011 http://en.red-dot.org/4566.html Medical Design Excellence Award 2008 http://www.pmpnews.com/article/news- novel-spray-package-wins-design-award

5. Marks & Spencer	MKS.L	FIRA Innovation Award 2011
		http://home.worldinteriordesignnetwork.
		  com/news/marks_and_spencer_wins_
		  fira_innovation_award_for_sonoma_
		  folding_wardrobe_111031/
		2006 Retail Interior Award for Food &
		  Supermarket Design of the Year
		http://corporate.marksandspencer.com/
		  media/press_releases/19092006_
		  marksspencerwinsretailinterioraward

6. Rolls Royce Group	RR.L	Reddot Award 2010
		http://www.autoblog.com/2010/04/02/red-
		  dot-design-award-honors-rolls-royce-
		  ghost-others/

7. Reckitt Bensicker	RB.L	Marketing Design Awards 2011 http://www.marketingdesignawards.com/
8. Mothercare plc	MTC.L	iF Product Award 2011
9. Kingspan Renewables	KSP.L	iF Product Award 2011

APPENDIX 5 – THE NZ DESIGN INDEX VS COMPARATIVE COMPANIES LIST

The NZ Design Index company is listed in bold, the two comparative companies are indented in Italics below their respective NZ Design Index company.

Company Name	NZX Sector	Notes
Air New Zealand (AIR)	Services > Transport	No other airline carrier in New Zealand
Freightways Ltd (FRT)	Services > Transport	http://www.freightways.co.nz/ http://www.mainfreight.co.nz/
Mainfreight Ltd (MFT)	Services > Transport	Global/en/Global-Home.aspx
Auckland Airport (AIA)	Services > Ports	No other airports listed on NZX
Port of Tauranga (POT)	Services > Ports	http://www.port-tauranga.co.nz/ http://www.southport.co.nz/
Southports New Zealand Ltd (SPN)	Services > Ports	
Comvita (CVT)	Services > Consumer	Produces natural health and skincare products
Pharmacybrands Ltd (PHB)	Services > Consumer	Retail pharmacy management company – http://
Goodman Fielder Ltd (GFF)	Services > Consumer	en.wikipedia.org/wiki/ Pharmacybrands
Fisher & Paykel Appliances (FPA)	Goods > Intermed & Durables	
Rakon Ltd (RAK)	Goods > Intermed & Durables	'One of the world's leading suppliers of energy saving,
Wellington Drive Technologies Ltd (WDT)	Goods > Intermed & Durables	electronically commutated (ECM) motors and fans' – http://www.wdtl.com
Fletcher Building Ltd (FBU)	Primary > Building	Only three companies listed in this sector
Nuplex Holdings Ltd (NPX)	Primary > Building	'Leading global manufacturer of polymer resins with
Steel & Tube Holdings Ltd (STU)	Primary > Building	operations in ten countries on four continents, our products are sold in over 80 countries' – http://www. nuplex.co.nz/

Company Name	NZX Sector	Notes
		'Largest distributor of steel and allied products in New Zealand' – http://www.steelandtube.co.nz/page/home.aspx
Kathmandu Ltd (KMD)	Goods > Textiles & Apparel	
Briscoes Group Ltd (BGR)	Goods > Intermeds & Durables	
Cavallier Corporation Ltd	Goods > Textiles & Apparel	'The Group's principal activities comprise two broadloom carpet businesses, a carpet tile business, a commission wool scouring operation and a wool procurement business' – http://www.cavcorp.co.nz/cbcorporate/corporate-overview/about-us.cfm
Methven Ltd (MVN)	Goods > Intermeds & Durables	
EBOS Group Ltd (EBO)	Goods > Intermeds & Durables	
Mercer Group Ltd (MGL)	Goods > Intermeds & Durables	One of its business units is the design, manufacture and distribution of a range of kitchen, bathroom and laundry products – http://www.mercers.co.nz/
Pumpkin Patch Ltd (PPL)	Services > Consumer	Children's clothing retail chain
Hallenstein Glassons Ltd (HLG)	Services > Consumer	Retail clothing chain Retail clothing chain (low cost)
Postie Plus Group Ltd (PPG)	Services > Consumer	
Skellerup Holdings Ltd (SKL)	Goods > Intermeds & Durables	Manufacturers of farming footwear and dairy farming equipment – http://www.skellerup.co.nz/
Scott Techno-logies Ltd (SCT)	Goods > Intermeds & Durables	Manufacturers of automated production machinery – http://www.scott.co.nz/

Company Name	NZX Sector	Notes
PGG Wrightson Ltd (PGW)	Primary > Agriculture	PGG Wrightson offers many more products and services than Skellerup. Not just consumables but offers business advice, financing, rural real estate etc – http://www.pggwrightson.co.nz/company_profile.html
Skycity Entertainment (SKC)	Services > Leisure & Tourism	Operates hotels, casinos, and movie theatres – http://www.skycity.co.nz
Tourism Holdings Ltd (THL)	Services > Leisure & Tourism	All-round tourism company. Operates scenic attractions and holiday rentals vehicles –
Millenium & Copthorne Hotels Ltd (MCK)	Services > Leisure & Tourism	http://www.thlonline.com/ http://www.millenniumhotels.co.nz/
Westpac Banking Corporation (WBC)	Overseas	Bank – http://www.westpac.co.nz
Australia & New Zealand (ANZ) Banking Group Ltd	Overseas Services > Finance & Other Services	Another Bank – http://www.anz.co.nz. BNZ is a subsidiary of National Australia Bank which is listed on the ASX. ASB is a subsidiary of Commonwealth Bank which is also on the ASX. National Bank of New Zealand is a subsidiary of ANZ. Kiwibank is an SOE. TSB Bank is a 'Trustee Bank'
Tower Ltd (TWR)		Insurance and savings / investment company – http://www.tower.co.nz
Xero Ltd (XRO)	Services > Finance & Other Services	Provides online or 'cloud' accounting services for businesses – http://www.xero.co.nz
AMP Ltd (AMP)	Services > Finance & Other Services	AMP is almost identical to Tower, offers insurance and investment / savings services – http://www.amp.co.nz
Smartpay Ltd (SPY)	Goods > Intermeds & Durables	

Company Name	NZX Sector	Notes
		Smartpay owns Cadmus, they distribute and maintain EFTPOS and retail infrastructure like cameras and radio – http://www.smartpay.co.nz/

1. Experimental Innovation ⟵relation⟶ Entrepreneurship
2. Apply failure lessons to Entrepreneur
3. How risk-taking differs in arts v. tech

7. Learning to fail: lessons from Happenstance
Chris Bilton

'That wasn't flying! That was . . . falling, with style!' (Woody, *Toy Story*)

In the introduction to this handbook we have argued that a creative approach to management strives to connect different competences and fields of endeavour. This chapter considers three such connections. First, the chapter will highlight the relationship between experimental innovation and entrepreneurial drive and purpose. Second, the chapter identifies the importance of failure and doubt in a creative process and applies this to entrepreneurial risk-taking. Third, the chapter considers differing approaches to entrepreneurial risk-taking in the arts and in technology. The chapter is framed by a case study of Happenstance, a funded research project exploring the relationship between technological and artistic processes and mentalities in three UK arts organisations.

Happenstance def

INTRODUCING HAPPENSTANCE

The Happenstance Project consisted of a series of creative technology residencies, placing three pairs of creative technologists into three UK arts organisations for approximately 12 weeks from March 2012 to June 2012. The project was conceived by Rachel Coldicutt at Caper, a digital agency with experience of running 'hack days', managing digital projects and devising digital strategies, and by Laura Sillars, co-director of Site Gallery in Sheffield, a small contemporary gallery with a rapidly changing programme of innovative exhibitions. The other two arts organisations were Lighthouse, a digital culture agency in Brighton with a gallery space, studios and office space, and Spike Island in Bristol, home to a gallery, artists' studios and rented spaces for artists, designers and associates, housed in a former tea factory near the harbourside. For a brief explanation of the day-to-day workings of Happenstance, see Box 7.1.

goal

The primary aim of Happenstance was to consider how digital technology and creative uses of technology can become 'embedded' in arts organisations. The project was one of eight pilot projects supported by the

BOX 7.1   EXPLAINING THE PROCESS OF
            HAPPENSTANCE

As the name suggests, the outcomes of Happenstance were left deliberately open-ended. However, there was an expectation that resident technologists would come up with some innovative applications of digital technology (hardware or software) to address specific problems with internal communication, corporate identity or external perception in each arts organisation. Hardware solutions included use of thermal receipt printers to respond to inputs from social media, using Kinect motion sensors to observe human traffic in the building, and embedding digital information about artists into artist postcards. Software solutions included 'Offbot', a communication tool designed to capture informal communication amongst staff – a kind of anonymised virtual office gossip; this data could then be aggregated and channelled, allowing the organisation to collectively reflect on individual, emergent ideas.

In the end the process behind these projects was no less significant than the outcomes. By making invisible, anonymous digital processes vivid and accessible, Happenstance residents made the arts organisations more aware of and confident with technology. At Lighthouse in Brighton, 'This Is A Working Shop' showed one of the residents writing code, making public the unseen craft behind the digital tools we usually take for granted. Meanwhile his co-resident ran lunchtime coding workshops and showed staff how to read and rewrite some of the code used on popular websites. In all three organisations, because the residents were working amongst them, in an open plan office or other public space, digital technology processes and methods percolated through to influence organisational behaviour. This chapter tends to focus on these intangible processes rather than tangible outcomes of Happenstance, in order to make some observations on the human side of enterprise – the people and attitudes which drive an entrepreneurial process.

Digital R&D Fund for Arts and Culture (a joint venture between National Endowment for Science, Technology and the Arts (NESTA), Arts Council England (ACE) and the Arts and Humanities Research Council (AHRC). A University of Warwick research team comprising Chris Bilton, Ruth

Leary and Katherine Jewkes was commissioned to observe and evaluate the project.

A full report on the Happenstance Project is available via the NESTA website.[1] This chapter will focus on the three aspects of the project noted above: the connections between experimental innovation and entrepreneurial impetus; the importance of risk-taking and failure within the entrepreneurial process; and the different ways in which technologists and arts organisations manage entrepreneurial and innovative behaviours.

ENTREPRENEURSHIP AND INNOVATION

Innovation is a composite process, combining the generation of novel ideas with their application to solve problems in a defined field (commercial, technical, artistic, social). In the application phase, which connects novel ideas into valuable outcomes, entrepreneurial traits and behaviours are a necessary input, as noted in Chapter 6. In practice the innovator and the entrepreneur could be one and the same person. In the schema of this handbook, moving from the earlier chapters on innovation to a discussion of creative entrepreneurship entails moving from an analysis of an innovative process towards a focus on the entrepreneurial people and attitudes which can turn innovative ideas into viable products.

The paradox within entrepreneurship, and the key to its creative character, is the bisociative combination of imaginative exploration and single-minded determination. Trait-based theories of entrepreneurship highlight this paradox – individual entrepreneurs appear to be open-minded, opportunistic and always ready to move on to the next project (hence 'serial entrepreneurship'); yet when attacking specific tasks and projects, they seem relentlessly driven, obsessively focused, to the exclusion of any external perspective or reality. At worst the entrepreneurial personality can be locked into one half of this duality, accused of short-term opportunism or mere tinkering on the one hand, or of being blinkered and rigid, incapable of converting a singular idea and vision into the more complex, multiple tasks and perspectives required to manage a large business with multiple objectives and accountabilities. This view of the entrepreneur as fundamentally different from managers is reflected in economic theories of the entrepreneur as a catalyst for economic change. In Schumpeter's theory of creative destruction, entrepreneurs are a necessary evil, disrupting the business environment, initiating the next phase in the economic cycle, opening up new markets, but pushed out to the margins as markets mature, leaving others to reap what they have sown. Schumpeter's model acknowledges the economic benefits of entrepreneurship while implicitly criticising the entrepreneurial enterprise for failing to mature into a sustainable long-term business. The entrepreneur in this model is trapped within a singular personality, unable to adapt and grow.

Trait-based theories of entrepreneurship have fallen out of fashion in academia. Certainly the very deterministic, personality-based profiling which divides the world into those who can or cannot become successful entrepreneurs appears unnecessarily limiting, and underestimates the importance of other contingent environmental factors which shape the entrepreneurial enterprise. However, entrepreneurship is by definition a personal approach to running a business and individual feelings of excitement, motivation, doubt or fear are powerful factors in the success and failure of any entrepreneurial enterprise. Some university courses (including Ruth Leary's Cultural Entrepreneurship module at Warwick) stress these personal aspects of entrepreneurship in curriculum design, seeking to articulate or develop the entrepreneur's self-perception and emotional commitment as much as the acquisition of basic business skills. In particular the self-perception of the entrepreneur as 'exceptional' (even if in reality they are not so different from the rest of us) seems to be a necessary source of perseverance and self-belief in the bruising struggle for business survival (McGrath et al. 1992, McGrath and Macmillan 1992). As Poettschacher discovered in his study of entrepreneurs in Vienna, this mythical sense of self is an important motivating factor and is bound up in a self-created mythology around the individual entrepreneur or entrepreneurial business. Unravelling this subjective feeling of exceptionalism (which to an outside eye might appear delusional) risks undermining the motivation and self-belief which drive the business forward (Poettschacher 2005). Consequently the subjective mythology survives even when it ceases to match reality.

Of course these identity myths can also have negative consequences. Strong intrinsic motivation and a belief in the unique character of the enterprise are rooted in formative experiences of the individual entrepreneur and of the business (Schein 1983). This makes it hard to reflect critically on the identity and character of the business, and harder still to change them. Entrepreneurs and enterprises can become so locked into their foundation myths and their self-efficacy beliefs that they are unable to take on board new ideas and new people, to delegate tasks or to confront the need for strategic change. The dream of exceptional individual talent can blind the entrepreneur to the harsh reality of long hours, low wages and a failing business, leading to self-exploitation and the unrealistic expectations of many entrepreneurs, especially in the cultural or creative industries (McRobbie 2002, see also Chapter 8 in this handbook). On the other hand, these self-perceptions reflect the 'self-efficacy' beliefs, often formed in childhood (Bandura 1997, Amabile 1998), which may be needed to drive entrepreneurial and creative behaviour.

What is perhaps needed here is an acknowledgement of the complexity and bisociative character of entrepreneurship. Bandura's self-efficacy beliefs and Poettschacher's 'foundation myths' serve a purpose in initiating and launching the entrepreneurial enterprise, inspiring purpose and confidence. But successful entrepreneurs must draw on other traits as they move onto the next stage in the business cycle – from entrepreneurial innovation to adaptive entrepreneurship – becoming more reflective and embracing uncertainty as well as purpose. The introduction to this handbook characterises this complexity as that of a 'diligent dilettante' – one who can be purposeful but also admit distractions and second thoughts.

Reflecting on the experience of the technologists on the Happenstance Project, the design of the project required them to initiate and sell new uses of technology to the host arts organisations. The project aims were comparable to Australia's 'Geek in Residence'[2] programme supported by the Australia Council, which invited technologists (and 'technologically confident artists') to pursue innovative projects with arts organisations. In both cases an ability to develop innovative uses of technology was only part of the challenge. An ability to work independently (either alone or in partnership with the other resident), to take risks and to develop and manage self-directed work, was arguably more important than creative flair and technical ability. Indeed at the recruitment stage, the fact that all the candidates had the basic technical skills was taken for granted; instead, the arts organisations were interested in the residents' attitude and their ability to 'make things happen' inside the organisation. In other words, the technologists in residence were not only expected to be innovative, they were also expected to be entrepreneurial. More specifically, the residency demanded a confidence that the work they were doing was not only 'innovative', but valuable, purposeful and transformative of the organisation.

Most of the residents were or had previously been self-employed and were used to project-based work, often following their own initiative and direction. Indeed, one of the intriguing culture clashes in Happenstance was when freelance, entrepreneurial individuals encountered the routines and procedures of formal organisations. On the other hand, not all of the technologists in residence had the confidence to take the initiative from the outset. One resident in particular admitted to a lack of confidence, half joking that perhaps they had appointed the wrong person (he claimed he didn't understand the label 'creative technologist' and certainly didn't feel this applied to him). Prior to working on Happenstance he had usually worked to a clearly defined brief. Working without rules or defined outcomes was unsettling. To begin with, he preferred to take a problem-solving approach to the residency, helping out with routine tasks rather than initiating projects, for example reconfiguring the gallery director's laptop, sorting out problems with the printer or the server, even agreeing to 'fix the Internet'. He played a similar, supporting role with his co-resident, allowing her to come up with ideas and then helping her to implement them, rather than taking the lead himself.

However, as the residency progressed, he became increasingly confident about his own role and abilities. He began to recognise that his ideas were valued and became more adventurous in taking the initiative. By the end of the residency he was able to envisage a new role for himself as a creative technologist and was determined not to fall back into his previous role as a worker for hire. Undoubtedly this personal transformation grew out of the support and trust from the arts organisation. The director of the organisation spoke of her belief that 'if you put brilliant people into an organisation, brilliant things will happen'. Meanwhile the residents both spoke of being 'given permission' to be creative, and appreciated the scope and freedom they were offered to take risks and try new things. For the arts organisations this interaction was comparable to curating artists in residence. While protecting the artist from external pressures and distractions, the host organisation also provides a sounding board for ideas and a framework of possibilities. Similarly for the technologists, the arts organisation provided a purposeful frame within which innovative technology (and the technologists themselves) could take on value and direction. Consequently the residents acquired a self-perception of themselves as 'creative technologists' who could not only innovate but could also add value to an organisation.

Following Happenstance, several of the residencies spoke of their new self-esteem or 'self-efficacy' as creative technologists. One resident initiated an arts project with the host organisation, one was hired as a resident technologist, another relocated in order to continue working with the ideas and people encountered through Happenstance. These personal transformations were not part of the Happenstance project design, which had been directed towards organisational outcomes rather than personal change. However, the fulfilment and personal development enjoyed by the residents in this pilot project might be significant motivating factors in any future iteration of Happenstance.

In order to initiate change, a measure of self-belief and confidence is required. But entrepreneurs must also learn to deal with doubt and failure. As the Happenstance residents moved from initiating projects (entrepreneurial innovation) to applying and developing them (adaptive entrepreneurship), a different set of traits and behaviours was needed to address new challenges.

LEARNING TO FAIL

Self-efficacy beliefs, intrinsic motivation and confidence represent only one side of the entrepreneurial personality. Entrepreneurs according to Frank Knight are prepared to take on 'uninsurable risk' (Knight 1921); they thus embark on risky projects, products and markets which conventional business might avoid. Entrepreneurs are able to be more tolerant of risk and failure than established businesses because they are less bound by external stakeholders and other accountabilities (Stevenson 1983). Entrepreneurial risk-taking may be driven by external conditions as well as by intrinsic choice, particularly in unstable markets, such as the commercial creative industries, where uncertainty and risk are inscribed in the nature of the production process and in the unpredictable, subjective nature of consumer demand (Bilton 1999). Attitudes to failure in Happenstance were shaped both by internal cultures and attitudes and by external circumstances.

The Happenstance resident technologists were used to building fast and building cheap, quickly assembling a piece of hardware or code, then hacking it in order to improve it. This iterative process of 'fast failing' – building a low-cost experimental prototype to find out what works, not as an end in itself but in order to learn for the next version – is not unusual in technology projects (for example software development) and in the arts, for example the process of theatre rehearsal (Ibbotson 2008, see also Chapter 13 in this volume). More recently the idea of 'deliberate mistakes' has been promoted more widely as a route to innovation and creativity (Schoemaker and Gunther 2006). It is important that mistakes are made quickly and cheaply. A protracted or expensive failure is more likely to discourage future experimentation and may exhaust the financial and human resources needed for a second attempt.

The arts organisations involved in Happenstance were publicly funded and their ability to take risks was constrained by resources and by relationships with external stakeholders. Apart from the financial risks, any failure would entail loss of time, energy and reputation, which would further implicate the organisation's relationships with funders, artists and audiences. Happenstance itself was a relatively high-profile project; the pilot projects were being observed not only by the funders but by other organisations which had either unsuccessfully bid for a pilot themselves or were planning future projects in the next funding round. While the arts organisations were used to taking artistic risks (for example including controversial material in an exhibition), organisationally they tended to be more risk averse. Organisational risks were associated with strategic planning for long-term projects – for example commissioning a new art work or exhibition. Such projects did not fit the iterative 'fast failing' model of software development or theatre rehearsal. Due to a combination of high stakes and greater accountability, the arts organisations were thus less likely to take risks, and less likely to discuss their attitudes to risk and failure; in the words of one organisation director, 'We're very bad at doing this – it's perceived as a threat to our relationships with stakeholders.'

Happenstance needed to provide a safe environment in which arts organisations can learn to fail. At the start of Happenstance, Caper (the digital agency behind Happenstance) introduced the idea of 'agile' development,[3] a flexible approach to software development which emphasises collaborative, adaptive teamwork practices, efficient software engineering and quick design cycles through self-organising, explorative work (Aoyama 1998, Schwaber and Beedle 2002) in an environment of mutual trust and respect (Agile Manifesto 2001). The key principles are flexible people, processes and technologies (Gunasekaran and Yusuf 2002) with a focus on 'collaborative work, concrete results, delivering value and minimising waste' (Shore and Warden 2007). This style of working allows for rapid prototyping and 'shipping' (Godin 2010) through continuous development of outcomes and team interaction. Although not all the arts organisations bought into all aspects of the methodology, many of the principles behind an 'agile' approach remained.

The arts organisation followed a 'deliberate' approach to planning, defining strategic objectives first, then implementing the strategy, then evaluating. Agile methodology aims to combine these phases, so that planning, implementation and evaluation proceed in parallel. Each day all the participants in a project report progress in a daily 'scrum' meeting. Outright success or failure is replaced by a relative measure of progress; if one task is temporarily blocked, the team may proceed to another. Planned outcomes may be adapted if new outcomes emerge. There are echoes here of Mintzberg's 'emergent' strategy model (Mintzberg and Waters 1985). Crucially the approach diminishes the fear of failure because, instead of waiting for a final deadline, progress and plans can be continually adjusted and updated. In this model, progress and outcomes may not follow a predicted path, but absolute failure is almost impossible. Provided the organisation is not too heavily invested (literally and metaphorically) in one particular pathway, it should be possible to learn from difficulties, address them and move rapidly on to another solution. The 'scrum' meeting allows the group to discard methods until something works, adapting quickly to setbacks and working around them.

In a technology context, it might be necessary to put a software development project on hold while awaiting a new piece of equipment or working around a specific technical glitch, then picking up the pace again once the problem has been resolved. Could this approach and attitude be applied to the process of planning an art exhibition or redesigning an arts organisation's website? Perhaps so – by disaggregating a larger crisis into a series of smaller problems, or by proceeding with one part of event planning while putting another task on hold until a viable 'workaround' has been identified. In the words of one Happenstance technologist, 'just because you don't know how to do something doesn't mean it's difficult.'

Agile methodology breaks down large projects into smaller components. Projects are considered as a set of operational challenges, and organisations are considered as an aggregate of motivated individuals. Again, this implies an 'entrepreneurial' rather than 'strategic' model. Thus the Agile Manifesto in its 'twelve principles behind the Agile Manifesto' (Agile Manifesto 2001) emphasises operational effectiveness over strategic goals ('working software is the primary measure of progress') and prioritises individuals over organisations ('build projects around motivated individuals. Give them the environment and support they need, and trust them to get the job done'). The latter gives a fairly accurate description of the position of the resident technologists during Happenstance.

One practical example of Agile during the residencies was the use of a software tool called 'Trello'. 'Trello' provides a 'trellis' framework for ideas and projects, depicted on a grid which can be accessed online by participants. Initially the two technologists used this software to map their ideas and projects during the residency. Each project was broken down into component parts which could be prioritised, completed, blocked or paused depending on progress and status on the Trello grid. Trello is also an open source planning tool which allowed the arts organisation staff members to update progress or reorder priorities, and so to organise each day's activities efficiently. This 'agile' approach to planning proved popular with the gallery staff and was introduced as an alternative method for updating and planning instead of more formal reporting and planning in staff meetings. Planning was here utilised as a verb (an active process) rather than as noun (a blueprint to be followed), and objectives were continually recalibrated and reordered in response to progress. Trello also reinforced a further principle of agile methodology, that users or 'customers' should be actively involved in the development process, allowing them to access work in progress rather than withholding judgement until the work is completed. The Agile Manifesto emphasises the importance of face-to-face communication, preferably on a daily basis, rather than formal reporting procedures. Most of the time the Happenstance residents were working alongside permanent staff in an open plan office, allowing a continual percolation of ideas between the arts organisation (users) and the technologists (producers).

goal:
put tech
into arts
orgs

The overall aim of Happenstance was for creative technology to become 'embedded' in the arts organisation. The residencies did produce a number of innovative products and practical outcomes.[4] However, the real value of the residencies was to introduce 'digital thinking' into the culture of the arts organisation. This was a social process rather than a technological one. Indeed, the Agile Manifesto specifically prioritises social interactions and individuals over technical processes and tools. Of course the arts organisations were used to working collaboratively in their creative output; what was new was applying a collaborative, social approach to organisational and technological processes. In particular the residencies demonstrated a link between communication and project planning, allowing goals and achievements to be continually discussed, shared and modified by project participants. This in turn allowed members of the group to be more confident and more open-minded when taking risks and less anxious about strategic planning. One of the senior arts managers noted that, following her experience on Happenstance, she no longer felt intimidated by planning large-scale technology projects and would see such projects as a natural extension of everyday problem-solving.

Overcoming fear of failure is no doubt part of the entrepreneurial capability of an organisation or individual. On the other hand, how we deal with failure after it has occurred is no less important. Here too, the Happenstance Project illustrated how an entrepreneurial mindset can be informed by the culture clash between technology and the arts.

LEARNING FROM FAILURE

The entrepreneurial virtues of resilience, diligence and relentless self-belief have a darker subtext. The drive that pushes the entrepreneur to take uninsured risks, to venture boldly into new markets and to challenge the conventional wisdom can blind the entrepreneur to their own weaknesses. In Danny Miller's *The Icarus Paradox* (1990), the entrepreneur becomes an empire builder, pursuing new ventures beyond any intrinsic abilities and resources; Miller's paradox is that success locks us into a pattern of repetition, simplifying our behaviour into what we take to be our strengths, stripping out the complexity and range which gave those strengths a meaningful context and purpose (Miller 1993). Conversely, failure inevitably stimulates change and experiment; failure thus might be the better teacher than success.

Like Miller, Clayton Christensen (1997) explores the paradoxical relationship between success and failure in his *Innovator's Dilemma*. Basing his study on computer hard-drive manufacturers, Christenson discovered that successful manufacturers became locked into certain technologies and customer bases, particularly in fast-moving markets. When new technologies emerged, the leading manufacturers found it difficult to adapt. They were heavily invested in the old technology, and their existing customers were reluctant to try something new. Consequently these manufacturers were overtaken by start-up companies with fewer resources and no real presence in the market, and hence with nothing to lose by investing whole-heartedly in the new technology. These new firms would themselves fall into the same dilemma as they found themselves similarly locked into technologies and customer expectations, and similarly threatened by the next generation of technologies and new entrants.

Within the Happenstance Project, the culture of experimentation and risk-taking required a willingness to fail. But it also required a willingness to learn from failure. The mantra of 'fail fast, fail often' requires a coda, 'don't make the same mistake twice'. One of the hardest tasks for any innovator or entrepreneur is to give up on an exciting new idea, when all of their entrepreneurial instincts drive them to proceed, diligently and doggedly, towards completion. After all, the previous section of this chapter argued that the entrepreneur presses on resolutely against the siren voices warning of trouble ahead. Surely this is precisely the meaning of 'uninsured risk'?

Knowing when not to persevere, when to let go, requires a measure of humility. Among writers, this is known as 'killing your babies' – cutting out the beautifully crafted opening sentence, the mysterious character, the dazzling dialogue, the parts of the script you are initially most proud of but which become an obstacle to everything else in the story. For the Happenstance technologists, this meant that a new piece of software or hardware which was technically innovative and in which they had invested considerable effort and imagination, might have to be dropped because the arts organisation had no use for it. At Site Gallery the technologists experimented with a 'polargraph' – a robotic arm which could draw in response to codes transmitted from a remote location. But the arts organisation could not identify any valuable purpose for this technology and the project was quietly shelved. Conversely, some of the technologies introduced by the residents were not in themselves innovative (for example using Kinect motion sensors to capture physical movement, or the Trello project management software alluded to above) but had the potential to be transformative as they took on a fresh purpose in the organisation. Very often the most transferable ideas were the simplest – a lunchtime coding workshop at Lighthouse, a 'design jam' at Spike Island, redesigning the online shop at Site Gallery. And very often the transformative effect came through the communication around the technology rather than the technology itself.

The humility and restraint required to surrender a promising idea, or to diligently work on an idea which initially appears unpromising, reflected a maturity amongst the residents. The capacity for self-doubt does not at first appear to be a characteristic of successful entrepreneurs. We only notice the single venture that they finally pursued to completion, not the many ideas and projects they discarded along the way. Yet when successful cultural entrepreneurs talk to students on the Cultural Entrepreneurship module at Warwick, they almost always begin by describing a catalogue of failures and false starts. Here it is the selection of the idea rather than the idea itself which drives the successful business; more specifically, it is necessary to accept failure in order to move on to the next possibility.

The core of the Happenstance process was the selection, retention and reapplication of promising ideas within the organisation. Selective retention of ideas connects with a Darwinian model of innovation (Simonton 1999) in which a diversity of inputs is selectively retained and absorbed into a continuously evolving system – in this case, the evolving system being the arts organisation's ability to make creative use of digital technology. Not all of the interventions proposed by the residents were useful or relevant. The residents would at times be excited by a particular technology (thermal printers, virtual drawing machines, tweeting kettles), but it was up to the arts organisation to identify the value of these ideas and either accept or reject them. In effect the functions of experimentation and adaptation were split between the technologists in residence and the arts organisations. The technologists generated promising ideas, and the organisations provided a purposeful frame within which these ideas could be applied, adapted or rejected (Figure 7.1).

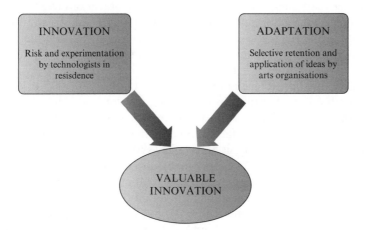

Figure 7.1   Creativity as a cooperation between innovators and adapters

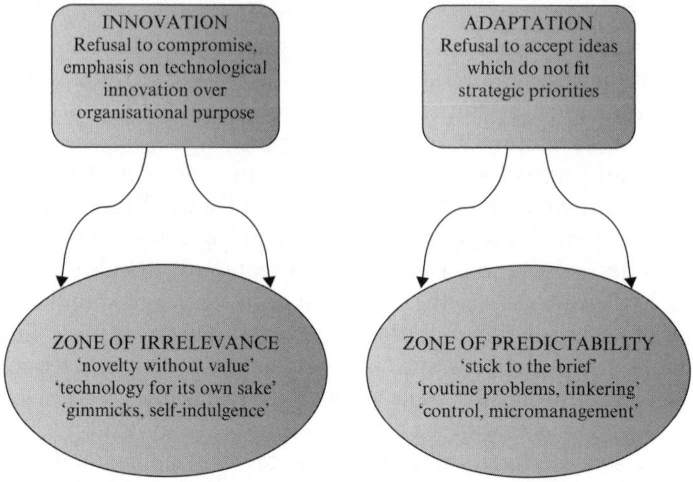

Figure 7.2   What happens when innovators and adapters fail to cooperate

For the model above to operate, both sides need to make compromises and be attuned to the other. This requires both humility and self-awareness on behalf of the technologists, and open-mindedness and trust on the part of the organisation. The entrepreneurial energy is directed inwards, framed by a common purpose. Where these personal qualities and shared purpose are lacking, the model can dissipate into dysfunctional outcomes and mutual mistrust (Figure 7.2).

Here the entrepreneurial energies are not directed inwards but towards diverging goals and priorities. Certainly we saw traces of these tendencies in Happenstance, and there were no doubt anxieties and frustrations on both sides. But the remarkable success of the project was to build mutual trust and allow both technologists and organisations not only to make mistakes but to admit when they got something wrong. In this way they were able to adjust to each other rather than pull in opposite directions. It is worth noting that this mutual respect was not just a happy accident. The three organisations had been selected (or self-selected) because of a shared curiosity about digital technology; the six technologists had been recruited not only on the basis of technical skills and creative input, but on the basis of their interest in the organisations. Curiosity and attitude were here more important than experience; several of the residents had limited experience of formal organisations and found the rituals of staff meetings and office email bizarre and irrational, but they were also motivated to intervene in these practices to improve them. The Happenstance Project was a product of deliberate planning by Caper, the digital agency behind

Happenstance, and the directors of the arts organisations. At the pre-production stage, this group established the working methods, principles and deadlines within which the participants could explore and learn. The entrepreneurial qualities and attitudes which drove Happenstance resulted from a combination of diligent, purposeful planning and a willingness to compromise, admit mistakes and to learn from failure rather than chase success.

THE HUMAN SIDE OF ENTERPRISE

This chapter has aimed to highlight the human qualities which characterise entrepreneurial behaviour and processes. Contrary to the stereotypical picture of the entrepreneur as a driven, even obsessive individualist, the Happenstance Project illustrates how entrepreneurial behaviour and outcomes can combine apparently contradictory qualities and can be distributed across individuals and organisations working together.

In particular the chapter has highlighted the importance of failure, self-doubt and compromise as the necessary counterweight to the entrepreneur's sense of purpose and conviction. These contradictory emotions and attitudes were identified amongst the six resident technologists who were charged with initiating digital innovation in the arts organisations. The technologists were increasingly confident and proactive over the 12-week residency in initiating ideas and taking risks. They were also occasionally racked by anxiety and self-doubt, feelings which allowed them to respond creatively to failures and to adapt to the needs and expectations of the host organisation. The transition from 'innovation' to 'adaptation' through the residency reflects the bisociative character of innovation and entrepreneurship. In trait-based theories of entrepreneurship and in Schumpeter's economic model, entrepreneurs are often identified with one half of this process, with the initiation of change rather than with continuity and adaptation, with strong intrinsic motivation and self-efficacy rather than with doubt and compromise. The Happenstance residents had to combine confidence and purpose with self-doubt and humility.

Organisations are less likely to embrace risk than individual entrepreneurs because they are more accountable to their stakeholders; the arts organisations were accountable to audiences, artists, funders and employees. Agile methodology provided a mechanism for managing risk and failure, allowing problems and setbacks to be absorbed into an evolving progress rather than loaded into a traditional planning and evaluation framework. For the arts organisations this approach offered an alternative way of managing risk and evaluating projects, breaking larger projects down into smaller steps and fostering a 'fail fast, fail cheap' mentality which acknowledges mistakes and readjustments as inevitable and necessary to effective progress.

Agile principles also highlight the social nature of entrepreneurship and innovation. Taking risks and sharing half-formed (occasionally half-baked) ideas is easier through regular face-to-face meetings than through formal reporting mechanisms. In Happenstance the sharing of ideas and the bisociative character of entrepreneurship was reflected in the relationship between the resident technologists and the arts organisations. The technologists were more likely to take risks and to initiate new ideas, the arts organisations were better placed to select and adapt those ideas, providing a purposeful frame for random innovations and converting them into valuable innovation (see Figure 7.1 above). Yet this neat division of roles only worked because both sides were capable of mutual adaptation, again underlining the importance of a bisociative mindset. The interaction between diligent purpose and self-doubt and compromise was played out both at the individual and the collective level.

Happenstance was designed as an exploration of digital innovation in arts organisations. This chapter has focused instead on the entrepreneurial attitudes and behaviours which drive innovation. As noted in the introduction to this chapter, innovation and entrepreneurship are two sides of a continuous process. The ability to take risks and to learn from failure is of course as necessary to innovation as to entrepreneurship. This handbook has framed entrepreneurship as the attitude and mentality which drives innovation towards successful outcomes. This chapter has highlighted the significant and necessary role of risk, failure and compromise (the bisociative opposites of drive and conviction) in that entrepreneurial mentality.

QUESTIONS FOR DISCUSSION

1. What are the entrepreneurial characteristics which drive innovation and adaptation? Are these different entrepreneurial characteristics mutually compatible? To what extent does entrepreneurial behaviour depend on personality, environment, experience?
2. Find an example of a 'successful failure' (a failure which led on to a success). How did the participants respond to success and failure and how did this influence the outcome?
3. How does 'fear of failure' influence your decision-making? How can big risks be broken down into small risks?
4. The Agile Manifesto describes a particular approach to project

management developed in the software industry. What can we learn about risk management from technologists, from artists or from other industry sectors? How might you adapt their methods to your own work?

NOTES

1. Available as PDF download at: http://www.nesta.org.uk/library/documents/Academic_report_Happenstance.pdf
2. http://www.australiacouncil.gov.au/grants/2013/geek-in-residence – Australia Council continues to support the Geek in Residence programme. Creative Scotland recently launched its own 'Geeks in Residence' programme in partnership with Culture Hack Scotland and sync (http://www.welcometosync.com/geeks/).
3. For an introduction to 'Agile' principles, see the Agile Manifesto: http://www.agilemanifesto.org
4. For a discussion of project outcomes see Bilton 2012, pp. 40–44.

REFERENCES

Agile Manifesto (2001), http://www.agilemanifesto.org.

Amabile, T.M. (1998), 'How to kill creativity', *Harvard Business Review*, **76**(5), **77**(12) (also available in *Harvard Business Review on Breakthrough Thinking*).

Aoyama, M. (1998), 'Web-based agile software development', *IEEE Software*, **15**(6), 56–65.

Bandura, A. (1997), *Self-efficacy: the exercise of control*, New York: W.H. Freeman.

Bilton, C. (1999), 'Risky business: the independent production sector in Britain's creative industries', *International Journal of Cultural Policy*, **6**(1), 17–39.

Bilton, C. (2012), *Happenstance Report*, London: NESTA, available at http://www.nesta.org.uk/library/documents/Academic_report_Happenstance.pdf.

Christenson, C.M. (1997), *The innovator's dilemma: when new technologies cause great firms to fail*, Boston: Harvard Business School.

Godin, S. (2010), 'The truth about shipping', http://the99percent.com/tips/6249/Seth-Godin-The-Truth-About-Shipping.

Gunasekaran, A. and Y.Y. Yusuf (2002), 'Agile manufacturing: a taxonomy of strategic and technological imperatives', *International Journal of Production Research*, **40**(6), 1357–85.

Ibbotson, P. (2008), *The illusion of leadership: directing creativity in business and the arts*, Basingstoke: Palgrave Macmillan.

Kettunen, P. (2009), 'Adopting key lessons from agile manufacturing to agile software product development – a comparative study', *Technovation*, **29**(6–7), June–July, 408–22.

Knight, F.H (1921), *Risk, uncertainty and profit*. Boston: Houghton Mifflin.

McGrath, R.G. and I.C. MacMillan (1992), 'More like each other than anyone else? A cross-cultural study of entrepreneurial perceptions', *Journal of Business Venturing*, **7**(5), 419–29.

McGrath, R.G., I.C. MacMillan and S. Scheinberg (1992), 'Elitists, risk-takers, and rugged individualists? An exploratory analysis of cultural differences between entrepreneurs and non-entrepreneurs', *Journal of Business Venturing*, **7**(2), 115–35.

McRobbie, A. (2002), 'From Holloway to Hollywood: happiness at work in the new cultural economy?', in P. du Gay and M. Pryke (eds) *Cultural economy*, London: Sage, pp. 97–114.

Miller, D. (1990), *The Icarus paradox: how exceptional companies bring about their own downfall*, New York: HarperBusiness.

Miller, D. (1993), 'The architecture of simplicity', *Academy of Management Review*, **18**(1), 116–38.

Mintzberg, H. and J. Waters (1985), 'Of strategies, deliberate and emergent', *Strategic Management Journal*, **6**, 257–62.

Poettschacher, E. (2005) 'Strategic creativity: how values, beliefs and assumptions drive entrepreneurs in the creative industries', *International Journal of Entrepreneurship and Innovation*, **6**(3), 177.

Schein, E. (1983), 'The role of the founder in creating organisational culture', *Organisational Dynamics*, **12**(1), 13–28.

Schoemaker, P. and R. Gunther (2006), 'The wisdom of deliberate mistakes', *Harvard Business Review*, June, 109–15.

Schumpeter, J.A. (1939), *Business cycles: a theoretical, historical and statistical analysis of the capitalist process*, New York: McGraw Hill.

Schwaber, K. and M. Beedle (2002), *Agile software development with Scrum*, Upper Saddle River, NJ: Prentice-Hall.

Shore, J. and S. Warden (2007), *The art of agile development*, Sebastopol CA: O'Reilly.

Simonton, D.K. (1999), 'Creativity as blind variation and selective retention: is the creative process Darwinian?', *Psychological Inquiry*, **10**, 309–28.

Stevenson, H.H. (1983), 'A perspective on entrepreneurship', in J.J Kao (ed.) (1989) *Entrepreneurship, creativity and organization: text, cases and readings*, Englewood Cliffs, NJ: Prentice Hall, pp. 166–77.

8. Good work? Rethinking cultural entrepreneurship
Kate Oakley

To adapt and horribly mangle Marx's great lines, cultural workers are entrepreneurial, but not as they please and not under self-selected circumstances (Marx 1852/2005). One of several paradoxes of a group of workers, alternately celebrated (Handy 1995, Florida 2002) and the subject of concern (McRobbie 2002, Ross 2003) is that, like Marx's revolutionaries, they are sometimes creating something that did not exist before, but in an environment of increasing precariousness and constraint. The entrepreneurialism they display is often of the forced, or at least adaptive, kind. They set up businesses because that is the easiest way to carry out their practice. They get premises because they need to work away from the kitchen table. They take on projects to pay the rent, and other projects on the back of that, because they now have new expertise. They socialise relentlessly to the point where it resembles work more than play. They often articulate social and political concerns about the kind of work they do; but they carry it out while exploiting themselves and others, often with the barest of acknowledgement.

This chapter looks at the phenomenon of the self-employed cultural worker, sometimes described as a 'cultural entrepreneur' or even 'culture-preneurs' (Lange 2006). In common with other writers (Naudin 2013), I am regarding entrepreneurship as encompassing aspects of self-employment, freelancing and portfolio working, as well as the more 'conscious' entrepreneurship of those who set up small businesses within the cultural sectors and seek to either work alone, or employ others as they grow. The chapter draws on many years of researching cultural entrepreneurs and considers the discourse of entrepreneurship and what it has meant to policymakers, advocates, critics and cultural workers themselves. It looks at various drivers of cultural entrepreneurship, including the growth and availability of digital technology, policy support for small businesses, and structural changes in the cultural sectors that have made the employment model a less stable one. It also looks at the growth of a more individualised attitude to work and the seeming willingness of cultural workers to take on the 'brave new world of work' (Beck 2000).

Alongside this, the chapter argues that the wider structural questions,

145

often ignored by advocates of small business-led growth, such as alternate consolidation and disintegration in the media and Internet industries, together with the growth of 'free work,' makes the conditions of the small-scale entrepreneur – all rhetoric aside – increasingly difficult. As Terranova puts it, the autonomous worker or the small-scale entrepreneur is always in danger of turning into 'the precarious worker' (2006: 33).

Yet the discourse of entrepreneurship and, behind this, some of the positive notions which we attach to cultural work, refuse to die. Even writers who have been critical of the over-promotion of entrepreneurship see some hope in new models of work, arguing that the growth of a critical form of social entrepreneurship could help to breathe new life into an idea that has become tarnished (McRobbie 2011). Others point to the growth of new worker organisations within the cultural industries as evidence of a new, more political, orientation among cultural workers (de Peuter 2011, Sawyer 2013), while theorists such as David Harvey (2012) see the 'exstensification' of work as proving an opportunity to link the politics of the workplace with that of the city, in new forms of radical organisation, such as the Occupy movement.

Thus, this chapter asks, in an environment characterised not just by economic slump, but by an over-supply of labour and increasing inequality and poor working conditions, is entrepreneurship a useful notion with which to discuss cultural work? What is its relationship to discussion of new business models, to social entrepreneurs or to new workers' movements, such as those that have formed around notions of precarity? And finally, is it a convenient way of disguising bad work or does it help us to recognise a continuing desire for a greater degree of self-determination in creative work?

DRIVING THE DISCOURSE OF ENTREPRENEURSHIP

As Barbrook has argued, while there is nothing new in the notion of entrepreneurship (Barbrook 2007), recent 'takes' on it tend to combine two forces: the growth of the Internet with its digerati (Brockman 1996), digital citizens, swarm capitalists (Kelly 1998), bobos (Brooks 2000) and netocracy; and the older notion of the bohemian, now reimagined as the 'creative'. Certainly the idea of the cultural entrepreneur, as it is often portrayed, is difficult to separate either from the changes wrought by the growth of digital technology or from the idea of individualism (McGuigan 2010).

Some of the more celebratory writing on entrepreneurship has often been infused with an uncritical excitement, especially with all things digital.

'Today, anyone who holds a job, and isn't looking for a side gig – or creating a business plan, writing a screenplay, or setting up shop on eBay – is out of touch,' proclaimed Dan Pink in his turn-of-the-century work, *Free Agent Nation* (Pink 2001: 6). Although just over a decade ago, it's difficult to imagine anyone writing a similar sentence today and not just because of the quaintness of the phrase, 'setting up shop on eBay'. The late 1990s and early 2000s saw a surge in interest, both in the newly minted creative industries (Hartley 2005) and in notions of entrepreneurship (Flores and Gray 2000) and, in many ways, we are still living with these expectations.

The 'dot-com' boom (or bust as it is now often known) lasted from around 1997 to 2000. As so often with stock market bubbles, the end of the boom can be dated fairly accurately to 10 March 2000, when the NASDAQ, a US stock market index largely composed of high technology stocks, peaked at 5132.52, before starting what became a fairly dramatic collapse. The period of the boom had seen the formation of thousands of what were called 'dot-com' firms, often with little more than an idea, a URL (or web address) and an unrealistic grasp of potential markets.

Many of these firms were in retailing – boo.com, one of the more notorious UK-based companies, was a pioneer of online fashion, for example; while pets.com in the US sold pet supplies to retailers (both went out of business). But the cultural possibilities of the net, the growth of videogames and websites, and the seemingly low to non-existent entry barriers to setting up a new company, meant that hundreds of musicians, comedians, magazine journalists and graphic designers also saw the possibilities of becoming self-employed (McRobbie 2002). McRobbie argued that the Internet drove a 'second wave' of cultural entrepreneurship, and distinguished this from the subjects of her earlier work on fashion designers (McRobbie 1998), not least in terms of what she saw as the 'despatialised' characteristics of those not used to working physically close to other workers. My own interest in cultural entrepreneurs started at around the same time (Leadbeater and Oakley 1999) and while I felt them to be considerably less seduced by the 'placelessness' that often surrounds digital discourse (Cairncross 1999) and indeed, rather rooted in place, it was nonetheless clear that the Internet boom was providing a huge fillip to what were longer-term trends in the cultural workforce.

The significance of this period is not in what it says about the longer-run 'creative destruction' of digital technology; in that story the year 2000 may be merely a blip. But the global discourse of 'cultural entrepreneurs' (Cunningham 2002, Lange 2006) owes much to the optimistic possibilities suggested by the turn-of-the-century dot-com boom. If the current global economic slowdown has put the dot-com collapse into the shade, it should perhaps be remembered more clearly. Not simply because many jobs were lost and businesses went under; it took until 2005 for employment in London's creative industries to recover from the effects of the bust, for example (GLA 2010), but because the positive association between small business entrepreneurs and digital technology – an association so central to the idea of cultural entrepreneurship – is one that still animates much talk of cultural entrepreneurship a decade later (UNCTAD 2010).

FORCED ENTREPRENEURSHIP

At the same time, debates about media ownership and concentration, which so animate writers on the media, particularly those within a political economy tradition (Hesmondhalgh 2002), often get less airing in this tradition of writing about cultural entrepreneurship, where the emphasis on small businesses, craft skills and self-employment remains strong. This is reflected in much of the policy literature in Canada, the UK and across the EU, where the stress is on helping entrepreneurs to start businesses; but there is very little recognition of the wider trends within the cultural industries which may affect these businesses (Murray and Gollmitzer 2012).

Thus, for all the cultural entrepreneurs in McRobbie's second wave who used the Internet to start new businesses, many others were created by wider structural changes within the cultural sectors themselves. Vertical disintegration, technological and, in some cases, regulatory changes mean that the core media industries, notably film and TV, have seen a huge growth in self-employed workers, who could be re-classed as entrepreneurs. As Blair has noted (2001), while the film industry has always had a great degree of freelance employment, at least outside of the Hollywood 'studio system', full-time, permanent jobs were a greater part of the television industry, particularly in European countries with a tradition of public service broadcasting. The contracting-out of more elements of TV production, and the growth of the independent TV sector, can be depicted on one hand as 'entrepreneurship', and on the other as the casualisation of formally secure employment.

McGuigan had rightly termed this 'the paradox of independence' (McGuigan 2010: 329) and it could be extended beyond TV into other cultural sectors. The core issue is that in this process of vertical disintegration, risk is passed from employers to workers, many of whom move from one short-term contract to another in situations of increasing insecurity. This has consequences in the exit of labour from these industries, particularly among older women, and at the entry level, a lack of diversity in terms of race, class and gender across all the cultural industries (Skillset 2010, Oakley 2013a, 2013b).

What might be called 'forced entrepreneurship', or the need for people in rapidly changing industries to adopt worsening working arrangements, lies behind much of the growth in entrepreneurship in the cultural sectors. While it could be argued that the term 'entrepreneur' ill-fits those who have never expressed any desire to be self-employed but have simply had to adapt, the cultural entrepreneurship literature is full of such conflicts and indeed often starts from the premise that entrepreneurship in these sectors is driven by a different set of personal motivations – autonomy, creativity – than in other allegedly more commercial sectors (Oakley and Leadbeater 1999, Banks 2007).

A blind spot in much of the rhetoric, and a failure of policy support for cultural entrepreneurs in the last decades, is that the focus on small businesses ignores wider national and international trends in media ownership, intellectual property and trade, in favour of a supply-side policy. Thus we have witnessed many starts-up in the cultural industries, for example, but, particularly in Europe, very few big or even medium-sized firms (KEA 2006). An iconic example of this would be the UK videogames sector, where I carried out a series of interviews in 1998/99, in what was at the time one of the top three countries in the world for videogames development (Leadbeater and Oakley 2001). Much of this was driven by a wave of first generation entrepreneurs, early gamers, who had grown up with programmable home computers such as the Sinclair Spectrum, which they could reverse engineer and teach themselves about in the classic, but nonetheless highly accurate, 'bedroom entrepreneurial' trope.

In many ways, videogames designers are classic cultural entrepreneurs; avid consumers of the products they want to develop, driven in the early days by a do-it-yourself culture which had built up a strong, but informal, shared knowledge base. But unlike those who work in the arts or as musicians, where the struggle to 'make it' had always been a perilous one, this wave of entrepreneurs stood at the beginning of their industry's development, just before a huge growth period which was to see videogames become one of the world's largest cultural industries. Rather than going on to develop global brands, however, over the next ten years, UK-based entrepreneurs lost competiveness, becoming reliant on global publishers to finance games development, and unable therefore to hang on to their own intellectual property (IP). As the games industry became more successful and more commodified, more reliant on sequels and genre games, publishers were commissioning less original IP development and therefore making it more difficult for small entrepreneurs whose 'creativity' was the source, not only of competitiveness, but of their interest in getting into the business in the first place (NESTA 2010). One way to read this is simply as an example of failed UK industry policy, which indeed it is; but my point is more that it is emblematic of the general disconnect between the discourse of cultural entrepreneurship and the reality of it.

While consolidation, concentration and disintegration have always been elements of the wider cultural industries, the growth of Internet mega-brands, what van Dijck (2013) has called GAFA (which stands for Google/Amazon/Facebook/Apple), sets a different set of challenges for creative work. Indeed, the current significance of 'free work' in the digital labour economy means that even to speak of things called employment or self-employment can be questioned (Scholz 2013). As freelance workers on the Huffington Post, unpaid interns on failing newspapers, games modders and spec workers have learned to their costs, 'whether all this activity can or should be classified as labour according to any traditional criteria of political economy' is now an open question (Ross 2013).

The problems of work in the cultural sectors have become more apparent, with even public industry bodies starting to pay attention to the lack of diversity in the industry and the explosive growth of unpaid work as an entry criterion (Cabinet Office 2009, Skillset 2010, 2011, Murray and Gollmitzer 2012). As Blair comments, the huge oversupply of labour in the cultural sectors gives particular importance to first jobs as a route in, as many of those who want to work in these sectors may never even get that far (Blair 2001). Given this, social contacts, including family links, play an important role in 'getting in', which obviously has undesirable consequences for the social and ethnic mix of the labour market. Similarly, the ability to sustain unpaid work, sometimes for lengthy periods, is clearly greater if one can draw on family resources.

One might expect that both the end of the initial Internet hype and the realisation of the hardship and inequality which characterises much cultural work would lead to a toning down of the promotion of cultural entrepreneurship and indeed some authors argue that this is the case (Lange 2006). But the idea remains a resilient one, not simply in the relentless promotion of government agencies, but in the minds of many young cultural workers themselves.

THE PLEASURES AND PAINS OF CULTURAL WORK

A distinctive, if not unique, feature of cultural labour markets is the degree of enthusiasm, even love that workers show for their job, which helps ensure that even casualised, insecure and often exploitative as these labour markets are, they are continually oversupplied with labour. McRobbie describes the 'passionate' attachment that such people have to their work as 'a space of romantic idealisation perhaps more rewarding than personal relationships' (McRobbie 2007: 1).

In her study of new media workers in the UK and the Netherlands, Gill (2007) speaks of the 'extraordinary passion and enthusiasm' that people have for their work and the many different elements of this passion: the sense of autonomy and opportunity, the playful and pleasurable nature of the work, and the opportunity for community and political activism. Indeed, as she argues, 'sociologists of work would be hard-pressed to find another group of workers who expressed similar levels of passion both for the work itself and for the field more generally' (2007: 14).

McRobbie connects what she calls the 'refusal of mundane work,' among these cultural workers with the autonomist notion of refusal of work and the feminist dynamic, by which this independent work becomes a potential source of self-realisation (McRobbie 2007).

Such enthusiasm continues to drive potential cultural entrepreneurs today, as anyone involved in small business support or teaching within higher education can testify. Yet in line with the stress of this volume on the contradictions and tensions within creative work, the enthusiasm and passion of entrepreneurs is rarely simple and can be mixed and even paradoxical. McRobbie points out that that professed pleasure in work often masks self-exploitation, and that this attachment to 'my own work' provides both a justification, and a disciplinary mechanism, for staying, often unprofitably, with cultural work and not abandoning it altogether (McRobbie 1998, 2007). In my own interviews with arts graduates (Oakley et al. 2008), most of whom were working freelance and in other entrepreneurial ways, alongside professions of pleasure in work, there are also appeals to an older, Romantic tradition of the 'importance' of the artist. And Naudin, in her work on higher education, notes the distaste that her interviewees often express for what are seen as the negative aspects of entrepreneurship, such as a focus on commercial gains at the expense of being socially useful, or selfish and anti-social behaviour (Naudin 2013). Her research with masters' students who are undertaking 'enterprise' education as part of their degree courses confirms the 'forced' aspects of entrepreneurship to which I have alluded. She quotes one student as saying of the idea of being a freelance worker, 'I'm trying to be comfortable with it, because I know it's going to happen to me' (post-grad student, quoted in Naudin 2013).

Research on art and design graduates suggests that while many of the aspects associated with entrepreneurship – self-expression, being able to use one's knowledge and skills fully and attachment to one's own creative practice – continue to motivate career aspirations for those in the cultural sectors, 'being my own boss' is in fact less of a driver than for workers in other sectors (Ball 2010). This research suggests that 'being able to work for myself' was 'very important' for just over 20 per cent of arts and design graduates, as opposed to 65 per cent who felt that 'making full use of knowledge and skills' was important, and even 60 per cent whose major motivation was to have a regular or stable source of income. This may reflect the optimism of newly minted graduates that they will be able to find scope for self-expression within employment, but again suggests that self-employment in the cultural sectors is about being able to find space for independent practices, not about the attractions of self-employment *per se*.

DOING GOOD WORK   *for no*

My own research with cultural entrepreneurs suggests that there is a subset who, rather than resenting a form of work that requires so much self-sacrifice, justify their decisions, not through pleasure, nor the possibility of future success, but through the importance that they attach to cultural expression. An ethical stance is often taken to justify 'being an artist' – the notion of artists as truth tellers, for example, is still in evidence – with the consequence that falling short is a personal, almost ethical failing (Oakley et al. 2008).

Banks has similarly argued for an ethical orientation to cultural work and workers (Banks 2006), again based on empirical work among small-scale cultural entrepreneurs. In doing so, he queries many of the accounts of cultural work, which he sees as portraying a 'moral vacuum at the heart of the cultural industries' (Banks 2006: 459). Such accounts, he contends, neglect the agency of cultural workers themselves, presenting a picture of self-exploitation that often steers close to a sort of false consciousness notion, while accounts of a 'new labour paradigm' (Miller 2004: 59) neglect the different social and spatial conditions in which cultural entrepreneurship takes place.

Banks' interviewees, by contrast, have a strong association with place, in this case Manchester, and are often involved in community activities, reflecting concerns about over-development and conservation and indeed keen to preserve some kind of diverse social mix in areas of gentrification. Others express a desire to give something back to the city in which they live and work: involving themselves in voluntary teaching or mentoring schemes, donating their services free to local arts events and, in one case, offering their recording studio free for local young people to use (Banks 2006).

Banks, also found entrepreneurs 'reflect in depth on ethical aspects of management/employment, particularly regarding the treatment and development of staff' (Banks 2006: 465).

In my own work, I've also heard both ethical and political concerns expressed freely among entrepreneurs; but unlike Banks, I have often found an exception to this in discussions of cultural work itself. Issues such as unpaid work, long hours and absence of standard work benefits are justified by cultural entrepreneurs on the grounds that, essentially, if they had to pay and provide benefits commensurate with other industries, they would not be in business at all (Oakley 2007, 2009, 2011). Instead, what many would argue are exploitative conditions are recast as the need for workers to 'demonstrate commitment'. Self-management, ability to deal with stress, long hours and often high levels of insecurity – what Ross (2003) calls the 'hidden costs' of cultural work – are what interviewees appear to take pride in and to look for in others. There is often little or no sense that relying so heavily on unpaid labour is either unfair or exploitative.

In his ethnography of the Wicker Park area of Chicago, Lloyd (2006) hints at a class-based element behind these justifications. While he is careful to make clear that although genuine material scarcity is not uncommon among all sorts of cultural workers, the 'voluntary' adoption of this material scarcity differentiates it sharply from the life of the genuinely poor, both in terms of social status, which is often quite high, and in terms of control over one's life.

> The neo-bohemians thus make a claim on status privileges typically denied to the urban poor. While poverty as it is normally experienced inhibits self-determination, the voluntary adoption of relative poverty by bohemians claims to increase autonomy. (Lloyd 2006: 161)

Interviewees of my own have made similar points, often stressing the fact that they do not work primarily for money; seemingly unaware that the 'voluntary poverty' of the cultural entrepreneur's lifestyle often serves to exclude working class people, who are less likely to see low incomes as a lifestyle choice, or to have the other assets that make such a life manageable.

Recent research on attitudes to unpaid work in the film and TV industries, however, reminds us that before generalising about 'cultural entrepreneurs' we need to pay more attention to the differences between types of cultural work – the self-employed community arts worker versus the freelance sound editor, for example. Different forms of cultural work have different histories of work organisation, and for those film and TV workers surveyed by Percival, a majority agreed that unpaid work in the industry was a source of injustice and not primarily because it undercut wages. The research also suggested an important distinction between paid and unpaid work, as clear distinctions were made by respondents between so-called 'no budget' film production, where everyone works unpaid, and budgeted production. Respondents generally agreed that if one worker on a particular film production was paid, everyone should be paid. This suggests possible ways forward for those thinking about how the arts economy, which has always had high levels of volunteers who are not seeking paid work, can distinguish between opportunities for volunteering and exploitation of unpaid workers.

The current prolonged economic downturn, however, may lead to a sea change in attitudes to, and types of, cultural entrepreneurship. Cuts in public funding, a shrinking public sector and decline in urban retail and leisure industries that are often used as a supplementary source of income while entrepreneurs are working on their own idea (Lloyd 2006) have left a generation of young, often highly educated, cultural workers vulnerable and insecure. This could suggest a turn away from the risks associated with entrepreneurship; or it could suggest new forms for it.

WHAT NOW FOR CULTURAL ENTREPRENEURS?

The expansion of higher education in recent decades, particularly in creative subjects, combined with increasing awareness of the problems of cultural labour markets and a growing 'politics of labor insecurity' (de Peuter 2011: 421) has led to a new generation of worker organisations, often focused around issues such as unpaid internships. De Peuter has analysed a variety of these cultural workers' movements, many of which either incorporate, or are driven by, the autonomous or self-employed cultural worker in a way that traditional trade unions, focused on a stand-ard model of employment, often had difficulty in doing (de Peuter 2011, forthcoming).

At what one might consider the 'higher end' of the cultural labour market, organisations such as Model Alliance and Freelancers Union NYC are tackling issues ranging from sexual abuse in the modelling industry to the need to provide health insurance to self-employed workers, a particular concern for those in the USA. Other groups attempt to bring lower-paid workers in the cultural sectors – often in the retail, leisure or hospitality industries – together with other low-paid workers. Such organisations have had some success, particularly with Living Wage campaigns, though these tend to have been observed by larger employers such as financial services companies and local governments, affecting cultural workers only in their second or third 'job', not in their primary mode of self-employment. In the UK, perhaps the most high-profile cultural labour market activism has been around the issues of unpaid work, which has seen a variety of students and younger workers developing campaigns on the issues of unpaid internships. Groups such as the Carrot Workers Collective, Precarious Workers Brigade, Intern Aware and Graduate Fog have run a variety of campaigns; at the time of writing, London Fashion Week was the scene for a campaign against unpaid internships in the fashion industry (Thorpe 2013). Such campaigns have undoubtedly had some success and have helped to bring in established trade unions; the National Union of Journalists has fought a successful legal case for 'back pay' for interns, while the Musicians Union campaigned (unsuccessfully) against professional musicians being asked to perform at the Olympics for free.

Others are looking not just to workers' organisation, but to the organisation of cultural work itself as a source of renewed creativity and political hope. McRobbie has called for a 'renewal of radical social enterprise and co-operatives' as a response to the high levels of unemployment and withdrawal of social support currently afflicting young people across Europe (McRobbie 2011: 33). She sees possibility in the growth of radical social enterprise and new forms of co-operative in the cultural sectors and beyond, particularly in the links between cultural work and social care and education. As such the 'instrumental' cultural policies of recent decades, which have stressed the links between cultural activity and responses to perceived social problems, may also be due for renewal, alongside the notion of entrepreneurship. Others see the salience of well-being in public policy as a possible avenue for renewed attention to working conditions, including those in the cultural sectors (Spencer 2007, Davies 2011).

Meanwhile theorists such as David Harvey (2012) see the 'extensification' of work as providing an opportunity to link the politics of the workplace with that of the city, in new forms of radical organisation. While Harvey argues that 'pacification and professionalisation' of the cultural workforce have blunted its once radical edges, he sees enough potential in its sub-cultures and growing discontent to believe it still makes fertile ground for leftist politics (Harvey 2012: 88). In doing so, he appeals to a timeless notion of culture as 'something so special' that it can both absorb and resist commodification. Eric Olin Wright in his study of what he calls 'Real Existing Utopias' similarly argues for the relevance of a basic income model for the arts, comparing it, in this case, with various kinds of caring activities and domestic labour as part of the social economy that should exist outside the market (Olin Wright 2010).

We are clearly a long way here from the notion of cultural entrepreneurship as simply starting a small business to produce websites. Many of these arguments call upon a notion of 'cultural work' greatly different from the sort of entrepreneurial creativity said to drive innovation in the wider economy. Instead, they suggest an intrinsic quality to cultural practices themselves that is capable of opening up other spaces of thinking or alternative views – ethically, politically and aesthetically. Indeed, the very notion of a 'culturepreneur' had always played with these differences, while often being used pragmatically to connote the kind of forced entrepreneurship I have been describing.

CONCLUSIONS: RETHINKING CULTURAL ENTREPRENEURSHIP — *Forced upon them*

This chapter has argued that the notion of the 'culturepreneur' was born at a particular historical juncture and yoked together the growth of high-tech small businesses, the desire for self-expression and the importance of cultural practices, and longer-term changes in the cultural industries, in a form that was always unstable and has now collapsed. Work in the cultural industries, including self-employment, needs to be rethought.

The notion of the cultural entrepreneur was adapted to serve a rhetorical function and pressed into service in the global spread of the creative industries or creative economy idea, but it has always concealed a multitude of different practices and experiences. More importantly, it relies on a model of economic growth and spending, both public and private, that is broken. The chapter has argued that the forced or adaptive models of entrepreneurship – the desire to carry on doing a certain kind of work after you've lost your job or the inability to fit your cultural practice into a paying job – has always been more characteristic of the figure of the cultural entrepreneur than the notion of the driven small business woman or man.

It is therefore useful to ask if there really is entrepreneurship in much of the cultural work we currently see around us. Calling the multifarious forms of contingent work 'entrepreneurship', particularly as these forms spread beyond the cultural sectors into huge parts of the economy, is meaningless, even deceptive. Autonomous workers, contingent workers, precarious workers – all these terms may capture the reality of self-employed cultural work better, but they have their own baggage and limitations.

In particular, the genuinely creative aspect of cultural work, the desire to make the world anew, is important to hang onto if we think that work, as it is currently experienced, can be improved. We cannot, and many would not wish to, rehabilitate 'standard' employment relationships –

historically contingent and demographically limited as they were. It is important not to sentimentalise cultural work; Banks (2007) reminds us that all work has a moral dimension, and there is no reason that cultural workers should be at the vanguard of more ethical forms of labour. But imagination is required to rethink our notions of good work in culture and elsewhere, and persistence will be necessary to bring this about – and both these are qualities of entrepreneurs.

QUESTIONS FOR DISCUSSION

1. Is it correct to label all self-employed cultural workers as entrepreneurs, or do we need a different term?
2. What do you think of the notion of 'forced entrepreneurship'? Does it correspond with your experience of work or self-employment, or those of people you know?
3. How can we make 'entrepreneurship' in the cultural industries genuinely open to all and more sustainable?
4. What policies might help with that and whose responsibilit(ies) are they?

REFERENCES

Ball, S. (2010), 'New class inequalities in education: why education policy maybe looking in the wrong place! Education policy, civil society and social class', *International Journal of Sociology and Social Policy*, **30**(3/4), 155–66.

Banks, M. (2006), 'Moral economy and cultural work', *Sociology*, **40**(3), 455–72.

Banks, M. (2007), *The politics of cultural work*, Basingstoke: Palgrave MacMillan.

Banks, M. and D. Hesmondhalgh (2009), 'Looking for work in creative industries policy', *International Journal of Cultural Policy*, **15**(4), 415–29.

Banks, M., A. Lovatt, J. O'Connor and C. Raffo (2000), 'Risk and trust in the cultural industries', *Geoforum*, **31**, 453–64.

Barbrook, R. (2007), *The class of the new: a Creative Workers in a World City project.* London: OpenMute.

Beck, U. (2000), *The brave new world of work*, Bristol: Polity.

Bilton, C. (1999), *The new adhocracy: Strategy, risk and the small creative firm*, in Research Papers, no.4, ed. Oliver Bennett. University of Warwick, Centre for Cultural Policy Studies.

Blair, H. (2001), '"You're only as good as your last job": The labour process and labour market in the British film industry', *Work Employment and Society*, **15**(1), 149–69.

Brockman, J. (1996), *Digerati: encounters with the cyber-elite*, Wired Books.

Brooks, D. (2000), *Bobos in paradise*, New York: Simon & Schuster.

Cabinet Office (2009), *Final report of the Panel on Fair Access to the Professions*, London: Cabinet Office.

Cairncross, F. (1999), *The death of distance: how the communications revolution is changing our lives*, Cambridge, MA: Harvard Business School Press.

Christopherson, S. (2006), 'Behind the scenes: how transnational firms are constructing a new international division of labour in media work', *Geoforum*, **37**, 739–51.

Christopherson, S. and M. Storper (1989), 'The effects of flexible specialisation on industrial relations and the labour market: the motion picture industry', *Industrial and Labour Relations Review*, **42**(3), 331–47.

Christopherson, S. and D. van Jaarsveld (2005), 'New media after the dot com bust', *International Journal of Cultural Policy*, **11**(1).

Cunningham, S. (2007), 'Creative industries as policy and discourse outside the United Kingdom', *Global Media and Communication*, **3**(3), 347–52.

Cunningham, S. (2002), 'From cultural to creative industries: Theory, industry and policy implications', *Media Industry Australia, Incorporating Culture and Policy*, **102**, 54–65.

Davies, W. (2011), *Happiness and production*, available at: http://www.opendemocracy.net/ourkingdom/william-davies/happiness-and-production [Accessed 21 March 2012].

De Peuter, G. (2011), 'Creative economy and labor precarity: a contested convergence', *Journal of Communication Inquiry*, **35**(4), 417–25.

De Peuter, G. (forthcoming), 'Confronting precarity in the Warhol economy: notes from New York City', *Cultural Economy*.

Flores, F. and J. Gray (2000), *Entrepreneurship and the wired life*, London: Demos.

Florida, R. (2002), 'The economic geography of talent', *Annals of the American Association of Geographers*, **92**(4), 743–55.

Gill, R. (2007), *Techobohemians or the new cybertariat? New media work in Amsterdam a decade after the Web*, Amsterdam: Institute of Network Cultures.

GLA (2010), *London's creative workforce: 2009 update*, Working Paper 40. London: GLA Economics.

Handy, C. (1995), *The empty raincoat: making sense of the future*, London: Random House.

Hartley, J. (ed.) (2005), *Creative industries*, Oxford: Blackwell.

Harvey, D. (2012), *Rebel cities*, London: Verso.

Hesmondhalgh, D. (2002), *The cultural industries*, London: Sage.

Kelly, K. (1998), *New rules for the new economy: 10 radical strategies for a connected world*, London: Penguin.

Lange, B. (2006), 'From cool Britannia to generation Berlin? Geographies of culturepreneurs and their creative milieus in Berlin', in C. Eisenberg, R. Gerlach and C. Handke (eds) *Cultural industries: the British experience in international perspective*. Online. Humboldt University Berlin, Edoc-Server. Available: http://edoc.hu-berlin.de.

Leadbeater, C. and K. Oakley (1999), *The independents: Britain's new cultural entrepreneurs*, London: Demos.

Leadbeater, C. and K. Oakley (2001), *Surfing the long wave: knowledge entrepreneurship in Britain*, London: Demos.

Lloyd, R. (2006), *Neo-Bohemia, arts and commerce in the post-industrial city*, New York: Routledge.

KEA Associates (2006), *The economy of cultural in Europe*, Brussels: KEA.

Marx, K. (1852), *The Eighteenth Brumaire of Louis Bonaparte*, Mondial. 2005 Edition.

McGuigan, J. (2010), 'Creative labour, cultural work and individualisation', *International Journal of Cultural Policy*, **16**(3), 323–35.

McRobbie, A. (1998), *British fashion design: rag trade or image industry?*, London and New York: Routledge.

McRobbie, A. (2002), 'Clubs to companies: notes on the decline of political culture in speeded up creative worlds', *Cultural Studies*, **16**(4), 516–31.

McRobbie, A. (2007), *The Los Angelisation of London: three short-waves of young people's micro-economies of culture and creativity in the UK*, available at http://eipcp.net/transversal/0207/mcrobbie/en [Accessed 11 February 2013].

McRobbie, A. (2011), 'Re-thinking creative economy as radical social enterprise', *Variant*, **41**, Spring.

Miller, T. (2004), 'A view from a fossil: the new economy, creativity and consumption – two or three things I don't believe in', *International Journal of Cultural Studies*, **7**(1), 55–67.

Murray, C. and M. Gollmitzer (2012), 'Escaping the precarity trap: a call for creative labour policy', *International Journal of Cultural Policy*, **4**(18), 419–38.

Naudin, A. (2013), 'Media enterprise in higher education: a laboratory for learning', in D. Ashton and C. Noonan (eds) *Cultural work and higher education*, Basingstoke: Palgrave Macmillan.

NESTA (2010), *The money game: project finance and video games development in the UK*, London: NESTA.

Oakley, K. (2007), *Better than working for a living? Skills and labour in the festivals economy*, London: City University.

Oakley, K., B. Sperry, et al. (2008), *The art of innovation*, London: NESTA.

Oakley, K. (2009), 'From Bohemia to Britart – art students over 50 years', *Cultural Trends*, **18**(4), 281–94.

Oakley, K. (2011), 'Good enough jobs and good enough workers', in S. Wright, J. Holden, J. Kieffer and J. Newbigin (eds) *Creativity, money, love*, London: Creative and Cultural Skills.

Oakley, K. (2013a), 'Making workers – higher education and the cultural industries workplace', in D. Ashton and C. Noonan (eds) *Cultural work and higher education*, Basingstoke: Palgrave Macmillan.

Oakley, K. (2013b), 'Absentee workers: representation and participation in the cultural industries', in M. Banks, S. Taylor and R. Gill (eds) *Theorizing cultural work*, London and New York: Routledge.

Olin Wright, E. (2010), *Envisioning real utopias*, London: Verso.

Paterson, R. (2001), 'Work histories in television', *Media, Culture and Society*, **23**, 495–520.

Pink, D. (2001), *Free-agent nation*, New York: Time Warner.

Ross, A. (2003), *No-collar: the humane workplace and its hidden costs*, New York: Basic Books.

Ross, A. (2009), *Nice work if you can get it: life and labour in precarious times*, New York: New York University Press.

Ross, A. (2013), 'In search of the lost paycheck', in T. Scholz (ed.) *Digital labor: the internet as playground and factory*, London and New York: Routledge.

Sawyer, S. (2013), 'What's in the fridge? Counter-democratic mobilization in post-industrial urban cultural development', in C. Grodach and D. Silver (eds) *The politics of urban cultural policy*, London and New York: Routledge.

Scholz, T. (ed.) (2013), *Digital labor: the internet as playground and factory*, Abingdon: Routledge.

Skillset (2010), *Women in the creative media industries*, London: Skillset.

Skillset (2011), *TV Labour market digest*, London: Skillset.

Spencer, D. (2009), 'The "work as bad" thesis in economics: origins, evolution and challenges', *Labor History*, **50**(1), 39–57.

Spencer, D. (2007), 'Job quality and the economics of New Labour: a critical appraisal using subjective survey data', *Cambridge Journal of Economics*, **31**(6), 941–71.

Terranova, T. (2006), 'Of sense and sensibility: immaterial labor in open systems', in J. Krysa (ed.) *Curating immateriality: the work of the curator in the age of network systems*, New York: Autonomedia, pp. 27–36.

Thorpe, V. (2013), 'London Fashion Week demonstration will highlight plight of industry's unpaid interns', *The Observer*, 10 February.

UNCTAD (2010), *Creative economy report 2010*, Geneva: UNCTAD.

Ursell, G. (2000), 'Television production: issues of exploitation, commodification and subjectivity in UK television labour markets', *Media, Culture and Society*, **22**(6), 805–27.

van Dijik, J. (2013), *The culture of connectivity*, Oxford: Oxford University Press.

Wilson, T. (2012), *Review of business–university collaboration*, London: Department for Business, Innovation and Skills.

9. Going all the way: the creativity of entrepreneuring in *The Full Monty*
Chris Steyaert

Over the past two decades, creativity and entrepreneurship have become twin notions to emphasise the increasing and by now crucial importance of creation for business life and society in general. From being considered a nice add-on, the paired concepts have become an imperative that should stimulate a whole series of professional groups and their creative role in developing organisations, communities and cities, and in transforming 'the economy' into a 'creative economy' (Florida 2002) and 'society' into an 'entrepreneurial society' (Steyaert and Katz 2004).

But this hype has lost any kind of historical perspective. Starting with Schumpeter (1994), one can trace a long-standing interest in relating entrepreneurship with creativity. Creativity is considered crucial for entrepreneurship, not only to spark it, but especially to perpetuate it. Even if creativity has sometimes been given a much reduced role or just been considered a personal feature or individual skill of the entrepreneur, there is increasing interest in a more radical conception that situates entrepreneurship within a creative process view (Sarasvathy et al. 2003, Steyaert 2007). This view engenders a fundamental rupture with mainstream approaches that conceive of entrepreneurship as being located in a stable world, that work with a logic of causation and that, consequently, emphasise entrepreneurial activities as a kind of allocation or discovery. Instead, researchers adopt the basic assumption of a becoming reality (Steyaert 2012) and try to explain entrepreneurship as the creation of artefacts by imaginative actors fashioning purpose and meaning out of contingent endowments and endeavours (Sarasvathy 2001). The verb 'entrepreneuring' has been suggested (Steyaert 2007, Rindova et al. 2009) to emphasise that entrepreneurship is an ongoing process and to explain its 'ways of worldmaking' (Goodman 1978) as one of its inherently creative contributions.

To reveal the creative process that enacts entrepreneuring, I will use a film from popular culture. Movies, like novels, have been considered valuable tools to understand social and organisational realities, although more such analyses have been conducted in organisation and management studies than in entrepreneurship contexts (Bell 2008). Moreover, novels have been considered important to study processuality. As Bakthin (1981:

7) puts it, the novel is '[t]he only genre which is in a state of becoming, therefore it more profoundly, essentially, sensitively and rapidly reflects the becoming of actuality itself'. To relate cinema to becoming, we must turn to an analysis, which 'diagnoses the affects and intensities that create us' (Colebrook 2002: 114).

To illustrate the various moments of the creation process – and the various affects and intensities that come with it – I will draw on the movie *The Full Monty*, made by Peter Catteneo in 1997 and later adapted both as a comedy play and a musical, which tells the story of six unemployed steelworkers who undertake an entrepreneurial project: setting up a male strip show. This low-budget movie has been one of the highest grossing UK films and received a BAFTA Award for best film and an Academy Award for best music among several more nominations. I have chosen this particular movie for several reasons. First, though a handful of unemployed men may not seem like the prime example of entrepreneurship, these non-heroic figures fit well with the non-elitist view of entrepreneurship I aim to develop here: the creator is not an individual genius, but an artistic collective. Second, the movie neatly exemplifies the transition from a production economy to one where creative capital is central, as the men evolve from blue-collar steelworkers into a group of performers. Third, the film lets me emphasise the increasing importance of the creative industries in understanding the role of creativity in entrepreneurship (studies) (see Bilton 2007, Henry 2007). With *The Full Monty*, we get a performance group that pre-figures the upcoming importance of the cultural and creative industries.

In the following, I will zoom in on different scenes of the movie to develop a theoretical understanding of the creative process of entrepreneuring. Practising what I would like to call 'theoretical bricolage', I will draw in the spirit of this book (see Chapter 1 and Chapter 15 this volume) on an almost forgotten model of creativity, described back in 1964 by Arthur Koestler in the *Act of Creation*, and connect it with one of the most original attempts at conceptualising entrepreneurship by Spinosa et al. (1997). The title of Koestler's book is still appealing: creativity is an act. Koestler competes with Einstein's $E=MC^2$ to develop one of the shortest explanatory formulations, in this case creativity as a triple variation of the letters A and H: Ah – Ah/a – H/aha. In short, his model says that creativity combines three unique human qualities – aesthetic, intellectual and humorous – which I will adopt and adapt to come to three episodes which sketch the creation process around emotional, social and historical relations. I will thus not use this model as a fixed scheme, but will give it new life and add to it, reconstructing entrepreneuring by fleshing out its AH-, AHA- and HAHA-quality. First, the AH-quality presents entrepreneurship as a way of 'wandering' into unexpected places and sensing possibilities which can overturn the usual ways of doing things. Second, the AHA-quality emphasises that entrepreneurship consists of an intensely social process which moves from apparently aimless wandering and vague intuitions to a deliberate, iterative process of rehearsal and hard work. Third, the HAHA-quality foregrounds the idea that entrepreneurship consists of redefining and reconfiguring a historical context, which works with, reinvents and turns upside down existing ideas and practices. Before going more in depth into each of these three qualities, I will first explain the framework by Spinosa et al. (1997), which will help me to deepen out and transform Koestler's initial notions.

ENTREPRENEURSHIP AS HISTORY-MAKING

To connect the creation process with entrepreneurship, I conceive of entrepreneurship by relating to the work of Spinosa, Flores and Dreyfus (1997), who understand it not as coming *ex nihilo* but rather as departing from existing frameworks and practices. Entrepreneurship thus forms an intervention which makes a connection between how (we speak about, understand and live how) the world is/has been and how (we say, conceive of and practise how) the world could be. Thus, we encounter a more nuanced understanding of creative destruction: rather than being dualistic, implying that a phase of destruction is followed by a phase of creation, the creation process literally produces a simultaneous multiplicity. That is, entrepreneurial practice draws upon and reuses current resources, forms, concepts and materialities as much as it engages with distancing, appropriating, questioning, rephrasing, overwriting or leaving all of that behind. For instance, as we will see in the film, the entrepreneurial team will take elements of the performance by the professional strippers, the Chippendales, and adapt them, but they will also go beyond this by doing a 'full monty'. They will also call their group 'Hot Metal', clearly drawing upon their past as steelworkers, but giving it a very different interpretation.

Spinosa et al. build their theory on the experience of anomaly, in which one relates to certain everyday practices and conceptions but also senses that they could be done differently and need to be altered. That is why the authors see entrepreneurial change as a form of history-making: because entrepreneurial endeavours intervene in our everyday styles of living and ways of understanding and thus always imply political choices, the authors ask how we encounter things in the course of our everyday practices and thereby bring new worlds into being. This process, which they call history-making, is predominantly reserved for those actions and events which fundamentally 'change the way in which we understand and deal with ourselves and with things' (p. 2). They are primarily interested in people's 'ability to appreciate and engage in the ontological skill of disclosing new ways of being' (p. 1). Disclosure is a general term for the coordinated practices which create an openness wherein things and people can show up; as disclosure excludes too, it is seen as opening a space that is bounded by a horizon (p. 191). Disclosure allows people to act upon, refine and even extend the traditional ways of doing things, which Spinosa et al. call the style of a disclosive space. Practices of disclosing require a sensitivity to detect the 'small perturbations that rule-followers miss' (p. 179).

In the case of entrepreneurship, this sensitivity moves persons away from simply pursuing rules since it takes the form of identifying the unique 'anomalies' in the disclosive space in which they find themselves. What makes change possible, then, is that entrepreneurs hold on to these anomalies long enough for their meaning to become clear; they can then reduce the given disharmony by changing the style in which those anomalies initially appeared. Hence, Spinosa et al. see articulation as a central disclosing activity of entrepreneurs: entrepreneurs bring marginal practices or concerns to the centre of people's attention by making them more important, and then reconfigure the practice of concern. This is how they make change. As the authors state about reconfiguration, 'successful entrepreneurs bring about social change by modifying the style of particular subworlds or the style of society in general'; they specify that the 'entrepreneur reconfigures the style of a disclosive space by installing a new product, service, or practice in that space' (p. 68).

Furthermore, disclosure is essentially about the embeddedness of creative processes: change only becomes possible if the actors involved are familiar with the disclosive space they want to alter. In the film, two disclosive spaces are connected. As we will see, the unemployed men start to question their usual practice of 'hanging out' waiting for 'a job to walk in', as Gaz, one of the strippers, puts it; instead they consider the possibility of (under)taking an entrepreneurial initiative by entering a process of questioning the sexual identity and relationship between men and women. Since each disclosive space has its own requirements, it is only by gaining an in-depth contextual sensibility that entrepreneurs are able to shift the customary ways that things are done. Here, we see, people need a distinct 'skill of intensified practical involvement' (p. 23) to notice the disharmonies that common sense would lead us to overlook. Thus, history-making is predicated mostly on a practice of 'involved experimentation' (p. 24) where change is stimulated as people continuously examine their lived experience of a given disharmony. In our example of *The Full Monty*, we can follow the men's ongoing involvement with their upcoming show, but the key experience is their experimentation with their self-understanding and their relationships to each other and to women, given that work, and urban contexts in general, are shifting dramatically. Along these theoretical framings, I will now give a reading of various movie scenes that turn *The Full Monty* team into a showcase for describing entrepreneurship as a process of exploring anomalies and paradoxes, bringing these to the surface and so reconfiguring the dominant way of framing the world.

ENTREPRENEURSHIP AS REFRAMING

The film opens with a short promotional clip, rolling from an old-fashioned projector, with pompous fanfare-style music, that presents Sheffield as 'a city on the move'. This opening sequence is taken from a 'real' promotional film from 1972, commissioned by the city's first-ever publicity officer, and praises the prosperity of urban life that came with Sheffield's steelworks in the early 1970s: Sheffield as 'the beating heart of Britain's industrial North' is developed based on modern town planning where 'Victorian slums have been cleared to make way for the homes of the future' and the city offers an exceptional quality of living and shopping and 'fun' leisure time. Indeed, it is 'thanks to steel' that Sheffield is 'on the move'.

Then, the film shifts ahead 25 years; now, instead of a thriving city, the image is a devastated landscape, an abandoned industrial site, a city on the dole. There, we meet Gaz, accompanied by his son Nathe and his friend Dave, wandering about their deserted former workplace, where only the brass band still seems to be active in an attempt to hold on to the past. Gaz and Dave, both unemployed, are trying to steal some rusting girders but fail to move them across a canal. The movie zooms out on Gaz and Dave balancing on a wrecked car floating in the water. The image of these two isolated men, who have lost everything and are about to drown, could not be more suggestive of their completely desperate and precarious situation. The question is indeed whether these complete losers can become entrepreneurial in what seems an utterly unmovable situation. At this moment in the film, we see little indication that they will take part in an entrepreneurial and ultimately successful endeavour. Thus, this point of departure for a creation process is hardly a *tabula rasa* situation; rather, there is a fixed frame, a particular kind of history, consisting of an urban narrative mixed with personal stories, which will need to be changed.

Their entrepreneurial initiative will entail a group of six (and a half) men developing a profitable strip show; it will require them to break with a state of being unemployed and looking for jobs to a situation where they create their own conditions of employment. Set against the 'unmovable' urban frame, we can follow the creative process through which an entrepreneurial endeavour becomes enacted, focusing on three episodes. In the first, I emphasise the affective immersion that opens up for a new idea by sensing an anomaly; in the second, I zoom in on how they develop and materialise this felt idea through social processes of improvisation and experimentation. In the third, I discuss how they further materialise the idea as they confront it critically and test its relevance for potential users.

AH: SENSING THE ANOMALY BY WANDERING AROUND

In the first episode, we follow Gaz, Dave and Nathan as they wander around in their neighbourhood. They are wet from rescuing themselves from the canal. As Dave is complaining about this, Gaz suggests that 'you should have taken your kit off', and insinuates that Dave might be too shy to do so, which Dave quickly laughs off: 'Don't! Shut it, all right?' At the same moment they pass a woman, and Gaz greets her with 'All right, babe?' and sizes her up: 'What do you reckon, Dave? Eight? Maybe even a nine?' In these few seconds, the film makes explicit its main point of departure with regard to male–female identity: women are objects, and men don't take off their clothes. However, on their walk, they run into a queue of women waiting to attend a male strip show by the Chippendales. As his son Nathe seems to know (all) about this and explains it to his father, Gaz's first response is to ridicule the whole thing. However, as Gaz realises that women have taken over the Working Men's Club and that even Dave's wife plans to attend, he realises they cannot let this pass: 'She's already got you hoovering! I saw it and I let it go! But this? No, no, no.' Even when his son says that this is a 'women only' event, Gaz will not be stopped: he climbs through the window. Having entered 'the Alley of Death', Gaz observes not only some elements of the performance, but also the hundreds of enthusiastic women and their raucous cheering of the strippers. Furthermore, Gaz has to flee into the gents' toilet when Dave's wife and two girlfriends sneak into the men's room to skip the line at the women's toilets. There, peeping through a keyhole, Gaz can watch how women behave in the toilet, and listen to their comments on the show and how they feel about it. Suddenly, the scene changes abruptly as one woman drops her underwear, hikes up her skirt, and starts to pee standing up, as men do. Gaz, who cannot believe what he has seen, finds his son and gets out as quickly as possible, leaving Dave's wife with them, saying that 'Auntie Jean is busy' enjoying the show.

The next day, Gaz is at the Job Club. The men, playing cards, are busy discussing Gaz's experience of the night before, instead of filling in job applications. We see more clearly the shifts these unemployed men have undergone as the changing economic situation has committed 'a series of assaults' on the 'male privilege' of them as fathers, husbands and bread-winners (Halberstam 2005: 138). For instance, Gaz has trouble keeping up with his alimony payments for his son and being a father who does 'normal things', as his son puts it; Dave has resigned from his job and has lost confidence in himself, even in his sexual potency. And Gerald, formerly the foreman over Gaz and Dave, has not told his wife that he is unemployed and cannot accept that he is 'just like the rest of us', as Gaz points out; instead, Gerald leaves home every morning pretending he still has a job. Against this background, the men discuss how men will no longer exist except in a zoo, as women will turn into men through genetic mutation. However, during the discussion, Dave points out that thousands of women were present the night before to look at those obsolete men. The men quickly calculate that if a thousand women would pay £10 each, they could take in £10,000 in one night. Gaz is overwhelmed at this, and replies to Dave: 'It's worth a thought, though, innit?' As they ponder themselves as would-be strippers, Gerald intervenes and kills the idea: 'Little and Large prancing round Sheffield with their widgers out. . . . Widgers on parade! Bring a microscope!' Dave defends the idea: 'I don't see why the chuff not!' And Gerald replies, 'Because you're fat and he's thin and you're both fucking ugly.' The scene quickly escalates into a fight.

These fragments illustrate how the creative process consists of sensing an anomaly. If the creativity of entrepreneurship starts with new ideas, at first these ideas are simply sensed, before they can be consciously formulated. Before anyone can articulate the idea that these men could become strippers, they must connect with an embodied experience from another world. Gaz, wandering around with his friend and son in the streets, suddenly encounters a world he did not know thus far: one where men can be objects of pleasure for women. If creativity, according to Koestler (1976), requires a form of bisociation where two habitually disconnected frames of reference are connected, Gaz actually 'creates' a new frame of reference by pushing himself through the window of the Men's Club and crossing new boundaries. Suddenly he is totally immersed in a different world, and he gets 'privileged' access to how women enjoy watching men strip, how they gossip about men, and how they even imitate and make fun of them in the bathroom. Once Gaz and his friends talk about this experience, it has a totally discomforting impact: they sense that things are changing even if they cannot pinpoint it. Then, rather paranoid (Halberstam 2005), they imagine how men will soon be obsolete: 'When women start pissing like us, that's it, we're finished, Dave, extincto.' Their talk does not really make much sense, but it reveals their profound emotional confusion because of something they cannot yet grasp. The creative process consists of sensing an anomaly that might lead to them engaging with a new project.

Thus sensing is first of all an emotional, aesthetic and embodied experience. Gaz's experience is based on his concrete, practical involvement of crossing a boundary and engaging with a different, unfamiliar world. They are all surprised and baffled. Being able to be surprised, to wonder how and why, to be astonished is indeed a primary quality of creativity. AH is the sound we make when something new comes to us. It gives us a sensation of wonder, of revelation, when something is disclosed. Creativity is indeed an act of opening up, of making things empty so the possible can enter. People experience the AH-quality through their senses.

The French philosopher Michel Serres (1995a) is a good help in pointing at the creative force of our senses. To fuel invention, he says, one must transcend the closed reference system of which one is a part. Serres believed in the role of the senses: 'if a revolt is to come, it will have to come from the five senses!' (p. 71). The first experience of anomaly and the creative impulse that this can be altered – in short, this emotional kind of knowing – comes through the body. The possible, the virtual and the imaginary are thus closely linked with the way we 'treat' our bodies. These days we place great trust in the visual and in images, but even before we have seen, we have already been in touch, we have smelled or heard or felt the phenomenon. As Paul Klee (1964: 310) famously wrote, 'One eye sees, the other feels.' Gaz has 'seen' many things that later will be used in their project, but at this moment, he holds an intense feeling that something is not right here and a burning question of how to deal with it.

Consequently, at this moment the friends do not yet say 'ah'; rather, they might say only 'oh', as they feel quite intimidated by their own feelings. However, this sense of anomaly turns into 'seeing' new possibilities and entering the level of the possible. In the fragment at the Job Club, this turnaround is the effect of a joint conversation. We can notice that becoming strippers is not the idea of a specific person. If any one person points at the financial potential, it is actually Dave, not really the smartest guy around the table. Yet overall, the idea gets formulated as the various men add elements to their joint articulations. And indeed, Gaz ends with a big smile on his face, turning his earlier worries into 'seeing' the potential in what felt at first like a cold experience of marginalisation. Indeed, he suggests that it might be worth a thought, letting himself be seduced by the AH-experience.

However, his words are hardly spoken when something very typical happens: Gerald kills the idea in a completely ironising intervention. Often, when a new idea is uttered, it is immediately criticised and what somebody imagines as possible is turned around as impossible with the simple utterance of a 'yes, but'. I like to call such a 'yes, but' a creative murder, as we explain why an idea is not possible and give all kinds of reasons, rather than say why it would be possible. Critique is important during a creative process (Bilton 2007), but it should not come too early on. For instance, we experience this response during creativity courses when we try out the six thinking hats of de Bono (1999), which is a model that highlights the different kinds of thinking involved in a creative process and in making lateral thinking possible. It often occurs that the black hat (giving a critical response) is immediately adopted when a creative idea is proposed (by someone wearing a green hat), before the white hat (giving facts and information), the yellow hat (giving positive support), or even the red hat (giving one's feelings about an idea) have had a chance to enter the conversation.

A long list of creative ideas and possibilities has been killed off prematurely by 'black hat thinking'. In 1962, Decca Records refused a contract to the Beatles, at that time still an obscure group, commenting to their manager Brian Epstein: 'Not to mince words, Mr. Epstein, but we don't like your boys' sound. Groups of guitarists are on the way out' (Barrow 2005: 19). The rejected demo, which contained ten songs from their audition on 1 January 1962, was found back in 2012, and auctioned for £35,000. In a similar vein, 12 publishing houses rejected J.K. Rowling's Harry Potter series, before Bloomsbury offered her a contract, supposedly at the insistence of the Bloomsbury chairman's 8-year-old daughter. Even before people can become aware of an anomaly, someone will have bounced away a new idea or intuition with a simple 'yes, but': that communicative move we have all mastered so well. 'Yes, but' doesn't sound at all like 'ah'. Every 'but' commits a new creative murder.

Will these lads be able to hold on to this sense of possibility? An entrepreneurial process doesn't seem very likely after Gerald's intervention. According to Spinosa et al. (1997: 41), 'the entrepreneurs worth thinking about are the ones who are sensitive to how the problem that they sense has its roots in our pervasive way of living, our lifestyle (. . .). The changes they bring about are the changes of historical magnitude because they change the way we see and understand things in the relevant domain.' Therefore, the idea of becoming strippers is not just a golden opportunity; it is anchored to the whole framework I have been describing, as the idea also relates to a paradigm shift in how these men relate to themselves, their own bodies. And thus the development of the idea operates on the level of a change of lifestyles, for themselves, for their families and friends, even their neighbourhoods. The question is: can they learn to see themselves as strippers and change their own form of dominant masculinity?

Thus, the creativity inherent in entrepreneurship is above all a form of sensing, a sensing that moves between the unspoken and the articulation, between the possible and the rejection (the impossible), between a feeling of anomaly and an opening up of the possible. Entrepreneurship, then, means entering the possible with regard to something that seems completely unmovable, overly coded and fixed. And here is where taking a risk is part of everyday life in entrepreneurship: one becomes vulnerable as one stands in front of the firing squad of those shouting 'yes, but!' to even the Beatles or J.K. Rowling. So the AH-quality also refers to the suspense and the necessary risk: it requires going for it, which comes with the necessary thrill and might produce a stretched out aaaaaaaaaaaaaahh. It requires taking one's chances while so many other chances are not taken, as one stands intimidated by the army of disbelievers who stand firm and say 'no'. But some do take the chance. They have the feeling of being pioneers. That's what forms the cutting edge of entrepreneurship: people enter the edge of what exists, and re-establish the first contact, which I call, inadequately, an emotional relation. That's why we can often call entrepreneurship a matter of pioneer-hood, based on a belief in the possible, as we can read again in the poetic words of Serres (1995b: 25):

> There are other possible worlds, I know other possible meanings, we can invent other forms of time. And this is why the philosopher broods over the possible as if it were a fragile newborn babe, like a bouquet of times, like a multibranched candelabrum, like a living network of veins and fibrils, he harkens to the noises and the ringing of changes.

Entrepreneurship, then, is about disclosing a possible world, hidden to most, but available to be sensed by some who haven't lost their sense for the sensible.

Let me summarise what I consider an AH-quality. It's an openness to the possible, the zero degree of being in the world, a receptivity to what comes to you, to what is strange, vague, chaotic. It's a quality of being able to begin, to follow what you feel, being able to recognise the access to the beginning. Here is a possibility . . . You say 'ah': it's the impulse to the virtual. It's the pulse of the imagination and the imaginary. It's the dream all people have when they sense the possible, when they open up to multiplicity. The AH-sound is about sensing the anomaly, having the 'pioneer' feeling of wanting to start something and taking a risk, breathing in and breathing out, followed by an 'ah', the door to one's *raison d'être*. Here an idea gets formulated and fed, as energies are accumulated. It's having a freedom to sense, a hospitality to ideas. In Flemish and Swedish we call it respectively *gastvrijheid/gästfrihet*; it's embracing ideas as your ideal guests . . .. . It's saying aahhh, therefore I am possible.

AH def

AHA: MATERIALISING THE IDEA THROUGH REPETITIVE EXPERIMENTATION

Gaz is mesmerised by this possibility and keeps thinking of the 'stripping project', even if he has not been able to convince Dave to step into it. For Gaz, who has taken the road toward petty crime by nicking a few cars, the entrepreneurial route would give him money to pay his alimony, so he can keep his partial custody of his son. In one of the next scenes, Gaz and Dave find themselves in their former workplace, hanging out with Lomper, a security guard who they earlier saved from a suicide attempt. To Gaz, Lomper is more than his desperate and depressed former colleague; through him, he realises, they would have a place to rehearse. Also he is a bugle player, which might come in handy for the show Gaz is still dreaming of. As they find Lomper's records in his car, Dave plays 'You sexy thing', a song from Hot Chocolate. Now Gaz starts to improvise, trying out some sexy movements under the 'spotlights' of the car lights. The attempt ends in utter chaos. Still Gaz seems to take pleasure in his first steps on the scene, even if his son begs him to stop. As Gaz thinks he would 'need an audience', Dave says, instead, 'you need a doctor'.

At this moment, one would see no future for this idea, as everybody keeps discounting it, and the first tryout was a disaster. But Gaz does not give up: for once he is 'serious'. He wins back his son who had run off, by telling him how much he loves him, a confession that does not come lightly for a macho lad like Gaz. Gaz and his friends are also trailing Gerald because he is an experienced dancer. While nobody is really convinced, Lomper and Gerald have joined up with Dave and Gaz; they organise auditions and manage to recruit two more mates, Guy and Horse. In one of the next scenes, we find the group rehearsing, against all odds. Nathe, the boy, is helping out with the music; Gerald is trying to get some choreography going while the other five are trying to simply stand in a straight line. When an irritated Gerald interrupts them again to correct them, Horse suggests that they imitate Arsenal players when they set up an offside trap. When they try out his idea, they form a perfect line and get an initial feel for how it could work.

Later, the group reunites in Gerald's home where Gaz instructs them to undress in front of each other. For each of them, this is an embarrassing moment, a boundary they try to cross with lots of moaning and self-loathing. Then they are interrupted by two men who have come to repossess Gerald's television because he is behind in his payments, but the five others show up in their underwear and scare away the visitors. Again, the group has a positive experience, and even Dave, usually the most sceptical one, remarks that 'It's not bad, this stripping lark, is it?'

With renewed energy, they go into a new round of rehearsals, struggling to get all the moves in the right order, slapping their belts into each other's faces, and stepping on each other's feet. Nathe is not just helping play the music; he is also giving the lads blunt feedback, like 'that were crap'. In the meantime, Gaz is transforming some borrowed costumes with Velcro so they can pull them off easily, something he saw the Chippendales do.

In the above scenes, we can follow how the felt idea of 'becoming strippers' is not aborted; instead, it is continued as the men give it direction and find a certain focus for it through experimentation and improvisation. With Koestler, who refers to the intellectual component as part of the creative process, we can speak of an AHA-experience. Indeed, at this stage, the idea is further conceptualised, which takes time and effort until the lads reach a breakthrough about how it all might work. This AHA-*Erlebnis* we all know from a story dating back to Greek times, when the Sicilian-born inventor Archimedes was able to solve the scientific problem he was chewing on by relating it to his observations about the way water moved when he took a bath: by connecting two unrelated frames in a process of bisociation, he finally could shout EUREKA!, I have found it. The difference between AH and AHA is only one letter, but moving from one to the next can take a lot of time – and blood, sweat and tears. In that sense, the conceptual development is not just based on cognitive and intellectual competences; above all, it relies on embodied practices, material translations and social interaction.

These activities of experimentation, improvisation and rehearsing – core activities in the social process of creativity – have been increasingly integrated in our understanding of the process of entrepreneuring. When we follow Gaz in his first attempts at 'stripping', a few things are remarkable. First, we find a typical situation of bricolage: one tries to accomplish something new by using existing resources in a new framework and combination (Baker and Nelson 2005). In many ways, like so many start-up situations from Apple to Google, from Amazon to Hewlett-Packard, the scene of this rehearsal is essentially a 'garage': with the lights of Lomper's car as spotlights and a record Gaz and Dave find in his car, they can create a rehearsal space for Gaz to try out what he has seen the strippers do at the club. As I mentioned earlier, this trying out is not just an intellectual activity, but something that Gaz experiences and performs through playing and role-playing. Bilton (2007) calls this a do-it-yourself aesthetic where everybody is learning and making it up as they go along. Gaz seems to be happy with his first performance, while the others look on in disbelief, and his son Nathe plainly refuses with a creative murder: 'Dad, don't.'

Indeed, as the team is extended, they continue its core activity of developing the concept of the show, through improvisation and trial and error.

As the team rehearses hard, they learn the moves and find a concept for the show. Here they must learn to do the movements in unison. This joint learning process is enacted with lots of mistakes and humour. When they repeatedly fail to move together, the reference to the Arsenal offside trap helps them to envision how to succeed. This bisociative thinking brings the worlds of football and stripping together to get them through their creative block. It reminds us of how Gutenberg's invention of the printing press was stimulated by his exposure to the workings of a grape press (Koestler 1964). Thanks to this bisociative move, the team succeeds in making a perfect line, and they experience their form of Eureka: 'that's easy.'

The team has another experience of working together successfully when they manage to chase away the men who would repossess Gerald's television. The emerging collaboration among the team members is primarily a matter of building trust in each other and convincing themselves that this is something they can – and want – to do. When they undress at Gerald's house, they literally experience how it feels to undress in front of others and they discover its new force. Thus, the team is testing everyone's involvement but also giving everyone enough space to try out this move on their own terms. In this sense, 'team-based innovation is an attempt to build a collective model of creativity and remains the key unit of activity in the creative industries' (Bilton 2007: 39).

By emphasising the collective creativity of the AHA-experience, we also import the idea that entrepreneuring is primarily a social process. This has been emphasised in the story of Jim Clark, a multiple entrepreneur of such companies as Netscape and Healtheon (Lewis 2001). Although some tend to place the entrepreneur Clark in the centre of the picture, he has emphasised that the team around him has done the bulk of the work to reach the Eureka moment based on what he sensed initially. For instance, in negotiating about Healthscape with a venture capitalist, Clark says, 'The problem I have with the way this discussion (. . .) has been going is that it is more or less in the abstract – that is, we're cooking up a business plan without a management team. This may be the way some companies are formed, but I'm more interested in finding bright people with a passion to change the way things are' (p. 109). Thus, invention requires a collective bath – and the AHA-quality requires in this way another kind of freedom, the freedom for collective search, social experimentation, trying out great 'casts'. In other words, the AHA-quality is far less a traditional intellectual one than a collective effort of a longer breath. Or to quote from the Clark story again: the point is not only 'to hire people bent on changing the world but to avoid hiring the people bent only on changing jobs' (Lewis 2001: 114). Collective experimentation is not a 9 to 5 job: the picture we get is that the work behind the scenes makes the entrepreneurial process into an intensive process where nurturing social relations is a daily activity. As Spinosa et al. (1997: 162) emphasise, the entrepreneurial team needs to 'hold on to this disharmony and live with intensity until it reveals how the common-sense way of acting out ought to take care of things and how it fails'.

Furthermore, the film gives us an insight into the everyday process of such a team forming itself, with all its ups and downs. Coming to an AHA-experience requires time, effort and patience. The 'actors' have to rehearse and learn by role-playing, if we follow the theatre metaphor that Bilton (2007: 29) endorses: 'The craft of acting is a useful metaphor for creative thinking and team-based innovation.' Indeed, this team is building up an intensive joint experience, trying out not only their roles as performers in the upcoming show, but also as creative performers and risk-taking entrepreneurs rather than unemployed steelworkers; thus they switch from being dominant males to taking up the position of a minority masculinity and exploring a series of dilemmas associated with femininity: 'the men worry about their bodies, their clothes, their ability to dance, and their desirability' (Halberstam 2005: 138).

Let me summarise what I understand as being an AHA-quality. Here sensing becomes transformed into sense-making, into finding a direction and a focus. The multiplicity of sensations requires refinement, repetitive work to make things visible, doable, to make them happen. There is no easy way. The AHA is the hard work. Let there be no doubt: they do not experience early winner's luck though they do need a lot of luck. The AHA requires working with people, making teams that are well connected, finding trust, taking up multiple roles and finding pleasure in trying out all kinds of roles. It's not enough to just put together the best and most competent people even if you are sensing and developing a vision and an imagination. All kinds of competencies must become connected and that process has to make sense to everyone who contributes. The freedom here is a freedom to engage in collective experimentation and search, a freedom to rehearse instead of performing.

HAHA: TURNING AROUND THE OLD ORDER

As the six men are building up inner confidence, they need to win over others in their community to step into the project, whether as funders or part of the future audience. Gaz first tries his luck at getting the Working Men's Club as a performance hall, which will cost him a deposit of £100. When the hall's owner asks him what they are up to, Gaz can only say that it is 'top secret'. As he does not have the money, he tries to borrow it from his former wife, encouraged by his son: 'The thing is, Mand, you have to speculate to accumulate, like in business. I'll get you it all back. I just need a tiny bit.' His wife is not willing to loan him any money, but does offer to start working in the packing section.

In the end, his son Nathe decides to take the £100 out of his savings – to his father's loud protests. In a very touching scene, Nathe says it is his money even if Gaz has to sign to retrieve the money. Gaz tells him to wait until he is 18 but Nathe wants to help:

> Nathe: You said you'd get the money back.
> Gaz: But you don't want to listen to what I say.
> Nathe: You said so. I believe you.
> Gaz: You do?
> Nathe: Yeah.
> Gaz: Blimey Nathe.

Nathe has moved from the one who told his father 'Dad, don't' when seeing him rehearse for the first time to the one who fully believes in him and funds his project. With renewed trust, we find the six men rehearsing. Their rehearsals are no longer so uptight. Under Gerald's guidance, they work out in an open field; they are having fun, playing some soccer, and teasing each other. Though their team confidence is rising, it is still diffi-cult to convince external actors. They have started to do some marketing, hanging posters on walls and mailboxes announcing the performance by the group 'Hot Metal' with the slogan 'We dare to be bare'. When two women approach them and ask what is so special about this event, as 'we had the real thing up here the other day', Gaz at first pretends that his friends are putting on this show, but he then blurts out that his mates are a better show as 'this lot go all the way'. 'The full monty,' the women reply, 'that would be worth a look,' and they walk off very amused. The other group members explode and tell Gaz he's gone too far; they fear they will become laughing stocks. However, Gaz says it's their choice whether to go back to the Job Club or maybe get rich. He gives them an ultimatum: 'are you in or are you out?' In the next scene, we see the group back in the queue collecting their unemployment cheques.

Now that the entrepreneurial team has built up an internal base of trust during rehearsals, we can follow, through the above fragments, how they leave their inner circle and confront the hard work of gaining trust outside. Here we have an almost classical 'step' in an entrepreneurial process of seeking and bringing resources together. However, finding investors is as much a matter of sound economics as of gaining and receiving trust. Such trust depends on people's ability to share their enthusiasm for the unfolding concept. This often implies a cold shower, when an entrepreneurial team has been working for a long time on their project, and other people seem not to follow automatically; in the end, it is the son Nathe who invests his money in this project. That comes as no surprise. Although he was once completely sceptical, he has also been following the process all the way. As a result, he has learned to see his father with new eyes, not as a loser, a petty thief with little perspective on a normal future, but as someone who is enthusiastic and dedicated to this new project. Like his father, Nathe comes to see the possibility in this project. In contrast, Nathe's mother and the owner of the club do not 'hear' the new part that Gaz is trying to play; they clearly do not believe what Gaz tells them. 'I can't believe this,' his wife cries, while the club owner would like to hear more about the project. However, Gaz is not prepared to tell him the full consequence of his new project, and to 'come out' as a stripper. The outside forms a mirror where entrepreneurs look into and experience what they have (not) yet become. The creative murders now come from outside, and they test how much the entrepreneurial team themselves believe in what they are saying.

Thus, the third quality – what we can call the HAHA-experience of the creative process – consists of an attempt to influence how other people, from investors to audience, can 'buy into the concept' but also to get outside feedback and critique. Spinosa et al. (1997: 167) point this out: '[t]he entrepreneur's anomaly speaks, then, for a historical possibility that has not been recognised, but that, when it is recognised through a new shared practice, will be recognised by most people in roughly the same way.' The HAHA-quality forms an intervention in the historical relations we have with a certain practice or style of living and often requires, as in a humorous action, that we turn around our usual conceptions and understandings of ourselves and the other: the idea that Gaz would become an entrepreneur would be almost comical if it were not also a bit tragic. However, this confrontation with external responses forms a necessary push through which new things can become visible and acceptable. New things play with the old habits and representations. The process questions all those who claim that they have always seen or done things in a certain way. The HAHA-experience complements the sensing and the sensemaking by dealing with all that is sensitive and by turning it around into a new sense that might at first look nonsensical. Entrepreneurs often have to work against prejudices or preliminary judgements, but at the same time this might also contain pertinent criticism or questioning that can inform the course of their project. An entrepreneurial breakthrough can only appear if the individuals can handle opposition, prejudice and critique. Thus these responses are crucial to finding out which is the 'real historical possibility' and whether the project can – with a loud laugh of 'haha' – oppose and question the dominance and colonisation of what is considered acceptable as practice. In turning around a historical relationship through creativity, we must expect some revolt, some uprising against the habitual ways of doing and seeing things – and we must make other people see this with us. For instance, the group in the film organises a sneak preview to which they have invited a few female friends so they can experience a 'real' audience and see how they respond. Crucially, the encounter with the women where Gaz oversells the group by suggesting the performance will include a 'full monty' shows that the core moments of the idea development happen in exchange with the future 'customers' or users of the performance.

For Koestler (1964), creativity is closely linked to humour and laughter as they also draw upon the bisociation where two frameworks collide. Through laughter, one allows for nonsense and for questioning the serious, whatever is considered important and habitual. For Koestler, laughter is a form of freedom; it creates revelation and freedom after confusion and misunderstanding. Humour is turning things upside down, or overdoing the expected. In a way, it makes strange connections no one would expect if they were reasoning logically. Humour, like creativity, requires lateral thinking, or going into the side paths of life.

As one laughs, one can let go of tensions. Laughter forms an important feeling to make creativity 'work'. Much more than through reasoning and arguing, laughter makes things possible and acceptable for others. Laughter is a form of communication that 'speaks' more than words. But laughter and humour are not just there to smooth things out. Humour, irony, persiflage, caricature, pun, satire, impersonation, parody and nonsense are as dangerous as poisoned daggers: they no longer take reality for granted and turn it upside down. In a way, the HAHA-experience can be compared with the practice of graffiti, where one literally inscribes another reality on the dominant use of a space or building. Graffiti is indeed what people have to write as protest in toilets and on walls as it is not heard within the established frames.

Let me summarise the HAHA-quality. Here, we meet a third kind of freedom: the freedom to oppose, to change the way things are. Humour, laughter and graffiti are important practices for lightening the tensions around a new reality so they eventually become acceptable. Entrepreneurship implies such a HAHA-quality. It involves laughing and poking at the ways things are done and simultaneously bringing in an alternative way. This kind of outsider position is difficult in many organisations, societies and cultures as it implies caring about what happens in the margins. One must use the HAHA-quality to gain credit and credibility from the sceptics.

CONCLUSION

To wrap up the understanding of the creative process of entrepreneuring, let me emphasise three elements. First, engaging with this entrepreneurial process entails identity work based on a sociocultural process of creativity (Glaveneau 2011): on the social level, identities are reframed as the protagonists change their relationships to themselves, to each other and to other significant social groups (such as women). Meanwhile, on the cultural level, existing artefacts (such as a Chippendale show) are altered as the actors create a new material reality by developing a new artefact: the 'full monty' version of a strip performance. Therefore, as a subtext in this chapter I have argued that the film's title, *The Full Monty*, also expresses the fact that creativity is always a matter of 'doing' a full monty. There is no such thing as a little bit of creativity; one must go all the way. Although creativity can be easily instrumentalised, I have proposed instead that habitual understandings and practices will be altered and that this will eventually alter conceptions of selves and worlds. The entrepreneurial process consists not only of the start-up process of the stripper group; it is, simultaneously, about tackling new gender relations and sexual identities. In the final scene of the film, it comes as no surprise when Gaz refuses to go on stage before a full house, one where some men have also sneaked in. After all, as the comic anti-hero, he

> ... has to grapple with the serious limitations of male masculinity in a world where feminism has empowered women, changes in the workplace have altered dominant conceptions of masculinity, and queer models of gender seem far more compelling and much more successful than old fashioned heterosexual models of gender polarity. Confronted with the failure of the masculine ideal, the male hero must accept economic as well as emotional disappointment and learn to live with the consequences of a shift of power, which has subtly but completely removed him from the center of the universe. (Halberstam 2005: 136)

Second, through this processual understanding of entrepreneuring, I have emphasised that creation is not a process that proceeds *ex nihilo*; rather it starts from existing practices, ideas, (self-)concepts and artefacts which form resources that, together with other resources, are used in a new combination during the creation process. The creativity of entrepreneuring, which draws upon a freedom to be free, has been sketched through three processes which are summarised in Table 9.1 and which intertwine practices of sensing, sensemaking and addressing the sensitive head on by allowing nonsense. Thus, creativity is about creating a place for three kinds

Table 9.1   The AH-, AHA- and HAHA-qualities of entrepreneuring

Qualities of creative process	AH	AHA	HAHA
Koestler's dimension	Aesthetic	Intellectual	Humorous
Adoption of Koestler's dimension	Emotional	Social	Historical
Relationship to Spinosa, Flores and Dreyfus	Sensing the anomaly in how things are enacted traditionally	Holding on to anomaly and living with it intensively	Finding broad recognition as a new shared practice
Core practices	Opening for the possible, sensing new worlds, being receptive to the vague	Sensemaking, finding focus and making it feasible in the team through hard work	Addressing the sensitive head on and provoking the taken-for-granted
Notion of freedom	Freedom to wander around (instead of being purposeful) and to begin something	Freedom to rehearse and make mistakes (instead of achieving results)	Freedom to oppose and revolt (instead of compliance and sticking to traditions)
Team dynamics	Developing curiosity and being open to cross unknown or unpleasant boundaries	Developing trust in each other, supporting each other to take risks, joint learning	Testing one's core assumptions and standing up to external critique and opposition
Requirements	A talent for chaos and disorganisation, being hospitable to new ideas, using one's intuition and imagination, letting go of inhibitions and resisting disbelief	A talent for improvisation, rehearsal and bricolage, an engagement with material translations and embodied practices, experiences of early success	A talent for humour, for opposing dominant practices, for learning from feedback and critique, for testing ideas and for convincing others of one's odd ideas

of freedom in the entrepreneurial process: the AH-freedom to wander around and sense something different; the AHA-freedom, which allows for collective experimentation and rehearsal; and the HAHA-freedom, which allows people to turn historically achieved practices upside down. In a nutshell, the creativity of entrepreneuring consists of opening up to the possible, making it feasible in a team and making it acceptable for others.

Third, I have situated the process of entrepreneuring in an urban context, making it into a form of urban entrepreneurship (Steyaert and Beyes 2009). The hypothesis I have elaborated concerning this entrepreneurial process is that *The Full Monty* team, if it wanted to succeed, had to change the city or, in fact, its relationship to the city. The context needed to be reframed as one where entrepreneurial modes of identity-making and its different forms of gendered practices were altered. This is probably best symbolised by the name of the show, 'Hot Metal', through which the worthless rusty girders seen at the beginning of the film have been turned into an invaluable, hot show. This urban frame, of a devastated Sheffield against which this process of creativity unfolded, can be said to anticipate one of the core and by now commonplace changes of the late twentieth and early twenty-first century: creativity is connected with an urban context through the concept of the creative city and the creative class (Florida 2002). The promotional clip used at the start of the film, a clear example of what is now called urban boosterism, clearly illustrates how entrepreneurial initiatives are closely linked with urban regeneration and governance (Steyaert and Beyes 2009). Thus the film illustrates a change towards a post-Fordist understanding of work and its meaning, which is related to (a change in) gender and class position. Before, work meant manual labour in a factory, which gave way to a dominant understanding of masculinity symbolised by steel and hard bodies (Halberstam 2005), but now the men experience loss and ambiguity, and the women have the jobs in the (upcoming) service industry and seem to have fun in their spare time, by attending shows in the Working Men's Club, of all places. According to Halberstam (2005: 17), the outcome of the change process is quite clear as the movie 'humorously foregrounds the relationship between alternative and dominant masculinities, and surprisingly credits alternative masculinities with the reconstruction of the terms of masculine embodiment'. It is against this changed urban context that we can say that entrepreneuring is about historic change. Not only will these men no longer be unemployed, but the city will know men who are less macho and also made it a slightly more diverse place.

QUESTIONS FOR DISCUSSION

1. How might the AH, AHA and HAHA stages be applied to your own experiences of entrepreneuring?
2. How has an entrepreneurial venture in your own city or community led to a change in attitudes to work, class or gender? And how has the experience of living in (or 'wandering around') the city or community shaped the entrepreneurial process?
3. What else can fictional descriptions of creativity and entrepreneurship add to our understanding?
4. Spinosa et al. describe entrepreneurs sensing and disclosing 'anomalies' in our experience of the world around us, and using these to reconfigure the way we conduct our affairs. Can you identify any such anomalies in your own experience? How might these lead on to entrepreneurial ventures?

ACKNOWLEDGEMENTS

Thank you to the students who have given me much inspiration to interpret *The Full Monty* in my classes on 'Creativity and Entrepreneurship', to Patrizia Hoyer for her encouragement to write this chapter all the way, to Helen Snively to make this text into a smooth reading, and to Chris Bilton and Stephen Cummings for their kindness and patience during this publication process.

REFERENCES

Bakhtin, M.M. (1981), *The dialogic imagination: four essays by M.M. Bakhtin*, edited by M. Holquist, translated by C. Emerson and M. Holquist, Austin, TX: University of Texas Press.
Baker, T. and R.E. Nelson (2005), 'Creating something from nothing: resource construction through entrepreneurial bricolage', *Administrative Science Quarterly*, **50**(3), 329–66.
Barrow, T. (2005), *John, Paul, George, Ringo & Me: the real Beatles story*, New York: Thunder's Mouth Press.
Bell, E. (2008), *Reading management and organization in film*, New York: Palgrave Macmillan.
Bilton, C. (2007), *Management and creativity: from creative industries to creative management*, Oxford: Blackwell Publishing.
Colebrook, C. (2002), *Gilles Deleuze*, Oxford: Routledge.
de Bono, E. (1999), *Six thinking hats*, Boston: Little, Brown and Company.
Florida, R. (2002), *The rise of the creative class*, Cambridge, MA: Basic Books.
Glaveanu, V. (2011), 'How are we creative together? Comparing sociocognitive and sociocultural answers', *Theory and Psychology*, **21**(4), 473–92.
Goodman, N. (1978), *Ways of worldmaking*, Indianapolis: Hackett.

Halberstam, J. (2005), *In a queer time and place: transgender bodies, subcultural lives*, New York: New York University Press.

Henry, C. (2007), *Entrepreneurship in the creative industries: an international perspective*, Cheltenham: Edward Elgar.

Klee, P. (1964), *The diaries of Paul Klee: 1898–1918*, Berkeley: University of California Press.

Koestler, A. (1976 [1964]), *The act of creation*, London: Hutchinson.

Lewis, M. (2001), *The new new thing: a Silicon Valley story*, New York: W.W. Norton & Company.

Rindova, V., D. Barry and D. Ketchen (2009), 'Entrepreneuring as emancipation', *Academy of Management Review*, **34**(3), 477–91.

Sarasvathy, S.D. (2001), 'Causation and effectuation: toward a theoretical shift from economic inevitability to entrepreneurial contingency', *Academy of Management Review*, **26**(2), 243–63.

Sarasvathy, S.D., N. Dew, S.R. Velamuri and S. Venkataraman (2003), 'Three views of entrepreneurial opportunity', in Z.J. Acs and D.B. Audretsch (eds) *Handbook of entrepreneurship research*, New York: Springer Science, pp. 141–60.

Schumpeter, J.A. (1994), *Capitalism, socialism and democracy*, London: Routledge.

Serres, M. (1995a), *Angels: a modern myth*, Paris: Editions Flammarion.

Serres, M. (1995b), *Genesis*, Ann Arbor: University of Michigan Press.

Spinosa, C., F. Flores and H.L. Dreyfus (1997), *Disclosing new worlds: entrepreneurship, democratic action and the cultivation of solidarity*, Cambridge, MA: MIT Press.

Steyaert, C. (2007), 'Entrepreneuring as a conceptual attractor? A review of process theories in 20 years of entrepreneurship studies', *Entrepreneurship and Regional Development*, **19**(6), 453–77.

Steyaert, C. (2012), 'Making the multiple: theorizing processes of entrepreneurship and organization', in D. Hjorth (ed.) *Handbook on organizational entrepreneurship*, Cheltenham: Edward Elgar, pp. 51–78.

Steyaert, C. and T. Beyes (2009), 'Urban entrepreneurship: A matter of imagineering?', in B. Lange, A. Kalandides, B. Stoeber and I. Wellmann (eds) *Governance der kreativwirtschaft. Diagnosen und handlungsoptionen*, Bielefeld: Transcript-Verlag, Bielefeld, pp. 207–21.

Steyaert, C. and J. Katz (2004), 'Reclaiming the space of entrepreneurship in society: geographical, discursive and social dimensions', *Entrepreneurship and Regional Development*, **16**(3), 179–96.

PART III

CREATIVE LEADERSHIP

Introduction to Part III: Creative Leadership
Chris Bilton and Stephen Cummings

> You say that you have no keenness of wit. Be it so; but there are many other things of which you cannot say that nature has not endowed you. Show those qualities then which are perfectly in your power: sincerity, gravity, patience, contentment with your lot, frankness, dislike of superfluity, freedom from pettiness. Do you not see how many [leadership] qualities you are immediately able to exhibit, as to which you have no excuse of natural incapacity and unfitness? (Marcus Aurelius, *Meditations*)

Marcus Aurelius' *Meditations* is one the earliest complete treatises on the nature of leadership. Thinking back to Chapter 5 of this handbook, you can see how Aurelius's writings – ascetic, rational, almost Confucian in tone – might appeal to both East and West. Ironically, however, *Meditations* is currently well known in China while it is now largely overlooked in the English-speaking world. Perhaps its assessment of good leaders as modest and unassuming does not square with modern Western views of leaders as charismatic heroes with big egos leading their lesser-than followers? Whatever the reason may be, it is a great shame, given that *Meditations* contains a passage that we believe best sums up the qualities required for leading the development of a creative enterprise: in two centring ways. The first is about such a leader being at the centre of things; the second is about being a leading force that is centred.

First, while innovation gives creativity a heart to move things forward and entrepreneurial drive gives it legs, it takes a quite different set of abilities to establish and lead an enterprise beyond the beachhead established through taking an innovation to market. In Parts III and IV of the book we will explore how moving on from the entrepreneurial launch to consolidate, sustain and move on to other beachheads requires a fertile organisational environment for innovators and entrepreneurs to continue to flourish and recreate. But, we believe that managing and leading this chaotically diverse and often necessarily egotistical band together requires a quiet, strong and relatively ego-free *centre*. The leadership that coordinates and inspires innovation, entrepreneurship and organisation comes from 'the middle', providing a solid centre for the diverse band that inspires creativity to hitch on to. If creative entrepreneurship is about providing force or impetus to the innovation that lies at the heart of the creative enterprise, leading others to be creative is about providing a gravitational hub to ensure that things don't spin out in conflicting orbits.

Second, the leadership of a creative enterprise requires someone, or a group, who is *centred*. The explanation of what we mean by this will take a little more time . . .

A question often asked is 'are leaders born or made?' Aurelius provides us with what we think is the best answer with regard to forming the lynchpin between innovation, entrepreneurship and organisation: they are neither.

Often people will claim that they are not leaders. They were not born with, or they failed to acquire, the attributes we routinely associate with our leaders: charisma, searing intellect, a strong jaw. However, to assume that leadership traits are heroic and either God-gifted or added in at a later stage, may be to miss Aurelius's most important point. We may lack an innate 'keenness of wit', for example. But the qualities Aurelius describes – sincerity, gravity, patience, contentment with your lot, frankness, dislike of superfluity, freedom from pettiness – are not traits we are born with; nor are they skills which can be acquired from training, consultants or business schools. These qualities are more like habits than traits or skills. They come slowly, and they come with experience and use. Aurelius would probably have classed them as 'virtues'; we must continue to restrain our baser instincts to enact them. They come to us as we become more sure of ourselves or 'centred'. Leaders are not born. Nor are they made. Leaders mature.

Hence, it is not so much, as is commonly purported now, that everybody is a leader. Or, alternatively, that nobody can lead apart from a sainted few. Aurelius indicates that everybody has the *potential to mature* into a leader. The qualities he describes are possible for any human; the challenge is to enact them consistently to the point where they become habitual and we become centred in this way.

This view of leadership has been backed up in recent times by a growing number of studies showing that most people would prefer a leader who is considerate and dedicated over one who is highly intelligent, and that many value the sort of mature leadership qualities that Marcus Aurelius alluded to: being down to earth, trustworthy and dependable.

In a 2007 article in *Scientific American Mind* called 'The New Psychology of Leadership', Stephen Riechler and his co-authors think through how this perspective might change leadership 'geometry': the case for leading not from the top or the front, but leading instead from the middle. In a world where leadership is about working to enable and shape what people want to do, rather than telling them or showing them what to do, leaders rely upon constituent support and cooperation. Leadership can thus no

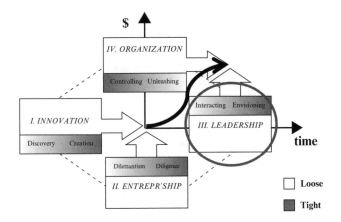

longer be a 'top–down' process, Riechler argues, relying on the leader's intelligence, charisma or other extraordinary traits to captivate and dominate the minds of followers. Rather, to gain the credibility necessary to attract followers, leaders must position themselves among the group, not above it. It follows then that the best leaders are those who best personify the shared values of a group rather than being in some way superior or extraordinary.

The idea of 'leading from the middle' also sits comfortably with the elements of the framework which related to leadership that we outlined in the introduction to this handbook. There we highlighted the importance of seeking *both* to cultivate an attitude to leadership that sought to skilfully interact with and among the organisation and its stakeholders in order to draw from this, *and* communicate back a clear vision of what the organisation was seeking to grow through its innovation and entrepreneurship programmes.

In their own ways, all four chapters in this part of the handbook advance this middle or both/and (rather than either/or) view of creative leadership. All of the authors put the leader, or the aspiring leader, not at the top or the front or on the outside looking in as an overseeing observer, but in the thick of it – in the middle.

The first, Lucy Küng's 'Leading for creativity in turbulent times', examines how fostering creativity has become an increasingly pressing priority for leaders of media organisations over the past decade. It outlines the key challenges for those seeking to promote creativity within organisations and it examines the approaches that can be taken to these challenges. It finds that while good creative leaders seem to blend both 'hard' and 'soft' characteristics, they do not confirm to a single type, and how looking for a single theory of creative leadership may be fruitless. Effective leaders draw upon a repertoire of leadership approaches, from 'hard' to 'soft', deploying different skills and styles to fit the situation – and what works in one scenario might be disastrous in another. Theories of creativity and theories of leadership both point to the importance of motivation and vision. But in order to achieve these outcomes it may be best to learn from your own experiences and the experiences of others to build your own creative leadership style.

Suze Wilson and Sarah Proctor-Thomson's 'Unleashed? Developing creativity-friendly leadership theory' runs a critical eye across the theories of leadership that dominated the twentieth century: theories that largely promoted the idea of the leader as a special or heroic individual leading from the top or the front; theories that may not be appropriate if the aim is to encourage creativity rather than followership. It then begins to think through and imagine how leadership theory could be different.

The third chapter in this section seeks to think differently about how leaders may be educated. Richard Hall and David Grant have been personally involved in one of the most innovative leadership programmes developed in recent times. Their contribution, 'Creativity in leadership development', reflects on what has been learned through developing and delivering a programme that gets developing leaders out of the classroom and out into the thick of where value is created: business around the world at various stages of their development.

Finally, after Richard and David's discussion of a general experiential programme to grow creative leadership skills, Vikki Heywood, Chris Bilton and Stephen Cummings' 'Promoting ensemble: creative leadership in practice at the Royal Shakespeare Company' seeks to distil Vikki's specific leadership experiences as she sought to blend the distinctive creative identity and traditions of the RSC with twenty-first-century management practice. Unlike the experience of many organisations in the creative industries, here good creative (in this case theatrical) practice, distinct to the organisation in focus, came to inform good management practice, rather than the other way around.

10. Leading for creativity in turbulent times
Lucy Küng

If there is a bottleneck in organisational creativity, might it be at the top of the bottle? (Intuit Founder Scott Cook)

The creative industries are in transition. Unceasing technological advance, convergence between once distinct sectors and profound changes in how consumers communicate and engage with content has brought dynamism, complexity and uncertainty, transforming virtually every aspect of established ways of doing business.

The most important change agent in any organisation is the leader. It is his or her task to analyse these developments, decipher their implications, set strategic priorities, and ensure the necessary organisational changes take place. The failure of legacy organisations to hold their pre-digital market position in a range of sectors indicates the difficulty of these tasks, and the challenges that face leaders of creative organisations.

There is surprisingly little research to help leaders of creative organisations surmount their difficulties, surprising because much public discussion about creative organisations centres on the aptitude, abilities or appropriateness of their leaders (think of News Corporation and Rupert Murdoch, Apple and Steve Jobs, Sumner Redstone and Viacom, John Birt and the BBC). The research that does address the field is fragmented and comes from different academic disciplines – organisational creativity, organisational technology, and leadership from management theory, and on the nature of the creative organisations and media industries from media management theory. This chapter attempts to pull these various strands together to create a cross-disciplinary picture of theoretical understanding of the task of leadership in the creative sectors, and reflect on their implications for leadership in creative organisations in particular, and more generally for all organisations needing to increase creativity and innovation in response to profound changes in their strategic environment.

This chapter starts by reviewing definitions of the creative and media industries. It then explores why the need for high levels of ongoing creativity, which one might expect to be an unchanging organisational requirement, is actually increasing in the current strategic environment and becoming a more pressing leadership priority. The role of leaders in fostering creativity is a key theme in this chapter, and the chapter starts by reviewing theoretical understanding of creativity in organisational settings and how levels can be influenced, with the discussion moving from theories that address all types of organisation to those that address how creativity can be increased specifically in creative organisations. Having explored the creative industries and creativity, the focus then shifts to leadership. It reviews key theoretical lenses by which leadership is understood, and the theory that focuses on leadership in creative organisations in particular. Points of connection or overlap between theories of creativity and of leadership are then explored. The chapter closes by revisiting the core theme of the chapter: the role of the leader in creative contexts during challenging times.

WHAT ARE THE CREATIVE INDUSTRIES?

There is no commonly accepted definition of the sectors that comprise the 'creative industries', nor is it easy to separate the creative industries from the neighbouring constructs of the cultural industries and the media industries. Hirsch (2000) delineates the cultural industries broadly as the organisational field that produces cultural products, and which ranges from talent agencies to communications satellites. It includes media, entertainment, design, architecture, advertising and marketing, public relations, information technology, performing arts, fine art auctions, galleries and museums.

Definitions of the media industry are equally confused. Even before convergence muddied the waters there was no commonly accepted definition of the 'traditional' media industries. European researchers generally tend to view the media industries as including broadcasting (radio and television), print (newspapers, magazines, journals and books), motion picture and recorded music. However, it should be noted that Garnham and Locksley's (in Blumler and Nossiter 1991) classification of the 'cultural industries' exactly matches this definition. US analysts often add gaming, sports and theme parks to this group (see, for example, Vogel 1999), which then becomes also known as the 'entertainment industries'. Sometimes the performing arts are included also, at which point the sector can sometimes become the 'cultural industries'.

WHY DO THE CREATIVE INDUSTRIES NEED MORE CREATIVITY?

A leader is the ultimate architect of an organisation's strategy. A central function of strategy is to align an organisation with its environment.

The creative industries, particularly media organisations, are currently confronted by a potentially lethal cocktail of 'first degree' environmental changes affecting virtually all aspects of their core business model.

The most fundamental dimension of change in the strategic context concerns technology. This is probably the most powerful influence on strategy currently – and also the one that leaders without a visceral sense of broad technology trajectories find the hardest to come to terms with. The creative industries normally see themselves and are seen as being primarily concerned with creating and disseminating content, but in fact they are technology industries as much as cultural ones. They emerged and developed in response to a series of first technical and later technological inventions. Unsurprisingly, therefore, recent revolutionary advances in technology associated with media (the Internet, digitalisation, incessant increases in computing power, bandwidth and storage capacity, plethora of mobile devices for media consumption, social media) have undermined virtually every aspect of their 'ways of doing business', from business models and revenue streams to distributing their products and engaging with consumers.

The impact of these developments can be seen clearly in value chains across all sectors of the industry where a consistent set of changes can be observed. First, value chains are becoming more fragmented and complex as new stages emerge (for example, new ways of handling 'news content' such as news aggregation, news curation, news packaging, user-generated content hubs) and more options emerge at each stage (think, for example, of the distribution in the TV industry, and of the number of different ways in which a programme can now be accessed by a potential viewer). Second, powerful new gatekeepers with feet in a range of converging sectors (notably Amazon, Apple and Google) are building strong positions at the consumer end of value chains, where they seek to transform how consumers acquire and consume content. These new gatekeepers have different strategic rationales and competitive assumptions than legacy players in the creative industries. Third, as the distribution stages of value chains get more complex and fragmented, media organisations are effectively being 'pushed back' along the chain to concentrate on the one area where they have unique competencies, the creation of content. This is their specialism and holds the greatest potential for strategic advantage.

CREATIVITY AS A LEADERSHIP CHALLENGE

This serves to underline the surprising increase in the strategic significance of creativity for the creative industries. Creativity is needed by all types of institutions, but is particularly vital for creative ones. This stems from the intrinsic nature of cultural goods. Because each one is unique and because customer demand is fickle, there is an incessant need for novelty (although this is not unique to organisations in the creative sectors; a pharmaceutical organisation must constantly engage in the process of creating new drug products and ensure it has a permanent pipeline of new ideas in developments). Viewed strategically, the higher the levels of product creativity, the greater the likelihood of market success and the stronger the competitive advantage.

A strong pipeline of creative products has therefore always been required – but in the emerging converged environment it becomes possibly the only ace in the industry's hand *vis-à-vis* its new powerful and massively resourced industry partners. Creativity has therefore moved to the top of the leadership agenda.

The need for creativity, of course, extends much further than the content and product sphere. When environments become more turbulent, all organisations need to become more creative, especially when that turbulence involves emerging technologies (Yoffie 1997, Brown and Eisenhardt 1998). In recent years the creative industries have needed not only to be more creative with their products, but also organisationally and strategically. They have needed to create new business models, understand and integrate entirely new platforms and types of services into their content offerings, and find ways to extend long-established professional skills, capabilities and professional values into entirely new arenas (see, for example, Dennis et al. 2006). Thus technological change and industry restructuring have not only reconfirmed the strategic importance of creative content in today's creative industries, but also expanded the areas of organisational activity where creative responses are required.

WHAT IS CREATIVITY, AND WHEN IS A PRODUCT CREATIVE?

Two bodies of theory deal with creativity in organisational context. The most substantial concerns theories of organisational creativity which apply to all types of organisations. It is rooted in a robust and precise definition of creativity:

> a product or response will be judged as creative to the extent that (a) it is both a novel and appropriate, useful, correct or valuable response to the task at hand, and (b) the task is heuristic rather than algorithmic. (Amabile 1996: 35)

By extension, a product that is creative needs to meet four criteria:

1. It needs to be original. In the jargon, the product should represent a heuristic rather than an algorithmic response to a task where there is no obvious or accepted path to a solution (Amabile 1983).
2. It needs to appeal to the public. A product that fascinates insiders but leaves the general public cold is not a successful creative entity according to this body of theory.
3. It receives critical acclaim. A creative product needs to be acknowledged as such by experts who know the field – a good indication for this is industry awards such as the Academy and Emmy Awards.
4. It meets organisational goals. A successful creative product must conform with the organisation's strategic objectives and fit available budgets and timeframes.

WHERE DOES CREATIVITY COME FROM?

Socio-constructivist approaches to organisations explore the relationship between the organisational context and creativity and are strongly influenced by the pioneering work of Amabile (Amabile 1983, 1988, 1993, 1996, 1998, Amabile et al. 1994, 1996, 2002). They see creativity as arising from the combination of three elements:

1. Creativity-relevant skills. These are cognitive abilities that allow individuals to think creatively and generate different alternatives. Particularly important are the ability to suspend judgement, to tolerate ambiguity and to reframe problems.
2. 'Domain-relevant skills'. This is essentially expert creative competencies in a particular field.
3. Intrinsic motivation. In terms of the building blocks of creativity, this is first among equals. Intrinsic motivation is central because our mental flexibility and ability to deal with complexity are highest when intrinsic motivation is high. In this 'flow' state, we are more likely to take risks, explore new cognitive pathways, and generate creative solutions.

CAN CREATIVITY BE FOSTERED?

The route to increasing creativity lies in increasing levels of intrinsic motivation. Creative thinking skills can be enhanced through training or reading (although improvements may be transitory). Expertise can be acquired. Intrinsic motivation, the key to increasing creativity, is a more ethereal entity and harder to 'increase'. However, research by Amabile (ibid.) highlights what can be done to influence levels of intrinsic motivation in work settings:

1. Encouragement. If creativity is required, those in charge must explicitly request it (for an example of best practice, consider HBO's strapline, 'It's not TV, it's HBO', which underlines to internal and external constituencies that creative 'differentness' is part of the organisation's DNA and a strategic priority).
2. The creative challenge and how it is framed. The creative challenge must be clear, unambiguous and feasible, and the team must be free to find their own path to a solution.
3. Autonomy. The creative team need to be free to get on with their task. Autonomy concerning process heightens a sense of ownership and therefore intrinsic motivation. This finding is echoed by a number of researchers of creative organisations. For Hesmondhalgh (2002: 55) an 'unusual degree of autonomy' is a defining feature of the 'complex professional era of cultural production'. Davis and Scase (2000) find that senior managers must not only provide autonomy but additionally be supportive and facilitative.
4. Resources. Time and money are critical and both need to be carefully judged. Financial resources should be sufficient but not over-generous since 'resource slack' will reduce focus (Nohria and Gulati 1996). If deadlines are too tight, there will be too little time to 'play' with concepts and solutions.
5. Team composition. The team working on the project must represent diversity of perspectives, expertise and backgrounds, and its working style encourage expertise to be shared (Kanter 2006) and emerging ideas to be fostered by debate and cross-fertilisation (Goffee and Jones 2000).

FOSTERING CREATIVITY IN CREATIVE ORGANISATIONS

A small body of research looks at creativity in creative organisations. Lampel, Lant and Shamsie (2000) note that defining creativity in organisations that produce creative products is difficult, because the creative quality of creative products is hard to judge since their consumption is a highly subjective experience (although Amabile's definition, which triangulates peer and market assessments, would seem to solve this difficulty). They distinguish between cultural organisations engaged in artistic endeavours and creative ones: whereas in cultural organisations, creative products must only satisfy artistic and cultural criteria, in commercial creative organisations, products must also meet commercial objectives. This places limitations on the scope of creativity because products cannot be too far ahead of consumer demand, leading to creative responses that combine new with familiar elements (Lampel et al. 2000).

Bilton (2007) notes that creative processes require boundaries, constraints and clear strategic targets. They also involve the mobilisation of a network of relationships between many diverse professionals (Burt 1992, Nohria and Eccles 1992). These contacts can be formal or informal and will cross organisational boundaries (Hirsch 2000).

Gil and Spiller (2007: 245–6), drawing on categories proposed by Caves (2000), identify eight distinctive characteristics of 'internal creative production', all of which pose management challenges:

1. An informational asymmetry between talent and management deriving from the fact that creative employees possess an expertise that management do not have. (Note: this is perhaps more accurately termed an 'expertise asymmetry'. Expertise is not the same as information, and, if 'nobody knows', as described below, all parties lack relevant information.)
2. Management cannot force the creation of high-quality work – only create conditions that are conducive to it being produced.
3. There are an infinite number of solutions to any creative challenge. Those posing the challenge cannot specify what solution is needed, and creatives cannot specify what will be produced.
4. The 'nobody knows' problem – the likely success of a creative product is virtually impossible to predict, and the majority of new products fail.
5. Creatives work on creative projects because of the sense of fulfilment or achievement it brings (in other words, intrinsic motivation). This means high levels of engagement and ownership, but also unwillingness to compromise. This can make management interventions difficult and lead to time and cost overruns.
6. There are high levels of uncertainty about how the task should be approached and how consumers will react to the finished product.
7. Creative projects can have high development costs. Should they go off track a decision must be made about whether to continue. Because market reactions are impossible to predict, there is always a chance

the product may succeed, so often a decision is made to continue with the project, rather than abandon it. This can lead to expensive market failures, known as 'ten-ton turkeys'.

8. Creative employees' expertise is a key strategic asset for the creative organisation, but can't be appropriated. This can limit the organisation's ability to further develop creative products or ranges.

CREATING CREATIVITY – THE CHALLENGE FOR LEADERS

Before moving on to leadership, it is worth summarising theoretical understanding of how creativity is defined, its origins and how it can be fostered. For socio-constructivist approaches to creativity a successful creative product has genuine originality, strong appeal in the market and to experts who know the field, and works within organisational goals and constraints. Three basic elements are required for a creative solution to emerge: creative thinking skills, expertise in the relevant field(s), and intrinsic motivation. Intrinsic motivation is the most critical. It cannot be increased on request, but rather via how creative tasks are set up. Specifically a creative response needs to be explicitly requested, the creative challenge needs to be clear, unambiguous and feasible, the team working on it needs autonomy, an adequate (but not over-generous) allocation of key resources such as time and money, a diversity of expertise and outlook, and needs to work in a way that encourages the free exchange and cross-fertilisation of ideas.

From research into creativity in creative organisations we learn that creative employees are embedded in networks of formal and informal, internal and external relationships and that the scope for creativity in commercial creative organisations is constrained because markets may reject products that are too original. A number of phenomena uniquely complicate the task of leading in creative organisations: that an expertise asymmetry exists between those working on creative projects and those assigning them; that the critical creative expertise belongs to the employees and cannot be appropriated by their organisations; that creativity cannot be increased on demand but only indirectly by altering the conditions that create creativity; that managers can only specify the challenge and not the solution and that creatives cannot predict what their solution will be; that the success of a creative product is virtually impossible to predict and this, coupled with high development costs, can lead to expensive mistakes; and that intrinsically motivated employees are committed and engaged but also unwilling to conform to organisational constraints.

WHAT DOES LEADERSHIP THEORY SAY ABOUT LEADING IN CREATIVE CONTEXTS?

Leadership theory (as a sub-set of management theory) is a substantial field with a clear development trajectory. A number of strands address leadership in creative contexts (Küng 2006, 2008) and these are summarised below. These are best understood as different lenses through which researchers have analysed and tried to understand leadership, rather than as options or alternative toolkits that practising leaders can use. Where relevant, it includes research findings from the creative or media sector relating to any particular approach.

Trait Approaches

Trait theories were some of the first scientific approaches to leadership. They see leadership as residing in a set of definable, measurable in-born traits found in 'natural leaders' (Jago 1982). The researchers sought to identify traits common to successful leaders, hoping that potential successful leaders could be identified by screening for these (Jago 1982). Although leadership researchers have moved on, trait thinking still influences analyses of media leaders' success, for example the media mogul is assumed to have natural entrepreneurial and risk-taking skills (see Tunstall and Palmer 1998). Early research into creativity was also trait based, where researchers looked for personality traits and intellectual abilities that were common to exceptionally creative individuals. This broadened into investigations of the skills underlying creativity and the contexts that support it, with an associated assumption that creativity is not simply the province of the talented few, but can be encouraged in all populations.

Skills Approaches

Skills approaches are more democratic: they see effective leadership as residing in a combination of skills, knowledge and competencies that can be learned (Jago 1982, Northouse 2004, Mumford et al. 2000a). As this approach developed, cognitive skills became a focus, particularly a facility with abstract and hypothetical ideas that allows a leader to identify complex relationships and predict future events from current trends (Yukl 2002), and find solutions to new, unusual and ill-defined problems (Mumford et al. 2000b, Northouse 2004).

Finding appropriate solutions to such problems gets harder as environments become turbulent because the risk of cognitive rigidity and erroneous conclusions increases in step with environmental instability. Leaders must become more structured and vigilant in environmental scanning and problem-solving (Ancona 1990), but also capable of revising operating assumptions and developing new heuristics (Tushman and Anderson 1986). This is central to the organisation's ability to adapt (Virany et al. 1992).

Failure to revise cognitive assumptions as the environment changed contributed to Michael Eisner's downfall at Disney (for full discussion, see Küng 2008). During his first decade the media industry was relatively stable; he applied the formula that had brought him success in previous roles: low budgets, no high-paid stars, a tight control on processes and costs, and a focus on the fields he knew well (Stewart 2005: 80). However, as technological advance and convergence transformed Disney's strategic environment, the assumptions that had brought success became hurdles. The industry had adopted blockbuster content strategies, but Disney stuck to its B-list approach and its products lost competitiveness as a result. Convergence brought growth opportunities far outside the traditional media mainstream, whereas Eisner preferred internal growth in fields he understood, and the financial markets penalised Disney as a result.

Skills approaches can be a valuable lens for analysing creative leaders. John Birt's director-generalship of the BBC (1992–2000) was at the time judged largely with respect to a large-scale strategic initiative he implemented called 'Producer Choice'. This was designed to answer vocal and dangerous criticisms from the government that BBC finances were over-generous and inadequately managed, and that the organisation was failing to meet the needs of those who financed it, a pressure that John Birt saw as so great that if the BBC had not undertaken such measures itself, 'the job would have been done for us'. Producer Choice was a highly analytic initiative that reflected John Birt's conceptual and intellectual approach to leadership, notably his ability to reduce complexity, predict patterns from incomplete data and reconcile conflicting demands. In essence he introduced a sophisticated trading system arranged around an 'internal market' that separated the purchasers of programming from the providers. Immediate goals were to allow all activities to be fully costed, inefficiencies to be highlighted, costs reduced and waste eliminated, thus ensuring that as much money as possible could be devoted to programme-making. The broader goal was to demonstrate to the government that the BBC was able to change, could operate efficiently and was, by extension, worthy of charter renewal (Harris and Wegg-Prosser 1998). Birt achieved these, and in 1997 the BBC was granted a new royal charter and its licence fee was extended for ten years. In addition, it was encouraged to develop its commercial activities and become globally active.

In terms of skills identified by researchers as important in creative sectors, Sternberg et al. (2003) have observed that the ability to integrate two ideas that were previously seen as unrelated or even opposed is important for creative leaders. Sanchez-Tabernero (in Küng 2006) sees the ability to 'build great teams' as important. Burns and Stalkers' (1961, reprinted 1994: 102) research into environments that promote innovation found that leaders need ability to grasp the changing strategic dynamics, particularly technological ones, and to recalibrate the internal organisation in response.

Cognitive skills, like analytic intelligence, strategic understanding or open-mindedness, provide another 'lens' for understanding leadership in creative organisations. This thinking moves beyond some of the limitations of 'trait-based' theories of leadership, yet remains predominantly focused on the leader. Style-based approaches open up another perspective on leadership, focusing not just on the leader but on the led.

Style Approaches

Style approaches stress the role of soft factors in leadership success. They look not simply at the leader, but also at his or her relationships with those led (Yukl 2002, Stogdill 1974, Jago 1982). Some of the earliest and most influential research on leadership style, the Ohio studies (conducted at Ohio State University in the late 1940s), looked at two dimensions of a leader's style: his or her relationship with followers (looking at communication, trust and warmth), and with groups (looking at how a leader organises relationships between group members, establishes channels of communication and the group's task). These dimensions were used to both develop leadership typologies and suggest the optimal leadership style.

Style approaches have been criticised because they can lead to overly simplistic analysis (the two by two matrix beloved of business schools) and prescriptive recommendations, but their simplicity has resonated with practitioners and with researchers from the media and creative management fields. It has been suggested that a consensus-based leadership style is most appropriate for media organisations because creative employees resent being told what to do (Davis and Scase 2000), will not accept unquestioningly direction from above (Lavine and Wackman 1988) and need editorial freedom and protection from managerial influence (Curran and Seaton 1981). Similarly, Mauzy and Harriman (2003) suggest that hierarchical, paternalistic management styles limit creativity, and inclusive ones that distribute creative decision-making throughout the organisation promote sustained creativity. Aris and Bughin (2005) identify two leadership styles for the media: an inspirational, charismatic, hands-on style, or a performance-orientated, structured style, involving systematic setting of strategic corporate and individual goals.

Transformational Leadership

A dominant approach to leadership in recent years, in both practical and theoretical domains, is 'transformational leadership'. This is credited to political sociologist Burns (1978), who identified a leader who achieves wide-scale change in an organisation by using levers in its social architecture to activate followers' intrinsic motivation, which can then be harnessed to realise stretching performance outcomes (Burns 1978, Bass 1985, Bass and Avolio 1994, Conger 1989, Bass and Steidlmeier 1999, Senge 1990). The transformational leader is a hybrid concept – it represents a particular style of leadership, but requires a specific palette of skills, some learnable and some, like charisma, probably in-born traits.

The leader's vision is central. This must be powerful enough to persuade individuals to behave in different ways (Senge 1990). Charisma is used to build followers' emotional commitment to a vision, activating higher-order needs and encouraging them to transcend self-interest to reach new goals (Bass 1985, Kotter 1996, Hitt et al. 1998).

Greg Dyke, Director General of the BBC from 2000 to 2004, is a classic example of a transformational leader (Kanter 2004). In 2002 he launched an ambitious strategic change initiative, 'Making it Happen'. His vision was to transform the BBC into the most creative organisation in the world within five years by harnessing the energy, commitment and ideas of all members of the BBC (Spindler and van den Brul 2006–7).

'Making it Happen' was intuitive, inclusive and sought to involve as many organisation members as possible. Dyke employed a number of strategies to build commitment and change behaviour (Spindler and van den Brul 2006–7). Brainstorming workshops were held where 10 000 staff made over 25 000 suggestions about the BBC's problems and how to solve them. A number of good ideas were implemented fast to show that the change agenda was serious and that staff involvement was valued. Dyke modelled the open, direct and non-bureaucratic communication style he wanted to instil by encouraging people to address him as Greg and reducing meeting documentation to a minimum. Staff were given a yellow 'referee' card stating 'Cut the Crap, Make it Happen' to bring out in meetings if they felt good ideas were falling victim to bureaucracy.

Dyke published a new set of BBC values, which he stressed should become the basis of the new culture. Staff teams were asked to investigate how the BBC could realise its new goals, and these ideas were combined into a BBC-wide change plan. The plan was presented to staff through a live, televised, interactive BBC-wide conversation involving 17 000 staff at over 400 meetings.

The concept of the transformational leader is present in the literature on creative industries. Bilton (2007) identifies 'visionary leaders', who are individualistic and favour bold, differentiated strategic responses that depart from received industry wisdom. In his exploration of how incumbent businesses threatened by digitalisation must change, Waldman (2009) proposes a leadership approach that mirrors many of the tenets of transformational leadership. He views the ability to 'bring people with you in challenging times' (2009: 130–31) as the essence of the leadership task. This requires clarity ('people need to know what is happening: why, how and when'), consistency ('don't just present a plan once; present it time and time again . . . you are leading people on a journey, not a set of random dance moves'), and collaboration ('getting people working with people from different parts of the business, tackling business problems collectively, is energising and constructive. It makes people feel they are part of something bigger').

Charismatic Leadership

Charismatic leadership is closely connected to, almost a sub-set of, transformational leadership (Hunt and Conger 1999). It involves a leader employing personal magnetism to evoke followers' trust and to influence them to act in certain ways in the pursuit of specific goals (Bass 1985, Yukl 2002, Conger 1989, Conger 1999, Conger and Kanungo 1998).

A vision that appeals to followers' higher-order needs and links with their own inner values and ideals is a central tool of charismatic leadership. To embed the vision the charismatic leader needs to model personally the behaviours and values that followers should adopt. Steve Jobs' (a prime example of a charismatic leader) vision for Apple was to build 'insanely great' machines that will 'make a dent in the world'.

Charismatic leadership, however, has a shadow side. Steve Jobs is frequently described by those who knew him as a 'jerk' and worse (see, for example, Isaacson 2011, Young and Simon 2005).

LEADING FOR CREATIVITY

There is relatively little research that explicitly addresses the links between creativity and leadership. Amabile and Khaire (2008: 102) found that the first priority of leaders seeking to increase creativity is to distribute the responsibility for creativity throughout the organisation, specifically to recast the relationship between leaders and those led. They propose that hierarchies can have a negative correlation with creativity because they limit the scope of autonomous groups and impede the exchange of ideas. Thus they found that Google has a higher success rate with ideas that have been executed in the ranks without support from above than with ideas that had been initiated by senior management.

Management control processes have also been widely found to limit creativity. Clayton Christensen (in Amabile and Khaire 2008) describes how 'powerful constituencies inside the company collectively beat things into a shape that more closely conforms to the existing business model rather than to the opportunity in the market'. Budget allocation processes, which indirectly reinforce a focus on improving the performance of established products along dimensions that mainstream customers in major markets traditionally value, are also detrimental to innovation (Christensen 1997).

Findings from research on the links between creativity and leadership in creative contexts reach broadly similar conclusions. Mauzy and Harriman (2003) find that traditional structures constrain the creative potential of an organisation because they assume that position equals knowledge. In reality all employees have potentially valuable knowledge and potential contributions to the creative process, and thus need to be engaged. Leaders can therefore increase the overall creativity of an organisation by spreading the responsibility and capability of creative leadership to every employee.

One of the best-documented cases of creative leadership concerns Michael Eisner's tenure at Disney. Eisner's eventual downfall at Disney is mentioned earlier in this chapter. But it is worth considering the entire span of Eisner's career at Disney and how leadership can contribute to both the rise and fall of an organisation. In 1984 Disney was a failing organisation, and 'Team Disney' – comprising Michael Eisner, as chairman and CEO, Frank Wells as president and COO, and Jeffrey Katzenberg as head of the film studio – was brought in to rescue the organisation. Between the mid-1980s and mid-1990s at the Walt Disney Company they orchestrated a remarkable turnaround. It became the number one ranked studio, *The Lion King*, released in 1994, became the second largest grossing film ever, and new businesses were developed. By 1987 Disney was a vertically integrated conglomerate with an operating income that had jumped from $300 million to nearly $800 million.[1] It was one of the most valuable brands in the world and admired for its tight internal management and aggressive exploitation of synergies. Eisner had a clearly articulated formula for creative leadership (Wetlaufer 2000) that corresponded with many of the principles of organisational creativity. Weekly meetings were held where staff were encouraged to contribute ideas. Creative staff were given time to incubate ideas, autonomy was fostered and diversity in creative teams explicitly furthered (Stewart 2005).

However, in 1994 things started to go wrong. Wells was killed in an accident and Katzenberg left to found Dreamworks SKG. Other studios' animated films started to outperform Disney's, live action films performed poorly, and video and merchandising income fell, as did earnings and stock price. A year later, Comcast launched a hostile bid, and negotiations with Pixar on prolonging a successful joint venture collapsed. Forty-five per cent of shareholders voted to withhold support for Eisner's re-election, and he subsequently announced his resignation.

At this point, entirely different accounts of Eisner's creative leadership started to emerge. Eisner was described as 'an oppressive force' that had 'extinguished the company's creative spark' (Young and Simon 2005: 311). Organisational politics were described as 'cut-throat' (Stewart 2005) and the focus on synergy had led to 'endless iterations of existing properties'.[2] It may well be that although Eisner did institute mechanisms to further creativity, other aspects of his management priorities undermined these. Theories of organisational creativity provide an explanation. In terms of the creative challenge, the profit-multiplier business model that was the engine behind Disney's financial strength (Slywotsky et al. 1997) also limited and prescribed the creative challenge. Tight financial control may have curtailed experimentation. Autonomy was compromised by Eisner's 'centralised and controlling management style' and propensity to 'sweat the details'.[3] This case underlines the context-dependent nature of the creative leadership task: a formula that brought success in a stable strategic environment created institutional rigidity in a more dynamic one. It also shows the subtle interplay between strategy, organisational processes and creativity. Eisner pioneered the multi-platform brand-based business models that today all legacy organisations are striving to achieve. However, while a tremendously creative strategic response, it was one that squeezed out creativity at lower levels of the organisation and reduced Disney's ability to adapt in step with the environment.

MOVING THEORY FORWARD

What additional insights on leadership in creative contexts can be drawn from the reviews of theories of organisational creativity and of leadership in this chapter? To begin we can identify three obvious contact points between general management theories of leadership and those of organisational creativity.

The first and most obvious point of connection concerns the organisational context in which creativity occurs. Creativity theory tells us this has a huge influence on levels of intrinsic motivation and therefore creativity. Leadership theory tells us that the leader is the architect of the work environment, dictating the nature of creative challenges, how resources are allocated, and establishing wider contextual elements such as structure, coordination mechanisms, business processes, and management. Transformational and charismatic theories explore how the leader creates intangible contextual elements important for creative responses – particularly culture and climate. These contextual elements in turn trigger a second connection point – intrinsic motivation.

2. Intrinsic motivation

Intrinsic motivation is central both to theories of organisational creativity and to transformational and charismatic leadership. It forms the second connection between theories of leadership and creativity. According to creativity theories, it catalyses expertise and creative-thinking skills to produce novel solutions. In leadership theories it makes followers receptive to higher-order goals and able to suppress the self-interest that might otherwise block their acceptance. Charismatic leaders can nurture this crucial ingredient of intrinsic motivation – but if taken to an extreme (towards a 'dark side' of control and manipulation), they can also overpower it.

3. Vision

A third link is vision. Vision is the starting point of transformational and charismatic leadership, and also, in the form of the initial creative challenge, of successful creative projects. The leader, whether of the organisation or of the creative project, crafts and promulgates a vision that is powerful enough to get followers to think differently, entertain new ideas and behave in different ways. The vision sets the creative challenge, fires up the creative team and establishes the scope of innovation.

Finally, a fourth connection emerges. Neither creativity nor leadership can be reduced to a formula. Leadership theories highlight the need to adapt style to context, both to the rapidly changing external environment and to the inner space of the leader's followers. Creativity theory points to a combination of release and control, vision and action, ideation and revision, in order to convert creative ideas into viable products and solutions. An ideal leadership formula for a particular industry and organisational context can morph into a significant obstacle should circumstances change.

CONCLUSIONS

What final conclusions can be drawn from this analysis of theory in the fields of creativity and leadership? The first conclusion is that this is an under-researched field. Taken together there is a substantial amount of work, but the overall picture is fragmented and too scattergun to provide guidance for practitioners.

There is, however, a highly coherent kernel at the heart of this theory, and that is the research findings on how organisational contexts influence creativity, and what kinds of environments best foster it. Here there is an unusual degree of triangulation between findings from general management theorists and specialists on creative sectors. Even more unusual, these findings are highly practical and applicable.

This is important because increasing creativity looks set to be *the* strategic imperative for organisations in the creative sector in coming years. As they get pushed back along the value chain, they will need to increase their creativity in the content area – this is realistically the only area where they have a unique strategic advantage *vis-à-vis* the massively well-resourced new players and gatekeepers. But as legacy business models collapse, they will also need to expand the scope of their creativity and innovate strategically and organisationally along the value chain as well.

In terms of leadership theory, it seems relatively well established that the leader plays a dominant role in increasing creativity. This starts with setting an explicit vision, creating emotional buy-in to the vision, modelling required behaviours, and then shaping the organisational context in such a way that intrinsic motivation is increased and structural blocks to innovation are minimised. Theory provides ample advice on how systems and projects can be fine-tuned to organise this.

The ideal leadership profile to achieve all this is less clear. The greatest areas of 'theoretical crossover' can be found between creativity theories and those of transformational leadership, suggesting that this approach to leadership may well be appropriate in environments where high levels of creativity are required.

This approach is, however, primarily focused on the leader's relationship with the internal organisation, against a context of a stable strategic environment. While transformational leadership approaches have the capability to create or fuel a 'creativity engine', they provide less guidance on how the leader deals with external environments, on what kind of 'hard' skills and competencies might be necessary to respond to complex, challenging and fast-changing strategic environments, and how these can be reconciled with the demands of fostering creativity and protecting the social architecture.

The ideal leadership profile is probably a composite of hard and soft, of skills and style approaches, although a leader with this combination would be a rare and special creature. A comparison between Birt and Dyke and their respective change initiatives at the BBC is instructive. When John Birt took over the BBC, he had to focus on the external environment and key stakeholders. The severity of the challenge facing the BBC and the complexity of the organisational changes mandated a complex, analytically based, top–down response. The steps necessary to ensure survival were simply too complex and uncomfortable to be arrived at by following a bottom–up, consensual approach. Similarly, his strategy for the BBC in terms of its Internet and digital activities was the result of his analytical skills and ability to synthesise complicated incomplete data and conceptualise its import. Today, thanks to John Birt, the BBC is arguably the only legacy media organisation that has managed to maintain a position in digital and Internet markets equivalent to the one it held in analogue ones (Küng 2005).

In contrast, Greg Dyke's leadership challenge was internal, to repair the scarring from Producer Choice, reduce the bureaucracy that had been created, and secure the BBC's future by increasing the quality of its programming and increasing its relevance to licence-fee-payers. His warm, open and intuitive leadership style, real liking for people and visceral approach to strategy was perfect for the task. Dyke would have been poorly suited to the task of reforming the BBC in response to government criticism (as evidenced by his painful departure from the BBC resulting from conflict with the government over the BBC's coverage of an incident during the build-up to the Iraqi conflict). Equally, Birt lacked the charisma, warmth and spontaneity to successfully carry through an initiative like 'Making It Happen'.

'Horses for courses' seems to be the appropriate cliché. The discussion in this chapter shows that leadership in creative environments, especially during turbulent times, is highly context dependent, and assessments depend both on the creative challenge and on the environmental challenge and are subject to revision with the benefit of hindsight. No single leadership approach is 'best' for creative organisations, since the need for creativity is embedded in the organisational context and unique combination of strategic imperatives. 'Best' is also open to interpretation. A leader that appears highly effective at one point in time may look less so when the context changes.

From a theoretical perspective, it's equally clear that no single theoretical lens is sufficient to analyse leadership. A leader's actions and achievements are based on a composite of inborn skills, acquired competencies, personality and relationship with self and with others, and need to be assessed within the organisation and strategic context. Research into leadership for creativity in turbulent times is not only a field ripe for research, but one that promises intriguing insights of potentially great value for any organisation or sector seeking growth through innovation and creativity.

QUESTIONS FOR DISCUSSION

1. Choose an organisation in a creative sector and analyse its strategic situation. As a second research task, uncover as much as you can about the present leader of the organisation.
2. Imagine you are a head-hunter required to find a successor to the organisation's current leader. Write the profile for this position. What skills, competencies or traits would be essential? What kind of experience would he or she need to have?
3. Using each of the theoretical approaches to leadership described in this chapter, analyse Steve Jobs' tenure at Apple.
   - Which lens provides most insights about his success?
   - Would you have liked to work on Jobs' senior management team? Explain the reasons for your answer.
4. When did the strengths of Eisner's leadership style at Disney become liabilities? What environmental factors caused this change of perspective?

NOTES

1. Increased profits stemmed from three main sources: raising admission prices at theme parks; greatly expanding the number of company-owned hotels; and distributing the animated classics on home video (Stewart 2005).
2. *Fortune*, 6 September 1999.
3. *Fortune*, 6 September 1999.

REFERENCES

Amabile, T.M. (1983), *The social psychology of creativity*. New York: Springer.
Amabile, T.M. (1988), 'A model of creativity and innovation in organizations', in B.M. Shaw and L.L. Cummings (eds) *Research in organizational behaviour*, Greenwich, CT: JAI Press, pp. 123–67.
Amabile, T.M. (1993), 'Motivational synergy: toward new conceptualizations of intrinsic and extrinsic motivation in the workplace', *Human Resource Management Review*, 3(3), 185–201.
Amabile, T.M. (1996), *Creativity in context*, Boulder, CO: Westview Press.
Amabile, T.M. (1998), 'How to kill creativity', *Harvard Business Review*, September, 77–87.
Amabile, T.M. and N. Gryskiewicz (1989), 'The creative environment scales: the work environment inventory', *Creativity Research Journal*, 2(1989), 231–54.
Amabile, T.M. and M. Khaire (2008), 'Creativity and the role of the leader', *Harvard Business Review*, 86(10), October.
Amabile, T.M., R. Conti, H. Coon, J. Lazenby and M. Herron (1996), 'Assessing the work environment for creativity', *Academy of Management Journal*, 39(5), October, 1154–84.
Amabile, T.M, C.N. Hadley and S.J. Kramer (2002), 'Creativity under the gun', *Harvard Business Review*, August, 52–61.

Amabile, T.M., K.G. Hill, B.A. Hennessey and E. Tighe (1994), 'The work preference inventory: assessing intrinsic and extrinsic motivational orientations', *Journal of Personality and Social Psychology*, **66**, 950–67.

Ancona, D. (1990), 'Top management teams: preparing for the revolution', in J. Carroll (ed.) *Applied social psychology and organizational settings*, New York: Erlbaum.

Aris, A. and J. Bughin (2005), *Managing media companies: harnessing creative value*, Chichester: John Wiley and Sons.

Bakhashi, H., E. McVittie and J. Simmie (2008), *Creating innovation: do the creative industries support innovation in the wider economy?* London: NESTA.

Bass, B.M. (1985), *Leadership and performance beyond expectations*, New York: Free Press.

Bass, B.M. and B.J. Avolio (1994), *Improving organizational effectiveness through transformational leadership*, Thousand Oaks, CA: Sage.

Bass, B.M. and P. Steidlmeier (1999), 'Ethics, character and authentic transformational leadership behavior', *Leadership Quarterly*, **10**(2), 181–217.

Bilton, C. (2007), *Management and creativity: from creative industries to creative management*, Oxford: Blackwell Publishing.

Blumler, J.G. and T.J. Nossiter (1991), *Broadcasting finance in transition: a comparative handbook*, Oxford: Oxford University Press.

Brown, S.L. and K.M. Eisenhardt (1998), *Competing on the edge: strategy as structured chaos*, Boston: Harvard Business School Press.

Burns, J.M. (1978), *Leadership*, New York: Harper and Row.

Burns, T. and G.M. Stalker (1994 [1961]), *The management of innovation*, Oxford: Oxford University Press.

Burt, R. (1992), *Structural holes: the social structure of competition*, Boston: Harvard University Press.

Caves, R.E. (2000), *Creative industries: contracts between art and commerce*, Cambridge, MA: Harvard.

Christensen, C.M. (1997), *The innovator's dilemma: when new technologies cause great firms to fail*, Boston: Harvard Business School Press.

Conger, J. (1999), 'Learning the language of leadership', *Human Resource Management International Digest*, **7**(2), 217–18.

Conger, J. (1989), *The charismatic leader: behind the mystique of exceptional leadership*, San Francisco: Jossey-Bass.

Conger, J.A. and R.N. Kanungo (eds) (1998), *Charismatic leadership: the elusive factor in organizational effectiveness*, San Francisco: Jossey-Bass.

Curran, J. and J. Seaton (1981), *Power without responsibility: the press and broadcasting in Britain*, London: Fontana.

Davis, H. and R. Scase (2000), *Managing creativity: the dynamics of work and organization*. Buckingham: Open University Press.

Dennis, E.D., S. Wharley and J. Sheridan (2006), 'Doing digital: an assessment of the top 25 US media companies and their digital strategies', *Journal of Media Business Studies*, **3**(1), 33.

Gil, R. and P. Spiller (2007), 'The organizational implications of creativity: the US film industry in mid-XXth century', *California Management Review*, **50**(1), 243–60.

Goffee, R. and G. Jones (2000), 'Why should anyone be led by you?', *Harvard Business Review*, September–October.

Harris, M. and V. Wegg-Prosser (1998), 'The BBC and Producer Choice: a study of public service broadcasting and managerial change', *Wide Angle*, **20**(2), 150–63.

Hesmondhalgh. D. (2002), *The cultural industries*, London: Sage.

Hirsch. P.M. (2000), 'Cultural industries revisited', *Organization Science*, **11**(3), May–June, 356–61.

Hitt, M.A., B.W. Keats and S.M. DeMarie (1998), 'Navigating in the new competitive landscape: building strategic flexibility and competitive advantage in the 21st century', *Academy of Management Executive*, **12**(4), 22–42.

Hunt, J.G. and J.A. Conger (1999), 'Charismatic and transformational leadership: taking stock of the present and future (Part II)', *Leadership Quarterly*, **3**(10), 331–4.

Isaacson, W. (2011), *Steve Jobs: the exclusive biography*, New York: Simon and Schuster.
Jago, A. (1982), 'Leadership: perspectives in theory and research', *Management Science*, **28**(3), 315–36.
Kanter, R.M. (2006), 'Innovation: the classic traps', *Harvard Business Review*, November, 73–83.
Kanter, R.M. (2004), *Confidence*, London: Random House Business Books.
Kotter, J.P. (1996), *Leading change*, Boston: Harvard Business School Press.
Küng, L. (2004), 'What makes media firms tick? Exploring the hidden drivers of firm performance', in R.G. Picard (ed.) *Strategic responses to media market changes*, Jönköping: Jönköping International Business School.
Küng, L. (2005), *When innovation fails to disrupt. A multi-lens investigation of successful incumbent response to technological discontinuity: the launch of BBC News Online*, Habilitationsschrfit: University of St Gallen.
Küng, L. (ed.) (2006), *Leadership in the media industry: changing contexts, emerging challenges*, JIBS Research Reports 2006–1, Jönköping: Jönköping International Business School.
Küng, L. (2008), *Strategic management in the media: theory to practice*, Los Angeles and London: Sage.
Lampel, J., T. Lant and J. Shamsie (2000), 'Balancing act: learning from organizing practices in cultural industries', *Organization Science*, May/June, **11**(3), 263–9.
Lavine, J.M. and D.B. Wackman (1988), *Managing media organisations: effective leadership of the media*, New York: Longman.
Mauzy, J. and R.H. Harriman (2003), *Creativity, Inc: building an inventive organization*, Boston: Harvard Business School Press.
Mumford, M.D., S.J. Zaccaro, F.D. Harding, T.O. Jacobs and E.A. Fleishman (2000a), 'Leadership skills for a changing world: solving complex social problems', *Leadership Quarterly*, **11**(1), 11–35.
Mumford, M.D, S.J. Zaccaro, M.S. Connelly and M.A. Marks (2000b), 'Leadership skills – Conclusions and future directions', *The Leadership Quarterly*, **11**(1), 155–70.
NESTA (2006), *Creating growth: how the UK can develop world class creative businesses*, London: NESTA.
Nohria, N. and R. Eccles (eds) (1992), *Networks and organizations: structure, form and action*. Boston: Harvard Business School Press.
Nohria, N. and R. Gulati (1996), 'Is slack good or bad for innovation?', *Academy of Management Journal*, **39**(5), 1245–64.
Northouse, P.G. (2004), *Leadership: theory and practice*, 3rd edition, Thousand Oaks and London: Sage.
OECD (1996), *The knowledge-based economy*, Paris: OECD.
Senge, P. (1990), *The fifth discipline: the art and practice of a learning organization*, London: Random Century.
Slywotsky, A.J., D.J. Morrison and B. Andelman (1997), *The profit zone: how strategic business design will lead you to tomorrow's profits*, New York: Crown.
Smith Institute (2006), *Creative nation: advancing Britain's creative industries*, London: Smith Institute.
Spindler, S. and van den Brul, C. (2006–7), '"Making it Happen", creative and audiences: a BBC case study', *NHK Broadcasting Studies*, **5**, 29–55.
Squire, J.E. (2004), *The movie business book*, 3rd edition, New York: Fireside (Simon & Schuster).
Sternberg, R.J., J.C. Kaufman and J.E. Pretz (2003), 'A propulsion model of creative leadership', *The Leadership Quarterly*, August–October, **14**(4–5), 455–75.
Stewart, J.B. (2005), *Disney war: the battle for the Magic Kingdom*, London: Simon & Schuster.
Stogdill, R.M. (1974), *Handbook of leadership*, New York: Free Press.
Towse, R. (2000), *Creativity, incentive and reward: an economic analysis of copyright and culture in the information age*, PhD thesis, Rotterdam: Erasmus University.

Tunstall, J. and M. Palmer (1998), *Media moguls*, London: Routledge.
Tushman, M.L. and P. Anderson (1986), 'Technological discontinuities and organizational environments', *Administrative Science Quarterly*, **31**, 439.
Virany, B., M.L. Tushman and E. Romanelli (1992), 'Executive succession and organization outcomes in turbulent environments: an organisation learning approach', *Organization Science*, **3**(1), 72–91.
Vogel, H.L. (1999), *Entertainment industry economics: a guide for financial analysis*, 4th edition, New York: Cambridge University Press.
Waldman, S. (2009), *Creative disruption: what you need to do to shake up your business in a digital world*, London: FT Prentice Hall.
Wegg-Prosser, V. (2001), 'Thirty years of managerial changes at the BBC', *Public Money and Management*, **21**(1), January–March, 9–14.
Weisberg, R.W. (1986), *Creativity: genius and other myths*, New York: Freeman.
Wetlaufer, S. (2000), 'Common sense and conflict: an interview with Disney's Michael Eisner', *Harvard Business Review*, January–February, 115–24.
Wolf, M.J. (1999) *The entertainment economy: how mega-media forces are transforming our lives*, New York: Times Books.
Yoffie, D.B. (ed.) (1997), *Competing in the age of digital convergence*, Boston: Harvard Business School Press.
Young, J.S. and W.L. Simon (2005), *Icon Steve Jobs: the greatest second act in the history of business*, New York: John Wiley.
Yukl, G.A. (2002), *Leadership in organizations*, 5th edition, Upper Saddle River, NJ: Prentice Hall.

11. Unleashed? Developing creativity-friendly leadership theory
Suze Wilson and Sarah Proctor-Thomson

All organisations, we are told these days, need more of two things: 1) strong leadership; 2) creativity. A closer look at influential leadership theories, however, quickly shows up their focus on leaders as the movers and shakers who drive new initiatives, while the role expected of followers is merely that of enthusiastic supporter. We think these leader-centric models are problematic given that, and as others in this volume have shown, fostering creativity in an organisation entails leaders embracing others' perspectives and allowing multiple parties to help shape the change agenda.

At a time when more and better leadership is sought as the solution for almost every problem, the possibility that leadership theory – and its potential flow-on effects to leadership practice – might sit in a relationship of conflict with enhanced creativity in organisations seems counterintuitive. Yet through tracing developments in thinking about leadership over the course of the last century, we show that central to the origins and assumptions of today's most influential leadership theories is a concern to ensure leader-driven control of employees which may be detrimental to creativity in organisations. To the extent that these theories inform practitioners' actions, leadership – as conventionally theorised at least – may in fact be a problem if our aim is to enhance creativity in organisations, rather than the solution we normally take it to be.

Thus, picking up where Lucy Küng left off in the previous chapter, we take a rather more critical approach in drawing the connections between extant leadership theory and the objective of enhancing creativity in our organisations. We propose an alternative set of underpinning assumptions to those we see informing dominant leadership theories today, thus repositioning leadership so it is more conducive to the promotion of creativity in organisations: leadership *for* creativity means tipping conventional assumptions on their head so that we:

- value creativity as a priority in the leader–follower relationship and the leadership process
- conceive of leadership as focused on unleashing others' creativity

- value follower agency and freedom to act and provide extensive scope for this
- assume follower creativity is as equally likely as leader creativity, and
- place a value on the free exchange of ideas and constructive critique as supporting mechanisms for creativity to flourish.

By privileging both creativity and followers as the focus of a creative leadership model, we see the leadership *process* as a facilitative mechanism, thus shifting attention away from the person of the leader and onto the individual and collective potential of the group. Heywood, Bilton and Cummings' case study of change at the RSC (Chapter 13) illuminates and expands on these assumptions, while Hall and Grant's chapter (Chapter 12) shows how we might go about developing leaders capable of both enacting creative leadership and leading creatively.

LOOKING BACKWARDS TO LOOK FORWARDS

In recent decades leadership has come to be understood as the potential panacea to much, if not all, that ails organisations and societies (Alvesson and Spicer 2011, Bolden et al. 2011). Leadership as THE solution has arisen at least in part in response to what was seen as the overly tight bureaucratic control of workers in earlier forms of management and organisation. Beginning from the late 1970s leadership in and of organisations has been associated with talk of 'vision' and 'transformation', of the creation of 'strong cultures' which reduce 'bureaucracy' to a bare minimum and in which employees are 'empowered' to achieve 'excellence' (e.g. Bennis and Nanus 1985, Burns 1978, Peters and Waterman 1982). Little wonder then that today we would simply presume more and better 'leadership' will result in more and better 'creativity'.

'Leadership' now carries with it connotations of a workplace where employees are both encouraged and allowed to give vent to their creative abilities and desires. For our part we accept there is ample evidence showing that employees managed from a distance, allowed autonomy and given the scope to explore new possibilities and question conventions tend to produce more and better innovations in services and products (Ryan 1992, Hesmondhalgh and Baker 2011). As others in this volume have highlighted, leadership enacting 'loose control', stimulation of ideas, promotion of teamwork and adequate recognition of creative workers provides the model for creative organisation (Amabile 1998). In turn, the leader's role in creativity becomes one of asking inspiring questions, seeking diverse perspectives and promoting teamwork and collaboration (Amabile 2008).

At first glance, dominant theories of leadership since the 1980s including 'transformational leadership' (with its intellectual stimulation, individualised consideration, inspirational motivation and idealised influence, Bass 1985a) – and 'authentic leadership' (with its self-knowledge, ethical standards of conduct, balanced processing of information and transparency, Walumbwa et al. 2008) appear to be well placed to lead creativity in contemporary organisations. Indeed recently, numerous research programmes have been developed based on the assumption of a natural link between transformational leadership and creativity (e.g. Cheung and Wong 2011, Jung et al. 2008, Zhang et al. 2011). However, we think this rather rosy picture is only a partial account of the relationship between 'leadership' and 'creativity'. The mainstream of leadership theorising may today be portrayed in words and phrases more acceptable to current sensibilities, yet we think a concern with control of others remains central to leadership theory – and potentially much leadership practice. To the extent that controlling another person's freedom of thought and action is detrimental to creativity, we therefore argue that the relationship between creativity and leadership, as conventionally theorised, may not be the easy marriage it is normally taken to be.

Our approach here builds on an assumption that discourses which claim to speak the truth constitute – when widely dispersed, accepted and acted upon – potent forces which shape our understanding and experience of the world and our very selves (Foucault 1977, 1979). Consequently, the study of such discourses offers us the opportunity to understand, reflect on and potentially resist the conventionally accepted wisdom that otherwise marks out the limits of what can be thought, spoken and done in the name of truth. Discourses on different truth topics arise in response to a phenomenon coming to be perceived as a 'problem' that requires attention, thus inviting inquiry into the emergence and development of ideas over time (ibid.). However, it is important to not only examine how discourses develop but also to explore what they do, in particular their effects for human subjectivity and relations of power between persons. By applying these methods of inquiry to leadership discourse we have found that a more ambiguous relationship between it and creativity emerges than is normally understood.

In what follows we begin by tracing the influence on today's dominant leadership theories of both the scientific management and human relations traditions of management theory, a heritage that has not previously been well understood. We show how these traditions gifted to modern leadership theory an orientation toward maintaining the unquestioned legitimacy of managerial authority and perfecting managerial control of employees.

We then turn to consider the underpinning assumptions and origins of visionary, transformational concepts of leadership which came to dominance in the mid-1980s and which remain highly influential today. We show how ideas underpinning this paradigm about the nature of 'leaders', 'followers' and their relationship are problematic in terms of fostering creativity, as they carry with them the effect of intensifying managerial control of employees.

We then assess a more recent theoretical development now rising to prominence in the field: authentic leadership theory. If a key priority for leadership in contemporary organisations is to foster creativity, we again find this approach of limited value. What our analysis of these limitations in extant theories leads us to is the uncovering of key assumptions which are needed to inform a model of leadership conducive to enhancing creativity.

We conclude by considering the potential impacts of these assumptions not only for enabling greater creativity but for changing our understanding of leaders, followers and the leadership process.

DEVELOPMENTS IN (MOSTLY AMERICAN) LEADERSHIP THEORY

Pre-1980s

Though it may seem surprising to us now, in the early part of the twentieth century 'leadership' was not connected to talk about organisational performance (Huczynski and Buchanan 2006, Parry and Bryman 2006, Wren 2005). At this time, largely US-based leadership researchers focused on identifying the traits of leaders by studying youth groups and students. Some of this early research sought to confirm the hypothesis that leadership was an inherited capacity, with influential leadership researchers such as Sir Francis Galton active in the then popular eugenics movement. Meanwhile, and quite separately, management theorists' focus was on controlling the bodies of workers via Taylorist techniques and ensuring management made decisions on 'rational' grounds, pursuant to Fayol's principles of management (Fayol 1930, Huczynski and Buchanan 2006, Parry and Bryman 2006, Taylor 1919). This early stage of organisation science sought to bring data, logic and 'reason' into the workplace and emphasised values of productivity, orderliness and efficiency (e.g. Fayol 1930, Taylor 1919). However, even in the 'land of opportunity', the 'scientific' division of labour promoted by Taylor and his supporters carried with it a division of rights, privileges and status which rendered workers subservient to management (Huczynski and Buchanan 2006, Wren 2005). Maintaining the desired subservience in the face of worker resistance was thus a key 'problem' that early management theorists sought to address (Bruce 2006, Bruce and Nyland 2011).

By the 1930s Mayo et al.'s human relations perspective began challenging the scientific management paradigm by posing an alternative set of means for achieving the same overall end (Bruce and Nyland 2011, Wren 2005). The earlier concern of scientific management to control worker bodies was however now widened to one of a general interest in securing their ready compliance with management wishes (Bruce and Nyland 2011, Huczynski and Buchanan 2006). The focus of human relations research at this time was on supervisory behaviours as the key labour–management interface and it aimed to enhance productivity and reduce labour–management friction while retaining the privileged status of management know-how and authority (Bruce and Nyland 2011, Huczynski and Buchanan 2006, Wren 2005). An underlying political concern was to eliminate the influence of unions and the perceived associated risk of socialism, with Mayo's research being backed by elites such as Rockefeller, who held that the interests of big business would be better served by the human relations approach (Bruce and Nyland 2011).

The connection between 'leadership' and 'management' in theoretical and research terms is largely a post-Second World War development, although it had of course attracted some limited interest prior to this time (e.g. Gowin 1915, 1918). However, quite suddenly in the late 1940s, leadership researchers shifted their focus away from identifying leader traits and started focusing on supervisory behaviours. While Stogdill's (1948) review of trait-based research is typically credited with bringing about this change, we suggest that a post-war antagonism toward ideas of inherited superiority was influential in shifting research attention to the much 'safer' territory of observable behaviour. Around this time in influential studies at Michigan and Ohio State Universities the supervisory work of managers was thus relabelled and reconceptualised as 'leadership', and research began aiming to identify and prescribe the most effective supervisory 'leadership' behaviours (Fleishman 1953a, Huczynski and Buchanan 2006, Parry and Bryman 2006). This work was directly informed by developments in management theory: Fleishman, who participated in the Ohio State studies, explicitly acknowledged the notion of 'consideration' used in the Ohio leadership model was a concept which 'comes closest to representing the "human relations" approach toward group members' (1953b: 154).

In entering into the workplace, leadership research adopted the same orientation of management research more generally: a presumption in the 'natural' authority of management in decision-making, the design of the work environment and the controlling and directing of others (Bruce and Nyland 2011, Reed 2006). Subsequent developments in the field through to the 1980s, adopting contingent rather than universal prescriptions for supervisory/leadership behaviours, maintained this managerialist perspective (Huczynski and Buchanan 2006, Parry and Bryman 2006).

Through to about the 1980s talk about 'leadership' was typically focused on supervisory behaviour. Even Mintzberg's (1973) influential study on managerial work only treated leadership as just one aspect of a CEO's role. Thus the primary focus of leadership research from around the 1940s through to the 1980s was control of operational-level employees, through supervisory behaviours that would solicit worker co-operation rather than dissent.

VISIONARY, TRANSFORMATIONAL LEADERSHIP: A NEW PARADIGM

By the mid-1980s a new conception of leadership had emerged and has since come to dominate mainstream leadership theory (Jackson and Parry 2011, Hunt 1999, Parry and Bryman 2006). This paradigm positioned leadership as the purview of those at the top of organisations and tied leadership closely to issues of strategy, vision, transformational change and the shaping of organisational culture. Early texts by a small set of key authors have shaped transformational leadership studies and continue to underpin this field today (e.g. Burns 1978, Bass 1985a, Bass and Avolio 1997, Bennis and Nanus 1985).

In this visionary, transformational conception of leadership (VTL), 'management' and 'managers' were rendered dull, orthodox and concerned with routine matters, while 'leadership' and 'leaders' were rendered extraordinary but essential to organisational survival and success (Bass 1985a, Bennis and Nanus 1985, Zaleznik 1977). Leadership became essentially synonymous with the role of senior management and with the persona of a successful senior manager.

A notable feature of the elevation of 'leadership' from the low and rather prosaic level of 'supervisory behaviours' through to the visionary transformational agent is that the concept of leadership changed from being a set of behaviours (e.g. Fleishman 1953a, 1953b) to something now understood as vested in and emanating from a human subject (e.g. Burns 1978, Bass 1985a). This subject in turn was understood as having an underlying personality and a set of values and goals which effectively compels them to act in a leaderful manner (e.g. Bass 1985a, Bennis and Nanus 1985, Peters and Austin 1985). For leadership theory this was in many ways 'back to the future', because trait theory also presumed an intentional subject 'behind' the observed 'traits' in a manner that was, from the late 1940s through to the 1980s, largely absent from leadership theory.

This return to a focus on the leader as a knowing, intentional subject in leadership theory offers a conception of leadership highly appealing to cultural norms which privilege individual action and individual interests: systemic inequality, collective values and impersonal structural forces are rendered largely invisible in such a perspective (Fletcher 2004). It offers a human face allowing all-comers the opportunity to 'try on' (at least in our imagination) the idealised leader persona in a way that conceptualising leadership as 'supervisory behaviours' simply did not encourage. By situating leadership back in 'the self' of the leader, albeit while claiming to conceive of leadership as a process, these developments simultaneously democratise leadership as something open to everyone at the same time as leadership is rendered the work of the elite whose position in the organisational hierarchy provides them with strategic responsibilities.

A much expanded scope of managerial control is encouraged in this 'new' conception of leadership, which remains the dominant perspective even today (Jackson and Parry 2011). Followers' minds and sense of self now come within the purview of leader-manager attention, as leader-managers are encouraged to 'manage meaning', instil appropriate values, promote self-belief and self-development in followers and in all ways ensure that followers put aside personal interests in favour of corporate interests (Burns 1978, Bennis and Nanus 1985, Smircich and Morgan 1982). Followers' ideas about 'who rules and by what means; the workgroup norms, as well as ultimate beliefs about religion, ideology, morality, ethics, space, time, and human nature' are here passed over for leaders to mould as they see fit, given their allegedly superior vision (Bass 1985a: 24).

The recommended techniques of leadership comprise encouragement, challenge, the presentation of the leader as a role model for followers to emulate, as well as the use of corrective feedback when followers fail to meet the leader's expectations (Bass 1985a, Bennis and Nanus 1985, Peters and Austin 1985). These mechanisms of control are almost always subtle, yet their expected persistence coupled with the intrusion into the follower's sense of reality, values and of self could hardly be more complete. Any act of resistance in this conception of leadership can be readily pathologised as arising from follower inadequacy or bad intent, because the unitarist assumption of common interest between leader and follower has been so deeply entwined with the managerialist assumption of the legitimacy and primacy of managerial interests.

The implications of the VTL concept for how leaders are to understand themselves are multifaceted. Change is said to be a compulsive requirement for leaders while routine work and matters of detail are an anathema, as they distract from the visionary focus that is said to be the hallmark of effective leadership (e.g. Bass 1985a, 1985b, Peters and Austin 1985). Leaders are expected to have unwavering confidence in their own abilities, possessing an 'inner strength' which compels them to act, without any scope for doubt (e.g. Bass 1985a, Bennis and Nanus 1985). The leader is expected to see further ahead than others, interpret with greater insight and explore possibilities more boldly and creatively (e.g. Peters and Waterman 1982, Bennis and Nanus 1985). In this paradigm leaders are associated with all that is good, desirable, effective and important and thus by implication distanced from all that is mediocre or bad, ineffective, mundane or modest.

In dealing with followers leaders are, according to the VTL paradigm, expected to connect with *their* values: at the same time it is asserted that followers' values are, in the absence of the leader's intervention, naturally self-serving (Burns 1978, Bass 1985a). In fact, followers are generally portrayed by proponents of VTL as persons of unrealised potential pending the leader's guidance and incitement to a course of action (e.g. Burns 1978, Bass 1985a, Peters and Waterman 1982). This passivity is, of course, a perfect counterweight to the energy of the leader as conveyed in this paradigm. This kind of dualistic thinking is in fact pervasive throughout this conception of leaders and followers. Table 11.1 identifies some of these dualities.

Table 11.1   Leader/follower dualities in VTL paradigm

Leader	Follower
● active	● passive
● motivator of others	● needs to be motivated
● serves the common good	● naturally self-serving unless leader provides guidance
● visionary	● has no vision
● bold	● cautious
● seeks to develop self and others to highest potential	● needs significant guidance to develop self to highest potential
● strategic thinker	● operational do-er

The implications of the VTL model for promoting greater creativity in organisations are concerning. By vesting such agency in the hands of leaders to determine reality, values and priorities, it remains for followers simply to execute the vision by following the agenda set by the leader. The dynamic of the leader–follower relationship conveyed by the VTL discourse positions leaders as the creative source of new visions and possibilities to which others merely respond.

However, the depiction of followers here compared with the depiction of creative workers in other literatures is one of stark contradictions. In his study of media work, Mark Deuze (2011) describes creative workers as passionate, pioneering, entrepreneurial and profoundly and emotionally tied to their work. Genius, relentless ambition, innovation and internal drive also endure as descriptions of workers across creative spheres including advertising, music and beyond (Bilton and Leary 2002, Nixon 2003, Negus and Pickering 2004).

Thus, the discursive attempt in the VTL literature to render followers passive and reactive is highly problematic for it encourages leaders to regard themselves as superior beings. Simultaneously, it places enormous pressure on leaders to function at super-human levels. This conception of leadership places such primacy on the leader as the centre of action that it results in a turning away from and a silencing of the creative capability of all others.

This shift in thinking about the nature of leadership emerged at a time when America had benefitted in recent decades from leaders whose visionary and charismatic approach had attracted strong support and who were widely perceived as bringing about major social change (e.g. Martin Luther King, Malcolm X, John F. Kennedy). America's post-Second World War economic dominance had also at this time come under such sustained challenge that the perception of the need for fundamental change in American business was widespread (Magaziner and Reich 1982, Peters and Waterman 1982). Meanwhile, the effects of the 1960s' counter-culture, along with the loss of confidence in political leadership arising from Watergate and the Vietnam War, also combined to help give rise to an environment in which traditional, positional authority no longer carried the same influence and respect as it had before (Ackerman 1975, Capitman 1973, Heath 1975, Roos 1972). For some commentators of the time, 'management' had come to imply authoritarian, conservative, rule-bound and inflexible modes of interaction (e.g. Cornuelle 1975, Peters and Waterman 1982). In the context of a culture long receptive to stories of heroic individual achievement, all of these factors coalesced to produce an environment open to this new conception of leadership.

Tasking leaders with the requirement of bringing about change, which is the central proposition of the VTL paradigm, means it is little wonder that we have now come to associate 'leadership' with 'creativity', insofar as change requires creative thinking. However, as our analysis of the key claims and assumptions embedded in the VTL paradigm has shown, this relationship is problematic insofar as it is the leader's assumed creativity which is emphasised, while followers' potential for creativity is obscured. There is little in this paradigm which encourages leaders to seek out others' creative potential, much less to defer to that. There is little sense of a two-way dialogue wherein followers' ideas bring about a change in the leader's vision; instead, the influence process is generally conceived as flowing one way, from the leader to the led (e.g. Bass 1985a, Peters and Waterman 1982).

The notion of 'empowerment' is a common feature of these texts and does mark an important shift from earlier thinking (e.g. Bennis and Nanus 1985, Peters and Austin 1985). However, we think it also important not to overlook the fact that the intended scope and focus of followers' freedom to act is still expected to be prescribed unilaterally by the leader and to be consistent with the vision, values and culture the leader has chosen for the group (e.g. Bass 1985a, Peters and Waterman 1982). The leash may have been let out; however, the leader still determines its length and retains the right to tug upon it at any time.

A further factor in the relationship between this leadership paradigm and creativity is the strong performativity orientation of this conception of leadership. The performativity that is sought from and by leaders in the VTL model is strongly aligned with the interests of capital in expanding markets, developing new products and services, and increasing productivity and profitability (e.g. Bass 1985a, 1985b, Peters and Waterman 1982, Kotter 1988). Consequently leaders who subscribe to this paradigm will likely encourage creativity only to the extent that it serves these interests and not for its own sake or for the sake of conflicting interests. This effect need not be understood as inherently problematic or venal, but it does nonetheless mean that the relationship between 'leadership' and 'creativity' in this model is one that functions within the constraints of that which is understood as serving business interests and is thus a limited relationship. If the aim is to value creativity for its own sake then adherents to the VTL paradigm are unlikely to act in support of such an outcome.

While the VTL model continues even today to dominate both scholarly and popular notions of leadership, over the last decade 'authentic leadership' (AL) has emerged as a new focus of scholarly research and practitioner action. Again, we think that the underpinning assumptions and key claims of this paradigm warrant scrutiny for their potential impacts on creativity in organisations, so we now turn to consider this recent development in leadership thinking.

AUTHENTIC LEADERSHIP

In recent years new, less leader-centric models such as distributed leadership (e.g. Gronn 2002) and relational leadership (Uhl-Bien 2006) have developed and established some support. Indeed, theoretical proliferation is now a marked feature of the leadership studies field, with Grint (2005) arguing that leadership is an 'essentially contested concept'. However, amongst the various new theories competing for attention and support, authentic leadership appears at this stage to be making particular ground (Jackson and Parry 2011, Ladkin and Taylor 2010).

Early advocates of authentic leadership theory include highly respected and influential scholars Bruce Avolio, Fred Luthans and John Gardner (see, for example, Luthans and Avolio 2003, Gardner et al. 2005). Seeking to respond to the examples of corruption and malfeasance by high-profile leaders such as Jeffrey Skilling of Enron, authentic leadership theory was early positioned as offering an increased focus on leader ethics: this connection to a matter of great contemporary salience along with the high standing of its early advocates has been crucial in advancing its development, despite the very limited number of empirical studies yet undertaken to test this theory (Jackson and Parry 2011).

While there is ongoing debate amongst proponents of AL as to its precise componentry and functioning, Walumbwa et al. (2008) have influentially argued it comprises four key elements: knowing oneself; using one's own moral compass; considering information in a balanced fashion; and taking a transparent approach to dealing with others. As with VTL, this model also positions a knowing, intentional subject at the centre of its conception of leadership; however, so-called authentic leaders are depicted as persons who are rather more down-to-earth than their charismatic, visionary predecessors (e.g. Avolio and Gardner 2005, Luthans and Avolio 2003, George and Sims 2007). The promise of 'authentic leadership' is that leaders act in accordance with their 'true' values and beliefs when leading others (e.g. Avolio and Gardner 2005, George and Sims 2007, Walumbwa et al. 2008). The silent opposite of 'inauthentic leadership' which this model conjures up is implicitly expected to be overcome by the more morally virtuous notion of leadership it claims to offer. This development does constitute a concerted scholarly effort to challenge the seemingly never-ending cases of corporate corruption, often by those previously lauded for their visionary and transformational leadership. Responding to this, leader ethics constitutes a central concern of the AL paradigm, in the same way that leading change was the central concern of the VTL paradigm, this in turn being a response to conditions prevailing at the time of its emergence. However, this move does leave unasked and unanswered the question of whether what has occurred constitutes a perversion of VTL or, more concerning, a predictable consequence of a model which credited leaders with such extensive powers (Tourish and Vatcha 2005).

[handwritten margin note: AL assumption Leader = Org goals]

The implicit assumption made by proponents of AL is that leaders' values will simply align with organisational interests (Ford and Harding 2011). In this regard the performativity constraints which we noted earlier limit VTL adherents to act only in accordance with business interests apply also to adherents of AL. These performativity demands, however, are somewhat 'softened': in 'relating transparently' to others AL prescribes a less utilitarian orientation than that of VTL (e.g. Walumbwa et al. 2008). It also places a greater emphasis on the intrinsic worth of each party to the leader–follower relationships and the value of non-coercive modes of interaction between persons than does VTL.

The model suggests a greater emphasis on relationships, leader accessibility and egalitarian values, narrowing the status distance that was implied between leaders and followers in the VTL paradigm. These shifts in thinking are potentially democratising in nature when compared with the depiction of visionary and transformational leaders as persons of almost magical abilities. Not only is the power imbalance between leaders and followers potentially reduced in rendering the leader persona less grandiose, the sense of 'common decency' embedded in the AL concept in turn suggests that leadership is something truly open to all (e.g. Avolio and Gardner 2005, George and Sims 2007, Luthans and Avolio 2003).

The mechanism of control in AL appears to work in the opposite direction to that of VTL, where the leader articulates the vision and then seeks to propel followers toward the achievement of that vision. In AL, however, it is the leader's very self which is said to be the source of attraction, with followers drawn toward the leader as a role model which they seek to emulate (e.g. Luthans and Avolio 2003, Walumbwa et al. 2008). Consequently, if VTL entails the leader *pushing* followers toward the leader's vision, then AL entails the leader *pulling* followers towards themselves as the template for replication. Despite this difference, however, the desired scope of control in AL remains as extensive as that of the VTL paradigm: authentic leaders too are to work on followers' sense of self to bring it into line with a standard determined acceptable by the leader, which in turn implies a standard acceptable to the commercial interests of the organisation (e.g. Avolio and Gardner 2005, George and Sims 2007, Walumbwa et al. 2008).

The leader subject as presented in the AL paradigm is one where it is solidity and stability of character and 'common decency' which warrants our appreciation and support. Authentic leaders are said to be 'confident, hopeful, optimistic, resilient, transparent, moral/ethical future oriented' persons (Luthans and Avolio 2003: 243). To the extent that these characteristics are conducive to creating an environment wherein new or different ideas can be openly considered, the relationship between AL and creativity would seem to be positive.

The other implications of the AL model for creativity are, however, less compelling. 'Leader self-knowledge', one of Walumbwa et al.'s (2008) four key components of AL, implies that leaders will at least understand their own creative predilections or lack thereof. However, whether that implies action to promote creativity in oneself or others is rather less certain. 'Using one's own moral compass', Walumbwa et al.'s (2008) second factor, seems to suggest no specific implications unless the leader's moral framework is especially pro or anti the moral worth of creativity. The third factor of 'balanced processing of information' (Walumbwa et al. 2008) implies creative ideas will be tested for the logical, practical, financial or other effects and will be neither automatically displaced nor privileged. Finally, transparency in relating to others (Walumbwa et al. 2008) implies that followers' creativity will be acknowledged and respected; however, whether it will attract active leader support seems less clear. Overall, creativity does not strongly feature as a value or priority in its own right or as a key attribute of leaders in the AL paradigm, suggesting that at best the linkage is fairly weak.

CONCLUSION AND IMPLICATIONS

In comparing the relationship between creativity and influential leadership theory in the form of VTL and AL, the key claims and assumptions of each paradigm and their potential effects are summarised in Table 11.2. What our analysis reveals is that the apparently strong and straightforward connection we have come to typically make between 'leadership' and 'creativity' is rather more vexed. Under a VTL paradigm, creativity is certainly prioritised so long as it has commercial value. But this model would have us rely exclusively on the leader's creativity and tends to downplay the potential creativity of followers, who are regarded as 'inherently' passive and deficient. In contrast, AL appears to imply an environment somewhat more conducive to follower creativity, yet creativity is not here positioned as a priority for leader and follower attention. Moreover, all four elements of Walumbwa et al.'s (2008) influential model of AL seem

Table 11.2   Comparison of the VTL and AL paradigms' relationship with creativity

Visionary, transformational leadership	Authentic leadership
Visionary capability of leader implies they are personally creative	Authentic leader characteristics seem conducive to an environment that is open to creativity
Strong emphasis on leader-driven change as the core of leadership, which also implies leader is personally creative	Walumbwa et al.'s model appears to suggest weak connections between AL and creativity
Strong emphasis on the value and broad scope of leader-initiated action, which in turn limits followers' scope of action and hence freedom to create	Softer performativity focus and less grandiose leader persona open up more space for follower input than is implied in VTL paradigm, which in turn may be positive for creativity
Assumes business interests take priority, hence interest in creativity is shaped by commercial considerations	Assumes business interests take priority, hence interest in creativity is shaped by commercial considerations
Positions followers as passive, reactive and naturally self-serving; implies follower creativity is either limited or irrelevant (unless directed by the leader)	Creativity not featured as a key concern, possibly implying a fairly neutral stance as to its value. Leader ethics is the primary concern

likely to have limited positive effects for workplace creativity. All in all the choices on offer, at least according to the mainstream of scholarly and popular depictions of leadership, are a heavy if not exclusive reliance on leader creativity which relatedly constrains follower creativity, or, alternatively, a fairly diffident view of creativity by leaders more focused on acting in a commercially viable yet still ethical way.

Moreover, if we assume a workplace populated by knowledgeable professionals who are motivated by intellectually stimulating work and peer respect, and who are cognisant of the organisational and market imperatives that will sustain the enterprise, much of the 'work' of leadership as conceived by proponents of both VTL and AL seems surplus to requirements. Instead a focus on group facilitation to sustain an environment conducive to individual and collective creativity would seem to be the priority.

To forge a stronger relationship between leadership and creativity we advocate for the re-conceptualisation of leadership guided by the following key assumptions:

- value creativity as a priority in the leader–follower relationship and the leadership process
- conceive of leadership as focused on facilitating others' creativity
- value follower agency and freedom to act and provide extensive scope for this
- assume follower creativity is as equally likely as leader creativity
- place a value on the free exchange of ideas and constructive critique as supporting mechanisms for creativity to flourish.

These elements constitute a dramatic shift in assumptions and values from the extant leadership models we have considered, suggesting that there is much that could be changed in terms of 'leadership' that would better support 'creativity' in our organisations. This alternative approach calls for different leader and follower behaviours and different values and priorities such that leadership functions to encourage, unleash and sustain creativity. Here, it is creativity rather than the leader that is privileged as the source of future value, while both followers and leaders alike are conceived as equally likely to make a creative contribution. Thus, it is through the interaction of followers and leaders that enhanced creativity might be achieved.

Theorising leadership as primarily a facilitative function would shift our focus to *process* rather than the attributes of the person facilitating the process. Such a facilitative role would involve aspects identified as central to the promotion of creative production in Küng's previous chapter and elsewhere (e.g. Amabile 1998, Hesmondhalgh and Baker 2011), including: posing stimulating creative challenges; mobilising fruitful networks of relationships; providing appropriate resources; ensuring worker autonomy and ownership of creative ideas and outputs. A conception of leadership which focuses on its facilitative functions also offers a model in which the holding of a formal position becomes a secondary consideration, thus embedding a more egalitarian assumption into our understanding of 'leadership'.

However, we also acknowledge that calling this facilitative work 'leadership' risks dragging in these extant conceptualisations which were clearly intended to deal with different needs and priorities and reflect different values. If creativity is indeed the most vital source material from which our organisations will sustain their ability to produce goods and services of value in the future, it is certainly critical that we think creatively about 'leadership' and what role, if any, we want it to play. As our analysis has shown, treating 'leadership' as inevitably necessary and automatically desirable is an assumption that demands greater scrutiny.

Looking forward, we suggest that organisations seeking to unleash the creative potential in their workforce would do well to carefully articulate what model, theory or conceptualisation of leadership, if any, they wish to promote. This is because, as our analysis has shown, influential notions of leadership as visionary, transformational or authentic do not readily lend themselves to the promotion of greater creativity.

Re-conceptualising leadership as fundamentally a facilitative function, as we propose, re-orients attention away from the person of the leader. By removing an idealised and prescribed identity script from our conception of leadership, this approach opens up a space for all persons to consider their leadership contribution in terms of how they can support their colleagues to achieve shared goals. In this, the presumption of control and superiority over others embedded in previous models is also removed. Leadership development in this approach would then necessarily shift away from developing star leaders to the promotion and formation of leadership constellations of multiple actors, or as Heywood et al. later describe in this volume (Chapter 13), leadership 'ensembles'.

By focusing on process, attention also goes to the very enactment of the creative effort, the experience of individual or collective struggle and resolution in solving a problem which lies at the heart of every creative breakthrough. Brilliant, exceptional individuals will, we think, always lead and inspire us with their unexpected insights and inventions. However, organisations whose very survival is reliant on consistently innovating their way forward would do well to consider how to unleash the creative potential of the great majority by adopting a leadership model which is not dependent on the exceptional individual.

QUESTIONS FOR DISCUSSION

1. Why has the study of leadership risen to such prominence in recent years?
2. Is the notion of leading others to be more creative a paradox? If so, how could this paradox best be managed?
3. Outline a set of three creative people that you most admire. Outline a set of three leaders you most admire. Outline a set of the creative leaders you most admire. Is there any overlap in the people in each of your three sets? If so, what are the characteristics of the people who appear in more than one set? Could you build a theory of creative leadership from these characteristics?

REFERENCES

Ackerman, R.W. (1975), *The social challenge to business*, Cambridge, MA: Harvard University Press.

Alvesson, M. and A. Spicer (eds) (2011), *Metaphors we lead by*, Abingdon, UK: Routledge.

Amabile, T.M. (1998), 'How to kill creativity', *Harvard Business Review*, **76**(5), 76–87.

Amabile, T. (2008), 'Creativity and the role of the leader', *Harvard Business Review*, **86**(10), 100–109.

Avolio, B.J. and W. Gardner (2005), 'Authentic leadership development: getting to the root of positive forms of leadership', *The Leadership Quarterly*, **16**, 315–38.

Bass, B.M. (1985a), *Leadership and performance beyond expectations*, New York: Free Press.

Bass, B.M. (1985b), 'Leadership: Good, better, best', *Organizational Dynamics*, **13**(3), 26–40.

Bass, B.M. and B. Avolio (1997), *Full-range of leadership development: Manual for the Multifactor Leadership Questionnaire*, Palo Alto, CA: Mind Garden.

Bennis, W.G. and B. Nanus (1985), *Leaders: The strategies for taking charge*, New York: Harper & Row.

Bilton, C. and R. Leary (2002), 'What can managers do for creativity? Brokering creativity in the creative industries', *International Journal of Cultural Policy*, **8**(1), 49–64.

Bolden, R., B. Hawkins, J. Gosling and S. Taylor (2011), *Exploring leadership: Individual, organizational and societal perspectives*, Oxford: Oxford University Press.

Bruce, K. (2006), 'Henry S. Dennison, Elton Mayo, and Human Relations historiography', *Management and Organizational History*, **1**(2), 177–99.

Bruce, K. and C. Nyland (2011), 'Elton Mayo and the deification of human relations', *Organization Studies*, **32**(3), 383–405.

Burns, J.M. (1978), *Leadership*, New York: Harper & Row.

Capitman, W.G. (1973), *Panic in the boardroom: New social realities shake old corporate structures*, Garden City, NY: Anchor Press/Doubleday.

Cheung, M. and C.S. Wong (2011), 'Transformational leadership, leader support, and employee creativity', *Leadership and Organization Development Journal*, **32**(7), 656–72.

Cornuelle, R. (1975), *De-Managing America: The final revolution*, New York: Random House.

Deuze, M. (ed.) (2011), *Managing media work*, Los Angeles: Sage.

Fayol, H. (1930), *Industrial and general administration* (J.A. Coubrough, trans.), London: Pitman.

Fleishman, E.A. (1953a), 'The description of supervisory behaviour', *Journal of Applied Psychology*, **37**(1), 1–6.

Fleishman, E.A. (1953b), 'The measurement of leadership attitudes in industry', *Journal of Applied Psychology*, **37**(3), 153–8.

Fletcher, J.K. (2004), 'The paradox of postheroic leadership: An essay on gender, power, and transformational change', *The Leadership Quarterly*, **15**(5), 647–61.

Ford, J. and N. Harding (2011), 'The impossibility of the "true self" of authentic leadership', *Leadership*, **7**(4), 463–79.

Foucault, M. (1977), *Discipline and punish: The birth of the prison*, New York: Vantage Books.

Foucault, M. (1979), *The history of sexuality* (Vol. 1), London: Allen Lane.

Gardner, W.L., B.J. Avolio and F.O. Walumbwa (2005), 'Authentic leadership development: Emergent themes and future directions', in W.L. Gardner, B.J. Avolio and F.O. Walumbwa (eds), *Authentic leadership theory and practice: origins, effects and development*, London: Elsevier, pp. 387–406.

George, B. and P. Sims (2007), *True north: Discover your authentic leadership*, San Francisco: Jossey Bass.

Gowin, E.B. (1915), *The executive and his control of men; a study in personal efficiency*, New York: The Macmillan Company.

Gowin, E.B. (1918), *The selection and training of the business executive*, New York: The Macmillan Company.

Grint, K. (2005), *Leadership: Limits and possibilities*, Basingstoke: Palgrave Macmillan.
Gronn, P. (2002), 'Distributed leadership as a unit of analysis', *The Leadership Quarterly*, **13**(4), 423–51.
Heath, J.F. (1975), *Decade of disillusionment: The Kennedy-Johnson years*, Bloomington: Indiana University Press.
Hesmondhalgh, D. and S. Baker (2011), *Creative labour: Media work in three cultural industries*, Basingstoke: Routledge.
Huczynski, A. and D. Buchanan (2006), *Organizational Behaviour*, New York: Prentice-Hall.
Hunt, J.G. (1999), 'Transformational/charismatic leadership's transformation of the field: An historical essay', *The Leadership Quarterly*, **10**(2), 129–44.
Jackson, B. and K. Parry (2011), *A very short, fairly interesting and reasonably cheap book about studying leadership* (2nd ed.), London: Sage.
Jung, D., A. Wu and C.W. Chow (2008), 'Towards understanding the direct and indirect effects of CEOs' transformational leadership on firm innovation', *The Leadership Quarterly*, **19**(5), 582–94.
Kotter, J.P. (1988), *The leadership factor*, New York: Free Press.
Ladkin, D. and S.V. Taylor (2010), 'Enacting the "true self": Towards a theory of embodied authentic leadership', *The Leadership Quarterly*, **21**(1), 64–74.
Luthans, F. and B.J. Avolio (2003), 'Authentic leadership: A positive developmental approach', in K.S. Cameron, J.E. Dutton and R.E. Quinn (eds), *Positive organizational scholarship* (pp. 241–61), San Francisco: Berrett-Koehler.
Magaziner, I.C. and R.B. Reich (1982), *Minding America's business: The decline and rise of the American economy*, New York: Harcourt Brace Jovanovich.
Mintzberg, H. (1973), *The nature of managerial work*, New York: Harper & Row.
Negus, K. and M. Pickering (2004), *Creativity, communication and cultural value*, London: Sage.
Nixon, S. (2003), *Advertising cultures: Gender, commerce, creativity*, London: Sage.
Parry, K.W. and A. Bryman (2006), 'Leadership in organizations', in S.R. Clegg, C. Hardy, T.B. Lawrence and W.R. Nord (eds), *The Sage Handbook of Organization Studies* (2nd ed., pp. 447–68), London: Sage.
Peters, T. and N. Austin (1985), *A passion for excellence: The leadership difference*, New York: HarperCollins.
Peters, T.J. and R.H. Waterman (1982), *In search of excellence: Lessons from America's best-run companies*, Sydney: Harper & Row.
Reed, M. (2006), 'Organizational theorizing: A historically contested terrain', in S.R. Clegg, C. Hardy, T.B. Lawrence and W.R. Nord (eds), *The Sage Handbook of Organization Studies* (2nd ed., pp. 19–54), London: Sage.
Roos, J. (1972), 'American political life in the 60s: Change, recurrence and revolution', in R. Weber (ed.), *America in change: Reflections on the 60s and 70s*, Notre Dame: University of Notre Dame Press.
Ryan, B. (1992), *Making capital from culture*, Berlin: Walter de Gruyter.
Smircich, L. and G. Morgan (1982), 'Leadership: The management of meaning', *The Journal of Applied Behavioural Science*, **18**(3), 257–73.
Stogdill, R. (1948), 'Personal factors associated with leadership: A survey of the literature', *Journal of Psychology*, **25**, 35–71.
Taylor, F.S. (1919), *The principles of scientific management*, New York: Harper & Brothers.
Tourish, D. and N. Vatcha (2005), 'Charismatic leadership and corporate cultism at Enron: the elimination of dissent, the promotion of conformity and organizational collapse', *Leadership*, **1**(4), 455–80.
Uhl-Bien, M. (2006), 'Relational leadership: Exploring the social processes of leadership and organising', *The Leadership Quarterly*, **17**(6), 654–76.
Walumbwa, F.O., B.J. Avolio, W.L. Gardner, T.S. Wernsign and S.J. Peterson (2008), 'Authentic leadership: Development and validation of a theory-based measure', *Journal of Management*, **34**, 89–126.
Wren, D.A. (2005), *The history of management thought* (5th ed.), Hoboken, NJ: Wiley.

Zaleznik, A. (1977), 'Managers and leaders: Are they different?', *Harvard Business Review*, **55**(5), 67–80.

Zhang, A.Y., A.S. Tsui and D.X. Wang (2011), 'Leadership behaviors and group creativity in Chinese organizations: The role of group processes', *The Leadership Quarterly*, **22**(5), 851–62.

12. Creativity in leadership development
Richard Hall and David Grant

Both business leadership and management education have come under increasing scrutiny and been the subject of extensive criticism over the past decade. In terms of leadership, there has been widespread talk of a crisis of leadership (Salaman 2011), the ascendency in contemporary business of a 'crude impoverished form of leadership' (Stern 2010), and of the corrosive effects of the heroic, celebrity CEOs who came to prominence in many high-profile corporations in the 1990s. After briefly surveying the experiences of Enron under Jeffrey Skilling, Rakesh Khurana wrote that: 'Today we stand at a crossroads where, it would seem, many corporations would do well to reconsider their models of leadership and ways of choosing leaders' (Khurana 2002: xi). In terms of management education there has been a sustained debate about, and strong critique of, the role of business schools and their MBAs in particular. Business schools have been criticised for being out of touch, for contributing to unethical business practices and for an overly narrow view of the role and responsibilities of business (Starkey et al. 2004, Bennis and O'Toole 2005, Podolny 2009). MBAs have been criticised for being overly theoretical, too focused on technical skills to the relative exclusion of generic skills and attributes and too fragmented in their approach, lacking a sufficient emphasis on integrated and practical application. The result, it is claimed, has been graduates who are too narrow in terms of their perspective, too fixated on short-term financial results and too dismissive of the role of values, ethics and other voices in business and the organisation (Mintzberg 2004, Datar et al. 2010).

Some, of course, have connected a narrow and technical MBA curriculum with the failings of contemporary business leaders.

> Combine agency theory with transaction costs economics, add in standard versions of game theory and negotiations analysis, and the picture of the manager that emerges is one that is now very familiar in practice: the ruthlessly hard-driving, strictly top-down, command-and-control focused, shareholder-value-obsessed, win-at-any-cost business leaders of which Scott Paper's 'Chainsaw' Al Dunlap and Tyco's Dennis Koslowski are only the most extreme examples (Ghoshal 2005: 85).

Evidently, this all puts a lot of pressure on leadership development – placed as it is at the very intersection of contemporary and future leadership practice and management education. Despite all the criticism, organisations show little reduction in their appetite for leadership development, although there may be increasing uncertainty as to what good leadership and good leadership development is. We might characterise the context of leadership development as one of flux, dynamism and scepticism, in which there is general consensus that established models are deficient, but little consensus as to better or best models or approaches for the future.

It was in this context, in 2007, that we were given the opportunity to develop a new approach and programme of leadership development as a key part of a new MBA programme. As academics with research backgrounds in the fields of organisation studies and management, rather than leadership studies *per se*, presented with something akin to a blank slate and without an existing legacy product or existing institutional commitment to a particular model, a degree of creativity was inevitable in this project. In one sense, then, this chapter invokes the notion of 'creativity in leadership development' as meaning innovation in our development of a new and relatively novel curriculum and programme in the area of leadership. There was a very clear expectation of product innovation (the programme needed to be very different from existing programmes offered in the market) and there was a very clear need for process innovation (the institution had no recent experience in the development, from the ground up, of a highly innovative programme of this kind in management education). A demand for creativity in this sense was clear: in terms of the celebrated formulation of creativity as being defined as both novel and useful (Sternberg 1999, Sawyer 2006), the first expectation was a high degree of novelty accompanied by genuine openness as to the content of the programme, and the second expectation was that the programme had to be successful, in the sense that it had to be rated as valuable and useful by participants.

This chapter speaks to the idea of 'creativity in leadership development' in a second sense also: the aspiration to design and deliver a programme that contributed to more creative leadership and more creative leaders. We certainly see leadership which is able to encourage and stimulate greater organisational creativity as embodied in these notions of 'creative leadership' and 'creative leaders' – in other words, leadership *for* creativity and innovation is seen as part of 'creative leadership'.

Having said that, 'creative leadership' was not an organising theme or leitmotif for the programme; this is not, and was never intended to be, a programme in creative leadership. Rather, we had some emergent views about a new and better style of leadership to that which we felt was a dominant form in both practice and teaching, and that that style was characterised by, amongst other things, a stronger emphasis on being creative and stimulating creativity.

The chapter seeks to illuminate both these senses of creativity in leadership development. The process of the development and thinking behind, as well as the content of, and approach taken in, a relatively innovative leadership programme is described. In the first section the key features of the leadership module are described. In the second we consider the ways in which our design and development of the programme required a degree of creativity. In the third section we consider how we have attempted to develop the creative leadership capacities of our participants through the module.

THE LEADERSHIP MODULE IN THE CONTEXT OF THE UNIVERSITY OF SYDNEY GLOBAL EXECUTIVE MBA

The Leadership module is the first in a series of six modules (see Figure 12.1) that constitute the Global Executive MBA run by the Business School at the University of Sydney. The first five modules are two-week, intensive residential face-to-face modules with the sixth, a capstone Executive MBA Report, being a supervised strategic change project undertaken by each participant focusing on a project associated with their employing organisation. The first two modules (*Leadership* and *Integrated Management*) are held in Sydney, Australia. The next three follow a life cycle of the firm model: the third module is held in Bangalore in India (*Creating and Developing New Opportunities*), the fourth in Silicon Valley in the US (*Managing Growth*) and the fifth in London, UK and the Languedoc region of France (*Turning around Mature Businesses*). The learning approach taken in the MBA is highly experiential. In the overseas modules, for example, the key learning experience is a team project in which small teams work on business projects for real clients, whose

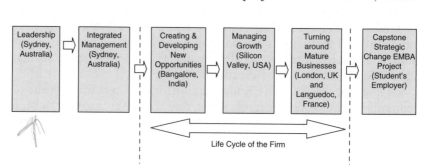

Figure 12.1   The six Global Executive MBA modules

projects are sourced exclusively for the programme. In the second module, while there is significant content devoted to the development and application of technical management skills (strategy, accounting, finance, marketing, data analytics, etc.), the major project is a consulting assignment for a not-for-profit client, again sourced exclusively for the programme. The highly experiential approach taken in the Leadership module is described in detail below.

The programme is designed for a small cohort, and cohorts to date have ranged from 15 to 20 participants. The programme is aimed at senior managers with at least 10 to 15 years' management and/or professional experience and admission is through interview. The average age of commencing cohorts has been approximately 40 years of age. Participants have been drawn from Australia, New Zealand and Southeast Asia, and the majority have significant international work experience. Participants are drawn from a variety of professional and sectoral backgrounds and have included entrepreneurs, managers from the not-for-profit sector and the public sector as well as private sector management. From our experiences at interview, and throughout the recruitment and selection processes, it is apparent that most participants are attracted by the experiential and applied nature of the learning, the exposure to overseas markets and conditions, the relative seniority and quality of the cohort, the novelty of the programme and the immersion in an intense learning environment for two weeks every three to four months across the 18 months of the degree programme.

CREATIVITY IN LEADERSHIP DEVELOPMENT

The authors developed, designed and have led the delivery of the Leadership module. The development process commenced in late 2007 with a pilot trial of the module conducted in early 2009. The module went live as the first unit of the MBA programme in 2010. The relevant academic director and principal architect of the overall programme set some general parameters for the design of the leadership module. The module was to be novel and experiential, and able to be delivered in block mode over a two-week period. In addition, the director suggested that we should consider a multidisciplinary approach to leadership and that we might want to consider how different disciplinary perspectives might illuminate leadership. He suggested that we explore perspectives on leadership drawn from diverse areas: philosophy, strategic studies, music and the arts were indicated as areas and perspectives we may wish to consider. It was also made clear by the director that the programme would need to be attractive to experienced managers and would therefore need to be seen as practical and useful.

We took the project parameters as constituting an invitation to be creative. The director's management of this invitation to creativity can be considered from the perspective of one of the key organising themes for this volume: Peters and Waterman's (1982) observation that excellent organisations exhibit 'simultaneously loose and tight characteristics'. The clear imperatives of novelty, value to users, an emphasis on experiential learning methods and a multidisciplinary approach to leadership development provided some 'tightness'. The 'looseness' was both promised and delivered through the director's encouragement and support for our ongoing innovations as the curriculum took shape. As developers we were granted a remarkable degree of freedom in terms of experimentation with new approaches to teaching and learning, new models to inform participant reflections on the practice of leadership and the introduction of ideas and concepts from diverse fields. Over time we increasingly adopted a similar 'loose-tight' approach to the management of our collaborative work with the many partners from different disciplines who helped us design and deliver the programme.

Bilton and Cummings (2010) argue that creativity in management needs to integrate four elements: innovation, entrepreneurship, leadership and organisation. As an example of creativity in management, our effort to develop and design the leadership programme certainly demanded something of each of these four elements.

Our approach to curriculum design was certainly innovative for our institution. In a very established teaching faculty such as ours, programme design was typically undertaken in the context of curriculum reviews. These reviews would customarily result in minor or more significant changes to course structures and curricula and, on occasion, result in the proposal of new programmes. However, these were often variations on existing programmes, typically seeking to better meet an emerging or growing market need. Revolutionary new programme designs were not part of the institutional memory. As might be expected in a university in which faculties were relatively strong and relatively segmented, cross-disciplinary programmes (even within the faculty, let alone beyond the faculty) were rare. The reality of departments and faculties competing for students meant that there were strong disincentives to collaborate and teach across disciplines. Our innovation was to initiate discussions with contacts we had, or were aware of, in other parts of the university and ask them if there were people in their area, or people they knew of, who might be interested in thinking about what their disciplinary area might be able to teach managers about leadership.

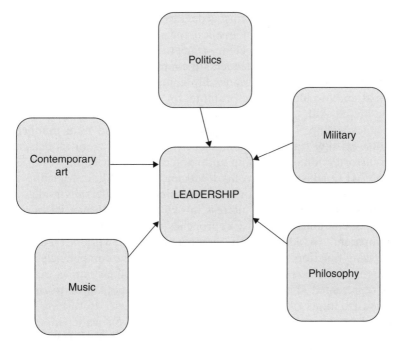

*Figure 12.2   The five domains used to develop and deliver the EMBA
Leadership module*

This process of seeking to initiate discussions with academics and practitioners from other disciplines quickly became a process akin to an entrepreneurial activity: we were venturing new ideas and seeking partners in a new educational product. Bilton and Cummings (2010: 107) note that entrepreneurs must be both dilettantes and diligent. We were open to speaking with anyone in a disciplinary area who was interested, but diligent in seeking to focus on the implications of their work for business leadership. Our entrepreneurial activities led us to constructive discussions with key people in the five domains, depicted in Figure 12.2: contemporary art, politics, the military, philosophy and music. Our key task at this stage was to build trust and confidence and to reassure our potential partners that we were committed to using their insights and expertise in the development of a leadership programme.

The translation of interesting conversations into a programme design demanded a degree of leadership. We described ourselves as 'module co-leaders' as distinct from the more customary 'unit of study coordinators'. In order to lead our partners and co-producers toward a common purpose, we also felt we needed an organising device or framework. Given that both business and universities understood the notion of 'competencies', we developed a leadership competency framework.

The development of our leadership competencies was not an attempt to create a comprehensive leadership competency framework as much as an attempt to identify and promote, for our developmental purposes, some of the skills, attributes and qualities we thought were central to better leadership. In this process we were influenced by a number of factors: existing leadership competencies as derived from models such as transformational leadership and related diagnostic frameworks such as the MLQ (Bass and Avolio 1990) and TLQ (Alimo-Metcalfe and Alban-Metcalfe 2005); critiques of contemporary leadership models and practices; and our shared interest in exploring the potential application of social constructionist approaches to leadership and leadership development. In addition, the competency framework served a key organising function: we considered how each of the competencies might or might not be explicated by each of the disciplinary areas our partners represented. This also forced us to think about how to organise the contributions of our cross-disciplinary partners. Returning to our original brief to consider different perspectives on leadership, in the process of discussions with our partners we identified the following six perspectives: military, political, philosophical, dramaturgical, ethical and musical. We then generated a matrix, Figure 12.3, in which we

	Military	Political	Philosophical	Dramaturgical	Ethical	Musical
Creative thinking and acting	▓			▓		▓
Critical reasoning			▓			
Strategic thinking	▓	▓				
Reflexive listening						▓
Identifying and managing power	▓					
Persuasiveness		▓				
Ethical decision-making			▓		▓	

Figure 12.3   Perspectives and skills, knowledge and attributes

identified where specific competencies might be expected to be strongly exemplified.

To both partners and participants we reiterated that the highlighted boxes in the matrix were only ever meant to represent hypothesised relationships and that we expected that many perspectives would more or less strongly exemplify many other competencies. For partners and external stakeholders, the matrix was an attempt to demonstrate a degree of coherence, or at least a reason for adopting the perspectives we did; for participants, it was designed to provoke thinking about each perspective and what they might bring to the practice of leadership. We encouraged participants throughout the module to actively and critically consider the extent to which each perspective illuminated or demonstrated each of the highlighted competencies and/or other competencies.

At another level of organisation, the module programme needed to conform to a curriculum design of two weeks' duration, suggesting the need to schedule topics and classes. We developed curricula with our disciplinary partners in different ways depending on their interests, expertise, access to other personnel and our mutual identification of potentially interesting topics and learning activities. Our lead partner on the military perspective was an ex-serving senior army officer with more recent teaching and research experience in leadership in the military context. He brought an impressive roster of current and recently serving army personnel at all ranks to the programme. Similarly, our lead partner from the political perspective was an ex-serving senior political leader who had then come to the university to head a school focusing on public sector management and government. He also brought access to serving and ex-politicians and bureaucrats. In both these cases curricula were based on a combination of two learning modes: 1) presentations from the leaders and experienced practitioners on leadership, strategy, development and decision-making in the respective fields of the military and politics; and 2) exercises or simulations in which participants responded to military or political scenarios. These sessions were designed to give participants insight into 'how we do things in the military/politics', thereby giving a sense of the distinctive culture of these institutions and their sense of leadership.

The curricula for the philosophical and ethical perspectives were organised differently but again in partnership with our lead partners – two philosophy academics. In the philosophy sessions the emphasis was on critical reasoning and the concepts of argument, evidence and reasoning. These concepts were illuminated through a blend of lecture material, team exercises based on working through philosophical conundrums, and activities including a debate. Particular attention was paid to the practical use and critical analysis of argumentative strategies: argument by analogy and the use of specific fallacies. Teams were set tasks of identifying particular 'moves' and strategies in a video and then transcript analysis of a televised debate. The ethical sessions introduced the classic ethical traditions of absolutism, consequentialism and virtue ethics through a series of ethical conundrums, and real and hypothetical ethical scenarios drawn from philosophy, medicine, public policy and business.

The dramaturgical curriculum was developed in partnership with three lead partners – all practising artists and art academics working in fields such as glass, conceptual and contemporary art practice and criticism. The key focus of these sessions was on the use of narrative and storytelling and performance using diverse communicative forms (including visual art, glassblowing, storytelling, recitation and slam poetry) as examples. Participants practised these disciplines by, for example, blowing glass, telling and reciting stories and performing in different contexts.

The structure of the musical sessions was organised around three phases designed to illuminate creativity, listening and performance. Working with practising musicians who were also academics at the Sydney Conservatorium, the sessions included a jazz improvisation workshop, a listening workshop (led by a singer) and a piano recital. To different degrees, in different sessions, participants were involved in listening, observing, critiquing, interpreting, playing and singing.

Given the diversity and novelty of these experiences at the heart of the leadership programme, issues of fragmentation, relevance and coherence have always featured prominently in the ongoing design/re-design and delivery of the programme. In addition to presenting the diverse perspectives in the framework of the competencies detailed in Figure 12.1, we have employed a number of other strategies in an attempt to enhance the integration, relevance and coherence of the perspectives. At the start of the programme when the idea of taking a multi-perspectives approach is introduced, a specific analytical/sensemaking approach is advocated to participants. Participants are asked to consider, throughout the programme as each perspective is encountered, the *concepts, techniques and values* which appear to be emphasised or privileged through each of the perspectives. By identifying the concepts used in each perspective, participants are encouraged to think about the forms of knowledge, organising questions and types of evidence that are thought to be important. By thinking about the techniques utilised and practised, participants are encouraged to identify ways of doing things, solving problems and achieving results. Finally, by focusing on values, participants are directed toward thinking about the different ways in which work is valued and evaluated and the attributions of meaning and significance that are characteristic of each perspective. The role of the module facilitators is critical in this endeavour. At the start of each perspective, the experiences are framed by a discussion of the competencies that might (or might not) be demonstrated by the impending experiences. At the end of each perspective the module leaders lead a discussion about the concepts, techniques and values that emerged as important for the participants. Throughout the module these debrief/ implications sessions become increasingly participant-led.

DEVELOPING CREATIVE LEADERSHIP

One of the central aims of the leadership module is the development of greater creativity in the leadership practice of the participants. Rather than adopting a single definition or central model of 'creative leadership' and then attempting to teach and develop a related set of competencies, we have been guided by the recognition that creative leadership is a contested, contingent and highly contextualised orientation to leadership practice. What counts as creative leadership will depend on the individual and their context. There are, however, distinctive meta-competencies, attributes and qualities that are associated with creative leadership. Bilton and Cummings (Chapter 1, this volume) define creativity as:

> A set of loose and tight processes, personal qualities and product attributes which lead to new and valuable outcomes. We further define creativity as a bisociative, a paradoxical concept which requires organisations and individuals to pull in different directions and to reconcile apparently contradictory concepts, purposes and frames of reference. This in turn requires an adroit ability to switch focus between frames of reference, and a tolerance for contradictions both conceptually (in our thought processes and perceptions) and organisationally (in our relationships and interactions with others).

This complex and subtle definition of creativity suggests a number of elements that might be needed in an attempt to develop creative leadership. First, it gives some much needed depth to our first leadership competency: 'creative thinking and acting'. It suggests that creative thinking and acting requires tolerance for ambiguity and a capacity to reconcile contradictions – conceptual, organisational, of goals and in ways of seeing. One aspect of this might be that leaders need to develop an appreciation and acceptance that organisational conditions are less likely to be rational, predictable and completely intelligible (as some accounts of management and leadership seem to assume) and more likely to be emergent, ambiguous, irrational and only partially intelligible. Yet, evidently, leaders cannot become paralysed by this ambiguity – they need to make sense of the environment in which they find themselves and in which their organisation operates. Following this logic, we invoke the notion of leadership as sensemaking (Pye 2005).

Second, it displaces the burden of leadership development from an accent on teaching a list of competencies as relatively specific behaviours (planning, measuring, directing, evaluating, etc.) to an emphasis on learning methods (experiencing, experimenting, reflecting, playing, implementing, etc.) – the *way* of doing things, rather than the *what* of doing things.

While this is a difficult and imperfect distinction, an example from our experience might be instructive. In working with our partners across the different perspectives we initially asked them in their sessions with participants to work towards explaining what their particular field or perspective implied for leadership, and/or what constituted good leadership from the perspective of their field. This was an attempt to identify what kinds of practices in music, philosophy, the military, etc. might be applicable to business leadership. Two things happened: our partners struggled to make this connection, as they felt constrained by a lack of familiarity with business processes and business leadership; and, secondly, it became apparent, from participant feedback, that participants were making important observations concerning the ways that partners, as practitioners, did things. For example, in both group and individual reflections on the military perspective, participants did not refer to military models of leadership or the way that certain military leadership behaviours might translate into business, as much as they noted that the way that military practitioners related to each other, analysed problems and issues and made decisions reflected a strong sense of respect for fellow serving or (ex-serving) personnel. This was seen to contribute to a strong culture characterised by 'mateship', mutual dependence and a sense of shared sacrifice and service.

This led to a re-conceptualisation of our pedagogic approach and a more complete acceptance of the importance of learning method rather than instruction in specific leadership competencies. Practically, this meant that we then asked our partners *not* to address implications for business leadership in future iterations of the programme, indeed not even to address leadership or business. Rather we asked them to focus on demonstrating, discussing and educating participants in their practice. Conceptually this also elevated the importance of the bisociative element of creativity, as one of the three key ways in which our learning method attempted to contribute to creative leadership, as explained below.

From the angle of developing creative leadership, and as shown in Figure 12.4, our learning approach appears to draw on three features that have proven to be important: an overarching bisociative element,

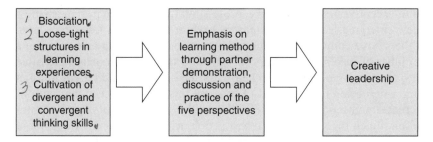

Figure 12.4   The EMBA Leadership module learning approach

the specific use of loose-tight structures in learning experiences, and the cultivation of divergent and convergent thinking skills.

Bisociation

Bilton and Cummings (2010: 5) appropriate the term bisociation from Koestler (1989) and define it as the process of making connections between or across different frames of reference, suggesting that assumptions can be questioned and novel solutions provoked through this process. One reason for adopting an organising analytical framework such as the simple concepts-techniques-values model was that it might give participants a structure by which to make comparisons across the different perspectives, thereby encouraging bisociation. At the most basic level, the observation that different perspectives evince different and distinctive concepts, techniques and values encourages participants to see the concepts, techniques and values routinely used in their own business practice as not fixed or given. Their prevalence in their business practice might be based on assumptions open to question. In a more direct way bisociation in our context might involve analogous reasoning (Tsoukas 1993). According to this logic participants might see elements of practice in an unfamiliar field they are studying as analogous to elements in their business world. When they see something working in the first setting, they might consider how an equivalent practice, behaviour approach or innovation might work in business.

Examples of the use of analogous reasoning in our programme have ranged from the direct to the more subtle. For example, from the military perspective, some participants have seen the army's practice of having a non-commissioned officer structure operating alongside the chain of commissioned officers as fairly directly applicable to business structures. Several have experimented with structures in which experienced non-executives (who might be professional experts) mentor or shadow new emerging leaders in an informal relationship. At a less direct level, others have commented on how the experience of seeing and studying a number of pieces of contemporary art and the idea that artists are often trying to 'solve problems' in their work has suggested a different mindset and orientation back at work. For some this is about accepting that different organisational members will have different views of any given situation, much the way that different people will have different views about the meaning of contemporary and conceptual art. For others it is about different ways of seeing as a key to creativity. This has led some participants to experiment with ways of getting diverse team and organisational members to brainstorm and otherwise generate multiple ideas, keeping a more open mind to the range of ideas that are generated.

As might be suggested by these brief examples, the core motivation for exposing participants to unfamiliar perspectives and their practices is to cultivate a greater 'open-mindedness'. This might lead to greater creativity on the part of participants as managers, strategists, decision-makers and problem-solvers, but perhaps more importantly, it might lead them to be more conscious of their role as leaders *for* creativity, seeing the cultivation of creativity and innovation in others as critical. After noting that the pace and complexity of contemporary change means that no one leader can hope to have all the answers, Puccio et al. (2011) argue that:

> . . . leaders must not only rely on their own creativity but must also be adept at facilitating the creative thinking of others, which implies that they possess the ego strength to admit that they do not have all the answers and the open-mindedness to entertain and support others' ideas (2011: 10).

Loose-tight Structures and Processes

Loose-tight processes are used throughout the programme in two ways: as a learning method and as an example of organising. In both modes learners/organisational members are required to exercise a fair degree of creativity in order to accomplish the task.

One example of using loose-tight processes as a learning method concerns the fluxus activity employed in the sensemaking sessions. Fluxus – which might be tentatively defined as a radical art community that emerged in the early 1960s and promoted experimentalism, play and ephemerality (see Friedman 2011 for an authoritative account) – spawned, amongst other things, a *Fluxus Performance Workbook* (Friedman et al. 2002), which contains hundreds of 'scores' amenable to performance. The activity involves teams of participants being asked to interpret sets of these scores. The tightness of this activity is constituted by the scores, the provision of a video camera and assistant technician, and the time limit of three hours by which time teams must return with all performances documented on video. The looseness is the scope for teams to interpret and enact the often obscure, contentious, even nonsensical scores. Amongst other things the activity is designed to promote reflection on creativity, interpretation, sensemaking and the nature of documentation.

An example of the use of loose-tight processes as an example of organising occurs in the jazz improvisation session conducted as part of the musical perspective. In this session participants watch and discuss with a jazz trio the process of improvising on a jazz standard. Following an account of some of the central timing, harmonic and rhythmic structures of the standard, the trio plays the standard 'straight' and then replays it with increasing degrees of improvisation. Tightness is displayed through the requirements of the standard and its basic structure as well as through the level of discipline with which trio members communicate with each other while playing, while looseness is exemplified through the improvisations led and then followed by the musicians. Participant reflections often highlight the importance of discipline, structure and a shared understanding (tightness) to successful improvisation (looseness).

Divergent and Convergent Thinking

The idea that creative leadership requires both the capacity to be open to new possibilities and ways of seeing and the capacity to focus on the most important, useful and practical responses and solutions is key to the creative problem-solving (CPS) model. Associated with the work of Alex Osborn in the 1950s and the subsequent work of Sidney Parnes and Ruth Noller at Buffalo State College in the 1960s and 1970s, CPS is based on the three conceptual stages of clarification, transformation and implementation. From this perspective, leaders are defined as creative problem-solvers (Puccio et al. 2011: 43). One of the critical features of the movement through these stages of creative problem-solving is the ability to systematically oscillate between divergent and convergent thinking. Divergent thinking concerns 'a broad search for many diverse and novel alternatives' and convergent thinking focuses on 'a focused and affirmative evaluation of alternatives' (Puccio et al. 2011: 56). Creative leaders need to be able to move from a divergent orientation to a more focused convergent orientation through each conceptual stage of clarification, transformation and implementation, focusing in turn on exploration then formulation at each stage.

While the Sydney Global Executive MBA Leadership programme does not explicitly seek to teach the cognitive and affective skills of CPS, the idea of encouraging, even compelling, participants to thoroughly engage in divergent thinking by exploring new frameworks and fields of practice, and then getting them to practise convergent thinking by constructively evaluating implications and formulating plans, resonates strongly with the programme approach. Indeed, the pattern of moving from divergent to convergent thinking applies to the leadership module as a whole, as well as to the facilitation of the experiences of each of the perspectives.

The sensemaking sessions, including the fluxus session discussed above, constitute an introductory, frame-breaking perspective which is designed to encourage heightened open-mindedness and divergent thinking. The often confounding and confronting experiences of interpreting and performing the fluxus scores, along with other sessions including interpreting, and listening to others' interpretations of, contemporary and conceptual art, encourage participants to be less certain of their assumptions and less confident in their immediate conclusions. The sensemaking sessions are therefore designed to be destabilising for participants and seek to prepare them for the diverse experiences that unfold throughout the remainder of the programme.

Divergent thinking is also explicitly encouraged as participants experience each of the perspectives – military, political, philosophical, dramaturgical, ethical and musical. Participants invariably struggle in these sessions, and in the prior sensemaking sessions, to see the direct relevance of the experiences to business leadership. As part of the facilitation process, participants are urged to defer the search for direct implications in exchange for immersion in the experiences. By 'staying in' the perspective and the experience, we effectively seek to reinforce two of the principles of divergent thinking: deferring judgement and seeking novelty[1] (Puccio et al. 2011: 87).

At the conclusion of each of the perspectives participants are given an opportunity to debrief and reflect on their experiences. Here participants are encouraged to engage in convergent thinking and to consider the positive and negative aspects of the experience and articulate the connections they may have made, or are making, to other perspectives and to their own leadership practice. Here the convergent thinking principle of 'applying affirmative judgment' is particularly important. Puccio et al. (2011: 96–7) contrast the process of applying affirmative judgement, in which positives and negatives are carefully balanced, with the process of 'faultfinding'. This is an important and difficult transition for many participants accustomed to finding fault in their roles as business executives.

The second major way in which convergent thinking is used is in the final assessment piece for the module – an individual reflective essay. In this task, completed approximately one month after the conclusion of the module, participants are asked to reflect at length on their experiences and identify the ways in which themes, experiences, and the concepts, techniques and values identified in the perspectives might have affected their thinking, behaviour and practice at work as leaders (and followers).

CONCLUSIONS

While the development of more creative leaders has not been the sole or even primary aim of the leadership module in the University of Sydney Global Executive MBA, creativity and its development has been vitally important to the programme. If we are right that leadership development and management education more generally is in need of change and new approaches, our design and delivery of a better leadership development programme has required a degree of innovation and creativity on our part. It is also the case that we are motivated by the ambition of helping to develop better leaders and a more compelling and constructive leadership practice. In place of the decisive, strong, assertive, heroic and charismatic leader-centred leadership models that have come to prominence over the past 30 years, we are seeking to develop leadership which is more modest, measured, authentic (Collins 2001), collective, collaborative and compassionate (Raelin 2003). This is entirely consistent with the cultivation of leadership for creativity. In their discussion of the strategic leadership of a creative enterprise, Bilton and Cummings (2010: chapter 11) advocate a kind of quiet leadership that is effectively 'leadership from the middle', rather than leadership from the top, or the front: 'leaders must position themselves among the group, not above it' (2010: 147).

Several aspects of creativity have decisively informed our curriculum and our practice of facilitation and leadership development. The use of loose-tight processes has been amongst the most important. Giving our participants significant freedom to explore and learn within some clear parameters and boundaries has encouraged engagement and deep learning. And those same loose-tight principles are directly applicable to leaders seeking to cultivate creativity and innovation in their people. The encouragement of bisociation and analogical reasoning has also been vital. We have found that exposure to unfamiliar and sometimes confounding experiences from different fields is energising and stimulating for our participants. We have also relied heavily on asking participants to embrace both divergent and convergent thinking, exploring new possibilities with

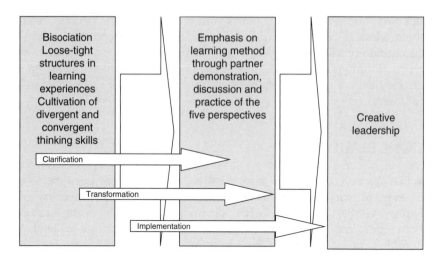

Figure 12.5   The EMBA Leadership module learning approach and the creative process stages

openness and then working together to formulate plans and practical, innovative strategies.

It is evident that there are general principles of creativity and of creative leadership. However, our contention and experience is that creative leadership cannot be learned in the abstract or at the cognitive level. Leadership is something that is done in a context. Therefore, what effective or creative leadership means will vary infinitely depending on that context. It follows for us that the most effective leadership development is that which engages with experiences, and which provides participants with the opportunity to critically reflect, as the basis for better leadership practice. In this way, and as shown in Figure 12.5, we seek to develop our participants' capacity to develop their own leadership practice using a learning approach that incorporates the creative process stages of clarification, transformation and implementation.

QUESTIONS FOR DISCUSSION

1. To what extent can leadership be taught?
2. Given your response to Question 1, in what ways might the programme outlined in this chapter be a better way to learn how to lead than conventional leadership classes, lectures and reading?

3. If the Sydney University programme described here is currently regarded as leading edge, what do you think that leading-edge creative leadership courses might look like in 20 years' time?

NOTE

1. The other principles of divergent thinking identified by Puccio et al. (2011) are 'going for quantity' and 'making connections'.

REFERENCES

Alimo-Metcalfe, B. and J. Alban-Metcalfe (2005), 'Leadership: Time for a new direction?', *Leadership*, **1**(1), 51–71.

Bass, B.M. and B.J. Avolio (1990), *Multifactor Leadership Questionnaire*, Palo Alto, CA: Consulting Psychologists Press.

Bennis, W. and J. O'Toole (2005), 'How Business Schools Lost Their Way', *Harvard Business Review*, May, 96–104.

Bilton, C. and S. Cummings (2010), *Creative strategy: reconnecting business and innovation*, Chichester: John Wiley and Sons.

Collins, J. (2001), *Good to great: why some companies make the leap . . . and others don't*, New York: Harper Business.

Datar, S., D. Garvin and P. Cullen (2010), *Rethinking the MBA: business education at a cross-roads*, Boston: Harvard Business School Press.

Friedman, K. (2011), 'Fluxus: a laboratory of ideas', in J. Baas (ed.) *Fluxus and the essential questions of life*, Hanover, NH: Hood Museum of Art, Dartmouth College, pp. 35–44.

Friedman, K., O. Smith and L. Sawchyn (eds) (2002), *The Fluxus performance workbook*, Digital supplement to *Performance Research*, **7**(3). www.performance-research.net/pages/e-publications.html

Ghoshal, S. (2005), 'Bad management theories are destroying good management practices', *Academy of Management Learning and Education*, **4**(1), 75–91.

Khurana, R. (2002), *Searching for a corporate savior: the irrational quest for charismatic CEOs*, Princeton, NJ: Princeton University Press.

Koestler, A. (1989), *The act of creation*, London: Arkana [1964].

Mintzberg, H. (2004), *Managers not MBAs: a hard look at the soft practice of managing and management development*, San Francisco, CA: Berrett-Koehler Publishers.

Peters, T. and R. Waterman (1982), *In search of excellence*, New York: Warner Books.

Podolny, J. (2009), 'The buck stops (and starts) at business schools', *Harvard Business Review*, June, 62–7.

Puccio, G.J., M. Mance and M.C. Murdock (2011), *Creative leadership: skills that drive change* (2nd edition), Thousand Oaks, CA: Sage.

Pye, A. (2005), 'Leadership and organizing: sensemaking in action', *Leadership*, **1**(1): 31–50.

Raelin, J.A. (2003), *Creating leaderful organizations: how to bring out leadership in everyone*, San Francisco, CA: Berrett-Koehler.

Salaman, G. (2011), 'Understanding the crises of leadership', in J. Storey (ed.) *Leadership in organizations: current issues and key trends*, Abingdon, UK: Routledge, pp. 56–68.

Sawyer, R. (2006), *Explaining creativity*, Oxford: Oxford University Press.

Starkey, K., A. Hatchuel and S. Tempest (2004), 'Rethinking the business school', *Journal of Management Studies*, **41**(8), 1521–31.

Stern, S. (2010), 'On management: a new way to lead', *Financial Times*, 10 May.
Sternberg, R. (1999), *Handbook of creativity*, Cambridge: Cambridge University Press.
Tsoukas, H. (1993), 'Analogical reasoning and knowledge generation in organization theory', *Organization Studies*, **14**(3), 323–46.

13. Promoting ensemble: creative leadership in practice at the Royal Shakespeare Company

Vikki Heywood, Chris Bilton and
Stephen Cummings

How do you direct innovation without stifling the emergent creativity of those that a creative organisation depends upon? At the same time, how do you lead change without undermining the things that people have grown to love about your organisation's identity? These two riddling questions must be faced by any leader of a creative organisation with any kind of tradition. The Royal Shakespeare Company may represent one of the world's most extreme cases: an iconic global brand whose product is intertwined with the very identity of a nation, confronted in recent years by increasing external competition and internal change. Creative leadership in such a setting would be quite a challenge.

In the final chapter of the leadership section of this book, we consider this extreme case of creative leadership in practice. The RSC is a cultural organisation as well as a creative one, and its leaders have taken the opportunity to connect the aesthetic culture of its products and production methods to the organisational culture of its people and processes. This connection was embodied in the partnership between the company's artistic director, Michael Boyd, and the executive director, Vikki Heywood. Under their joint leadership, the company rejuvenated the principles of 'ensemble' and spread it from the rehearsal room, to the organisation as a whole, and beyond this to the organisation's relationship with audiences. In this book we have argued that creativity depends on an ability to make unexpected combinations and connections between different frames of reference and thinking styles when confronted by problems and opportunities. Applying this logic to leadership, 'creative leadership' requires the connecting of different styles or modes of leadership to adapt to changing circumstances, ranging across bottom–up interaction to top–down vision, through 'leading from the middle'. Considering how creative leaders combine internal and external relationships with 'visionary' and 'active' roles led us to identify four creative leadership capabilities. Internally directed, active **promoting** of ideas allows leaders to 'suss' out or

249

encapsulate a unique vision. That vision is then directed outwards, **linking** to interact with stakeholders and **mapping** a way forward by relating the organisation's strategy to competitors, consumers and collaborators. Ensemble draws many of these aspects of creative leadership together.

Having described the 'ensemble' leadership model elsewhere in other publications (Bilton and Cummings 2010), we returned to the company shortly after Heywood and Boyd announced their departure in 2012. The chapter is based on reflective conversations with Vikki Heywood in 2011 and 2012, focusing on the evolving process of creative leadership during her tenure at the company, from 2003 to 2012. As will become apparent, this creative leadership required a combination of different perspectives and capabilities, adapted to the emerging challenges facing the organisation. In analytical retrospect, Vikki's experiences can be divided into four main aspects. We outline these below and then relate them to a framework called the Creative Leadership Keypad. The RSC is a unique and, as we have said, an extreme case. We do not, therefore, present Vikki's experiences as 'the way' that others should act when seeking to lead a creative organisation. We do, however, believe that this depiction of Vikki's story will help others to reflect on their own experiences and develop their own approaches to future creative leadership challenges.

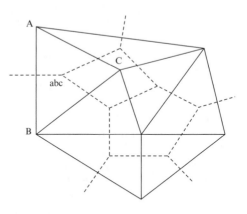

CREATIVE LEADERSHIP 1: PROMOTING FROM WITHIN: BUILDING AROUND THE CONCEPT OF ENSEMBLE

It was very clear that there was an urgent business need to get everyone in the company working together on a shared and articulated vision for the future. It was also very important to regain a sense of pride and through collective pride stimulate collective ambition. It was quite clear that there was a paradox at the heart of the organisation. It described itself as having a set of values and principles 'the whole being greater than the sum of its parts', but the process of the recent implementation of change management had appeared to be very 'top down' and had not been able to match that rhetoric. People had lost faith in what was, and was not, truth. In order to focus people on the future in a positive way, we had to provide clear leadership by rearticulating those principles and then very clearly demonstrating that we would work within those parameters, to achieve the changes that were needed. (Vikki Heywood, June 2012)

The initial challenge for Heywood and Boyd was to rebuild morale following an ambitious and ultimately unsuccessful attempt to reinvent the company under the previous regime. Company members were understandably suspicious of grandiose strategic plans and consultants' top–down interventions; some had first-hand experience of the jargon and gimmickry of generic change management programmes. Rather than attempting to 'make waves' in the organisation, Boyd and Heywood had to become more like surfers, picking the best waves to ride and waiting for the right one to break at the right time. This meant tapping into internal values and principles rather than importing or imposing their own.

It also meant rethinking the shape of the organisation. Creative work is characterised by flat hierarchies, with teams cooperating intuitively to solve problems rather than being told what to do. We might visualise a creative organisation as a series of flat surfaces where everybody can contribute to the creative process from different angles. Whereas this approach and structure might have described the creative work of rehearsals, the RSC at the time was characterised by vertical divisions and barriers separating different organisational functions. An especially high wall was erected between the creative work of making theatre and the organisational tasks of management and administration.

This was critical – the divisions and resentments between artistic and administrative staff in cultural organisations have been well documented (Parrish 2006) and the RSC was not exempt from these challenges. The first task for Boyd and Heywood was to bridge the divisions between the acting company and the administrators, and to unite the organisation around a distinctive set of values (Hewison et al. 2010).

The solution was found in the company's own internal process of rehearsal. An experienced director trusts the actors to express their own beliefs and values rather than articulating an overarching vision, and draws out stories, perspectives and ideas gradually to accumulate a shared understanding of the play. In order to fully engage the company – including the administrative staff – it was necessary to strip away the vocabulary of objectives and plans and use instead a more intuitive language of 'conversation' and 'our philosophy'. Boyd in particular was unafraid to use words such as 'love', 'forgiveness' and 'trust' in company board meetings. At this stage in the leadership process, the emphasis was on method rather than models – finding a way to communicate openly and imaginatively about the company's future and drawing out latent energies and directions from within.

At this stage too there was no explicit reference to organisational change – even if this would eventually be the end result. Indeed Heywood comments that the new leadership profited from a perception of 'no change'. Ironically, the return to core principles and beliefs would come to represent a much more radical transformation than the proliferation of new initiatives which typically heralds a new leadership broom. But the reassuring sense of continuity and regression to first principles helped to win trust in these early exchanges.

'Ensemble' emerged out of a year's worth of laborious discussion and interaction. It became clear that the idea of a company of people working towards a common goal applied not only to the actors but to the company as a whole. Heywood describes this realisation as a 'lightbulb' moment. The idea of ensemble encapsulated a feeling of equality and of 'one organisation'. It also required everybody in the organisation to become more engaged in a collective creative process, thinking of themselves not as cogs in somebody else's machine, but equal participants whose decisions and actions are all potentially 'creative', having the possibility to influence creative outcomes elsewhere in the organisation. This transition reflects the different ways of conceptualising different individual contributions to organisational creativity, illustrated in Figure 13.1 (Legge 2003).

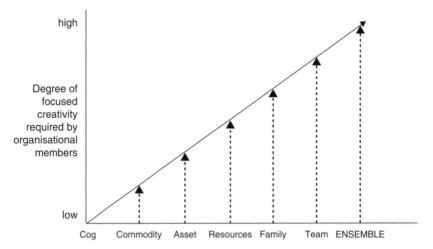

Source: adapted from Legge 2003

Figure 13.1   Mapping employee engagement against organisational creativity

Heywood compares the challenge of engaging with the RSC staff to similar initiatives in other organisations, such as the BBC's 'Make It Happen' culture change programme under Greg Dyke a few years previously (Schlesinger 2010). The RSC's relatively small scale gave Heywood an advantage in engaging the workforce – with around 700 employees it was possible for her to talk to most of her staff face to face within a year, rather than relying on 'personal' memos or mass emails (although Heywood is quick to point out that engagement can work in any scale of organisation, including the BBC, 'you just need a different methodology'). And whereas employers such as Mars or Disney might reward enterprising individual workers with a chance to pitch new product ideas to senior managers, at the RSC the conversation between leaders and workers was a genuine interaction, open to all and not just the inspired minority. The extent and depth of this engagement would later be borne out in company surveys which highlighted the sense of pride and shared purpose across the RSC.

The first paradox in the leadership cycle of the RSC was that transformation began from digging down into the company's past and present, not from envisioning the future – and that a new strategic direction emerged from a profound mistrust of strategic plans and planning. The key was interaction – working with the grain of the organisation and listening to the confused and sometimes challenging voices within.

RSC paradox
solution was starting...
to roots

CREATIVE LEADERSHIP 2: BEING A BRIDGE: MAKING AND ENACTING THE ENSEMBLE VISION

Any business that has to manufacture and sell products is no different than the RSC. Both have an identity that they seek to promote to their customers and they align their products to that corporate identity. The RSC has a 'commodity', Shakespeare, that is not unique to it alone and therefore it needs to make sure, perhaps even more so than its peer organisations, that it has an identity that current and future audiences can relate to. RSC customers need to know that if they book to see an RSC production it will have an allegiance, or a special difference, if you like, to other Shakespeare productions. The company had found itself in one big and all-encompassing identity crisis. Analysing what the company identity was and then how to project it, for its staff, its customers and its funders, became fundamental to the future success of the organisation. (Vikki Heywood, June 2012)

The next challenge for the RSC leadership was taking the vision of ensemble further, making it visible and vivid to the organisation. While Michael Boyd was able to embody the spirit of ensemble in the rehearsal room, the task of extending the ensemble vision to the organisation as a whole fell to Heywood. As executive director, she was the bridge connecting the theatre ensemble to the management and administration, as well as to a broader range of stakeholders including audiences.

Heywood attributes her success as a leader of creative organisations to her willingness to sponsor different viewpoints. She argues that the leader's role here is to provide sufficient context and freedom in which creative people can flourish; by bridging between different perspectives, leadership becomes a collective process in which business principles and creative processes are interdependent rather than antagonistic. One of the new perspectives Heywood brought into the organisation was that of Dr Mee Yan Chung Judge, a Cambridge academic who helped to establish the 'systemic principles' behind ensemble and supported Heywood's rejection of conventional management tools. There are echoes here of Billy Beane's leadership of the Oakland Athletics, bringing in an unconventional voice to challenge business orthodoxies and initiate a new organisational culture. Judge also helped to articulate the principles of ensemble in a jargon-free, vivid language.

There are many ways of representing a vision – Karl Weick refers to story-telling (Weick 1995), whereas for too many organisations strategy is articulated in the dry corporate language of the mission statement or five-year strategic vision. For an idea or vision to be 'sticky', brevity is important (Gladwell 2000). Furthermore, as a theatre company, the RSC leadership recognised both the power of language and the importance of action to lend weight and conviction to the right words.

Evolving an internal language became another bridge between actors and administrators, and a crucial stage in building internal consensus around the values of ensemble. Under Boyd's direction, the cast and crew of the acting company were contracted to work together on a series of plays over a 30-month cycle. Principles of tolerance, trust, commitment and humility were well understood by the actors. Boyd proved to be an articulate champion of the company's new identity (he preferred the word 'identity' to the more corporate connotations of 'brand'). The eloquence and sensitivity of Boyd's words cut through the dead language of company mission statements and spoke to the organisation in words they could understand and accept. Heywood's challenge was to extend this language beyond the acting company to the administrative staff:

> There were so many words that were 'not allowed' – 'route map, strategy, brand, matrix' being just some of them! I had to find ways to get buy-in without

any jargon and allow the company to invent its own. There were many anxieties around the word 'ensemble', as not having any meaning to the majority of
people outside the company – but in the end we decided to be brave, believe in
it and own it. (Vikki Heywood, June 2012)

Sometimes in the theatre actions speak louder than words. One way for
Heywood to make the principles of ensemble vivid to administrative staff
was to embody these values in her own behaviour. She remembers a conversation with another executive who was astonished that Heywood and
Boyd would fly economy rather than business class to New York, even
when they faced a gruelling schedule of work during the company's residency at the Park Avenue Armory. Similarly, Heywood made a point of
not parking in the reserved places at the company's Stratford base. For a
company claiming to represent unity and trust, the sight of a senior executive pulling rank would have sent out all the wrong signals; conversely,
seeing the company's executive director behaving like 'one of us' was
equally powerful. There could be no 'us and them' in an ensemble; and
Heywood could not be seen to break her own rules, even at the cost of her
own discomfort and inconvenience.

Embodying organisational values requires a measure of self-
consciousness. The leader becomes a visible symbol of the organisation.
Heywood describes the moment when she became conscious of herself as
a leader, when she was working in another theatre organisation and found
herself promoted into this more visible role. Until that moment, she 'didn't
realise I was something'; she had considered herself a backroom person,
invisible and insignificant. In her position at the RSC, Heywood recognised the symbolic weight of the leadership role. Her behaviour could
change the behaviour of those around her. For example, many modern
firms claim to be 'learning organisations'. For Heywood, the simplest way
to embody this rhetoric was to start walking around the organisation with
a book or article in hand and to talk enthusiastically about what she was
reading and learning herself.

No doubt it helped that Heywood and Boyd were respected insiders.
Boyd was a highly regarded theatre director who had paid his dues in
regional theatre. Amongst the actors we spoke to, he was recognised as
a director who trusted actors to take risks and express themselves, rather
than bending them to his directorial will. Heywood had arrived from
a successful tenure at the Royal Court Theatre but had also worked
for the RSC before as a stage manager. There has been a tendency
in Britain's major arts organisations to import senior managers and
board members from outside the cultural sector, on the assumption that
blue-chip commercial companies breed a sharper business sense than

subsidised arts organisations. Whether or not this is true, these outsiders are more likely to arrive with their own prescriptions and perceptions for organisational change, and must work harder to win the trust of the workforce.

Heywood's position as both a trusted figure inside the RSC and a respected manager with an impressive CV in other creative organisations allowed her to bridge the gap between an internal conversation and a public image. Heywood and Boyd were both ideally positioned for this bridging role, drawing together and promoting ideas from across the organisation, and making collective values vivid and immediate in their own behaviour and their interactions with others.

The idea of ensemble which emerged from this process of envisioning and interacting went beyond a vague democratic impulse. Heywood is keen to emphasise the robust and rigorous nature of ensemble:

> There were some people who decided that our consultative behavioural require-
> ment meant you could not lead, or make decisions. Those folk fortunately got
> lost in the majority rush towards this better, clearer and articulated manage-
> ment style that related back to the core identity of the company. It forced man-
> agers to behave in inclusive ways and it weeded out the weaker folk who felt
> their leadership and team management were threatened as a result. Teams that
> were not being managed in an inclusive and consultative way became jealous
> of those that were. I guess there are always excuses for deriding any change
> programme, but I found the internal sarcasm around 'ensemble equals weak
> management' hard to take some days, as it was not the truth. (Vikki Heywood,
> June 2012)

Boyd and Heywood were happy to pull people up on behaviour which fell below the ensemble's expected standards of mutual respect and commitment. The RSC had in the past tended to refer to itself as 'a family' – a term which Heywood had instinctively mistrusted for its implications of hidden hierarchies, dysfunctional relationships and condoned eccentricities. Ensemble did not mean 'anything goes', it set standards of behaviour towards each other which were insistently upheld by the leadership.

The second paradox of creative leadership under Boyd and Heywood is that distance does not always produce clarity of vision and purpose. A singular vision for the RSC emerged not from a single leader, but from a leadership prepared to embrace and interact with the workforce and to reflect the organisation's shared values back to them boldly and uncompromisingly. 'Sussing' a shared vision began with Heywood and Boyd bridging across different voices from across and outside the organisation to articulate the values of ensemble, then developing a common symbolic language to give that vision substance and weight.

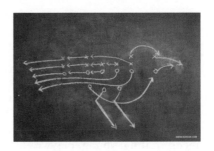

CREATIVE LEADERSHIP 3: MAPPING A PATHWAY TO THE OUTSIDE WORLD AND A BETTER FUTURE STATE

> Over the years we worked to ensure that the company's product, vision and values were clearly identifiable for our audiences, our funders and our competitors to help us ensure the message was coherent, different and of value to them. I believe this had a wide and positive effect and has contributed to the RSC now being the best known theatre brand in the UK. (Vikki Heywood, September 2012)

Up to this point the leadership focus had been internal, towards a rebuilding of confidence and unity after a battery of initiatives had left many employees confused and demotivated. Having 'sussed' a clear vision and purpose for the organisation, Heywood and Boyd set about communicating this externally and redefining the RSC's relationship with funders and audiences.

We describe this third phase of creative leadership as 'mapping' – redrawing the relationship between the organisation and the world around it. This is also the point where the vision of ensemble takes flight, forging better relationships with external stakeholders and envisioning a better future for the organisation. As a nationally funded organisation, it was important that the RSC stood for a distinctive approach to theatre. This approach extends beyond the success (or failure) of individual plays. The ensemble idea helped to define a compelling vision which funders and sponsors could identify with, and which extended beyond the relatively short cycle of individual productions or seasons. The continuity and consistency of the RSC brand was especially important for an organisation whose output is essentially project-based.

According to Heywood, the RSC 'brand' became more successful because external stakeholders could recognise a clear and coherent identity, one with which they were happy to identify themselves. The relationship with the major funder, Arts Council England, improved and investment for the ambitious redevelopment of the company's Stratford base was secured. Sponsors too recognised a vision and ethos with which they could associate themselves. 'Mapping' the organisation relative to its environment relates to Porter's vocabulary of strategic positioning and competitive advantage (Porter 1996). In Heywood's phrase, the leadership task was 'defining difference'.

The 'ensemble' identity was exported to New York and incorporated into fundraising and sponsorship activities. It was used to inform the company's education work, in particular the way the company worked with schools and supported teachers. It also became possible for the RSC to define a new approach to working with contemporary writers, incorporating young playwrights into the company's ensemble ethos and making connections between new work and Shakespearean themes; support for new writing had always been part of the RSC's mission, and the connections between contemporary plays and Shakespearean theatre were embedded into the ensemble's repertoire. The company curated 'The Complete Works', a season of Shakespeare productions from around the world, covering the complete works and drawing together a huge variety of nationalities, acting styles and theatre companies. These activities communicated a vision of the RSC as a vibrant, inclusive community and redefined its relationship with other theatre companies and writers. Whereas before the RSC might have represented a 'heritage' idea of Shakespeare and a rather isolated, elite position outside contemporary performance practice, the new mapping of the RSC ensemble positioned the company in the forefront of a more experimental and contemporary theatrical practice.

The remapped relationship with audiences was physically embodied in the new building at Stratford, opened in 2010. The new architecture was designed to be more open and accessible, from the frontage and foyer areas to the café and the layout of the auditoria. The main auditorium and thrust stage bringing actors and audience closer together and the open plan building were all engineered to follow through the principles and culture of an ensemble organisation. Apart from establishing a more friendly relationship with local residents and a stronger presence in the town of Stratford, the new building represented a closer relationship with a wider audience beyond the immediate neighbourhood. As she and Boyd prepared to leave the RSC, Heywood was planning to map this new relationship, asking audiences for their opinions about the RSC and its future – something the old RSC would surely not have dared risk. Again the more open style of communication reflected the organisation's confidence in its own identity and values. By remapping the relationship with its immediate surroundings, the RSC leadership subtly recast the organisation's identity and purpose.

By mapping a clear identity for the organisation that married physical, cultural and philosophical principles, the RSC leadership was able to communicate a clear vision to its partners and collaborators, from the funding bodies and sponsors to fellow theatre companies, actors, schools, teachers and audiences. The company's embrace of social media has been symptomatic of this new confidence and clarity. Social media challenge the old idea that organisations can control their public image through carefully designed marketing and PR. Increasingly audiences use online fora and microblogging to carry on a conversation in which the organisation is only a minor player; and if an organisation gets on the wrong side of the 'twitterati', negative gossip and rumours spread like a virus. In the past the proliferation of Twitter and Facebook chatter would have been profoundly threatening to a traditional, hierarchical organisation such as the RSC. Heywood recalls the anxiety of the press office when she first started at the RSC, with staff monitoring negative stories and trying to control the public perception of internal problems.

Trying to control today's online social media is impossible – the conversation will happen with or without the organisation's consent. Rather than seeking to control or 'moderate' social media, organisations such as the RSC are learning to trust in their own values and purpose. If they can communicate their values and vision clearly and confidently, the odd negative story is unlikely to disrupt or deflect the general flow of opinion and debate. No doubt the RSC will receive its share of criticisms, but by steering its own course it can avoid being battered by the kind of social media storms which occasionally blow up and blow over contemporary organisations. The worst response to such a storm is paranoia, retreat or inconsistency; no organisation can be popular all the time, but a quietly consistent direction and purpose are more likely to succeed than angry rebuttals and over-engagement. Again, the leadership is remapping the relationships between the RSC and the external world; no longer heroically isolated, the RSC appears more engaged and open.

The third paradox of creative leadership is that integrity and consistency of purpose are more likely to win over external stakeholders than an excess of external communication or knee-jerk re-branding. The most persuasive way of engaging with today's consumers is by listening to the conversation rather than attempting to lead it. Conversely a confident internal sense of purpose allows the organisation to be more open and accessible and to construct new relationships with audiences and collaborators. The remapping of its relationships with national and international consumers, contemporary theatre-makers, funders and social media users has been the third phase in the transformation of the RSC, drawing on the internal confidence of 'promoting' and 'sussing' to redraw a new competitive position for the organisation.

CREATIVE LEADERSHIP 4: CONNECTING THE NODES INTO A NETWORK THAT WILL LIGHT UP FUTURE DEVELOPMENT

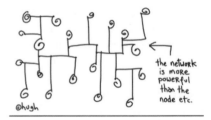

the network is more powerful than the node etc.

©hugh

> You're not telling me that those employees out there selling those sub-prime mortgages didn't know there was a fundamental problem – but who asked them? Who in the board rooms of those organisations thought it would be to their personal and corporate advantage to create a culture where permission to say what you thought, throughout the company, was encouraged? Everyone became complicit in denial of the facts before their eyes and as a result a collective agreement to do something that was so self-evidently crazy took hold. The change programme at the RSC was ahead of the curve in this respect – now everyone sees the value of corporate collective communication, self-awareness and responsibility. (Vikki Heywood, September 2012)

The RSC's new awareness of its audiences and of the wider world of communication beyond press releases and strategy statements signals a fourth phase in the leadership cycle. As the company seeks to re-animate and re-energise its values and ethos, the company is drawing new impetus from new recruits and new partnerships. Heywood and Boyd began their leadership by interacting and connecting with the internal staff, bridging the different factions and drawing out the shared ethos and values beneath the surface differences. Now they are closing the loop, connecting the other phases together, providing a conduit between the company's internal values and a wider constituency outside the organisation. The leadership function has circled back to interaction, this time not only bouncing ideas around within the organisation but across a wider network of collaborators and consumers. Leadership becomes the pinball which lights up the nodes in the network, sparking ideas in other organisations and bringing new ideas to bear on the company's future.

We call this leadership phase 'linking'. The approach involves interacting and 'leading from below' rather than from the top – entrusting the workforce to uphold the company's ethos rather than imposing this from above. Instead of the leaders setting the direction, in today's RSC they are as likely to be held to account by new recruits asking challenging questions, or by colleagues who, in Heywood's phrase, 'could do my job tomorrow'.

This form of 'distributed leadership' is not uncommon in arts organisations (Ibbotson 2008, Mumford et al. 2002), where the specialised nature of the work and the precarious career structure of the creative industries mean that employees are likely to mature into a role rather than being promoted into formal leadership positions. This highly specialised and highly experienced cadre of senior staff, typically at head of department level, are jealous guardians of the company's values. Such a group may of course represent an obstacle to organisational change – Heywood jokes that external management consultants would be 'spat out in five minutes' by her colleagues. But in the case of the RSC 'ensemble', where Heywood and Boyd went out of their way to engage these people in the company's vision from the outset, they are also the leadership's best allies, acting as critical friends and connectors to future possibilities and problems. Heywood describes her colleagues as 'at the top of their game' and suggests that as she prepares to leave, they are primed to engage in a new conversation about the company's future.

'Leading from below' reflects the maturing of the ensemble organisation and the RSC leadership. Several leadership theories describe this transition in leadership from 'instructing' to 'delegating', mapping a more devolved style of leadership against a progressively more engaged and responsible attitude among employees (Hersey and Blanchard 1977). 'Mapping' and 'linking' to those outside the organisation requires a level of confidence and mutual trust (acquired through the earlier phases of 'promoting' and 'sussing' from within). Opening the RSC to outside influences and perspectives might have been destructive if initiated earlier in the leadership cycle.

More recently Heywood suggests that the internal dynamic of the RSC has become self-sustaining as existing staff continue to buy into the ensemble ethos. In order to challenge and sharpen the company's vision, she notices a new relationship with those outside the organisation. New recruits expect the RSC to stand for certain principles, and will hold the company accountable to these values. Heywood describes new employees asking about the RSC's environmental policies; these may be questions she has not anticipated but she welcomes the challenge. She also observes how older employees who have returned to the RSC having worked elsewhere, especially members of the acting company, recognise and replenish the company's distinctive culture.

By 'linking' to those joining or re-joining the company from the outside, from new board members to returning actors and junior members of the back office, the RSC leadership is able to re-animate and redefine its values. This does not mean that 'anything goes' – the underlying principles are clearly established. But the newcomers are more likely to come up with a new interpretation of the established principles. Their expectations provide continuity but at the same time challenge complacency. Heywood makes an analogy to employees caught up in the global financial crisis. When an organisation is not behaving ethically, it is the responsibility of the workers and the non-executive directors or board, not just the leaders, to hold it to account and challenge the collective dereliction of principles. Sometimes those on the fringes of the organisation are better placed to connect with a wider agenda and so to question internal habits and logics – for example looking beyond profit maximisation as the sole rationale for a financial institution.

For the RSC, Heywood argues that a shared ethos implied a sharing of the burden of corporate responsibility beyond the leader, to include board members, junior administrators, actors and technicians. She is conscious of the symbolic power of leadership, as in her own symbolic behaviour when choosing how to present her leadership role; by the same token, there is a danger that organisations will be 'seduced by the cult of the leader' and remain silent when the leaders abandon collective principles. Linking to values and ideals outside provides checks and balances against the leadership's internal logic and assumptions. In the end this more open exchange of views between leaders and followers is more likely to inspire loyalty, creativity and mutual respect – the values that Elizabeth Murdoch felt had been lost by the British media and needed to be rediscovered through a new relationship between media producers and audiences (see box below).

The argument for collective responsibility, leadership from below and holding leaders to account shades into a discussion of who might succeed Boyd and Heywood at the company. Heywood argues that the company's values are sufficiently entrenched that a new leader is unlikely to want to challenge them and start again, even if they could. On the other hand, the company is confident enough in its own direction to allow a new person scope to reinterpret these values in their own way. By 'linking' outwards to new perspectives and challenges, Heywood and Boyd have already indicated they are prepared for their vision to be reinvented and re-animated by whoever succeeds them. They have also allocated more than a year between the announcement of their departure and the eventual handover to the new leadership, allowing sufficient time for an orderly transition rather than the drastic 'new broom' approach which had proved so destructive in the past.

'Linking' takes the leadership cycle full circle. Having begun their leadership by 'promoting' ideas from within, Heywood and Boyd are now 'linking' to draw in new ideas and people from the outside, integrating these back into a coherent vision. Whoever succeeds them (the new artistic director, Greg Doran, was announced in April 2012 and Heywood's

LINKING: FROM VALUES TO ETHICS

It is increasingly apparent that the absence of purpose – or of a moral language – within government, media or business, could become one of the most dangerous own goals for capitalism and for freedom. (Elizabeth Murdoch, 23 August 2012)

In her MacTaggart Lecture at the 2012 Edinburgh International Television Festival, Elizabeth Murdoch acknowledged the effects of the UK phone-hacking scandal on her parent company, News Corporation. Rather than trying to blame one or two 'rogue' individuals for unethical journalism, she argued that senior management also had to take responsibility, since 'any organisation needs to discuss, affirm and institutionalise a rigorous set of values based on an explicit statement of purpose'. In the complex collaborative ecosystem of global television, this task of 'articulating purpose' has become more critical. Murdoch criticised her brother James for attacking the BBC and claiming in a previous MacTaggart Lecture that 'profit' was the only true guarantor of an independent media. 'Profit without a purpose', she argued, was 'a recipe for disaster'. The irresponsibility and 'dearth of integrity' in the UK press had engulfed other institutions, transmitted through the corrosive and self-serving relationships between media, politics, police and banking. In order to heal these wounds, independent companies (such as Elizabeth Murdoch's company, Shine) would have to rediscover a sense of value and purpose, and build new relationships with audiences. As with the RSC, Murdoch claimed that audiences in the YouTube generation were now part of the conversation, participating through social media, connecting producers and consumers in new communities and holding media corporations to account. And any great creative organisation had also, according to Murdoch, to be an ethical organisation, 'a place of honesty and integrity and an environment where curiosity and enthusiasm are the norm' (Murdoch 2012).

Less than three months after Murdoch's Edinburgh speech, the BBC Director General, George Entwistle, was forced to resign, having apparently allowed 'rogue' reporters at an external investigative news bureau to make sensational but wildly inaccurate allegations against a senior political figure on one of the BBC's flagship news programmes. Few of the BBC's critics believed that the BBC itself was fundamentally corrupt or that Entwistle was himself responsible for a poor piece of journalism. Yet in today's networked television ecosystem, the BBC's journalistic values had to be directed outwards as well as inwards. The BBC leadership was accused of failing to communicate its values through its extended network of subcontractors, partners and outsourcing relationships. 'Linking' to an external network has become a critical task for leadership in today's networked organisations. Values have to be communicated and shared if they are to be effective. In this respect, Heywood argues that the RSC was ahead of the curve.

successor as executive director, Catherine Mallyon, in May 2012), Boyd and Heywood have established a solid platform for the RSC leadership. There is continuity and trust, but there is also space for diversity and renewal; the next leadership will follow its own cycle of vision and inter-action, internal engagement and external definition, but will be working within a coherent organisational culture rather than having to invent one.

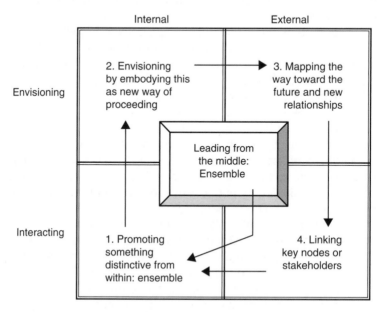

Figure 13.2   The leadership keypad at the RSC

CONNECTING LEADERSHIP TO ORGANISATION   *Summary*

In this chapter we have described 'creative leadership' at the RSC working through a series of phases over a ten-year period. The initial phase was more inwardly directed, **promoting** ideas from below through interaction with all members of the organisation, aiming to build up a shared vision of the company's direction. The next phase was **sussing** that vision – condensing and articulating a coherent set of principles and giving symbolic weight to these values through the actions of the leaders. Attention then moved towards a more external articulation of the company vision, **mapping** a definable difference which other stakeholders (funders, audiences) could recognise and buy into and redefining the relationships between the company and its partners and competitors. Finally, the company moved towards **linking** with a new generation of stakeholders, including audiences, new recruits and ultimately with a new leadership.

These different phases are presented separately to indicate a progression through the ten-year leadership of the company and to reflect an evolution in confidence and clarity of vision. Boyd compared leading an organisation to a heart pumping blood through the body, opening up to draw ideas in, then contracting to force these ideas through the arteries. The initial opening up was necessary to recruit the commitment and trust of the workforce, promoting ideas from below, the sussing and mapping phases condensed and drove that shared vision forward, and the final linking phase showed the company reopening the conversation about the company's future, confident enough to allow others to play a part in redefining the organisation.

However, these analytical categories should not imply a straightforward linear progress. Throughout their time at the RSC, Boyd and Heywood were able to draw on different modes of leadership and styles of communication to suit the needs of the moment. The essence of creative leadership *essence of creative ILS @RSC* is an ability to combine apparently contradictory ways of thinking and frames of reference. So Boyd and Heywood were simultaneously interacting *and* envisioning, leading from below by promoting and linking, *and* leading from above by articulating and symbolising a shared ethos, directing their attention and energy inwards to colleagues and stakeholders, *and* referring outwards to new partners and collaborators. Promoting ideas from within was necessary in order to 'suss' the collective vision; mapping that vision outwards allowed the RSC to 'define difference' and redefine its relationships with other companies, audiences and funders but also helped to further 'suss' or sharpen the internal vision. Linking to external viewpoints and promoting internal ideas can be seen as mutually reinforcing 'leading from below', but only made sense in relation to the higher-level 'sussing' and 'mapping' which drew these disparate influences together and made sense of them.

Nor does the 'leadership cycle' have to start at any given point on the circle. For Heywood and Boyd, starting at the bottom and starting with the people inside the organisation was the logical entry point. Whoever succeeds them is just as likely to begin somewhere else. The new artistic director, Greg Doran, is an internal appointment and over the past ten years has already witnessed the 'promoting' and 'sussing' of the internal culture (indeed his appointment is a reflection of that process). It may accordingly make more sense for him to focus on 'mapping' external relationships with other artists, venues and collaborators rather than focusing inwards. For external consultants, 'mapping' (analysing relationships, value chains, competitors) is very often the starting point because it fits the consultant's analytical skills and perspective; yet it may not be the best fit for the organisation. Each leader will need to start somewhere on the cycle, based on the organisation's particular predicament, and adapt their approach as the organisation (and its leadership) grows in maturity and strength.

Leadership at the RSC has thus been paradoxical or bisociative according to the terms set out in our introduction, combining different capabilities and perspectives to serve the needs of the time. It has also been extremely effective, measured both in the artistic successes such as the company's Histories cycle, the residency in New York or the Complete Works festival, and in the financial stability which allowed the company to rebuild its main theatres and remain viable and ambitious through a challenging period for UK arts funding and for the wider economy. At the time of writing the company is producing the World Shakespeare Festival as part of the cultural programme for the 2012 London Olympics.

Creative leadership is also the bridge into creative organisation. By defining and redefining the values and ethos of the RSC, Boyd and Heywood established a sustainable organisation with a coherent identity and vision extending beyond their own stewardship. They also created space within that organisation for a diversity of opinions and for a fresh round of innovations and entrepreneurial initiatives to re-animate and re-orientate the organisation in the future. The ultimate achievement of a leader is to make leadership appear invisible or unnecessary. Looking to the future, Heywood and Boyd can reflect that they have succeeded in taking the leaders out of leadership, and allowing the creative organisation of the RSC to prosper without them. This leads us on to the final section of this book: the creativity of organisation.

QUESTIONS FOR DISCUSSION

1. If you were to lead a creative organisation such as the RSC, what would you seek to achieve in your first 100 days, and how would you seek to achieve this? Can you identify your starting position on the 'creative leadership keypad'?
2. What are the key lessons about leading organisations in the creative sector from Vikki Heywood's experiences? Do you think that these lessons would apply to leading organisations in other sectors too?
3. Definitions of 'creative industries' and 'cultural industries' are contested in academic circles, and debates over their validity and scope have recently been revisited in UK cultural policy discussions. How helpful are these terms in understanding leadership at the RSC?
4. Reflecting back on all of the chapters in this section, develop four principles of creative leadership that you could apply.

REFERENCES

Bilton, C. and S. Cummings (2010), *Creative strategy: reconnecting business and innovation*, Chichester: Wiley.

Gladwell, M. (2000), *The tipping point: how little things can make a big difference*, London: Little, Brown.

Hersey, P. and K. Blanchard (1977), *The management of organizational behaviour: utilising human resources*, London: Prentice Hall International.

Hewison, R., J. Holden and S. Jones (2010), *All together: a creative approach to organisational change*, London: Demos.

Ibbotson, P. (2008), *The illusion of leadership: directing creativity in business and the arts*, Basingstoke: Palgrave Macmillan.

Legge, K. (2003), 'Strategy as organizing', in S. Cummings and D. Wilson (eds) *Images of strategy*, Oxford: Blackwell, 74–104.

Mumford, M.D., G.M. Scott, B. Gaddis and J.M. Strange (2002), 'Leading creative people: orchestrating expertise and relationships', *The Leadership Quarterly*, 13(6), 705–50.

Murdoch, E. (2012), James MacTaggart Memorial Lecture, Edinburgh International Television Festival, 23 August 2012 (available at: http://www.mediaweek.co.uk/news/1147079/Elisabeth-Murdochs-full-MacTaggart-speech/).

Parrish, D. (2006), *T-shirts and Suits: a guide to the business of creativity*, Liverpool: Merseyside ACME.

Porter, M. (1996), 'What is strategy?', *Harvard Business Review*, November–December, pp. 61–78.

Schlesinger, P. (2010), '"The most creative organisation in the world": The BBC, "creativity" and management style', *International Journal of Cultural Policy*, 16(3), August, 271–85.

Weick, K. (1995), *Sensemaking in organizations*, Thousand Oaks, CA: Sage.

PART IV

CREATIVE ORGANISATION

Introduction to Part IV: Creative Organisation

Chris Bilton and Stephen Cummings

The final part of this handbook considers the organisational structures and conditions which frame innovation, entrepreneurship and leadership. Discussions of creativity and management tend to position creativity as a specialism within an organisation rather than as a characteristic of the organisation as a whole. This section considers how we organise for creativity, and how this is itself a creative act.

Paul Kohler is a veteran of the video games industry. In 2007 he decided to make creativity in the video games industry the subject of a PhD.[1] Speaking to managers, developers and designers, he established that creativity was a relative concept – games had to be 'creative enough' for the market. This led him to the concept of a 'creative continuum', with highly original games at one end of the spectrum and re-workings or adaptations of existing games at the other. A new game, aiming to transform the market and initiate a new franchise – literally a 'game changer' for the company – would require a heavy investment of resources (time and money). A movie spin-off would require less creative input and hence less investment. Spending too much time on a sequel and overachieving on quality would be a waste of resources; investing too little on an original game was likewise a category error. Leadership had to know when to give the creative teams a free rein, and when to impose tighter budgetary and technical constraints. In the creative industries, organisations very deliberately define the terms within which creative thinking will occur. Of course, success and failure remain unpredictable – but the organisational constraints define the terms within which success or failure will be judged. Organisations can push innovation towards active creation or passive discovery; they can respond to visionary leadership from the top or interactive/distributed leadership from below; they can be driven by entrepreneurial diligence or inspired by entrepreneurial dilettantism. Creative organisation is thus both the cause and effect of creative management and caps the preceding sections of this handbook.

At the beginning of this book we outlined two largely forgotten ideas: one from a study of management; the other from a study of creativity. The creativity idea was Koester's notion that creativity comes from

2 Ideas.
Bisociation
Loose-Tight

bisociations: the combination, or bringing to bear, of opposite and seemingly contradictory aspects. The management idea was that good organisations often exhibit simultaneously loose and tight characteristics. These have been themes that have run throughout this handbook, but they come to a head here in this final section. The question posed to the contributing authors was 'how can an organisational environment be developed that continues to encourage creativity?' And the answers supplied in response all have something of that loose/tight flavour.

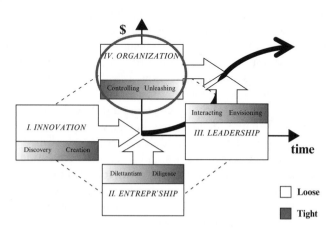

Doris Eikhof's chapter 'Transorganisational work and production in the creative industries' begins this section by arguing that the sort of managerial concerns once seen as the opponents of creativity – deadlines, budgets, control mechanisms – can actually stimulate creative people and groups and foster innovation. It looks at how people in the creative industries are advantaged by transgressing across their own organisational borders, to move in and out and to make new points of contact that help the development of new ideas and initiatives. And it examines how these findings from the creative industries can inform our understanding of creativity and management more widely.

Torkild Thanem and Sara Värlander's 'Fun-parks or *parkour*?: The ambiguities and paradox of planning pro-creative office design' investigates recent trends in office design that suggest that the key to promoting creativity in organisations is to tear down the walls and promote an atmosphere of 'fun'. Their research into the experiences of workers in two quite different organisations subjected to this kind of design suggests that tearing down walls, opening things up, and promoting fun may in fact not lead to greater creativity. They suggest creative people (such as urban freerunners or *parkour* enthusiasts) are likely to be inspired by boundaries and barriers – getting over or around them is part of what they do and part of the creative process. It may be better, then, to spend a lot of that money allocated to an office overhaul to hiring more really good people. (We think it is worth stressing that *parkour* is promoted here as a metaphor for mental dexterity and combinative play rather than something that should actually and physically be attempted in an organisation: in fact, such a notion was recently parodied in the US comedy series *The Office*.)

Over a decade ago David Oliver, Loizos Heracleous and Claus Jacobs pioneered a practical method of encouraging creative play, risk-taking, strategy-making and team-building among people in organisations by promoting building with LEGO as a proxy for real organisational tasks. In 'Balancing divergence and convergence: stimulating creativity through hybrid thinking' they reflect back and theorise why such an approach was (and still is) an extremely useful tool for promoting creative practices.

They outline how the 'serious play' afforded by directed tasks using LEGO enables the kind of 'hybrid thinking' that includes both the opening up to new ideas as they emerge and refocusing on important goal-oriented tasks. They argue that this divergent/convergent thinking is a key component in effective creativity and this kind of creativity is increasingly key in strategy-making in all organisations in the twenty-first century.

In the final chapter in this section on creative organisation, Giovanni Schiuma suggests that in order to provide space and time for creativity, organisations need to combine 'loose' and 'tight' properties and that this can best be achieved by integrating emotional aspects of the organisation with technical, rational systems through 'arts-based initiatives'. This brings artistic projects or attitudes into the organisation to trigger bisociative thinking. Giovanni's contribution, the last in this handbook, titled 'Shaping creative organisational environments through the arts', examines how this approach can be enacted and the benefits that can accrue.

The themes in these four chapters echo – and in this way will bring us back around to – the ideas promoted in the first section of this book on innovation. This is by design, and we shall discuss this design and its implications for a holistic approach to the management of creativity in a brief review chapter after the end of this fourth and final section of the handbook.

NOTE

1. Paul Kohler, *Creativity in video games: a creativity model set illustrating the creative process with theoretical and practical implications*, doctoral thesis, Centre for Cultural Policy Studies, University of Warwick.

14. Transorganisational work and production in the creative industries
Doris Ruth Eikhof

Academic and practitioner debates on managing creativity typically centre on how to facilitate people and groups being creative, how not to constrain their inventiveness, imagination and originality. To understand how creativity can be managed, a range of studies have focused on individual creativity, its antecedents, conducive environments and management techniques as well as potential constraints (e.g. Amabile 1996, Drazin et al. 1999, Oliver et al. (in this volume), Schiuma (in this volume), Sutton 2001). The underlying assumption of much of this debate is that management implies planning, organising and controlling processes of production and marketisation whereas working creatively requires freedom from tight schedules and space for imagination, unpredictable developments and play (e.g. Bilton and Leary 2002, Davis and Scase 2000, DeFillippi et al. 2007, see Thanem and Värlander in this volume for a discussion of whether office design can help provide such spaces for creativity). Where creativity is to be managed in an at least partly economic context, i.e. in relation to markets for product, finance (be it venture capital or public funding) or labour, the allegedly conflicting logics of management/ business on the one hand and of creativity, artistic ambition or cultural innovation on the other tend to be the focus of the discussion. But while management and creative practice do follow different logics (Eikhof and Haunschild 2007), a growing number of studies show that their relationship is by no means one of pure antagonism. As for instance Barrett (2004), Eikhof (2010) and Grabher (2002) show for software production, theatre and advertising, deadlines, finite budgets and management control can provide the boundaries that condense creative practice and facilitate innovative explosions and progress. Consequently, in their introduction to this volume, Bilton and Cummings expose dichotomist conceptualisations of management and creativity as too reductionist and as limiting our understanding of the real-life complexity in both management and creative practices. They call for conceptual and empirical approaches that capture the complexity of management and creativity.

This chapter heeds the call for an appreciation of such real-life complexity by analysing the work and production context that creativity and management are embedded in. The analysis focuses on a sector in which creativity is the key resource: the creative industries, or those industries 'supplying goods and services that we broadly associate with cultural, artistic, or simply entertainment value' (Caves 2000: 1). In these industries, constraining, let alone crushing, creativity would endanger the success of the respective creative enterprise, be it for- or not-for-profit. These industries therefore provide a particularly useful empirical setting for analysing the management of creativity in relation to its complex context of work and production.

Focusing on work and production uncovers an important aspect of managing creativity in the creative industries that has so far not been systematically addressed: the transorganisational character of work in these industries. In various ways, work and production in the creative industries transcend organisational boundaries and link the individual directly with structures at the macro-levels of field and society. Similarly, organisational practices link directly into such macro-structures, for instance where individual performance appraised in industry-wide processes of reputation-building rather than in intra-organisational exercises. The implications of transorganisational work and production in the creative industries for the management of creativity have so far not been explored, and the chapter will use the examples of recruitment and retention to discuss them. In so doing the chapter demonstrates how understanding the management of creativity requires understanding much more than an allegedly antagonistic, or at least ambiguous, relationship between management and creativity.

In order to analyse the real-life complexities of managing creativity in the creative industries, this chapter, firstly, focuses on the organisation of creative work and production. Drawing on an extensive range of empirical studies, work in the creative industries is characterised as transorganisational: as happening in and in relation to, but simultaneously transcending, organisations. Secondly, the chapter discusses how the transorganisationality of creative work and production influences the management of creative human resources. The chapter concludes by identifying avenues for future research and by discussing how findings from the creative industries can inform our understanding of creativity and management more widely.

THE ORGANISATION OF WORK AND PRODUCTION IN THE CREATIVE INDUSTRIES

Influentially defined by the UK's Department for Culture, Media and Sport as those industries that 'have their origin in individual creativity, skill and talent' (DCMS 2001: 5), the creative industries are typically thought to include architecture and design, film, television, video, radio and publishing, fine arts, music and the performing arts, software and computer gaming, advertising and crafts (e.g. Caves 2000, DCMS 2001). Although the organisation of production across these industries varies, there is, as Hesmondhalgh (2007: 24) points out, a 'collective nature of these industries that matters' and that can thus be analysed across the creative industries. Focusing on the commonalities of these industries, several characteristics stand out: individual creativity and talent are the key resources, intellectual property rights play a crucial role, workers are driven by intrinsic motivation and the production of material outputs is overlaid by the production of meaning (e.g. Bilton 2007, Caves 2000, Hesmondhalgh 2007, Howkins 2001). For the management of creativity, however, two other features characteristic of the creative industries are more important. Firstly, the first unit of production incurs high sunk costs. Music recordings, a computer game or the first opening of an exhibition require high initial investment, only a fraction of which is required for their (mass) reproduction. Secondly, product success depends on changeable subjective taste, trends and fashions, and is difficult to engineer – a characteristic termed the creative industries' 'nobody knows' property by Caves (2000: 2). Consequently, only a small percentage of creative products are profitable. High initial sunk costs and risky product markets mean that to be viable, production in the creative industries has to be as flexible as possible: a flexible organisation of production reduces sunk costs and therefore potential losses. Constituting a significant part of the real-life context of management and creativity, the work and production context in the creative industries is thus one of a flexible organisation of production (Eikhof and Warhurst 2012). The following subsections review a range of existing empirical studies to describe this work and production context more systematically. This review focuses on three aspects: the organisation of production; the relationship between organisations, creative workers and the immediate context of production; and labour markets.

Production in Collaborations

Reviewing existing studies with respect to the organisation of production shows that the single most obvious characteristic of the creative industries is a focus on what is commonly called a project (e.g. Caves 2000, Davis and Scase 2000, Faulkner and Anderson 1987). Production and labour processes are designed to produce a certain product or service within a given period of time, which can be a fixed deadline or the achievement of a certain output. A book, a movie, a TV show, a theatre play, a painting, a sculpture, a radio show or a song can be seen as a project, and might themselves be a part of a larger project, e.g. a theatre repertoire, a TV or radio programme, a series of books or paintings. The outcome of these projects may be subject to further distribution, promotion, merchandising or exhibition, but the core process of production is designed and understood as a project, undertaken by specifically assembled teams.

In management and organisation studies, however, the term project has been colonised by the debate on project management in which 'projects are seen as tools, not as organisations' (Packendorff 1995: 324) and which focuses on the efficient use of projects as management tools (e.g. Lundin and Söderholm 1995). Alternative terms such as 'temporary organisations' (Lundin and Söderholm 1995) or 'project ecologies' (Grabher 2002) prioritise organisational and resource perspectives, respectively, over a focus on the organisation of production and work. We therefore use the term collaboration to refer to the temporary, output-defined structures of production and work in the creative industries.

Collaborations dominate production and work across all creative industries: a range of partners come together for a limited time to produce a certain creative output. In the performing arts, sequences of rehearsals from first readings to dress rehearsals including light, costumes and sound culminate in a premiere and a series of shows, after which the collaboration ends and partners disband (Broughton 2001, Dempster 2006, Eikhof 2010, Haunschild 2003, Sgourev 2011). In film, TV and radio, teams of creative professionals, technical professionals and support workers shoot or record the raw material, which is then edited, distributed to movie houses or broadcasters and released to the public. Production teams disband after the shooting/recording stage and a network of specialist subcontractors completes the subsequent stages of production. These industries are particularly indicative examples of how the 'production process is organised around those individual projects rather than any permanent production company per se' (Blair et al. 2001: 172, see also Baker and Faulkner 1991, Baumann 2002, Blair 2001, Christopherson and Storper 1989, Davis and Scase 2000, DeFillippi and Arthur 1998, Dex et al. 2000, Faulkner and Anderson 1987, Jones 1996, Starkey et al. 2000, Sydow and Staber 2002, Windeler and Sydow 2001). Evidence from the music and advertising industry shows that here, too, collaborations as temporary structures constitute the relevant context of work and employment (Davis and Scase 2000, Gander and Rieple 2002, Gander et al. 2007, Grabher 2002, 2004, Hesmondhalgh 1996, 2007, Lee 1995, Lopes 1992, Lorenzen and Frederiksen 2005, Petersen and Berger 1971, 1975, Thompson et al. 2007). Although stable organisations in the form of record labels and advertising agencies are important players in these industries, Grabher (2002: 247) describes a 'projectification' of advertising work and Davis and Scase (2000: 67) characterise the music industry as 'complex, network-based and built around short-term contracts'. Lastly, even in the visual arts or publishing, where creative outcomes are attributed to individuals, a closer look reveals that production is structured around temporary collaborations of, for example, freelance painters, sculptors or writers, technical support staff, gallery owners and editors (Caves 2000, Davis and Scase 2000, Granger et al. 1995, Kammertöns 2007, Stanworth and Stanworth 1997, Wijnberg and Gemser 2000). Contemporary visual artists such as Damien Hirst, Olafur Eliasson or Ron Mueck, for example, produce work that is publicised in their individual names with teams of up to 80 people (Diez 2007, Foundation Cartier pour l'art contemporain 2006, Rauterberg 2006, Timm 2007).

Depending on the type of output and the scale of the creative endeavour at hand, collaborations differ with respect to their complexity and the intensity with which individual work practices are interwoven with those of other collaborators. Even though a fiction writer, for instance, might collaborate closely with an editor, their everyday work practices will be less entwined than those of an opera director with the respective singers and musicians. Likewise, an action movie shot at several locations in parallel will require more complex schedules and communication structures than a short, one-location TV documentary. But despite these differences in complexity and intensity, the structural context of work throughout the creative industries remains temporary and output-focused and involves constantly changing teams of collaborators. Reviewing existing studies with respect to the organisation of production and work therefore exposes collaborations as a first characteristic of the context in which creativity is managed in the creative industries.

Organisations, Collaborations and Creative Workers

In describing the organisation of creative production as collaborations, we have already alluded to the fact that the context of creativity and management in the creative industries transcends organisational boundaries. Because of this transcendence, two relationships become relevant: the employment relationship between organisations and creative workers and the relationship between organisations and collaborations.

Across creative industries the employment relationship between creative workers and organisations typically exhibits three characteristics. Firstly, these industries feature a high percentage of freelance workers and self-employment (e.g. European Commission 2006, Menger 1999). While average rates of freelance employment across all creative industries and occupations are estimated between 33 per cent and 50 per cent (e.g. Davis and Scase 2000), in industries such as film and TV up to 90 per cent of workers are freelance (Skillset 2010). The European Commission (2006: 100) concludes that 'artists (performing artists, writers, directors, visual artists, craftspeople, composers, musicians, designers and others) are usually self-employed freelancers' (see also Benhamou 2000). Secondly, when creative workers do find themselves in employment, these employment contracts tend to be temporary (European Commission 2006, Menger 1999). Often lasting only a few days or weeks (Dex et al. 2000), temporary contracts mean that many creative workers spend as much time looking for work as they spend in employment (Blair et al. 2001, Dex et al. 2000, Skillset 2008, 2010). Thirdly, creative workers are often involved in more than one collaboration at a time (Bain 2005, Blair et al. 2003, Dex et al. 2000, Menger 1999, Randle and Culkin 2009). In theatre, for instance, actors on temporary contracts with one theatre will frequently take on additional work as freelancers at the same time (Haunschild and Eikhof 2009). Similarly, Gill (2002) describes new media workers as typically working on two to three projects in parallel, none of which occupy all their time or provide all the income they need.

These three characteristics may vary across creative industries, countries or professions. For instance, because the allocation of subsidies to arts organisations and projects is organised differently in the UK and Germany, British actors, ballet dancers, singers or musicians tend to have much lower job security and higher rates of short-term, freelance employment than their German counterparts (e.g. Broughton 2001, Haak 2008). Similarly, some big broadcasting corporations still boast considerable shares of permanently employed creatives while in small independents the same tasks are undertaken by freelancers, temporary workers or interns with little to no employment security (Davis and Scase 2000, Hesmondhalgh 2007). However, focusing on the commonalities across the creative industries, two key points arise:

- The relationship between organisations and individuals tends to be temporary, freelance and not necessarily full-time. It is thus considerably looser than in other industries and, importantly, participation in collaborations is not necessarily linked to organisational membership.
- These loose relationships between employers and creative workers are characteristic not only for creative workers on the periphery of the production process who can easily be substituted, but also for those workers whose input is crucial to the creative outcome, such as lead actors, singers or dancers, directors or conductors.

With respect to the relationship between organisations and collaborations, it tends to be organisations that initiate collaborations and provide financial resources and organisational infrastructure. But how closely these collaborations are then integrated into any one organisation's processes and structures differs widely across the creative industries internationally. The Anglo-American film industry, for instance, comprises a complex web of large corporations, small and micro enterprises and freelance workers with one-off collaborations as their focal points. Producers initiate collaborations, but the production itself is spread across various actors and locations, all of which are only loosely linked to the producers via a network of temporary contracts. Subcontractors such as script writers, sound studios or editors use their own organisational and material infrastructure and any material resources required on set (sets, props, scaffolding, vehicles, catering, etc.) are hired from specialist companies. Although the production processes may be similar for most collaborations, they are specifically designed to meet the requirements of each individual film. Organisational processes and structures may intersect with collaborations, but are largely irrelevant: the Anglo-American film industry has become completely projectified and consists of a dynamic series of ever changing collaborations (Blair 2001, Christopherson and Storper 1989, Hesmondhalgh 2007, Paul and Kleingartner 1994).

In continental European performing arts, on the contrary, organisations play a much more prominent role (e.g. Broughton 2001, Haunschild 2003, Eikhof 2010). Stable organisations such as theatre, opera or ballet companies usually occupy architecturally prominent city centre premises and employ a substantive number of administrative and support staff on long-term contracts. Artistic staff such as actors, directors, stage, costumes and light designers work on contracts either for a season or for one production. Companies devise a season programme of shows, each of which constitutes a collaboration. Teams are assembled specifically for each collaboration and disband after the last performance. Typically, several collaborations run in parallel at any given time, so a season's worth of performances resembles a complex web of collaborations at different stages of development, rehearsal and exhibition. As the companies initiate, co-ordinate, resource and market these collaborations, the organisation–collaboration relationship is a comparatively close one in the performing arts. Collaborations are integrated into organisational processes and structures such as the programme of shows, rehearsal timetables or marketing and public relations activities. Although each show is produced as a distinct and idiosyncratic entity and although the performing arts are explicitly structured around these collaborations and their teams, companies as organisations dominate the industry's overall appearance.

Other creative industries occupy various places on this continuum from close to loose integration of organisations and collaborations. Similar to performing arts, collaborations in advertising are closely integrated into agencies as organisations (e.g. Davis and Scase 2000, Grabher 2002, 2004). The new media industry (e.g. Gill 2002, Pratt 2005) and Anglo-American theatre (e.g. Dempster 2006) resemble more the film industry, with collaborations only loosely linked to organisations. The TV and recorded music industries, finally, show a split structure (e.g. Baumann 2002, Davis and Scase 2000, Dex et al. 2000, Hesmondhalgh 2007, Starkey et al. 2000, Sydow and Staber 2002, Windeler and Sydow 2001). Where big broadcasting houses or record companies lead productions, collaborations are more closely intertwined with organisational structures and processes. But production in independent companies is as projectified as in the Anglo-American film industry.

Although in some industries collaborations may be more closely integrated into organisational processes, they remain distinct from these. It is an important feature of production in the creative industries that collaborations as the immediate context of production are distinct from general organisational procedures and processes. In many cases collaborations are initiated and resourced by organisations, but proceed without any direct interaction with organisational structures, processes and practices. To understand management and creativity in these industries we therefore need to take not only the relationship between organisations and creative workers into account, but also between organisations and the creative workers' immediate work context, the collaborations. Analysing these two types of relationships exposes comparatively loose ties between organisations, collaborations and creative workers as a second characteristic of these industries.

Labour Markets

The previous two sections revealed that work and production in the creative industries are organised in collaborations and that relationships between organisations, collaborations and creative workers are comparatively loose. Temporary constellations and loose relationships between the key actors make for a fluid and dynamic context of managing creativity in the creative industries. Who occupies which positions in this fluid and dynamic context is co-ordinated via the labour market. In traditional industrial production, organisations recruit the required human resources from an external labour market and screen them using various selection tools, for example interviews or psychometric tests. In addition, skilled and professional workers commonly find themselves in internal labour markets that match labour demand and supply within an organisation (Osterman 1987). Often offering promotions and career opportunities as well as a change of job, internal labour markets can help organisations retain valuable human resources. In the creative industries, however, where collaborations transcend organisational boundaries, processes of recruiting creative workers into collaborations differ markedly from such traditional matching of labour supply and demand.

Depending on the collaboration at hand, different types of inputs – creative, technical, business, administrative, support – are needed. These inputs are provided by workers with different skillsets and backgrounds who may be working as employees, freelancers or self-employed with their own micro-enterprise or SME ('freelancers' are sole traders, whereas 'self-employed' can have employees or be part of a practice). In completely projectified industries such as film and TV where collaborations almost entirely comprise freelancers and self-employed creatives, participation in collaborations is co-ordinated via what is traditionally understood as external labour markets. Initiators of collaborations contract creative workers for the duration of the collaboration or for the provision of specified inputs or services, and once this duration or output is achieved, the contractual relationship ends (e.g. DeFillippi and Arthur 1998, Faulkner and Anderson 1987, Randle and Culkin 2009). Such decisions about participation in collaborations are traditional recruitment decisions in the sense that they match demand and supply for a specific quality and quantity of labour via a traditional external labour market. Notably, though, because most collaborations only last for a relatively short time, these recruitment decisions occur substantially more often than in other industries. Where, on the contrary, creative workers are employed with an organisation, for instance with an advertising agency or as ensemble members in a performing arts organisation, decisions about participation in a collaboration can be understood as casting decisions: directors or managers choose a team for a collaboration from an existing cast of employees, similar to a football manager choosing the team for a match from the full squad. In these cases, employment and participation in a collaboration overlap, but they are not synonymous; creative workers can be employed by an organisation without participating in a specific collaboration.

Neither internal casting decisions nor external recruitment are internal or external labour markets in the traditional sense. Two aspects are particularly relevant here. Firstly, even where collaborations are comparatively closely integrated with organisations and creatives work as (temporary) employees, collaborations comprise substantive shares of freelance workers. These freelance workers pose direct competition to employed creatives, most prominently in the performing arts where directors regularly favour a freelance, 'guest' actor, singer or musician over an ensemble member. Casting decisions are thus not limited to internal labour markets, but regularly transgress organisational boundaries. Secondly, the decision-makers who recruit participants into a collaboration are not necessarily members of the organisation that initiates and resources the collaboration. In film, for instance, recruitment decisions are taken by freelance heads of departments, directors and casting agencies, all of which are only loosely linked to the production company (Blair 2001, Randle and Culkin 2009). Similarly, in the performing arts freelance directors decide on the cast for operas, plays and concerts that are produced and marketed in the respective opera, orchestra or theatre company's name (Dempster 2006, Haunschild and Eikhof 2009, for media Sutton Trust 2006). To a significant degree not only the creative workers who are subject to recruitment decisions, but also the decision-makers are at best loosely aligned with the respective organisation. The distinction between external and internal labour markets thus becomes meaningless. Like collaborations as the immediate context of work and production, the mechanisms for co-ordinating participation in collaborations transcend organisations. With respect to the real-life complexities of management and creativity, these transorganisational labour markets therefore constitute the third relevant characteristic of creative industries.

Transorganisational Work

The previous subsections have described three characteristics of the real-life context of management and creativity in the creative industries, focusing on the organisation of production, the relationship between organisations, creative workers and the immediate context of production, and labour markets. Analysis of the creative industries with respect to these three aspects reveals three characteristics:

- Creative production and work are undertaken in temporary structures: collaborations. Workers with diverse skills and undertaking diverse tasks come together for a limited stretch of time to produce a certain project output. This output determines the processes designed for the collaboration, its duration and its cast of creative workers and other partners. As collaborations are idiosyncratically designed to suit the creative endeavour at hand, the context of management and creativity constantly changes. Importantly, collaboration-specific processes and schedules constitute the main frame of reference in which creative capacity is turned into creative output; organisational structures or production processes are of lesser or no importance.

- Organisations, collaborations and creative workers are only loosely coupled. Organisations can be influential partners in collaborations but collaborations need not be closely linked to any one organisation or integrated with organisational processes. Likewise, creative workers do not have to be members of a particular organisation to partake in collaborations; on the contrary, organisation-individual relationships are typically governed by short-term, flexible contracts.
- Teams for collaborations are recruited via labour markets that transcend organisations. Internal and external labour markets in the traditional sense amalgamate to form transorganisational labour markets that reconcile the supply of creative workers with the collaboration-driven demand for creative labour.

These three characteristics – collaborations as the key context of creative work and production, loose coupling of organisations, creative workers and collaborations, and transorganisational labour markets – denote what we term the ideal type of transorganisational work. This definition highlights that work in the creative industries transcends organisations in a way that makes distinctions between internal and external workforces or labour markets obsolete. For understanding the real-life complexities of management and creativity in the creative industries, the status of creative workers as members of organisations becomes less important; it is superseded by their involvement in a series of creative collaborations. In other words: what counts in the creative industries is who is involved in which collaborations, in which role and with what success. The underlying contractual arrangements of employment or between organisations and collaborations are of, at best, secondary interest.

In the following section we will explore the implications of transorganisational work for the management of creative human resources. Before proceeding with our analysis, however, we need to draw attention to ideal types as a tool of theoretical enquiry. Following Weberian tradition, the ideal type of transorganisational work was constructed by 'abstracting and synthesising those characteristics that a set of empirical phenomena have in common' (Weber 1922/1972: 193, author's translation). Ideal types provide a theoretically guided and focused analysis of social phenomena and thus prevent empirical research from remaining a mere collection of individual case data (see also Kluge and Kelle 1999). Instead of minutely mirroring real practices of work and production in a particular creative industry's setting, the ideal type of transorganisational work offers 'a foil against which unique contextual features can be more easily seen' (Neumann 2000: 34). It is in this sense that we employ the ideal type of transorganisational work in the remainder of this chapter and suggest it be used for further empirical analysis within and outwith the creative industries.

MANAGING CREATIVITY, MANAGING A TRANSORGANISATIONAL WORKFORCE *per Ideal Type*

As outlined at the beginning of this chapter and in Bilton and Cummings' introduction to the handbook (Chapter 1), management and creativity are typically discussed as antagonistic. The underlying assumption is that management's need to plan, monitor and control limits creative freedom and thus constrains the quality and innovativeness of creative work. While such dichotomist views have been exposed as too simplistic (e.g. Bilton 2007, Eikhof 2010, Grabher 2002), management and creative practices do indeed follow different and distinct logics, which we have elsewhere described as artistic and economic logics (Eikhof and Haunschild 2007). Balancing or reconciling these logics is crucial to managing workers in the creative industries (e.g. Bilton 2007, Davis and Scase 2000, Barrett 2004). However, analysing work in the creative industries as transorganisational draws attention to a range of other pertinent aspects of managing creativity. These other aspects are the focus of the following discussion.

Because creativity is provided by individuals, a substantial share of managing creativity is managing human resources. The key task of human resource management (HRM) is to ensure that, firstly, the right quality and quantity of human resources are available for production and that, secondly, this workforce converts its potential into actual productivity. A variety of HRM tools can help facilitate this task: HR planning, recruitment and selection, performance monitoring and appraisal, retention and dismissal. Notably, though, the majority of these tools are premised on a long-term perspective and assume that employees stay with organisations for at least some length of time. Traditionally, the underlying assumption of recruitment, training, performance monitoring and appraisal and retention is that the employee will remain with the respective organisation long enough for these HRM investments to pay off. In the transorganisational work and production context of the creative industries, however, organisation-individual relationships are typically neither that tight nor that stable. Organisations and individuals are only loosely connected and their relationship is typically of a temporary nature. These features of transorganisational work and production have important implications for the management of creative human resources, which will be discussed in the following.

A first major implication of transorganisational work and production is that although in the creative industries, managing creativity equals HRM, traditional systematic training approaches are absent. As short-term relationships between organisations and individuals do not allow organisations to recoup substantial training investments, on-the-job training tends to be in the form of unpaid or low-paid internships without clear pathways from education to employment. Although on-the-job training, as opposed to training provided by further and higher education institutions, is seen as vital in these industries (e.g. Grugulis and Stoyanova 2009, Randle and Culkin 2009), a 'grow your own' approach to creative human resources is not lucrative for most creative industries employers. Large organisations with an explicit training and development approach, such as the BBC, for instance, remain the exception. Initiatives such as the Skillset internships and Skillset Academies in the UK try to establish more systematic industry-based training schemes, but unpaid work experiences continue to dominate routes into the industry (e.g. Skillset 2010).

A second implication of transorganisational work and production for the management of creative human resources concerns retention. As unemployment is typically high in the creative industries, retaining creative workers once they have been recruited into a collaboration is typically not a problem. Instead, the focus shifts from retention in the traditional sense to securing the availability of a pool of qualified creative human resources that can be recruited into collaborations as and when needed. At this point, the recruitment mechanisms prevalent in the creative industries come into play. Recruitment into collaborations – whether, as distinguished above, as recruitment in the traditional sense or as casting decisions – is overwhelmingly through the personal networks of those who artistically/creatively lead on a collaboration. Directors and producers build a team of collaborators they either know themselves or who have come recommended by trusted third parties, be those industry insiders or agencies (e.g. Blair 2001, Haunschild and Eikhof 2009, Randle and Culkin 2009, Sutton Trust 2006). In more complex collaborations, e.g. film productions, key collaborators such as heads of camera, sound or lighting departments recruit their crew through their own networks (Blair 2001). Recruitment through personal networks serves as a quality assurance mechanism: in collaborations with tight project schedules there is little to no room for correcting appointments, so making the right recruitment choices is crucial. Personal networks supply vital information not only on whether a specific individual can do the job, but also on their work ethic and what they are like to work with (Grugulis and Stoyanova 2009). Given these recruitment practices, the success of collaborations depends on the networks of the collaborations' decision-makers and on whether these networks can draw on a broad and deep enough pool of creative human resources.

From the point of view of organisations that initiate collaborations, this dependence on the collaborations' artistic decision-makers creates an interesting shift in the management of creative human resources: the collaborations' decision-makers are often not members of the organisation either. Directors, producers or conductors typically work as freelancers, with contracts often not extending beyond a single collaboration. An organisation's access to the desired quality and quantity of creative resources thus depends on individuals the organisation itself has got only loose ties with. These loosely linked individuals control the organisation's access to those resources that are most crucial to its creative and therefore business success. Compared with traditional HRM, this is quite a remarkable implication of transorganisational work and production. Themselves a consequence of organisations' attempts to minimise the business risks of creative production, transorganisational work and production result in organisations surrendering direct control over their core resources – a situation that runs counter to any management approach borne out of the influential resource-based view (e.g. Barney 1991, Penrose 1980), which sees tight control of core competencies and resources as crucial to organisational success.

To understand why organisations can risk such low control over core resources, the situation of individual creative workers needs to be taken into account. Two aspects are important in this regard. Firstly, the creative industries' transorganisational labour markets are fiercely competitive and constantly feature a significant over-supply of creative labour.

With contracts typically short term and often limited to single collaborations, creative workers spend a substantial amount of their time looking for employment instead of actually working on collaborations. For instance, 74 per cent of film workers surveyed by Skillset (2008) had been unemployed and sought work at some stage in the 12 months prior to the survey, with 30 per cent spending a substantial 11–29 weeks out of work. Creative human resources of higher quality will be more in demand and less readily available, but overall only a small percentage of those working in the creative industries can afford to be choosy about the collaborations they will get involved in.

Secondly, because collaborations are so central to the creative industries, careers are perceived as sequences of collaborations, too: films worked on, shows starred in, exhibitions contributed to. Career success is then assessed by the artistic clout attached to these collaborations (Boutinot 2012, Cameron 1995, Faulkner and Anderson 1987, Hirsch 1972, Jones 2002): what was the respective worker's role in the collabora-

tion, e.g. lead or supporting role, group or solo show? What is the reputation of the other collaboration partners involved, both in the absolute
sense of industry-wide reputation and in relation to the creative worker
in question (e.g. working with established artists reflects positively on a
novice while a collaboration staffed with no-names can damage the good
reputation of a mid-career creative)? How did critics asses the collaboration's artistic output, e.g. was it awarded any prizes or awards, featured at
festivals? What genre did the collaboration's output belong to and where
did it thus position its collaborators artistically within their industry?
What was the audience and market response, e.g. was a computer game or
advertising campaign commercially successful? Through such evaluations
of collaborations a creative worker has been involved in, individual artistic
reputations are built. Partly such reputations are driven by the individual
desire to make a particular artistic or creative contribution to the industry
(e.g. Bain 2005, Svejenova 2005). Creative workers define themselves as
dedicated to specific artistic genres and creative causes, which in turn give
meaning to their professional trajectories. At the same time, though, the
quest to establish one's artistic reputation is linked to the need to market
one's labour power (Bain 2005, Eikhof and Haunschild 2006, Haunschild
and Eikhof 2009). Creative workers have to clearly stand for a certain
authentic artistic contribution that decision-makers can recognise as valuable to a collaboration. A distinctive individual reputation is thus both an
outcome of artistic motivations and aspirations as well as a necessity for
winning opportunities to convert these motivations and aspirations into
actual artistic output by participating in collaborations.

From the point of view of an organisation initiating a collaboration,
this individual focus on artistic reputation is important. In order to be
(artistically or commercially) successful, an organisation has to initiate
collaborations that constitute an attractive opportunity to build artistic
reputation. Constellations need to be attractive to creative workers generally, but in particular to those who can lead them and can recruit other
creatives into the collaboration. Attracting collaboration leads is a task
typically undertaken by organisations' artistic or creative directors, which
means that an organisation's capacity to attract good collaborators is
again dependent on a particular individual's contact book. When artistic
and creative directors move, their contacts typically move with them and
the organisations' standing within the respective creative industry is up
for reassessment. To a certain extent such constant change induced by
the merry-go-round of creative human resources is deliberate: the prevailing ethos in the creative industries is one of development, transformation
and renewal, all of which are regarded as conducive to creative innovation (Boltanski and Chiapello 2005, Howkins 2001). Such beliefs might

contribute to creative industries organisations being less concerned about the long-term retention of creative human resources in the traditional sense. But managing creative human resources in the creative industries, both in a specific collaboration and in terms of organisations initiating portfolios of collaborations, requires careful maintenance of both personal contacts and artistic reputation.

Analysing the implications of transorganisational work and production thus uncovers an important dyad for managing creativity in the creative industries: the simultaneous importance of the individual creative worker and industry-wide mechanisms of reputation-building. At any given time, the micro-level of the individual is directly linked into the macro-level of the industry: individual action cannot be understood without linking it into industry-wide structures of personal networks, formal and informal performance assessment and reputation-building. This micro-macro dyad is important for those managing creativity in two ways. Firstly, it has to be taken into account in the management of creative workers. How an individual creative worker will behave on a collaboration in the day-to-day running of it, how committed they will be to it, how much of their energy and creative attention they will allocate to it will depend on how that collaboration is positioned within the transorganisational, industry-wide structures of networks and reputation-building. They might have been recommended to the collaboration by an influential contact within the industry, in which case they are likely to be motivated to live up to the expectations and the trust in their creative ability expressed through that recommendation. Equally, they might in parallel be working in a second collaboration that promises comparatively higher pay-offs in terms of artistic recognition, in which case they are less likely to contribute to the first collaboration with full energy. A manager has to be able to understand such individual but transorganisational concerns in order to shape collaborations, i.e. the context of creative work, in a way that makes it attractive for the creative workers to be most dedicated to the collaboration at hand.

Secondly, the micro-macro dyad needs to be taken into account when making strategic artistic or creative decisions, such as designing programmes, commissioning work or investing in individual artists. The industry-wide networks, perceptions of artistic quality, trends or criteria for creative innovation that are crucial for such strategic management of creativity cannot be understood without recourse to individuals' creative outputs and agendas, influential judgements or personal alliances (e.g. Alvarez et al. 2005, Jones 2010). To appreciate, for instance, how genres, and with them individual artists, are developed, the actions of critics, patrons and other influential industry insiders or 'cultural mediators'

(Bourdieu 1983a, 1983b) need to be considered. Rüling and Strandgaard Pedersen (2010), for instance, outline how film festivals can be understood as 'field-configuring events' in which the festival directors' or programming committee's programming decisions draw on existing perceptions of genres and artistic quality and at the same time challenge, confirm or alter these perceptions. In doing so, they influence both the context for individual careers and the evaluation of creative output throughout the industry. Similarly, managers need to understand the interplay of individual artists and key gatekeepers that drive the trends and form the genres a manager might want to orient production towards.

In this micro-macro dyad, organisations play a role, but not necessarily the decisive one. Individual action and industry-wide structures and processes include organisations, but they transcend them. In their daily working lives, individuals are concerned both with their immediate collaborators and with their embeddedness in the industry. Both are relevant and influence individual action at the same time. Vice versa, industry structure and action is always related to concrete individuals. This micro-macro dyad is thus a key aspect of the real-life context of managing creativity – and one that emerges from analysing work and production in the creative industries as transorganisational.

CONCLUSION

The aim of this chapter was to open up the analysis of managing creativity in a way that appropriately captured the real-life complexity of management and creativity. This analysis was deliberately situated in the creative industries, where creativity is the decisive resource and its management thus crucial to organisational success. Drawing on existing studies, the chapter has argued that work and production in the creative industries are transorganisational. Work and production are undertaken in collaborations as temporary structures that are designed towards producing a defined project output. Organisations, collaborations and creative workers are only loosely coupled, and recruitment into collaborations is via transorganisational labour markets that transcend what traditionally would be called internal and external labour markets. In a second step the chapter then analysed how the transorganisationality of creative work and production influence the management of creativity. In the creative industries, managing creativity largely means managing human resources, but because of the transorganisationality of creative work and production, HRM deviates from traditional HRM practices. Long-term orientations in recruitment, training, performance appraisal and retention are replaced by dynamic and flexible relationships between individuals that transcend both organisations and collaborations and are always oriented towards the industry as a whole. Analysing HRM practices in the creative industries thus revealed a context of work and production that is at the same time focused on industry-wide structures, i.e. the transorganisational structures of work and production, and on individual creative workers and decision-makers, each with their own artistic reputation. Managing creativity, both as managing individual creative workers and as strategically managing creative programmes and outputs, requires awareness of this micro-macro dyad.

possible new research

Analysing management and creativity in the creative industries from the perspective of transorganisational work and production opens up two new pathways for future research into the real-life context of management and creativity. Firstly, it broadens our understanding of such management in the creative industries themselves. In creative industries research, managing creativity is predominantly discussed as balancing tensions between art and business, or artistic and economic logics. Although this aspect is clearly important for managing creativity, this chapter has demonstrated that the transorganisationality of work and production in the creative industries impacts management and creativity in ways that lie beyond balancing potential conflicts between art and business. For understanding management and creativity in their real-life context in these industries, both the relationship between art and business and the micro-macro dyad have to be taken into account. What happens at the level of individuals, organisations, projects and industries amalgamates into a complex context against which we need to understand the actions of creative workers and managers. Research into a particular collaboration, for instance the production of a show or a record, cannot be limited to the narrow empirical setting of the collaboration itself, but has to be linked into the wider industry and societal context, exploring, for instance, links between recruitment and reputation or performance and positioning in the industry.

Secondly, appreciating the implications of transorganisational work and production for management and creativity in the creative industries allows asking new questions of contexts in which the management of creativity is important, but the (potential) art-business conflict is not. For instance, in academia or corporate research and development, technological, scientific or intellectual creativity are vital resources. Distinguishing between the art-business relationship and the micro-macro dyad in the creative industries allows analysing which HRM practices are attributable to which influence, and can then help analyse to what extent transorganisationality of work and production impacts the management of creativity outwith the creative industries. Existing studies on knowledge-intensive work already hint at transorganisational aspects of such work, for instance with respect to employment practices or with respect to organisational knowledge creation (e.g. Carnoy et al. 1997, Cohendet and Simon 2007). Another prominent example is academia. University strategies require their researchers to collaborate with other institutions because such collaborations increase their own institutional reputation and their capacities for attracting funding. Nevertheless, in their daily operations universities often still fail to address the practicalities of staff working transorganisationally, i.e. across institutions, geographies and time zones, in a way that facilitates rather than constrains academic creativity. The perspective of transorganisational work could be used to analyse the degree to which organisational strategies of capitalising on field-wide networks of creativity and knowledge-generation need to be (and currently are) supported by administrative organisational policies and practices. Further, and similar to the creative industries, HRM in knowledge-intensive work equals the management of workers who creatively generate and apply knowledge. Again, applying a transorganisational work perspective could help better understand how such workers develop and exercise loyalties towards employers *vis-à-vis*, for instance, professions, and what the implications are for an organisationally driven management of creativity.

In making these two contributions to future research within and outwith the creative industries, the chapter has proposed new conceptual avenues for understanding the real-life context of management and creativity. As a conceptual perspective, transorganisational work and production allows better appreciating the complexity of managing creativity. Research using this perspective can therefore generate new understanding of the real-life practices in a substantial share of contemporary and future workplaces, and can thus provide insights that are relevant to academics and practitioners alike.

QUESTIONS FOR DISCUSSION

1. What challenges might one expect when managing a team of transorganisationally-oriented creatives and organisation-focused support staff?
2. What are the advantages and disadvantages of transorganisational careers for the individual creative worker?
3. What might be the property-rights implications of a business strategy explicitly aimed at capitalising on transorganisational networks of creativity?

4. If transorganisational work and production dominate an industry, how can industry organisations (e.g. employer federations, sector skills councils, unions) attempt to ensure the availability of creative resources to that industry as a whole?

REFERENCES

Alvarez, J.L., C. Mazza, J. Strandgaard Pedersen and S. Svejenova (2005), 'Shielding idiosyncrasy from isomorphic pressures: Towards optimal distinctiveness in European film making', *Organization*, **12**(6), 863–88.
Amabile, T. (1996), *Creativity in context*, New York: Westview.
Bain, A. (2005), 'Constructing an artistic identity', *Work, Employment and Society*, **19**(1), 25–46.
Baker, W.E. and R.R. Faulkner (1991), 'Role as resource in the Hollywood film industry', *American Journal of Sociology*, **97**(2), 279–309.
Barney, J. (1991), 'Firm resources and sustained competitive advantage', *Journal of Management*, **17**(1), 99–119.
Barrett, R. (2004), 'Working at Webboyz: An analysis of control over the software development labour process', *Sociology*, **38**(4), 777–94.
Baumann, A. (2002), 'Informal labour market governance: The case of the British and German media production industries', *Work, Employment and Society*, **16**, 27–46.
Benhamou, F. (2000), 'The opposition between two models of labour market adjustment: The case of audiovisual and performing arts activities in France and Great Britain over a ten year period', *Journal of Cultural Economics*, **24**, 301–19.
Bilton, C. (2007), *Management and creativity. From creative industries to creative management*, Malden, MA: Blackwell Publishing.
Bilton, C. and R. Leary (2002), 'What can managers do for creativity? Brokering creativity in the creative industries', *International Jorunal of Cultural Policy*, **8**(1), 49–64.
Blair, H. (2001), '"You're only as good as your last job": The labour process and labour market in the British film industry', *Work, Employment and Society*, **15**(1), 149–69.
Blair, H., S. Grey and K. Randle (2001), 'Working in film. Employment in a project based industry', *Personnel Review*, **30**(2), 170–85.
Blair, H., N. Culkin and K. Randle (2003), 'From London to Los Angeles: a comparison of local labour market processes in the US and UK film industries', *International Journal of Human Resource Management*, **14**(4), 619–33.
Boltanski, L. and E. Chiapello (2005), *The new spirit of capitalism*, London: Verso.
Bourdieu, P. (1983a), *The field of cultural production. Essays on art and literature*, New York: Columbia University Press.
Bourdieu, P. (1983b), 'The field of cultural production, or: The economic world reversed', *Poetics*, **12**, 311–56.
Boutinot, A. (2012), 'Reputation-building in the French architecture field', in C. Matthieu (ed.), *Careers in the creative industries*, London: Routledge, pp. 163–84.
Broughton, A. (2001), 'Collective bargaining in the arts and culture sector: an examination of symphony orchestras in Germany and the UK', *European Journal of Industrial Relations*, **7**(3), 327–45.
Cameron, S. (1995), 'On the role of critics in the cultural industry', *Journal of Cultural Economics*, **19**, 321–31.
Carnoy, M., M. Castells and C. Benner (1997), 'Labour markets and employment practices in the age of flexibility: A case study of Silicon Valley', *International Labour Review*, **136**(1), 25–48.
Caves, R.E. (2000), *Creative industries*, Cambridge: Harvard University Press.
Christopherson, S. and M. Storper (1989), 'The effects of flexible specialization on industrial

politics and the labor market: The motion picture industry', *Industrial and Labor Relations Review*, **42**, 331–47.

Cohendet, P. and L. Simon (2007), 'Playing across the playground: Paradoxes of knowledge creation in the videogame firm', *Journal of Organizational Behavior*, **28**(5), 587–605.

Davis, H. and R. Scase (2000), *Managing creativity*, Buckingham: Open University Press.

DeFillippi, R.J. and M.B. Arthur (1998), 'Paradox in project-based enterprise', *California Management Review*, **40**(2), 125–39.

DeFillippi, R., G. Grabher and C. Jones (2007), 'Introduction to paradoxes of creativity: Managerial and organizational challenges in the cultural economy', *Journal of Organizational Behavior*, **28**(5), 511–21.

Dempster, A. (2006), 'Managing uncertainty in the creative industries: Lessons from Jerry Springer the Opera', *Creativity and Innovation Management*, **15**(3), 224–33.

Department for Culture, Media and Sport (DCMS) (2001), *Creative industries mapping document*, London: DCMS.

Dex, S., J. Willis, R. Paterson and E. Sheppard (2000), 'Freelance workers and contract uncertainty: the effects of contractual changes in the television industry', *Work, Employment and Society*, **14**(2), 283–305.

Diez, G. (2007), 'Atelierbesuch Olafur Eliasson', *ZEITmagazin Leben*, **34**, 40–42.

Drazin, R., M.A. Glynn and R.K. Kazanjian (1999), 'Multilevel theorizing about creativity in organizations: A sensemaking perspective', *Academy of Management Review*, **24**(2), 286–307.

Eikhof, D.R. (2010), 'The logics of art: analysing theatre as a cultural field', in B. Townley and N. Beech (eds), *Managing creativity: exploring the paradox*, Cambridge: Cambridge University Press.

Eikhof, D.R. and A. Haunschild, A. (2006), 'Lifestyle meets market. Bohemian entrepreneurs in creative industries', *Creativity and Innovation Management*, **13**(3): 234–41.

Eikhof, D.R. and A. Haunschild (2007), 'For art's sake! Artistic and economic logics in creative production', *Journal of Organizational Behavior*, **28**(5), 523–38.

Eikhof, D.R. and C. Warhurst (2013) 'The promised land? Why social inequalities are systemic to the creative industries', Employee Relations, **35**(5), 495–508.

European Commission (2006), *The economy of culture in Europe*, Luxembourg: KEA European Affairs.

Faulkner, R.R. and A.B. Anderson (1987), 'Short-term projects and emergent careers: Evidence from Hollywood', *American Journal of Sociology*, **92**, 879–909.

Foundation Cartier pour l'art contemporain (2006), *Ron Mueck*, London: Thames and Hudson.

Gander, J., A. Haberberg and A. Rieple (2007), 'A paradox of alliance management: Resource contamination in the recorded music industry', *Journal of Organizational Behavior*, **28**(5), 607–24.

Gander, J. and A. Rieple (2002), 'Inter-organisational relationships in the worldwide popular recorded music industry', *Creativity and Innovation Management*, **11**(4), 248–54.

Gill, R. (2002), 'Cool, creative and egalitarian? Exploring gender in project-based new media work in Europe', *Information, Communication and Society*, **5**(1), 70–89.

Grabher, G. (2002), 'The project ecology of advertising: tasks, talents and teams', *Regional Studies*, **36**(3), 245–62.

Grabher, G. (2004), 'Learning in projects, remembering in networks? Community, sociality, and connectivity in project ecologies', *European Urban and Regional Studies*, **11**(2), 103–23.

Granger, B., J. Stanworth and C. Stanworth (1995), 'Self-employment career dynamics: The case of "unemployment push" in UK book publishing', *Work, Employment and Society*, **9**(3), 499–516.

Grugulis, I. and D. Stoyanova (2009), '"I don't know where you learn them": skills in film and TV', in A. McKinlay and C. Smith (eds), *Creative labour*, London: Palgrave, pp. 135–55.

Haak, C. (2008), *Wirtschaftliche und soziale Risiken auf den Arbeitsmärkten von Künstlern*, Wiesbaden: VS Verlag für Sozialwissenschaften.

Haunschild, A. (2003), 'Managing employment relationships in flexible labour markets: The case of German repertory theatres', *Human Relations*, **56**(8), 899–929.

Haunschild, A. and D.R. Eikhof (2009), 'Bringing creativity to market. Actors as self-employed employees', in A. McKinlay and C. Smith (eds), *Creative labour. Working in the creative industries*, Basingstoke: Palgrave Macmillan.

Hesmondhalgh, D. (1996), 'Flexibility, post-Fordism and the music industries', *Media, Culture and Society*, **15**(3), 469–88.

Hesmondhalgh, D. (2007), *The cultural industries*, London: Sage.

Hirsch, P.M. (1972), 'Processing fads and fashions: An organization-set analysis of cultural industry systems', *American Journal of Sociology*, **77**(4), 639–59.

Howkins, J. (2001), *The creative economy*, London: Penguin.

Jones, C. (1996), 'Careers in project networks: The case of the film industry', in M.B. Arthur, and D.M. Rousseau (eds), *The boundaryless career. A new employment principle for a new organizational era*, Oxford: Oxford University Press, pp. 58–75.

Jones, C. (2002), 'Signaling expertise: how signals shape careers in creative industries', in M. Peiperl, M. Arthur and N. Anand (eds), *Career creativity: explorations in the remaking of work*, Oxford: Oxford University Press.

Jones, C. (2010), 'Finding a place in history: Symbolic and social networks in creative careers and collective memory', *Journal of Organisational Behavior*, **31**, 726–48.

Kammertöns, H.B. (2007), 'Atelierbesuch Jörg Immendorff', *ZEITmagazin Leben*, **24**, 44–6.

Kluge, S. and Kelle, U. (1999), *Vom Einzelfall zum Typus: Fallvergleich und Fallkonstrastierung in der qualitativen Sozialforschung*, Opladen: Leske + Budrich.

Lee, S. (1995), 'Re-examining the concept of the "independent" record company: The case of Wax Trax! Records', *Popular Music*, **14**(1), 13–31.

Lopes, P.D. (1992), 'Innovation and diversity in the popular music industry, 1969 to 1990', *American Sociological Review*, **57**, 56–71.

Lorenzen, M. and L. Frederiksen (2005), 'The management of projects and product experimentation: Examples from the music industry', *European Management Review*, **2**, 198–211.

Lundin, R.A. and A. Söderholm (1995), 'A theory of the temporary organization', *Scandinavian Journal of Management*, **11**(4), 437–55.

Menger, P.-M. (1999), 'Artistic labor markets and careers', *Annual Review of Sociology*, **25**, 541–74.

Neumann, W.L. (2000), *Social research methods. Qualitative and quantitative approaches*, 4th ed., Needham Heights: Allyn and Bacon.

Oakley, K. (2004), 'Not so cool Britannia: the role of the creative industries in economic development', *International Journal of Cultural Studies*, **7**(1), 67–77.

Osterman, P. (1987), 'Choice of employment systems in internal labor markets', *Industrial Relations*, **26**, 46–67.

Packendorff, J. (1995), 'Inquiring into the temporary organization: New directions for project management research', *Scandinavian Journal of Management*, **11**(4), 319–33.

Paul, A. and A. Kleingartner (1994), 'Flexible production and the transformation of industrial relations in the motion picture and television Industry', *Industrial and Labor Relations Review*, **47**, 663–78.

Penrose, E.G. (1980), *The theory of the growth of the firm*, 2nd ed., Oxford: Blackwell.

Petersen, R.A. and D.G. Berger (1971), 'Entrepreneurship in organizations: Evidence from the popular music industry', *Administrative Science Quarterly*, **16**, 97–106.

Petersen, R.A. and D.G. Berger (1975), 'Cycles in symbol production: The case of popular music', *American Sociological Review*, **40**, 158–73.

Pratt, A.C. (2005), 'New media: work organisation and place', paper presented at 23rd Annual International Labour Process Conference, Glasgow.

Randle, K. and N. Culkin (2009), 'Getting in and getting on in Hollywood: freelance careers in an uncertain industry', in A. McKinlay and C. Smith (eds), *Creative labour*, London: Palgrave, pp. 93–115.

Rauterberg, H. (2006), 'Heiß auf Matisse', *DIE ZEIT*, **17**, 17–20.

Rüling, C. and J. Strandgaard Pedersen (2010), 'Film festival research from an organizational studies perspective', *Scandinavian Journal of Management*, **26**, 318–23.

Sgourev, S. (2011), '"Wall Street" Meets Wagner: Harnessing Institutional Heterogeneity', *Theory and Society*, **40**(4), 385–416.

Skillset (2008), *Feature film production. Workforce survey report 2008*, London: Skillset.

Skillset (2010), *Creative media workforce survey*, London: Skillset.

Stanworth, C. and J. Stanworth (1997), 'Managing an externalised workforce: freelance labour-use in the UK book publishing industry', *Industrial Relations Journal*, **28**(1),43–55.

Starkey, K., C. Barnatt and S. Tempest (2000), 'Beyond networks and hierarchies: Latent organizations in the U.K. television industry', *Organization Science*, **11**(3), 299–305.

Sutton, R. (2001), 'The weird rules of creativity', *Harvard Business Review*, **79**(8), 94–103.

Sutton Trust (2006), *The educational background of leading journalists*, London: Sutton Trust.

Svejenova, S. (2005), '"The path with the heart": Creating an authentic career', *Journal of Management Studies*, **42**(5), 947–74.

Sydow, J. and U. Staber (2002), 'The institutional embeddedness of project networks: The case of content production in German television', *Regional Studies*, **36**(3), 215–27.

Timm, T. (2007), 'Atelierbesuch Jeff Koons', *ZEITmagazin Leben*, **38**, 46–8.

Thompson, P., M. Jones and C. Warhurst (2007), 'From conception to consumption: Creativity and the missing managerial link', *Journal of Organizational Behavior*, **28**(5), 625–40.

Weber, M. (1922/1972), *Wirtschaft und Gesellschaft*, Tübingen: Mohr (1st ed. 1922; 5th ed. 1972).

Wijnberg, N.M. and G. Gemser (2000), 'Adding value to innovation: Impressionism and the transformation of the selection system in visual arts', *Organization Science*, **11**(3), 323–9.

Windeler, A. and J. Sydow (2001), 'Project networks and changing industry practices – collaborative content production in the German television industry', *Organization Studies*, **22**(6), 1036–60.

15. Fun-parks or *parkour*? The ambiguities and paradox of planning pro-creative office design
Torkild Thanem and
Sara Winterstorm Värlander

Over the past century open office design has taken a number of forms, of which the open-plan office and office landscaping may be the most well known. The open-plan office, which traditionally was adopted in work environments housing white-collar workers such as typists and book-keeping assistants, lines up workstations to expose individuals to supervision (Hofbauer 2000). Conversely, office landscaping is less linear, more informal, and organises employees in circles and groups to facilitate communication and interaction. Nevertheless, it often organises workstations to make different groups easily recognisable, and employs principles of distance and visibility to inscribe differentials in status and authority between employees at different hierarchical levels (ibid.). While dividing walls and doors and private offices are at odds with any school of open office design, both the open-plan office and office landscaping are underpinned by a formal definition of office space, its use and purpose. But in recent years organisations have started to adopt distinctive forms of office design that give a new edge to openness in the workplace. By removing spatial and social structures by design, these approaches are typically intended to increase performance by fostering openness, sponta-neous interaction and learning: like a fun-park. And, as such, many have associated this new way of organising with increased creativity.

Many trace the beginnings of this workplace architectural revolution to the invention of Apple Computers. Apple made much of not being IBM, and they did not want any corporate uniforms, strict timetables or rigid job descriptions. Nor did they want their employees to sit alone in an allocated office box. New terms such as 'hot-desking' and 'hoteling' entered the vocabulary of office design, and an increasing number of workplaces have come to contain 'chill-out rooms' and fitness centres (Bell 2007). By 2001, a UK government report entitled 'Tomorrow's Workplace: Fulfilment or Stress?' (Moynaoh and Worsley 2001) used the recent past as a guide to the future and envisaged the twenty-first-century office as a 'recreational centre' where the toys and tasks differed little from those found at home. Today, much has been made of Google's revolutionary and autonomous organisational processes. Many hold it up as a beacon that should be leading other organisations away from the traditional, closed spaces of organisational architecture. However, as underlined by the Google CEO Eric Schmidt, there is only a small part of Google that works like this: the parts where new ideas and innovations are developed. Most of the organisation is very 'tight' and very conventional. The company could not function otherwise (Bilton and Cummings 2010).

The substantial increase in open office design has prompted growing interest amongst researchers into the values it offers organisations and individuals. However, research within this stream remains divided and contradictory (Maher and von Hippel 2005). Some researchers maintain that open office design impacts negatively on employee satisfaction, leading to loss of privacy, job dissatisfaction, impaired performance (Sundstrom et al. 1980, Block and Stokes 1989, Hofbauer 2000, Maher and von Hippel 2005, Oommen et al. 2009), and increased labour control (Hofbauer 2000). Conversely, Kornberger and Clegg (2004) have argued that negative control can be turned into a positive power through 'the generative building' which houses a number of open spaces and meeting places. In their view, the generative building stimulates open-ended use and spontaneous encounters between people from different organisational levels and departments. Similarly, others have contended that open office design constitutes a flexible space which allows for reduced set-up and renovation times, accommodates greater numbers of employees in smaller volumes of space (Brennan et al. 2002), and facilitates social interaction and communication (Zahn 1991). On the whole, this has been seen to improve job satisfaction, staff morale, information exchange and productivity (Brennan et al. 2002).

In summary, some of the more recent accounts have tended to highlight the power of open office design to shape, control or otherwise facilitate particular forms of employee behaviour and unleash their creativity, while others have warned against a one-dimensional view on open office design as enabling creativity and efficiency. Although previous research has argued against spatial determinism and acknowledged that open spaces may be enacted by employees in a variety of ways (e.g. Sundstrom et al. 1980, Hatch 1987, Elsbach 2003), this remains an under-researched topic. In particular, little attention has been given to the 'new spirit' of open office design that is explicitly geared towards boosting fun and creativity and to the ways in which the intentions of this 'pro-creative' office design may be subverted and resisted.

In this chapter, we investigate how pro-creative forms of open office design may afford a broader range of behaviour than originally intended.

More specifically, we argue that it may undermine the kind of spontaneous interaction and creativity that it is intended to foster, and instead lead to subversive practices through which its incumbents express alternative forms of creativity. More specifically, we argue that greater spatial openness may inhibit difference and originality and thwart 'liberation' from conventions and habits as employees re-invoke spatial and social structures and boundaries.

To do this we introduce three perspectives that help us investigate the unintended consequences of this 'new spirit' of open office design: Gibson's theory of *affordances* to study the connection between office design and behaviour without invoking spatial determinism; Foucault's notion of panoptic surveillance in combination with Gabriel's notion of the glass cage to examine the disciplinary politics of office design; and de Certeau's notion of *tactics* to highlight the ambivalent ways in which people may challenge and *subvert* the intentions of office design. We then investigate two examples that problematise the positive values currently prescribed to open office design and its promotion of spontaneous interaction, creativity and learning. The first example draws on our study of open office design and work practices at a Swedish occupation pensions specialist. The second example draws on our study of open office design and work practices at a new model call centre in another European country. Finally, we conclude that a more fruitful approach, if organising for creativity really is the aim, is an organic mix of open and closed, new and old, private and public spaces and the concept of *parkour*, or transgressive free running within, between and across these spaces.

UNDERSTANDING THE AMBIGUITY OF PRO-CREATIVE OFFICE DESIGN

Affordances

Gibson's (1979) concept of affordances provides a way to avoid spatial determinism without ignoring the power of space and spatial design. In other words, it provides a way to understand how spatial design features affect people without determining social behaviour, interaction and practice. The concept of affordances concerns what the environment offers its inhabitants – what it provides, furnishes or affords. In other words, it suggests that the environment affords, suggests and makes itself available to certain uses while constraining others. For example, a stairway affords walking more than it does sleeping, a bench with a backrest affords comfortable sitting more than a bench without a backrest, and, as in the

Figure 15.1   An 'anti-homeless' bench in Japan

example from Japan in Figure 15.1, we can see how this 'anti-homeless' bench affords sitting but not lying down.

In this sense, affordances are functional and objective aspects of the environment (Hutchby 2001: 448). But affordances are also relational and subjective aspects of the environment: what an environment affords is different for different users. What is afforded depends both on the environment and the user (Gibson 1979: 129). For example, perceived and attained boundaries in bipedal stair-climbing are affected by body size and body proportions as well as by hip-joint flexibility and relative leg-strength (Meeuwsen 1991). Moreover, affordances are a result of people's past knowledge and experiences (Lakoff 1987, Norman 1988, Jordan et al. 1998), and the use afforded by certain environments and artefacts are governed by social or technical rules that must be learned by its users (Hutchby 2001). For example, for fellow employees to stop and talk to each other in the photocopier room or by the water-cooler they must feel that this is socially acceptable (Fayard and Weeks 2007).

The importance of learning and knowledge is further emphasised through the concept of dynamic affordances. In management and organisation theory, this concept has been introduced to understand how learning, knowing and knowledge emerge through dynamic interaction with the world or with an artefact, a technology or a discourse in the world (Cook and Brown 1999, McNulty 2002). However, this can be further applied to understand the affordances of an environment. As dynamic affordances 'emerge as part of the (dynamic) interaction with the world' (Cook and Brown 1999: 390), learning, knowing and knowledge do not merely result from learning rules or from past experience and knowledge. People learn, know and develop new knowledge about an artefact or environment and how to use it by interacting with it – and what is afforded changes with the interaction. Changes or developments in dynamic affordances create facilities or frustrations. The theory is that facilities result when more is afforded and frustrations result when less is afforded. Hence, we might think that greater open space would afford more creativity. A room without chairs, for example, offers many possibilities.

While the concept of affordances makes it possible to analyse how particular features of open-space office design are materially constituted and how an open-space office is spatially organised to afford certain uses and users more than others, most affordance research presumes a simplified and depoliticised understanding of the human subject and social relations among humans. This may be the case because affordance research has primarily concerned itself with relations between humans and the natural or technical environment, ignoring how affordances may affect social relations between humans. Arguing that the alteration of the natural environment by humans has made life easier for humans and acknowledging that humans thereby have 'made life harder for most of the other animals', Gibson (1979: 130) does not recognise that these alterations may profoundly alter relations between humans, frustrate rather than facilitate human relations, and make life harder for some humans. This is a problem of power relations which remains largely neglected in recent organisational research on 'social affordances' (see Fayard and Weeks 2007). Although the notion of social affordances recognises how spatial and social features of a setting combine to promote or hamper social interaction, a more politically conscious re-articulation of affordances is needed to understand how open office designs are embedded in the spatial politics of organisations – that is, how open office designs are infused with power in ways that facilitate certain uses, users and social relations but frustrate others.

Disciplinary Politics

Since the 1980s Foucault's (1977) studies of panoptic surveillance have had a significant impact on the understanding of power and control mechanisms in contemporary organisations. Panoptic forms of surveillance have been found in a number of management technologies, from accounting, to information technology, to human resource management and teams (see e.g. Miller and O'Leary 1987, Zuboff 1988, Townley 1994, Sewell 1998). While it may seem obvious that the lack of dividing walls and doors in open office design makes its inhabitants visible to colleagues and managers, the notion of panoptic surveillance remains a powerful tool in helping us shed light on the politics of affordances and understand the visual logic and power relations of open office design (e.g. Visker 1995).

Gabriel's (2005) notion of the glass cage extends Foucault's understanding of panoptic surveillance and further problematises the visualisation of contemporary society and organisations. 'Like the panopticon, the glass cage acts as a metaphor for the formidable machinery of contemporary surveillance' (ibid.: 18), which exposes employees to the gaze of colleagues and managers through a range of electronic, spatial, psychological and cultural technologies. As such, the glass cage is an entrapment, but it is more fragile and 'affords greater ambiguity and irony' than the panopticon (ibid.). The glass cage 'seeks to hide the reality of entrapment rather than display it' (ibid.: 20), and constitutes a display case, container or glass palace which highlights 'the uniqueness of what it contains rather than constraining or oppressing it' (ibid.). At the same time, Gabriel, like Foucault, acknowledges that power is not without resistance. However, the glass cage provokes 'more subtle and nuanced acts of disobedience and defiance' as employees seek to 'create spaces that are sheltered from continuous exposure or, at least, are only semi-visible from the vantage of power' (ibid.: 18).

Tactics of Subversion

Several studies have shown that the spatial layout of organisations is central to understanding power relations within the workplace and that managers perceive space as a tool to control employees through various forms of visualisation techniques such as self-surveillance or peer-surveillance (Perin 1991, Collinson and Collinson 1997, Ezzamel et al. 2001). At the same time, it has been shown that attempts to implement organisational change through office re-design often provoke resistance as employees feel their identity (Elsbach 2003) or status (Baldry 1999) is under threat. Thus, management control over spatial settings of work is limited (Fleming and Sewell 2002).

However, the particular ways in which employees resist and subvert open office design remains under-theorised. In this chapter, de Certeau's (1984) notion of tactics enables elaboration on how people may resist and subvert open office design.

> A tactic insinuates itself into the other's place, fragmentarily, without taking it over in its entirety, without being able to keep it at a distance [. . .] A tactic is a calculated action determined by the absence of a proper locus. No delimitation of an exteriority, then, provides it with the condition necessary for autonomy. The space of a tactic is the space of the other. Thus, it must play on and with a terrain imposed on it and organised by the law of a foreign power. (De Certeau 1984: xix, 37)

Tactics, then, are ways of operating that seize the opportunity and 'make do' (or create) by combining the heterogeneous materials at hand. More specifically, this may include 'victories of the "weak" over the "strong"', 'knowing how to get away with things', clever tricks, manoeuvres, and joyful discoveries. Furthermore, the quote above underlines the close connection between tactics and 'imposed space', and shows how this enables, encourages and stimulates the use of tactics among the inhabitants of space. Within imposed places, tactics create space, and while strategic place can be described as disciplining and normalising (e.g. Hjorth 2004), tactics are forms of resistance towards such places.

Underlining the emergence and unpredictability of tactics, De Certeau (1984: 37) stated that 'it must vigilantly make use of the cracks that particular conjunctions open in the surveillance of the proprietary powers. It poaches in them. It creates surprises in them. It can be where it is least expected. It is guileful ruse.' Tactics, then, are a different form of power from the strategies of the dominant: 'occupying the gaps or interstices of the strategic grid, tactics produce a difference or unpredictable event which can corrupt or pervert the strategy's system' (Colebrook 1997: 125). Thus, tactics give rise to emergent and unexpected outcomes, which makes it suitable for understanding how office design that is imposed on employees may also encourage employees to use tactics creatively, as creative resistance, rather than unequivocally produce intended creative behaviours.

Research in organisation studies has actualised the use of tactics in organisational life by focusing on how employees may resist dominant notions of subjectivity. Kondo (1990) has investigated how female part-time workers in a Japanese factory resist corporate culture by retaining it on the surface yet using humour and irony when talking about it amongst themselves. Similarly, Collinson (1992) has shown how shop-floor workers at a UK heavy vehicles manufacturer expressed resistance by cynically distancing themselves from managers, management and management values and culture in order to retain an autonomous sense of masculine, working-class identity. Further, Fleming and Spicer (2003: 166) have argued that workers may submit to job requirements and overtly endorse organisational roles, norms and values, but cynically reject or distance themselves from the ascribed corporate culture through clandestine countercultural expressions.

While these studies highlight the mobilisation of tactics in the pursuit of alternative subjectivities, tactics can revolve around spatial dimensions of organisational life. For instance, in the case of 'physical distancing', male shop-floor workers worked 'flat out' in the mornings to maximise their bonus but withdrew to the toilets in the afternoons to play cards and read pornographic magazines out of sight from management (Collinson 1992). In a somewhat different vein, it has been argued that entrepreneurial practices may tactically play in and with the spatial settings of organisations (Hjorth 2004). In this chapter, we show how employees mobilise spatial tactics as a response to open office design in ways that rearticulate and modify the social and spatial dimensions of work organisations.

In summary, our theoretical framework enables us to avoid spatial determinism in design–behaviour relations and highlight the unintended consequences of pro-creative forms of open office design. While Gibson's concept of affordances enables us to investigate what uses, behaviours and interactions pro-creative forms of open office design might afford, a combination of Foucault's, Gabriel's and De Certeau's work enables us to elaborate the control mechanisms of open office design and how they may be subverted. This is not to suggest a dichotomy between the power of open office design to control behaviour and the power of employees to resist open office design. Rather, this enables us to highlight the ambiguous ways in which open office design – and spatial design more broadly – is mobilised and re-mobilised to create multiple and contradictory effects.

INVESTIGATING THE LIVED EXPERIENCE OF PRO-CREATIVE OFFICE DESIGN

Our aim in this research is to study a contemporary phenomenon in an area where there are some largely unquestioned assumptions in play: particularly the idea that the freedom provided by open spaces and an emphasis on fun promotes creativity. Our empirical investigation seeks to use the theoretical lenses described above to explore the relationship between the practice of opening space in organisations and organisational creativity.

To study the case of pro-creative office design we therefore employed the principle of purposeful sampling (see e.g. Strauss and Corbin 1990, Bickman and Rog 1998) to select two organisations that had worked systematically to promote fun and creativity through the implementation of open office design. One is a Swedish occupational pensions specialist and the other is a UK call centre (other aspects of their identity have been disguised). More detail on the method of these investigations is provided in Appendix 15.1.

Example 1: Office Re-design at OPS

OPS manages the pension savings of 1.6 million individuals. There are 600 employees working at the head office and in 2004 the company undertook a complete re-design of these facilities – out with the many small rooms, dusty drawers and old-fashioned fixtures which were associated with a rigid, bureaucratic organisation as opposed to a modern, transparent and creative organisation. The aim of the re-design was not only to become more 'space efficient' but also to facilitate spontaneous interaction, creativity and learning. Almost all employees now sit in open office landscapes, the only exception being staff doing calculation work as this is considered to require quietude. One manager underlined his conviction that the new design would produce favourable learning outcomes: 'when employees sit together in a shared space they are in the middle of the information flows. They are constantly exposed to what is going on, and they can speak more freely with each other.'

Prior to the re-design, employees worked in isolation in separate offices. With the open office design, workspace is allocated on the principle of 'hot-desking'. Hot-desking enables employees to easily change workspace when moving between projects or when taking on new tasks or positions within the company. In general, employees change workspace a couple of times a year.

Whereas the old design only housed one canteen, each floor of the head-quarters building now houses a large flashy kitchen where employees can meet and gather for a fast bite to eat or a cup of tea or coffee. Comfortable sofas and chairs have also been put in to encourage employees to spend more time talking and interacting. Adjoining this informal meeting area is a number of isolated meeting rooms for formal meetings.

Even the CEO and the managing director have left their top floor private offices and now sit in one of the open office areas. Before the re-design, many employees were hesitant to approach and talk to senior management unless they had a clear purpose for doing so. Now the new office design makes it difficult to avoid bumping into them or spontaneously exchanging ideas. Most of the managers work in the open office environment, and we were told that the few who do not create much frustration because they are not seen to 'practise what they preach'. That managers sit in the open space office environment was regarded positive because it reflected a sense of equal treatment. However, as emphasised by one employee: 'naturally, when you have your desk beside your manager, you cannot avoid feeling that they have their eyes on you.'

Have spontaneous interaction, creativity and learning between employees been enhanced, then, with the office re-design? Well, some findings could support this argument, but there are also contradictory findings that seem to suggest that this may just as well be hampered by open office design. Arguably, our interviews suggested that the feeling of being a team had been strengthened since the employees within a project or a department see each other frequently and are therefore forced to conform to certain social codes of conduct, such as greeting each other with a hello or a goodbye.

However, sharing the same space also created problems within the team which may not have occurred in a traditional office design. Our respondents claimed they had difficulties ignoring what their colleagues did in the open office area. As one respondent said: 'In the beginning it was almost unbearable; I spent so much time and energy looking at what my colleagues were doing. Now after a year it is easier, but I still get annoyed several times a day.'

There was also much irritation between employees as not everybody conformed to the behavioural rules which had been developed step-by-step by the employees to cope with the increased noise levels and disturbances resulting from the new office design. These rules were written down and distributed to all employees. Eating and drinking was prohibited in the open area. And to avoid co-workers being disturbed by loud conversations, telephone use and interaction was restricted. It was also not allowed to bring additional chairs to individual desks, even when two or more people were working together on the same task or when experienced staff were involved in the training of new staff members. Instead, meetings and training sessions were supposed to be conducted inside the formal meeting rooms. Indeed, when people violated these rules – by making private phone calls, talking loudly or gobbling and slurping at their desk – arguments frequently broke out as co-workers were quick to remark on and rectify such behaviour.

Furthermore, quarrels were triggered by certain employees seeking to monitor the work schedules of their colleagues – counting the actual time spent working and commenting on arrival and departure times as well as on the number and duration of coffee breaks and cigarette breaks. Thus, teamwork was not always facilitated by the open office design. But at the same time, the number of sick days among employees had decreased significantly after the re-design. Two competing interpretations may be given to this phenomenon: Firstly, it may be that employees were more satisfied with the new setting, feeling more involved, empowered and

*Figure 15.2   The open social area adjoining the kitchen at a Swedish
occupational pensions specialist*

motivated to work; but secondly (and this is gloomier), it may be that the
increased visibility brought about by the new design had amplified the
panoptic eye. This panopticism does not emanate from an epicentre of
management control. Rather, it is a decentralised form of panoptic control
where everybody controls everybody through the internalisation of peer
surveillance as 'auto-surveillance'. In a place where employees are defined
in terms of seeing and being seen, *not* being seen is more conspicuously
noticeable than in a setting where employees typically work in separate
offices.

Our interviews and observations at OPS suggest that spontaneous
interaction, creativity and learning were not an automatic effect of the
new open design. On the one hand, the open design was apt at promoting frequent spontaneous meetings between employees – it made it easy
for employees to spot one another from afar and pop by for a chat. The
kitchen areas and the adjacent seating areas situated on each floor also
made it easier for employees to engage in spontaneous conversations over
a cup of coffee. On the other hand, employees engaged in loud discussions
risked disturbing their colleagues. So even though the landscape potentially affords spontaneous interaction, this was considered so disturbing

that employees were requested to relocate to continue their 'spontaneous' interaction inside the meeting rooms. Consequently, the meeting rooms tended to be overbooked. At the same time, the new kitchen areas on each floor made employees interact less with other departments, creating a stronger feeling of group belonging and 'us-and-them' mentality. In order to counter this sense of group segregation, employees actually started to make personal visits to sort out queries with colleagues in other departments instead of using email and the telephone.

Furthermore, the surveillance afforded by the open design made some employees adopt a more strictly professional identity at work, feeling that it left less room for their private selves. As one employee stated: 'You feel that you have to play your professional role for the whole day, at least this is the case for me, as I don't want to become too private with my colleagues. This can be really exhausting sometimes, to always keep up the façade. I often feel that I would like to have a small private space where I could think clearly and silently without thinking about how I behave, just to be myself for a short while.'

Such sentiments led employees to tactically manipulate the flexi-time arrangement at OPS, working more from home than before the re-design. In summary, then, our findings from OPS suggest that their open office design hindered rather than encouraged spontaneous interaction and creativity.

Example 2: Office Design at CC

Whereas OPS had re-designed their existing headquarters, CC had gathered their call centre operations in a new state-of-the-art open-space facility known as 'the dome'. The dome combined the pursuit of feel-good, fun, vibrancy and creativity with open-space office design. In a recruitment ad CC portrayed itself as 'a fun place to work, with a fantastic team atmosphere – we all work hard, play harder and take great pride in celebrating our successes'. While we did not directly discuss the notion of creativity with staff, CC viewed the open design itself and its indoor facilities as a creative approach to recruit and retain creative and highly motivated employees capable of improving sales and customer satisfaction. Spatial boundaries and clear-cut structures were avoided. Rooms were large and open, encouraging employees to move between and interact with colleagues in different workspaces. Like OPS, CC applied the principle of hot-desking. Moreover, CC's dome contained open, flexible and undefined spaces located between work areas. For example, drink machines and kitchenettes were strategically located on busy passages, near elevators and bathrooms, to help generate spontaneous interactions

Source: Architen Landrell Associates Limited

Figure 15.3   Inside 'the dome', an open design call centre in the UK

between employees and create, and set in place, positive relational patterns. There were also a number of activity rooms with different themes, including a sports-themed room with table soccer, pinball and 'Nerf' balls and a Mediterranean café.

The architects that built the centre described it on their website as follows under the title 'Creating an environment that helps to attract and retain employees':

> [The company's] vision for their operation was to create a vibrant and fun call centre that would accommodate 1000 people. Their goal was to attract and retain the highest quality personnel . . . .. The scope of [our] work was wide. Before designing the environment, we determined the ideal configuration of teams to gain maximum efficiency. The teams are mostly made up of staff aged 18–23 so we developed a concept that appeals to them.

So, was this workspace fun? It certainly appeared that many employees were enjoying themselves. There were regular competitions to meet performance targets and announcements made to declare winners. There was certainly a lot of noise or 'buzz'. Most of the teams seemed very tight-knit, engaging in much gossiping and socialising. The teams would generally hang out together. As noted above, hot-desking was promoted in principle, but in practice most groups – particularly those who were most competitive and those who had been in place for a while – would establish a spatial and social position in these principally non-territorial office arrangements, marking out their spatial territory with posters, slogans and personal artefacts and moving furniture around to create their own personalised space. We saw nobody seeking to move into the personalised space generated by other teams. Teams would use the 'fun rooms', but much the same way as any group would use a more conventional cafeteria: at regular times in accordance with the desires of the most established groups. Moreover, employees tended to stick to their own teams, interacting very little with other teams. And they reinforced team boundaries and identity and enacted and created spatial structures by putting up posters and slogans and relocating furniture.

Was this workspace creative, then? It was certainly competitive, and this led to some interesting team tactics being used to inspire victories over other teams, such as holding back on calling 'good targets' if a 'game' was tight and the end of a competitive period (which was determined from above) was near. Indeed, any competition requires the rules and criteria for performance to be established in advance and generally from above: target numbers such as going after particular demographic or geographical segments or cross-selling. We did not observe any questioning or thinking differently about performance targets at the operative level and the workers that we spoke to claimed to have not thought to question or adapt these.

Further, cultural and sub-cultural norms were strong, with teams developing a shared identity which often meant socialising with members of their group during breaks and after hours, and gossiping about members of other groups. It seemed very difficult to step outside of these norms and 'cross-fertilise' or socialise with other teams and team members – partly, it seemed, because the boundaries between social groups and work groups had become blurred as these groups had built their own structure around themselves to create efficiency and order within the space provided by the organisation.

Certainly, while the open space had enabled different groups to generate their own structures and flows, these were quickly synchronised with the flows of others. For instance, groups did not all arrive in the same 'fun spaces' at the same times. There were definitely flows that appeared to have originated from employee behaviours rather than decreed by management. But, because of this, people seemed to be more wary and shy about going against 'the flow' than they may have been in a more conventional structure imposed from the top–down, as their actions would be more obvious to their norm-setting co-workers.

At the same time, many claimed that the bright, open environment was wearing. Unusually perhaps for such a large building, there was little personal space. Indeed, the open-space office design here seemed to deprive employees of any homely space or individual haven and social interaction was imposed on the employees. An interesting issue that surfaced at CC was the problem caused by the sharp light created by the initial open design. On the one hand, the carefully designed glass ceilings brightened the whole building and visualised the space by letting in solar lighting. But on the other, it led to complaints from staff who found it too bright and somewhat overpowering. After some time, managers had to take employees' concerns into consideration, despite their persuasion that the lightness was beneficial for efficiency. The employees did not share the same perspective, and claimed that the brightness in the building was repressive on sunny days. The architects that won the contract to fix the problem explain their task on their website as follows: 'In a call centre for a major [. . .] company, staff were complaining that the solar glare was hindering their work. [We were] approached to install some skylight diffusers to control the glare and blend into the industrial style of the open plan office.'

In summary, the open-space office design adopted in this call centre did not necessarily afford a more creative workspace than other more normal spaces that we have visited. To some extent, the fun rooms afforded employees to engage in games and play and have fun at work. And the Mediterranean style café, for example, afforded what many agreed was a 'feel-good atmosphere'. The sports room was claimed to be 'good for bonding'. But, the open-space design itself may be seen to have afforded surveillance, control and normalisation, but this was initiated by the employees themselves more than their managers. Moreover, it appeared difficult for an individual or group of employees to resist these tactics, and instead of increased socialisation, which was supposed to foster a creative and dynamic organisation with high team spirit, some employees claimed that the organisation was more fragmented and inter-group boundaries and differences even more visible than at other organisations they had worked for.

While the design afforded employees unobstructed movement between different areas of the call centre building, it also made employees highly visible to each other. Indeed, the open design made performance, success and failure visible. Thus, employees were able to monitor their own behaviours, movements and performances as well as those of their colleagues and other teams. This seemed to play an important role in shaping employee behaviour, movements and performance. Employees used fun rooms and recreational spaces according to fairly structured schemes that largely complied with what had been established as mainstream expectations of work breaks, work behaviour and performance, and they typically strived to copy the 'best practices' of other groups they observed or heard about.

This suggests that the visualisation afforded by the open-space design enabled employees and teams to exercise self-control in pursuit of a normalised form of work performance and best practice and divide and separate themselves from others. While this took place in a competitive environment, the lack of interaction also helped teams avoid conflict. Hence, these are not just social affordances affecting social interaction within teams and between teams. They are micro-political affordances too, affording power, surveillance and control to be exercised. The importance of the team structure suggests that the surveillance and control afforded was more a matter of neo-liberal self-surveillance and self-control than management surveillance and control. It further suggests that the use afforded by the open-space office design in this case was not static but dynamic. Inhabiting this workspace afforded employees to change the space and change and adjust their behaviour. As employees working in the dome experienced sunlight as a problem, the sun screens that were installed to deal with this changed the spatial design of the dome. And as employees watched other teams and top performers in their own teams, they changed and adjusted their own behaviour to copy and maximise their own performance rather than create anew. Inhabiting the workspace therefore afforded creativity, learning and changes in behaviour, but not necessarily in the ways that were initially intended.

DISCUSSION

Rather than providing universally generalisable findings, our cases help us rather explore and question the ambivalent affordances and politics of pro-creative office design. Despite their architectural and organisational differences, our two cases of pro-creative open office design show a number of similarities in how they were enacted by employees, fostering other outcomes and different kinds of creativity than what was originally intended by the organisations. Almost 50 years ago, Koestler (1964) stated that: 'It is obvious that innovation or discovery takes place by combining ideas. The Latin verb cogito for "to think" etymologically means "to shake together".' This casts doubt on the assumption that openness facilitates creativity, suggesting instead that ongoing creativity requires a combination of light and dark, openness and secrets, an operation across and shaking together of mainstream worlds and marginal other-worlds. We should therefore carefully think through the unintended, and sometimes counterproductive, consequences of exposing everything in an organisation out in the open, even (or perhaps especially) when it is done in the name of creativity.

Affordances are typically evaluated in terms of how they facilitate certain behaviours while frustrating others (see e.g. Gibson 1979). The pro-creative open office design implemented at OPS and CC did not unequivocally afford and facilitate creativity through an increase in spontaneous interaction, a fun atmosphere, and exciting learning proc-esses. Indeed, our findings suggest that they set in motion differential and dynamic affordances that facilitated a range of different responses which also changed over time as employees interacted with and within these office environments. In part, we found that the pro-creative open office designs at OPS and CC afforded surveillance and control of employees by colleagues and managers – and ultimately an auto-surveillance whereby employees disciplined themselves – in ways that frustrated rather than facilitated spontaneous interaction, fun and learning.

Previous research has highlighted that post-bureaucratic organisation may produce post-bureaucratic forms of 'concertive control' (Barker 1993). But whereas the shop-floor workers at the medium-sized US manu-facturing company in Barker's study 'concertively' developed written rules to enhance peer surveillance and team performance, the written rules developed by employees at OPS were rather a direct response to cope with the strains of the pro-creative open office design. Furthermore, Barker (1993) and others (see e.g. Sewell 1998) suggest that peer surveillance may be more repressive (from an employee perspective) and more effective (from a management perspective) than management surveillance. Indeed, at OPS the open design did make employees tone down the personal and instead adopt a more professional identity which they thought would be more in line with management expectations. And at CC, the open design did seem to facilitate a competitive and performance-oriented team culture.

However, and more intriguingly, employees at both OPS and CC crea-tively and tactically responded to and subverted the frustrations created by the panoptic 'glass cage' architecture of the pro-creative open office design. Rather than simply accepting the enhanced surveillance afforded by the open design, employees managed to avoid or at least reduce sur-veillance from co-workers and managers by introducing and imposing spatial and social structures and boundaries that streamlined, normalised and formalised social interaction. Similar to Collinson's (1992) notion of 'physical distancing', at OPS more employees started to work from home after the re-design or they gathered in the enclosed meeting rooms, and at CC different teams regularly withdrew to the play rooms and cafés, thereby avoiding not only interaction with co-workers and other teams but also avoiding management surveillance.

This is also in contrast with former studies that highlight how employees modify the physical aspects of open office design by using personal artefacts such as personal photos and calendars or gym wear to affirm a personal or team identity and to claim or mark out a distinct personal space in open and non-territorial office arrangements of hot-desking and hoteling (see e.g. Elsbach 2003, Edenius and Yakhlef 2007). Sure, employees at OPS and CC would sometimes claim a spatial or social position in the open office environment to avoid surveillance or affirm team identity. But they did not merely subvert the open office design by making physical modifications to the space. The structured ways in which CC teams used common areas, the increase in OPS employees working from home, and the frequent booking of meeting rooms also suggests that the open office designs were subverted by employees mobilising and imposing *social* structures.

Rather than leading to more social interaction and to the disruption of norms of behaviour, interaction and performance, as might have been an expected effect of the pro-creative open office designs, employees therefore responded to the open office spaces with tactics to avoid and regulate socialisation. These socio-spatial tactics are therefore also somewhat different from the tactics described by De Certeau (1984) and by later applications of his work in organisation studies (see e.g. Hjorth 2004). Tactics are typically seen to involve people playing with, subverting and moving in and out of strategically organised places in unstructured, dynamic and unpredictable ways. Although the particular ways in which OPS and CC employees enacted the new office designs might not have been predictable from the perspective of top managers and architects, they engaged with these designs through creative and subversive tactics that eventually turned out to be rather structured and predictable. Indeed, employees moved in and out of the strategically organised open office areas and they moved between these areas and their adjacent enclosed rooms according to formal booking schemes (OPS) or at regular times and intervals (CC).

This further complicates conflicting arguments about fun, play and creativity pursued in previous organisational research. On the one hand, Hjorth (2004) has argued that play may be tactically staged in heterotopian spaces of organisation which blur the boundaries between art and work so as to facilitate creativity and entrepreneurship. On the other hand,

Fleming (2005) has problematised the power of organisations to stage fun and play through blurring the boundaries between work and non-work, even when physically heterotopian elements such as kindergarten-style colour schemes and fluffy mascots are introduced into the office environment. Rather, Fleming argues, this creates widespread employee cynicism. In contrast to Hjorth's argument, our findings suggest that employees at OPS and CC undermined the fun, play and creativity which management and architects intended to facilitate through pro-creative open office design, but not quite in the ways argued by Fleming. Rather than playfully enacting the space or cynically dis-identifying from the ascribed corporate culture, they creatively and tactically restructured social interaction within the space.

Now, is it possible to argue that employees at OPS and CC tactically restructured rather than playfully enacted social interaction within these spaces because they were not heterotopian spaces but homogeneously open spaces and therefore strategically organised places? In other words, that had they been heterotopian spaces then employees would have inhabited them in more playful ways? No, we don't think so. Although our findings argue against overestimating the ability of organisations to create and stage heterotopia, the open office designs at OPS and CC and, more importantly, how they were enacted by employees, did actually incorporate certain heterotopian elements. Firstly, the enclosed meeting rooms and common areas adjoining the open office areas indicate that neither the OPS head office nor the CC dome were unequivocally open-space environments. Secondly, the attempt at staging fun and creativity in a work environment indicates that neither OPS nor CC were unequivocally designed as work environments. But thirdly, we would argue that employees at OPS and CC added heterotopian dimensions to the pro-creative office designs by tactically and creatively imposing socio-spatial structures. And in the case of certain OPS employees starting to work more frequently from home, this expanded the heterotopia to include the space of the home as well as the space of the OPS head office.

The organisation studies literature on resistance tends to associate resistance with opposition to and subversion of organisational goals (see e.g. Collinson 1992, Fleming and Spicer 2007). Our findings do not echo this. While the tactics mobilised by OPS and CC employees subverted the intentions of the new designs, they did not seem to subvert the overarching organisational goals of OPS or CC. Rather, their allegedly subversive introduction of socio-spatial structures actually seemed to facilitate the achievement of overarching organisational goals, improving efficiency, productivity and performance. Interestingly, these structures seemed to harden into established norms that it was difficult to challenge and shift because they were enacted by the very same employees who produced them.

CONCLUSION

The new lenses that we have employed in this study – the dynamic of affordances, the effects of disciplinary 'glass cage' visibility, and the serious tactics which impose rather than disrupt structures – have highlighted both the limited power of organisations to stage and promote certain ideas, values and behaviours in the workplace and the limited politics of employee tactics in so-called 'pro-creative' workplaces. Previous studies have already warned against the difficulties in crafting politically effective resistance tactics when organisations transform initially non-work things such as fun, playfulness and creativity into organisational variables to be exploited in the interest of work and organisational performance (see e.g. Fleming 2005). In a sense, the picture indicated by our findings is even gloomier. Employees do not necessarily dis-identify with the ascribed corporate culture of fun, playfulness and creativity, but they do impose structures that help them both avoid surveillance and the intensification of work performance.

The question, then, is not so much whether or not employees can still have fun at work, but to what ends employees put these tactically created structures. In our two examples, the planned and intentional nature of these structures (for organised fun) made them, paradoxically, effect anti-social, mean-spirited and even inhuman behaviours. And even though these structures may be futile in terms of the resistance they afforded, they draw attention to the creative and tactical use of space as a potentially important aspect of resistance. Indeed, the fact that the structures imposed in response by employees at OPS and CC helped them avoid surveillance from peers and managers suggests that employees may learn to mobilise such structures in the pursuit of alternative ends. In a nutshell, if we see creativity as new, unforeseen or unpredicted developments of lasting value, the investment in shiny new fun and open workspaces may not make employees more creative for an organisation. Paradoxically, such investment may even reduce the likelihood of such an outcome.

Our response to this finding, and an alternative suggestion to those organisations interested in creativity (rather than predictable intended outcomes), resonates with Daskalaki et al.'s (2008: 51) notion of *parkour*, or 'free running'. They use this notion as a metaphor to discuss the need for spatial structures in the workplace that are not planned, regimented and limiting, but instead exist to encourage the kinds of chance,

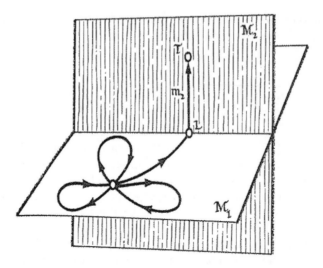

Figure 15.4   Koestler's diagram (1964) explaining the creative process related to novel discoveries such as Archimedes' 'Eureka' moment (T)

interaction, imagination and change that can lead to creativity. Indeed, free-runners, or '*traceurs*' (a derivation of the verb 'tracer', or to trace, in French) can be at their most creative in the most mundane environments, with the focus on what an individual can do within the limitations of an environment rather than what the environment does to or makes him or her do. This is about people overcoming and adapting to mental obstacles as well as physical barriers rather than these obstacles and barriers being removed by an overseer (see Foucan 2008, Belle 2009).

Indeed, the *parkour* metaphor reminds us of some of the diagrams used by Arthur Koestler to describe the creative process in the 1960s, such as Figure 15.4, which describes Archimedes moving around on a single plane (what was known about the science of volume) until the juxtaposition with a second plane of thought/experience (taking a bath) helped him find a creative solution to the problem of how to determine the actual volume of a coin.

Consequently, the best way for organisations to organise for creativity might be to plan or organise less and just let things happen more. Indeed, much in the architecture literature encourages mixed space: open and closed, public and private, urban and rural, new and old, indoor and outdoor (Bell 2007). Given that getting around barriers, obstacles and divergences are often key stimulants in the creative process, it may be that such organic bricolage mixtures can allow employees to do more of the sorts of things that lead to genuine unpredicted or 'surprising' creativity: to follow or trace a line of thought while transgressing or flowing across pre-determined boundaries (Csikszentmihalyi 1997). Perhaps 'free-running', then – transgressing between and across different spaces – may help employees create their own fun and creatively resist existing organisational strategies to create the new. And our findings would therefore suggest that it would be better to invest in creative people and creative practices (such as those described in the next two chapters) rather than completely new architecture to promote the serious play of creativity. Ironically, less 'pro' intentionality may be more in seeking to achieve what was supposed to be the end of pro-creative office design: more creativity.

QUESTIONS FOR DISCUSSION

1. What are the challenges with organising for flexibility, i.e. encouraging 'free-running'? How can organisations use space to achieve this?
2. Provide examples of what an organisational space constituted of mixed spaces could look like.
3. The current chapter illustrates a view on space as affording rather than determining organisational members' behaviour. Discuss how this view enables us to understand emergent and unexpected outcomes of spatial design. Drawing on your own experience, provide examples of emergent uses of spaces.

ACKNOWLEDGEMENT

We would like to thank Stephen Cummings, who worked closely with us in the preparation of this draft and for furnishing the *parkour* analogy. This paper draws on a previous paper by Thanem, Värlander & Cummings entitled 'Open space = open minds? Unintended consequences of pro-creative office design' in *International Journal of Work Organisation and Emotion* 4(1) January 2011. We gratefully acknowledge Inderscience Publishers for letting us reuse parts of that paper for this chapter.

REFERENCES

Baldry, C. (1999), 'Space – the final frontier', *Sociology*, **33**(3), 535–53.
Barker, J.R. (1993), 'Tightening the iron cage: Concertive control in self-managing teams', *Administrative Science Quarterly*, **38**(3), 408–37.

Bell, J. (2007), 'Game over! Back to work', *Wallpaper*.

Belle, D. (2009), *Parkour*, Paris: Intervista.

Bickford, S. (2000), 'Constructing inequality: city spaces and the architecture of citizenship', *Political Theory*, **28**(3), 355–76.

Bickman, L. and D.J. Rog (1998), *Handbook of applied social research*, Thousand Oaks, CA: Sage.

Bilton, C. and S. Cummings (2010), *Creative strategy: reconnecting business and innovation*, Oxford: Wiley.

Block, L. and G. Stokes (1989), 'Performance and satisfaction in private versus nonprivate work settings', *Environment and Behavior*, **21**(3), 277–97.

Brennan, A., J.S. Chugh and T. Kline (2002), 'Traditional versus open office design: A longitudinal field study', *Environment and Behavior*, **34**(3), 279–99.

Clegg, S.R. and M. Kornberger (2006), *Space, organizations and management theory*, Malmö: Liber.

Colebrook, C. (1997), *New literary histories: New historicism and contemporary criticism*, Manchester: Manchester University Press.

Collinson, D.L. (1992), *Managing the shopfloor: Subjectivity, masculinity and workplace culture*, Berlin: DeGruyter.

Collinson, D.L. and M. Collinson (1997), 'Delayering managers: Time-space surveillance and its gendered effects', *Organization*, **4**(3), 375–407.

Cook, S.D.N. and J.S. Brown (1999), 'Bridging epistemologies: The generative dance between organizational knowledge and organizational knowing', *Organization Science*, **10**(4), 381–400.

Cooper-Marcus, C. and C. Francis (1998), *People places: Design guidelines for urban open space*, New York: Wiley.

Cross, R.L., A. Yan and M.R. Louis (2000), 'Boundary activities in "boundaryless" organizations: A case study of a transformation to a team-based structure', *Human Relations*, **53**(6), 841–68.

Csikszentmihalyi, M. (1997), *Creativity: Flow and the psychology of discovery and invention*, New York: Harper Perennial.

Dale, K. and G. Burrell (2008), *The spaces of organisation and the organisation of space*, Basingstoke: Palgrave Macmillan.

Daskalaki, M., A. Stara and M. Imas (2008), 'The "parkour organisation": inhabitation of corporate spaces', *Culture and Organization*, **14**(1), 49–64.

Davis, T.R.V. (1984), 'The influence of the physical environment in offices', *Academy of Management Review*, **9**(2), 271–83.

de Certeau, M. (1984), *The practice of everyday life*, Berkeley, CA: University of California Press.

Deleuze, G. (1988), *Foucault*, Minneapolis: University of Minnesota Press.

Deutsche, R. (2002), 'From evictions: Art and spatial politics', in G. Bridge and S. Watson (eds) *The Blackwell city reader*, Malden, MA: Blackwell Publishing, pp. 401–8.

Donovan, R. and J. Rossiter (1982), 'Store atmosphere: an environmental psychology approach', *Journal of Retailing*, **58**(Spring), 34–57.

Edenius, M. and A. Yakhlef (2007), 'Space, vision and organizational learning: The interplay of incorporating and inscribing practices', *Management Learning*, **38**(2), 193–210.

Elsbach, K. (2003), 'Relating physical environment to self-categorizations: Identity threat and affirmation in a non-territorial office space', *Administrative Science Quarterly*, **48**, 622–54.

Ezzamel, M., H. Willmott and F. Worthington (2001), 'Power, control and resistance in the factory that time forgot', *Journal of Management Studies*, **38**(8), 1053–79.

Fayard, A.-L. and J. Weeks (2007), 'Photocopiers and water-coolers: The affordances of informal interaction', *Organization Studies*, **28**(5), 605–34.

Fleming, P. (2005), 'Workers' playtime? Boundaries and cynicism in a "culture of fun" programme', *Journal of Applied Behavioral Science*, **41**(3), 285–303.

Fleming, P. and G. Sewell (2002), 'Looking for "the good soldier Svejk": Alternative modalities of resistance in the contemporary workplace', *Sociology*, **36**(4), 857–73.

Fleming, P. and A. Spicer (2007), *Contesting the corporation*, Cambridge: Cambridge University Press.

Fleming, P. and A. Spicer (2008), 'Beyond power and resistance: New approaches to organizational politics', *Management Communication Quarterly*, 21(3), 301–9.

Fleming, P. and A. Spicer (2003), 'Working at a cynical distance: implications for power, subjectivity and resistance', *Organization*, 10(1), 157–79.

Foucan, S. (2008), *Free running*, New York: Michael O'Mara.

Foucault, M. (1977), *Discipline and punish*, London: Allen Lane.

Foucault, M. (1980), *Power/knowledge*, C. Gordon (ed.), Hemel Hempstead, UK: Harvester Wheatsheaf.

Foucault, M. (1984), 'Space, knowledge and power', in P. Rabinow (ed.) *The Foucault reader*, Harmondsworth, UK: Penguin, pp. 239–56.

Gabriel, Y. (2005), 'Glass cages and glass palaces: images of organizations in image-conscious times', *Organization*, 12(1), 9–27.

Gibson, J.J. (1979), *The ecological approach to visual perception*, Boston: Houghton Mifflin.

Griffin, M. and M.R. McDermott (1998), 'Exploring a tripartite relationship between rebelliousness, openness to experience and creativity', *Social Behaviour and Personality*, 26(4), 347–56.

Hatch, M.J. (1987), 'Physical barriers, task characteristics, and interaction activity in research and development firms', *Administrative Science Quarterly*, 32(3), 387–99.

Hjorth, D. (2004), 'Creating space for play/invention – concepts of space and organizational entrepreneurship', *Entrepreneurship & Regional Development*, 16(September), 413–32.

Hofbauer, J. (2000), 'Bodies in a landscape: On office design and organization', in J. Hassard, R. Holliday and H. Willmott (eds) *Body and organization*, London: Sage, pp. 166–91.

Holahan, C.J. (1978), *Environment and behavior*, New York: Plenum Press.

Hutchby, I. (2001), 'Technologies, texts and affordances', *Sociology*, 35(2), 441–56.

Jordan, T., M. Raubal, B. Gartrell and M.J. Egenhofer (1988), 'An affordance-based model of place in GIS', in T. Poiker and N. Chrisman (eds) *Eighth International Symposium on Spatial Data Handling*, Vancouver, Canada, pp. 98–109.

Koestler, A. (1964), *The act of creation*, London: Penguin.

Kondo, D.K. (1990), *Crafting selves: power, gender, and discourses of identity in a Japanese workplace*, Chicago: University of Chicago Press.

Kornberger, M. and S. Clegg (2004), 'Bringing space back in: Organizing the generative building', *Organization Studies*, 25(7), 1095–114.

Lakoff, G. (1987), *Women, fire and dangerous things: What categories reveal about the mind*, Chicago: University of Chicago Press.

Maher, A. and C. von Hippel (2005), 'Individual differences in employee reactions to open-plan offices', *Journal of Environmental Psychology*, 25(2), 219–29.

McNulty, T. (2002), 'Reengineering as knowledge management: A case of change in UK healthcare', *Management Learning*, 33(4), 439–58.

Meeuwsen, H. (1991), 'Variables affecting perceptual boundaries in bipedal stair climbing', *Perceptual & Motor Skills*, 72, 539–43.

Miller, P. and T. O'Leary (1987), 'Accounting and the construction of the governable person', *Accounting, Organisations & Society*, 12(3), 235–65.

Moynaoh, M. and R. Worsley (2001), 'Tomorrow's workplace: Fulfilment or stress', *United Kingdom Government report prepared as part of the 'Tomorrow Project'*.

Norman, D. (1988), *The design of everyday things*, New York: Doubleday.

Oommen, V., M. Knowles and I. Zhao (2009), 'Should health service managers embrace open plan work environments? A review', *Asia-Pacific Journal of Health Management*, 3(2), 37–43.

Perin, C. (1991), 'The moral fabric of the office: Panopticon discourse and schedule flexibilities', in P. Tolbert and S. Barley (eds) *Research in the sociology of organizations*, Greenwich, CT: JAI Press.

Sewell, G. (1998), 'The discipline of teams: The control of team-based industrial work through electronic and peer surveillance', *Administrative Science Quarterly*, 43, 397–428.

Shalley, C.E. (1995), 'Effects of coaction, expected evaluation, and goal setting on creativity and productivity', *Academy of Management Journal*, **38**(2), 483–503.

Spradley, J.P. (1979), *The ethnographic interview*, Orlando, FL: Harcourt Brace Jovanovich.

Stahl, M.J. and M.C. Koser (1978), 'Weighted productivity in R & D: Some associated individual and organizational variables', *IEEE Transactions in Engineering Management*, **25**, 20–24.

Strauss, A. and J. Corbin (1998), *Basics of qualitative research*, 2nd edition, Thousand Oaks, CA: Sage.

Sundstrom, E., R. Burt and D. Kamp (1980), 'Privacy at work: Architectural correlates of job satisfaction and job performance', *Academy of Management Journal*, **23**(1), 101–17.

Townley, B. (1994), *Reframing human resource management: Power, ethics and the subject at work*, London: Sage.

Vischer, J. (1999), 'Will this open space work?', *Harvard Business Review*, **77**(May/June), 28–36.

Visker, R. (1995), *Michel Foucault: Genealogy as critique*. London: Verso.

Woodman, R.W., J.E. Sawyer and R.W. Griffin (1993), 'Towards a theory of organizational creativity', *Academy of Management Journal*, **18**, 293–321.

Yin, R. (2003), *Case study research design and methods*, Newbury Park, CA: Sage.

Zahn, L.G. (1991), 'Face to face communication in an office setting: The effects of position, proximity and exposure', *Communication Research*, **18**(6), 737–54.

Zuboff, S. (1988), *In the age of the smart machine: The future of work and power*, New York: Basic Books.

APPENDIX 15.1: RESEARCH METHODS

Case data was generated through interviews, observations and documents, and both organisations and respondents have been heavily disguised in the interests of anonymity. At the occupational pensions specialist (OPS), one of the authors spent a full day observing the re-designed facilities and interviewing members of staff. Semi-structured face-to-face interviews were conducted with four representatives: the vice CEO and three employees in various positions. During these interviews we used a general interview guide designed by the authors. The guide included questions about the underlying intentions of the office re-design, employee attitudes towards it, and how employees enacted the new office environment. Each interview lasted for 20–60 minutes. Further, the semi-structured interviews fostered a conversational style and elicited open responses in such a way that the conversation itself rather than the interview guide dictated the order in which the various issues were discussed. All interviews at OPS were tape-recorded and transcribed.

At the UK call centre (CC) two academics were invited by company representatives to spend a day observing operations, and open access was granted to talk to a range of staff (from senior managers to telephone operators) about their work and the new open office environment. We asked a range of questions about the intentions and design of the new facilities and about work practices at the new facilities. In total we interviewed five members of staff. We were not given permission to tape-record our interviews or take photographs at CC, but notes to remember key issues were taken during and shortly after returning from the visit. According to Holahan (1978), the impact of design is often subliminal. Furthermore, Donovan and Rossiter (1982) insist that the effects of design are difficult to verbalise and to recall. Therefore, we also conducted observations with the aim to capture aspects of office design which it may be difficult to articulate, and to gain a *self-experienced* understanding of how the open office design affected creativity.

Ten hours spread over two days were spent in the occupational pensions specialist, and five hours were spent at the call centre. During these observation sessions, we focused on how the offices were designed and how employees behaved and interacted in the offices, and both discursive and visual material was collected in the form of notes and photos. In addition, we generated data through textual and photographic material made available by the two organisations, including corporate reports, policy manuals and company descriptions from their websites. In the case of CC, we also generated documentary data through job advertisements and through architectural reviews as their new office facility has been widely discussed in architectural circles. While we are aware that the amount of time spent in each organisation is too short to get a deeper understanding and record repeating patterns within the setting (Spradley 1979), the observations and documents enabled us to complement our understanding of the interview material.

How 2 embed Hybrid thinking
What LS skill most imp to support hybrid.

16. Balancing divergence and convergence: stimulating creativity through hybrid thinking

David Oliver, Loizos Heracleous and Claus D. Jacobs

Creating a climate that fosters organisational creativity is a critical challenge for many managers today. We know for example that strategic uniformity across organisations leads to reduced returns, whereas difference leads to higher performance (Nattermann 2000). Creative thinking is an important component of developing such uniqueness in an organisation, both in terms of its strategic positioning as well broader internal understandings (Jacobs and Heracleous 2005, 2006).

Incentive structures that favour short-term results, combined with limited budgets and the notorious difficulties associated with quantifying creativity payoffs (Amabile and Khaire 2008), pose significant challenges to managing for creativity. At the same time, the long-term survival of most organisations in dynamic business environments will ultimately depend on their ability to nurture and mobilise creativity, that is, to generate outputs and outcomes that are both *novel* and *valuable* (Ford 1996). While standardised strategy tools and techniques can provide useful inputs for strategic analysis, the ability to move beyond 'dry' analytics and make a creative leap is often essential to developing strategies with sufficient distinctiveness and uniqueness to confer competitive advantage. The creative process itself can energise managers and motivate them to exert discretionary effort.

Managers often face a variety of challenges when attempting to stimulate creative thinking and implement innovative strategies in their organisations. Today's increasingly diverse and complex organisations can hinder the intersubjective sensemaking among individuals and groups necessary to develop a negotiated order (Drazin et al. 1999) favourable to creativity. It has been well documented that diversity is a necessary condition for real creativity; that is, only by bringing together individuals from diverse backgrounds and with diverse views can true novelty emerge. Further, simply hiring more creative people is not enough; research suggests that in unstructured settings, people tend to interact mostly with people similar to themselves (Ingram and Morris 2007). It is also easy

325

for organisations to fall into habits, and for subcultures and managerial structures and systems to tend toward conservatism, thus impeding the incentive to participate in collective creativity. It is not always clear how managers can most effectively foster processes, subcultures and managerial systems that might play a direct and important role in encouraging individuals to participate in collective creativity (Drazin et al. 1999).

Many managers also lack effective mechanisms or intervention techniques for facilitating the generation of more novel and valuable outputs in their work environments. This chapter is focused on this issue, as we examine intervention techniques aimed at enhancing collective – not merely individual – creativity, and harnessing it to address real organisational challenges. We begin by reviewing a number of conventional management intervention techniques that purport to facilitate the development of creative outputs. We first focus on interventions that we propose draw on 'divergent thinking'. We define divergent thinking as a process of expanding the pool of ideas and incorporating different perspectives and assumptions, within a fluid framework or parameters, without directly seeking to address a specific business challenge. Brainstorming, mindmapping and storyboarding are some examples of divergent techniques that we will discuss.

We contrast this review by looking at other intervention techniques that focus more on their ability to converge and integrate inputs into manageable and useful results. We define such 'convergent thinking' as a process of focusing on particular ideas, perspectives and assumptions, within a structured framework or parameters, to achieve a specific business outcome. Many of these techniques come from the world of strategy. In this chapter we will discuss two such techniques: formalised strategic planning and management simulations.

Finally, we describe what we refer to as 'hybrid thinking', which includes both opening up (divergent) and refocusing (convergent) components. We define hybrid thinking as synthesising relevant ideas, perspectives and assumptions into a coherent whole in a way that provides a direction ahead, with respect to a specific business challenge. We provide a detailed example of one hybrid approach – serious play – that is designed to engender high levels of organisation-specific inquiry and engagement, ultimately generating outputs that are both novel and useful.

A CLOSER LOOK AT 'DIVERGENT' APPROACHES TO MANAGEMENT CHALLENGES

The first set of intervention techniques we explore relates to those focused on the generation of a wide range of novel ideas in a divergent fashion, that is, in a way that does not seek to integrate these ideas and does not aim to directly result in a resolution of a specific challenge. These techniques all share a focus on having participants give voice to and acknowledge the legitimacy and equal plausibility of different viewpoints (Schein 1996), a process of 'divergence'.

Brainstorming

Brainstorming is a commonly used creativity enhancing technique developed in the 1950s. It was originally designed as an intervention technique that involved individuals, groups and organisations following four key rules to generate ideas: 1) generate as many ideas as possible, 2) avoid criticising any of the ideas, 3) attempt to combine and improve on previously articulated ideas, and 4) encourage the generation of 'wild' ideas or 'free-wheeling' (Osborn 1957).

One of the purported strengths of brainstorming is its capacity to generate a significant number of high-quality ideas, due to its encouragement of participants to build on each other's contributions. Whether brainstorming indeed generates higher-quality ideas, however, remains to be demonstrated empirically (Girotra et al. 2010). Indeed, brainstorming has been critiqued for a number of shortcomings, starting with free riding – as not everyone is obliged to participate, and the quality of the output is generally measured at the group level. Further, despite encouragement to not criticise the ideas of others, evaluation apprehension – i.e. failure to speak due to fear of negative reactions of others – has also been observed. Finally, production blocking may occur when one person dominates the exercise while others must wait in order to speak (Diehl and Stroebe 1987).

Indeed, although people who participate in brainstorming may feel that they are being more creative than when they work individually, face-to-face team brainstorming has been shown to produce fewer results than individuals generating ideas alone (Paulus et al. 1995, Paulus and Brown 2003). While the breadth of ideas generated collectively through this technique can be impressive, it can be challenging to subsequently draw such disparate ideas together into coherent messages that can be useful for an organisation. While brainstorming groups may generate a large number of ideas, the quality of the ideas can be highly variable and of ambiguous relevance to the organisation's challenges, making it hard to select the 'best' idea (Girotra et al. 2010).

A variety of mechanisms have been suggested to improve idea quality generated from brainstorming. The use of information technologies in 'electronic brainstorming' – developed to facilitate idea generation in contexts where people cannot be co-present – helps mitigate the production

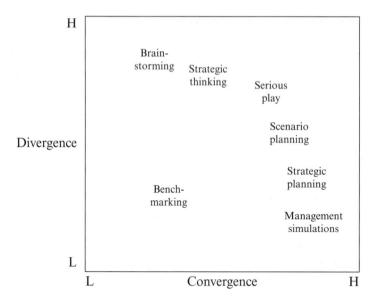

Figure 16.1   Mapping of intervention techniques along the dimensions of divergence and convergence

blockage issue. However, such groups are transformed into sets of individuals with lower group interaction richness (Potter and Balthazard 2004), and indeed the problem of drawing together the ideas in the end remains. Litchfield (2008) has recommended the introduction of goals to brainstorming in order to improve both idea quality and targeting to management problems, although the feasibility of this attempt to foster idea convergence lacks empirical support for the time being.

In summary, brainstorming is an approach that is strong on divergence (generation of a variety of ideas from various perspectives) but weak on convergence (bringing these ideas together in a coherent whole which indicates a direction to address a specific challenge). Figure 16.1 illustrates the mapping of brainstorming and other approaches we refer to in this chapter.

Mindmapping and Storyboarding

Mindmapping (Buzan 1983) is another divergent means for generating strategic ideas. Starting with a key problem in the centre, participants work outward in a random, yet somewhat organised fashion to ultimately produce a complex 'map' of the issue. Even though the resulting maps appear integrated by virtue of several interconnections, as with brainstorming, it can be difficult to pull the disparate maps of different individuals together in a coherent output that can help to address a specific challenge. A variant of brainstorming, storyboarding involves attaching ideas to a wall or whiteboard, and using them to construct a story (Higgins 1996). While this technique provides a more structured means of pulling together ideas at the end of the process, it is monological, dependent on written textual representations of complex ideas whose connections may be multi-faceted. Further, it can be difficult to group unrelated ideas into a coherent story using this method.

In sum, brainstorming, mindmapping and storyboarding are examples of divergent creativity intervention techniques that can be used for strategising. All three generate a wide variety of perspectives and ideas, but limited mechanisms for pulling them together into a coherent plan, strategy or framework.

A CLOSER LOOK AT 'CONVERGENT' APPROACHES TO MANAGEMENT ISSUES

Convergence of ideas requires negotiation of meaning, often leading to the development of shared mental models and a common understanding (Oliver and Jacobs 2007). Many conventional techniques aim to provide such structured convergence in order to enable shared strategy insights. We argue that techniques that emphasise convergence in the absence of prior divergence, however, may lead to premature closure of debates about strategic direction or other challenges facing the organisation, with the result that suboptimal decisions may be taken and political support for implementation not sufficiently developed. Approaches that are strong on convergence but weak on divergence run the risk of becoming routine annual rituals (such as the strategic planning cycle) where real, incisive insights into customers, markets and competition are not substantively pursued or expected.

Strategic Planning

Strategic planning has been criticised as a time-consuming, programmatic, formalised process which rarely results in creative outputs, a process which, rather than helping organisations effectively respond to environmental turbulence, merely offers the illusion of controlling such turbulence (Mintzberg 1994). McKinsey found that only 45 per cent of their sample of executives said they were satisfied with their strategic planning process, and only 23 per cent said that major strategic decisions were taken within this process (Dye and Siboni 2007). Some proposed remedies include starting with debating the issues rather than the numbers, involving the right executives in the conversations, focusing on effective execution, paying attention to the implications of the plan for people development, and adjusting planning practices to the needs of different business units (Dye and Siboni 2007). Despite these challenges and the gradual reduction of academic interest in the topic, strategic planning is a prevalent tool, being used by more than 80 per cent of organisations (Whittington and Cailluet 2008).

The perceived importance of the practice has resulted in the appointment of chief strategy officers in many organisations. Going beyond the rather limited idea of strategy as planning, however, chief strategy officers and their colleagues perceive strategy as a multi-faceted, contextually specific, metaphorical concept, intimately bound up with their identity as strategists and as a resource to be employed when institutionalising new practices in organisations (Paroutis and Heracleous 2013). Planning has even been viewed as learning if carried out in an exploratory, inquisitive spirit (de Geus 1988), transcending Mintzberg's critique that strategies seemed to be emergent and based on learning rather than in-advance planning (Mintzberg 1991). The traditional understanding of planning remains, however, as a numbers-driven endeavour which is often intended to operationalise already decided strategies rather than to generate radically new ones (Heracleous 1998).

Management Simulations

Simulations work by creating an artificial or synthetic environment that serves as the context for managers to experience 'reality'. Computer-based simulations involve simulating reality in an effort to understand the future impact of various strategic ideas, including product design (Vaccaro et al. 2011), organisational architecture (Ethiraj and Levinthal 2004) and organisational structure (Marengo and Dosi 2005). 'Wargaming' simulations are frequently used to enable managers to 'experience' competitive dynamics in their industry and think more creatively about the future, in an effort to test strategic ideas (Schwarz 2011). They are also widely used to teach strategic management (Wolfe and Rogé 1997).

Simulations are high on convergent thinking as in most cases 'players' must make decisions within a framework defined and constrained by computer algorithms in order to deal with organisational or strategic issues. The effectiveness of simulations depends considerably on the granularity of problem framing, that is, the decomposition (or not) of the question into a variety of sub-problems (Vaccaro et al. 2011). Although participants in multi-player simulations interact in order to generate some competitive dynamics, the result of these interactions continues to be mediated by the computer algorithms built into the simulation.

In sum, convergence techniques are grounded in assumptions that tend to reduce complexity and lead to somewhat narrowly focused collective outputs. Such techniques may lead to useful and practical insights, but in many cases not novel ones. Furthermore, some of these outputs can also be relatively standardised, whereas in order to be effective, strategic plans and organisational change initiatives need to take account of organisational particularities. They also frequently suffer from participant disengagement with the process, even though it is well documented that people are most creative when they are involved, excited and challenged by a task, i.e. when they are intrinsically motivated (Amabile 1996).

UNDERLYING ASSUMPTIONS OF DIVERGENT AND CONVERGENT THINKING

March (1979) distinguished between technologies of reason that insist on the necessity of consistency among action and give primacy to instrumental rationality, with technologies of foolishness that acknowledge the emergence, ambiguity and open-endedness of action and relax – at least temporarily – the instrumental imperative. We suggest that convergent approaches to creativity in organisations tend to be grounded in technologies of reason, whereas divergent approaches tend to lean towards technologies of foolishness. While the former might overly constrain creative thinking and force premature closure (inducing the risk of myopia), the latter approaches might open up too much and neglect the need for closure (inducing the risk of confusion). Thus, hybrid approaches to creativity aim at balancing technologies of foolishness with technologies of reason so that the generation of options (opening up) is supplemented with the necessary gesture of assessing, prioritising and selecting the most viable options (closure) (see Table 16.1).

To summarise our argument to this point, managers need creativity interventions that avoid both the risk of premature closure (myopia) as well as unlimited opening up (confusion), that balance an orientation to exploitation with exploration, as well as foolishness with reason. While brainstorming and other divergent techniques are useful for opening up, and strategic planning and more convergent techniques tend to operate on a set of given convergent assumptions about issues such as market trends and organisational competencies, hybrid approaches would appear most able to question established assumptions and aim to envision new futures.

Table 16.1   Key assumptions of divergent and convergent thinking

	Divergent approaches	Convergent approaches
Mode of rationality	Frivolous, foolish, but with a serious purpose	Functional, following the instrumental imperative
Mode of thinking	Synthetic	Analytic
Main risk	Confusion, lack of direction	Myopia, lack of breakthroughs
Main orientation	Exploration-oriented generation of novel options	Exploitation-oriented work on existing options
Degree of structuredness of approach	Low to medium	High
Degree of directiveness of approach	Low to medium	High

HYBRID THINKING: BOTH DIVERGENT AND CONVERGENT

Our review above identifies a significant need for creativity intervention techniques that allow for both processes of divergence and convergence in order to develop novel and useful strategic organisational insights. This is consistent with findings in other organisational domains, which indicate that it is beneficial to balance alternative approaches. For example Girotra et al. (2010) have found that 'hybrid' structures, in which the group works individually for some time and then works together, is superior to having the team work together the entire time. We now review intervention techniques that mobilise this insight, as well as the understanding that convergence which follows active, broad divergence is more likely to lead to creative insights because it brings into the decision-making process a broader set of influences.

Scenario Planning

Developed in the 1970s at Royal Dutch Shell, scenario planning has been adopted in a wide number of organisations operating in contexts of environmental uncertainty (van der Heijden et al. 2002). It involves the identification of key strategic issues and contextual variables, around which a number of scenarios are developed and their consistency and plausibility evaluated. Thinking is initially divergent, as environmental trends and their likely interactions are identified and debated, until these crystallise in different scenarios. Ultimately, a script or narrative of each scenario is written which provides a detailed and rich description of its contingencies (Schoemaker 1995). The concluding phase of scenario planning involves selecting strategies which would be viable in any of the key likely scenarios identified, rather than a single scenario.

Scenario planning has been critiqued due to its dependence on use of rational analysis to project into the future, although there have been more recent calls to integrate higher levels of intuition and creativity (van der Heijden et al. 2002). We classify this form of scenario planning as hybrid, as it concludes in a convergent fashion, having begun with divergent thinking.

Strategic Thinking

Strategic thinking as a divergent, synthetic, creative thinking process has been suggested as a necessary antidote to the programmatic, convergent nature of strategic planning (Heracleous 1998). Strategic thinking can be aided by various types of tools and frameworks, including scenario planning, even though scenario planning as proposed by Schoemaker (1995) can be seen to contain a stronger element of convergence than divergence. Frameworks act as ways to stimulate thinking about the big picture of the industry landscape, strategic options and feasibility in terms of organisational capabilities, people, organisation design and values, as for example the ESCO model (Heracleous et al. 2009) recommends. By exploring both the big picture and long-term trends, as well as organisational realities and feasibility, strategic thinking can integrate divergence and convergence, analysis and synthesis. Schoemaker (2012) clarifies the capabilities involved in strategic thinking. He notes that effective strategic thinkers are able to look ahead and anticipate what might happen in the industry, can think critically beyond conventional wisdom, can interpret data and situations effectively through seeking patterns and avoiding quick heuristics, are able to take a stand and reach difficult decisions, can align various stakeholders behind a certain direction by understanding their agendas, and can learn from both successes and failures.

SERIOUS PLAY INTERVENTION TECHNIQUE

The notion of serious play refers to an approach to adult learning – initially suggested by Plato – that combines a playful mode of interaction with a serious intent. Central to its effective use is a clearly defined goal of the construction process ('the serious issue') that will then be carried out in several steps. A first, important step consists of so-called warm-up exercises aimed at mitigating or reducing conceptual resistance that some participants may experience when working manually and with unusual objects, such as toy construction materials. Thus, a more playful exploration of the material at hand tends to create a sense of comfort with the material if less serious issues are explored initially. For instance, asking participants to build a particular model of some kind, followed by a model representing their job or family, will enable them to appreciate the expressive potency of the materials at hand. Carefully debriefing these models in terms of the level of the artefact (what do we see?), the meaning of it (what is it supposed to mean?) as well as the process (how did it come about?) shows the systematicity of the construction and debriefing process.

A second important step then consists of individually constructing a model of the serious issue (e.g. build a model of your organisation; your current team climate; your role as a leader; an effective planning process; what your organisation will stand for in five years, etc.). The framing of the issue is crucial here: it should be sufficiently broad to allow for interpretive variation and adaptation, but focused enough to allow for cross-individual comparisons. In the best case, such instruction is brief, precise and clear, although in contexts where the issue is less clearly defined, the facilitator may adopt somewhat more ambiguous questions (e.g. build a model of your team experience in the MBA programme) in order to generate a wider breadth of interpretations. The resulting individual models should be debriefed in detail and probed into by others.

A third step consists of building a collective construction of the issue at hand. This process typically starts by inviting participants to explore the individual models of the serious issue in terms of differences and commonalities, as well as to discuss whether and how these might be meaningfully integrated in a joint model. It is here that the distinction between artefact and its meaning is most helpful. Even if the models differ at the artefactual level, their intended meanings might actually converge. Allowing sufficient time for these meaning negotiations in terms of exploring and appreciating divergent viewpoints in order to then explore opportunities for a shared, convergent take on the serious issue is crucial. Debriefing the model provides another opportunity to 'triangulate' the narrative of the serious issue. Typically, we ask several participants to debrief the model – deliberately to again check for divergent and convergent interpretations. Lastly, and while the three-dimensional endeavour can create positive team dynamics, it is crucial to capture the key insights gained in a two-dimensional way (typically through flipcharting), related both to the focal issue and other insights triggered by the models beyond the actual focus of inquiry.

A quick note on materials – although serious play was developed using toy construction materials, i.e. LEGO, it is not necessarily limited to using these objects. Over the years, we have experimented with a wide range of materials, including those without preconfigured meaning, such as wooden bricks or clay. Such materials have the benefit of a 'white sheet' effect, that is, the meaning is mainly, if not exclusively, attributed by participants; although creation 'from scratch' also tends to be a bit more time-consuming. On the other hand, materials with preconfigured meanings such as construction toys have the benefit of swiftly providing participants with an image-rich repertoire, but may influence or constrain participants' imaginations. We suggest that depending on the object of inquiry and time constraints, one might opt for the former or the other with respect to choice of materials.

SERIOUS PLAY AS AN EXAMPLE OF HYBRID THINKING

The serious play technique thus combines elements of both divergent and convergent approaches to organisational creativity. As with divergent thinking techniques, participants draw heavily on intuition and play in developing constructions based on original metaphors and analogical reasoning. Much of the outputs are narrative-based, which emphasises the contextual uniqueness of the situation, as well as the reflexivity involved in telling the stories (Tsoukas and Hatch 2001). Processually, it is also more democratic than many of the convergent techniques, as it provides a common platform on which individual participants may freely contribute their perspectives and voices into the process – it is structured in such a way that no single perspective dominates. The insights developed are anchored in stories that prove more memorable than bullet point lists or statistics generated by other techniques. The process itself stimulates the generation of unexpected and insightful content (Bürgi and Roos 2003, Statler and Oliver 2008).

However, the serious play technique also includes elements that are more convergent. The subject of discussion is the organisation in its environment – thus it is more particularistic and grounded than techniques more divorced from specific organisational realities. The analogical reasoning that takes place is facilitated by what is built in the constructions (source domain), which represent specific organisational challenges or dimensions (target domain). The stories developed during serious play sessions integrate diverse considerations and evaluations, as expressed by the group participants, and point towards a direction for resolving the challenge that serious play was employed to address. Thus, at the end of the session, implementation of the solutions has already started, since agents are involved in constructing the story and making sense of the challenge and how it might be resolved.

To illustrate the combined divergent and convergent aspects of serious play, in the next section we provide three case vignettes of workshops run using the technique.

Vignette 1: ChemInc

The management team from ChemInc, the speciality chemical division of a mid-sized Swiss company, was responsible for developing a three-year strategic plan. The team engaged in a traditional strategic planning process and developed a plan that closely resembled ChemInc's previous three-year strategy, despite the fact that the company's customer base was rapidly changing. Corporate management decided ChemInc's plan lacked ambition and originality, so it sent its management team back to the drawing board to develop one that was more innovative. The team embarked on a two-day serious play process intervention in order to develop a more original strategy. The first day of the workshop involved the six-member management team (the VP of strategy and five functional heads) constructing individual representations of the identity of ChemInc, and narrative accounts describing these constructions. The use of the 3D construction materials allowed for a wide diversity of constructions, and indeed each team member developed a very different (and divergent) initial representation of his or her organisation, including a magician operating behind a barrier, a highly mobile vehicle with tube-like structures, a surveillance tower surrounded by threatening polar bears, and a factory controlling scattered sales people through use of an antenna.

Subsequently, the team was asked to combine their models into a single construction. This more convergent exercise proved difficult; they slid their individual constructions into the centre of the table, and only after much debate constructed a highly elaborate structure representing three main parts of the business connected by clogged communication channels or 'tubes'. After additional discussion, the group agreed that operational complexity was indeed a key element of the company's identity. Subsequently, participants constructed representatives of competitors, suppliers and other players in their business environment, which were all then positioned around and linked to ChemInc. In a final step, the group added communication channels connecting three key customers with logistics that bypassed the rest of the organisation. These 'tubes' subsequently formed the basis of a new element of the strategy plan involving the need to implement key account management (i.e. 'build more tubes') to circumvent organisational complexity and improve the company's

Figure 16.2   Resultant construction for ChemInc including tube-like structures

customer orientation. The emergence of these tubes was a result of 'hybrid thinking', in that they first appeared in an unrestrained individual construction but subsequently became part of a convergent structure, in which they played a major role in the subsequent strategy revision.

Vignette 2: PaintInc

A European paint company, PaintInc, had a well-established brand identity in its home market, and had recently embarked on an extensive international expansion. Senior management had launched a new customer-focused strategy as part of a broader effort to improve customer service, which included the objective of promoting the company's brand identity in its newer markets. One of the co-authors was hired to provide a two-day workshop using serious play to help managers from across the company better understand their company's brand identity and its role in the new strategy. The 20 workshop participants were divided into two groups of 10, each of which included participants from a variety of different company operations, although the company's 'international operations' were disproportionately represented in Group 2. Following some warm-up activities, each participant was asked to build an individual model of PaintInc's identity and present it to their group for discussion. These models included a divergent variety

*Figure 16.3   Group 2's representation of PaintInc, including critical
            elements*

of metaphors, including mazes, skeletons, red flags, networks, ninjas,
tightropes and bridges. Several of these representations were critical of
the organisation; a fact that several participants indicated to facilitators
during the break had surprised them.

Subsequently, each table was asked to build a collective model representing the identity of PaintInc. Group 1 quickly built a single con-
solidated model of company identity, which eliminated everything of
a critical nature that had been included in the individual models. The
model consisted only of a 'peacock' (representing adaptability, friendli-
ness and professionalism), 'heart' (representing compassion within the
company, a kindly and helpful attitude toward customers, and concern
for the environment) and 'family' (representing the founding family,
a 'family-style' way of working internally, and treating customers
like 'family'). The model constructed by Group 2 was quite different,
showing much more complexity and including many critical elements,
while no mention was made of peacocks or hearts. Each of the two
tables then described its identity representations to the other.

At this point, strong disagreements between the groups ensued, leading
several participants to become visibly tense and upset, with several
members of Group 2 commenting that Group 1 appeared to be living

in a 'dream world'. In particular, one participant from China insisted that the peacock and heart symbols were simply not relevant in her part of the organisation. Following further discussion, however, Group 2 began to integrate these symbols into a revised model of PaintInc's identity. Further animated discussion ensued when the groups were then asked to build models showing perceptions of the company's most important customers. A wide diversity of perceptions became evident, which was a painful revelation for some of the managers from head office. Indeed, one appeared on the verge of tears at this point of the workshop. The group ultimately converged on the view that while its brand identity might usefully be highlighted in its new customer-focused strategy in Europe, other aspects of the company, such as attention to pricing, would have to be prioritised in its new markets such as China.

Vignette 3: MobileInc

A European mobile telephone company, MobileInc, was dealing with a number of major strategic challenges related to a significant debt burden linked to its acquisition of expensive 3G licences, and its recent acquisition by a large competitor. Assured of a high degree of autonomy by its new owner, MobileInc senior management decided to engage in a two-day serious play workshop in order to develop some principles to guide its future strategic decision-making. Ten managers participated in the workshop (seven from strategy and three from human resources). Following some warm-up exercises, participants built individual constructions showing key organisational characteristics of MobileInc. A number of differing individual views of the organisation's identity were presented, including boat-like figures, towers and assorted plat-forms, yet consensus over a shared representation of the firm proved difficult, as the metaphors and individual identity representations were quite different from one another. The significant differences in assumptions and viewpoints became highly visible, which led to a lowering of overall energy in the room.

The second day began with some in-depth conversations among team members concerning the root causes of these differences. These conversations enabled team members to inquire into their own and others' privately held assumptions in a non-threatening way, leading the overall energy level to gradually increase as commonalities began to be discovered. Ultimately, the group converged on a shared identity representation drawing on the metaphor of 'a flotilla of ships'. The next step involved the construction and addition of 'agents' in the company's landscape – for example, important customers, competitors and regulators – then building connections between these agents and the shared MobileInc identity representation. Subsequently, group members individually generated some possible unexpected events that could emerge on this landscape, which were then 'played out' by the team using the model on the table. The playing out process included working through *how* the team should respond to the event, and then *why* such a response was most appropriate. With some help from the facilitator, the answer to the 'why' question would go on to lead to the development of the following guiding principles: 'be the meaning machine', 'take control of the complete narrative', 'maintain our difference' and 'be thought leaders'. When the guiding principles were discussed and developed at the end of the second day, the energy level in the room remained high. Many participants expressed satisfaction with the overall outcomes of the workshop, and the guiding principles would go on to be invoked many times by members of the strategy team in the days following the intervention.

In contrast, five months later and following some major organisation changes, the group – joined by some new individuals – decided to use a more conventional, discussion-based method to develop guiding prin-

Figure 16.4   Serious play intervention at MobileInc

ciples, involving break-out groups, PowerPoint templates, and hours of wordsmithing of the final phrases. The output of this second process involved a one-day workshop followed up by two half-day meetings of a designated 'committee' to refine the output. The result was a 12-page PowerPoint presentation, which follow-up discussions revealed had little buy-in from participants in the exercise, and was quickly forgotten.

In sum, the three vignettes each include elements of both divergent and convergent thinking, which led in each case to outputs that were both creative and useful to the organisations concerned (see Table 16.2).

Table 16.2   Summary of divergent and convergent thinking in serious play organisational vignettes

	Task	Divergent thinking	Convergent thinking	Consequences
ChemInc	Revise strategy	Magician behind wall; surveillance tower with polar bears; car including tubes	Shared representation of organisation as complex entity with 'tubes' symbolising new strategic objective	Strategic plan modified to include objectives for more key account management (i.e. 'tubes')
PaintInc	Improve customer service by expanding brand identity internationally	Individual symbols such as mazes, skeletons, red flags; also differing interpretations of core org identity symbols such as peacocks and hearts	Shared view of core organisational identity but diversity of customer perceptions across countries	Collective understanding of brand perception in international markets – directions for how to improve
MobileInc	Develop strategic 'guiding principles'	Elaborate boats, towers, platform-like structures	Shared metaphor of a flotilla of ships; four shared guiding principles	Guiding principles integrated into organisational conversations and decision-making

DISCUSSION AND CONCLUSION

Hybrid thinking serves as a useful approach to generating organisational creativity as its divergent side encourages novelty, while its convergent side ensures that the discoveries will be valuable to the organisation. On their own, divergent approaches may ultimately cause frustration on behalf of participants if the ideas produced are difficult to implement, which may lead to reduced ownership. On the other hand, overly convergent techniques may close off creative opportunities due to the predetermined, probabilistic reasoning often embedded in these processes.

The hybrid approaches we discuss in this chapter attempt to draw benefits from both sides (see Table 16.3). For example, serious play generates outputs related to 'traditional' management problems that are imaginatively rich and build on multifaceted metaphor and narratives. Serious play allows for concepts to be physically manipulated and interconnected during process, adding a tactile dimension to conceptual notions such as

Table 16.3   *Comparison of serious play to divergent and convergent*
intervention techniques

	Divergent techniques (e.g. brainstorming)	Convergent techniques (e.g. planning)	Hybrid techniques (e.g. serious play)
Types of outputs	Oral and textual	Oral and textual	Physical construction of conceptual ideas, narratives represented in constructions
Breadth of participation	Based on objective of session	Usually narrow – confined to top managers	Broader, allowing for inputs from diverse organisational members
Level of engagement in process	Medium	Medium/low	High
Commitment to result	Low to medium, low level of convergence	Variable, low sense of ownership	High, as there is high sense of ownership
Primary mode of engagement	Cognitive	Cognitive	Cognitive, emotional, embodied
Element of creativity and surprise	Intended but often accomplished to a limited degree	Not intended, plans aim to reduce surprise and variance	High, outputs are emergent and surprising

'organisation' and 'strategy' that has been found to be better retained by participants than more cognitivistic approaches.

It should be noted that hybrid approaches such as serious play include some risks similar to those found with divergent techniques. These approaches are more difficult for senior management to control – the process can generate unpredictable outputs that some might find threatening. For example, serious play frequently generates unanticipated outputs that draw on tacit or unconscious understandings of organisational phenomena (Oliver and Roos 2007). We also note that while such outputs are potentially useful in generating creative solutions to conventional problems, the insights gained still need to be operationalised using more conventional frameworks so that they can enter the realm of action rather than stay in the realm of imagination and creativity. In conclusion, we agree with Heracleous (1998) that imaginative techniques should be seen as complementary and mutually reinforcing with more conventional techniques, rather than opposing them.

QUESTIONS FOR DISCUSSION

1. What other management techniques appear to draw on 'hybrid' thinking?
2. How can hybrid thinking as a strategic capability be organisationally embedded and institutionalised – if at all?
3. What challenges might you expect to encounter if implementing 'hybrid' techniques such as serious play in an organisational setting?
4. What skills or personal characteristics of a change agent or an organisation development practitioner do you believe would be most useful in implementing hybrid thinking?

REFERENCES

Amabile, T.M. (1996), *Creativity in context*, Boulder, CO: Westview Press.
Amabile, T.M. and M. Khaire (2008), 'Creativity and the role of the leader', *Harvard Business Review*, **86**, 101–9.
Bürgi, P. and J. Roos (2003), 'Images of strategy', *European Management Journal*, **21**, 69–78.
Buzan, T. (1983), *Use both sides of your brain*, New York: Dutton.
De Geus, A. (1988), 'Planning as learning', *Harvard Business Review*, March–April, 70–74.
Diehl, M. and W. Stroebe (1987), 'Productivity loss in brainstorming groups: Toward the solution of a riddle', *Journal of Personality and Social Psychology*, **53**, 497–509.
Drazin, R., M.A. Glynn and R.K. Kazanjian (1999), 'Multilevel theorizing about creativity in organizations: A sensemaking perspective', *Academy of Management Review*, **24**, 286–307.

Dye, R. and O. Sibony (2007), 'How to improve strategic planning', *McKinsey Quarterly*, **3**, 40–48.

Ethiraj, S.K. and D.A. Levinthal (2004), 'Bounded rationality and the search for organizational architecture: An evolutionary perspective on the design of organizations and their evolvability', *Administrative Science Quarterly*, **49**, 404–37.

Ford, C.M. (1996), 'A theory of individual creative action in multiple social domains', *Academy of Management Review*, **21**, 1112–42.

Girotra, K., C. Terwiesch and K. Ulrich (2010), 'Idea generation and the quality of the best idea', *Management Science*, 56, 591–605.

Heracleous, L. (1998), 'Strategic thinking or strategic planning?', *Long Range Planning*, **31**, 481–7.

Heracleous, L., J. Wirtz and N. Pangarkar (2009), *Flying high in a competitive industry*, Singapore: McGraw-Hill.

Higgins, J. (1996), 'Innovate or evaporate: Creative techniques for strategists', *Long Range Planning*, **29**, 370–80.

Ingram, P. and M. Morris (2007), 'Do people mix at mixers? Structure, homophily, and the pattern of encounters at a business networking party', *Administrative Science Quarterly*, **52**, 558–85.

Jacobs, C. and L. Heracleous (2005), 'Answers for questions to come: Reflective dialogue as an enabler of strategic innovation', *Journal of Organization Change Management*, **18**, 338–52.

Jacobs, C. and L. Heracleous (2006), 'Constructing shared understanding – the role of embodied metaphors in organization development', *Journal of Applied Behavioral Science*, **42**, 207–26.

Jacobs, C. and M. Statler (2006), 'Toward a technology of foolishness', *International Studies of Management and Organization*, **36**, 77–92.

Litchfield, R. (2008), 'Brainstorming reconsidered: A goal-based view', *Academy of Management Review*, **33**, 649–68.

March, J.G. (1979), 'The technology of foolishness', in J.G. March and J.P. Olsen (eds) *Ambiguity and choice in organizations*, Bergen: Universitetsforlaget, pp. 69–81.

Marengo, L. and G. Dosi (2005), 'Division of labour, organizational coordination and market mechanisms in collective problem-solving', *Journal of Economic Behavior and Organization*, **58**, 303–26.

Mintzberg, H. (1991), 'Learning 1, planning 0: Reply to Igor Ansoff', *Strategic Management Journal*, **12**, 463–66.

Mintzberg, H. (1994), 'The fall and rise of strategic planning', *Harvard Business Review*, Jan–Feb, 107–14.

Nattermann, P.M. (2000), 'Best practice is not best strategy', *McKinsey Quarterly*, **2**, 22–31.

Oliver, D. and C. Jacobs (2007), 'Developing guiding principles: an organizational learning perspective', *Journal of Organizational Change Management*, **20**, 813–28.

Oliver, D. and J. Roos (2007), 'Beyond text: Constructing organizational identity multimodally', *British Journal of Management*, **18**, 342–58.

Osborn, A.F. (1957), *Applied imagination*, New York: Scribner.

Paroutis, S. and L. Heracleous (2013), 'Discourse revisited: Dimensions and employment of first-order strategy discourse during institutional adoption', *Strategic Management Journal*, forthcoming,

Paulus, P.B. and V.R. Brown (2003), 'Enhancing ideational creativity in groups: Lessons from research on brainstorming', in P.B. Paulus and B.A. Nijstad (eds) *Group creativity: Innovation through collaboration*, New York: Oxford University Press, pp. 110–36.

Paulus, P.B., T.S. Larey and A.H. Ortega (1995), 'Performance and perceptions of brainstormers in an organizational setting', *Basic and Applied Social Psychology*, **17**, 249–65.

Potter, R.E. and P. Balthazard (2004), 'The role of individual memory and attention processes during electronic brainstorming', *MIS Quarterly*, **28**, 621–43.

Schein, E.H. (1996), 'Kurt Lewin's change theory in the field and in the classroom', *Systems Practice*, **9**, 27–47.

Schoemaker, P.J.H. (1995), 'Scenario planning: A tool for strategic thinking', *Sloan Management Review*, **36**, 25–40.

Schoemaker, P.J.H. (2012), '6 habits of true strategic thinkers', *Inc.*, 20 March, http://www.inc.com/paul-schoemaker/6-habits-of-strategic-thinkers.html, accessed 20 November 2012.

Schwarz, J.O. (2011), '*Ex ante* strategy evaluation: the case for business wargaming', *Business Strategy Series*, **12**, 122–35.

Statler, M. and D. Oliver (2008), 'Facilitating serious play', in G. Hodgkinson and W. Starbuck (eds) *The Oxford handbook on organizational decision-making*, Oxford: Oxford University Press, pp. 475–94.

Tsoukas, H. and M.J. Hatch (2001), 'Complex thinking, complex practice: The case for a narrative approach to organizational complexity', *Human Relations*, **54**, 979–1013.

Vaccaro, A., S. Brusoni and F. Veloso (2011), 'Virtual design, problem framing, and innovation: An empirical study in the automotive industry', *Journal of Management Studies*, **48**, 99–122.

Van der Heijden, K., R. Bradfield, G. Burt, G. Cairns and G. Wright (2002), *The sixth sense: accelerating organisational learning with scenarios*, Chicester: Wiley.

Whittington, R. and L. Cailluet (2008), 'The crafts of strategy', *Long Range Planning*, **41**, 241–7.

Wolfe, J. and J. Rogé (1997), 'Computerized general management games as strategic management learning environments', *Simulation and Gaming*, **28**, 423–41.

17. Shaping creative organisational environments through the arts
Giovanni Schiuma

This chapter follows the notion introduced at the beginning of this handbook, that in order to provide space and time for creativity, organisations need to combine 'loose' and 'tight' properties. I will argue that this can be achieved by integrating emotional aspects of the organisation with technical, rational systems. From this perspective the creative environment is considered as a platform supporting and catalysing bisociation processes, shaped by managers who integrate emotional and rational knowledge. In order to influence this synthesis, managers need to consider the aesthetic dimensions of the organisation. One instrument for nurturing a creative environment might accordingly be the instrumental use of the arts in the form of 'arts-based Initiatives' (Schiuma 2011). They bring artistic projects or attitudes into the organisation to trigger bisociative thinking. I will illustrate this process by analysing the use of arts-based initiatives at Elica, an Italian company and a world leader in the design and production of kitchen hoods. In order to create an organisational context which could nurture human potential and creative thinking, Elica has adopted the arts as an instrument to support the development of a creative organisational environment.

CREATIVE ENVIRONMENTS

Global trends are transforming today's competitive environment and forcing organisations to develop new capabilities (Friedman 2005, Held et al. 1999, Mau and The Institute Without Boundaries 2004, Meredith 2007). Increasingly an organisation's capacity to deliver competitive products is not only linked to the establishment of efficient and consistent organisational systems, as traditionally postulated by modern management, but it is increasingly tied to the definition of adaptable and resilient systems that are able to meet changing market demands and continuously emergent business problems (Hamel 2007).

In the new business age companies are challenged to be more and more flexible, agile, intuitive, imaginative, resilient and creative in order to face an increasingly turbulent competitive environment. In other words, they have to be able to develop a capacity to respond creatively to discontinuous changes. This poses a major challenge for organisations: how to nurture a creative environment in which change is a 'state of mind', where employees have the capacity to be imaginative and motivated to give the best of themselves and embrace transformation, continuously accepting and searching for new valuable solutions. Accordingly a creative environment can be interpreted as an organisational context in which people can discover and express their potential so that by deploying and exploiting their full cognitive capabilities they can find novel valuable solutions to problems and challenges at hand.

Organisations – by shaping a creative environment and mindset – can both absorb external changes, according to an adaptive approach, and nourish internal transformational processes in order to proactively project and induce changes in the external economic ecosystems. Companies such as Google have been able to create a capacity for change and innovation by shaping organisational contexts in which creativity could flourish. This is achieved firstly through human resource management. Employees are encouraged to continuously search for new solutions to emergent and potential business problems; to achieve this, the company gives every employee time and space to cultivate and express their creativity. Secondly, Google pays great attention to the aesthetic properties of the workplace through interior design and the aesthetic experiences of the workforce, configuring the physical environment in order to inspire and energise employees' creativity. The design and beautification of the workplace is enriched with playground areas (equipped with bar football and table tennis tables), and services for employees including free meals during the day, coffee corners, gym, spa, meditation and resting areas, and rooms where people can play music. All these solutions are aimed at shaping a space in which human senses can be stimulated, creating positive employees' experiences which in turn may certainly influence their emotive states. As a result Google is one of the best companies in the world to work for, attracting and retaining talents, and pragmatically enhancing employees' productivity and creativity. Indeed employees stay longer hours at work, are more satisfied and are engaged to use their creativity to conceive new product solutions.

The development of a creative environment within organisations starts with the acknowledgement that organisational systems are essentially living organisms whose capacity for being intuitive, imaginative, resilient, creative and adaptable is based on their human nature (Hamel 2000, Schiuma 2011). In fact, an organisation's ability to be intuitive and imaginative is related to its employees' willingness and ability to exercise their creativity and imagination in daily work activities. On the other hand, an organisation's flexibility, resilience and toughness are linked to employees' capacity to tackle negative emotions such as stress, anxiety or fear of failure.

The interpretation of the organisation as a living organism aims to move beyond a traditional management view of organisations as inherently rational and efficient. The defining principles of this traditional and rational-based management perspective are: control, standardisation, efficiency, measurability and forecasting. These pillars of organisational design and development have led to the development of organisations that tend to operate as machine-like systems. Rational management models, approaches and tools are deployed to impose a *tight* control over the organisation's value-creation mechanisms. In such a framework people have been traditionally asked to apply their technical knowledge and develop their know-how in order to make sure they can deal with the tasks in hand, usually, in accordance with predefined procedures and rules.

To illustrate the relationship between managerial control and a more intuitive and creative response to change, we might consider the analogy of an airplane cockpit, in which the manager plays the part of the pilot. Like pilots, who have to steer an airplane towards a specific destination, managers are expected to drive an organisation towards identified performance and business objectives. To govern the airplane pilots use a comprehensive cockpit, equipped with various indicators and automated systems, which provide data and information about the state of the aircraft as well as of its flying conditions in the external environment. Similarly, managers adopt the paraphernalia of rational-based models and tools, developed by the management discipline, to provide information and control mechanisms to manage the company towards predefined directions. Like the pilots, managers use these mechanisms and data to make strategic decisions and operational actions. Their models and tools have integrated scientific- and engineering-based principles and approaches, which implicitly assume that the success can be achieved through the deployment of rationality as a tight driving mechanism.

This assumption works well in stable or quasi-stable ecosystems. But when organisations find themselves in a more complex, dynamic, turbulent and chaotic environment they need to complement *tight* rational control-based mechanisms with more *loose*, creative-oriented methods. Consider the cockpit metaphor. When pilots are flying in very stable environmental conditions, they can even switch on the automatic pilot and let the airplane be entirely governed by automatic mechanisms. But when the weather conditions become rough, pilots must draw upon their experiences and intuition. If the situations in which they operate are very complex, such as for example a crash landing, they are challenged to use not only their technical skills and available rational tools, but also their emotional intelligence and creative capabilities. Similarly, in today's economic climate, managers confront challenges and problems which require the integration of rational-based 'tight' mechanisms with emotive-based 'loose' mechanisms. Certainly, this is an important feature not only for managers, but for all employees working in organisations as they are asked to be engaged in their workday activities and to deploy their full intelligence. Consider the enhancement of employees' productivity. The traditional use of incentive systems has to be integrated with approaches recognising that people achieve high performance when they are happy and engaged in their work activities. People work better and more productively when they enjoy their job and have fun and are energised in their workplace.

In order to integrate the rational and emotive dimensions within an organisation, it is necessary first and foremost to recognise that the people are at the heart of the organisation, and they have emotional as well as rational needs. Commitment, empathy, motivation and imagination contain an emotional component. Engaging these emotional aspects is essential to any human-based organisation and requires in turn that managers provide space and time for people to fully express their potential. Such a 'creative' environment offers scope for employees to develop imaginative solutions to unexpected problems.

This chapter aims to investigate how organisations can shape creative environments by adopting the arts as a management instrument. Recognising the techno-human nature of organisations, the arts can be used as a managerial means to shape and affect organisations' environments so that they can fully mobilise, convey and manage people's willingness to give the best of themselves in order to contribute to the company's success.

In the next sections, first the notion of techno-human organisation is introduced as a conceptual framework addressing the centrality of people for companies' value-creation mechanisms. This represents a fundamental assumption in order to integrate the rational-based view with a perspective which highlights the relevance of emotions in organisational life. Then, the organisational creative environment is interpreted as the creation of an ideal platform promoting a conversation between the rational and emotive organisational dimensions in order to reconcile tight and loose elements fostering change, creativity and innovation. Second, arts-based initiatives are introduced and proposed as a management instrument to shape organisational creative environments. Finally, the case example of the Italian company, Elica, is presented. Elica, a world leader in the design and production of kitchen hoods, has adopted the arts as an instrument to support the integration of emotions and rationality in order to shape a creative environment capable of sparking, fostering and developing human potential and creative thinking.

THE HUMAN-BASED ORGANISATION

The modern management paradigm implies that it is possible to design and govern an organisation essentially as an efficient system able to achieve the targeted business objectives through control, standardisation and planned changes. Accordingly innovation has been recognised as a key factor for success, but its development has been mainly associated with the organisational capacity for managing technical knowledge, developing core competences, and making sure people deploy their know-how to solve problems. This view has worked well enough through the twentieth century in a business climate characterised by quasi-stable economic growth. However, the twenty-first century business landscape appears beset by ambiguities, uncertainties, dynamism and unpredictability that call for a renewed interpretative perspective of the organisation and management systems (Hamel 2007, 2009, Mol and Birkinshaw 2008).

In the new business age, organisational success cannot be considered as the mere ability to define and manage technical efficiency. Organisations need to integrate rational-based management systems with approaches and tools that acknowledge the nature of organisational life and components (Adler 2010). They are challenged to develop a continuous tension for change and innovation and acquire new capabilities to survive and prosper. In particular, they have to become agile, intuitive, imaginative and resilient to change. This requires that employees are fully engaged both to give the best of themselves and to exercise their creativity in order to solve existing problems as well as to generate new valuable business opportunities. For this reason organisations need to foster the development of workplaces in which people can feel good and be in touch with their positive emotions.

Emotion and Engagement in Creative Environments

The interpretation of a creative environment as an organisational context in which people can discover and express their potential essentially recognises the centrality of people and their role in the creative processes. In turn, the employees' capacity of being creative and innovative is very much related to their level of engagement in what they do. Traditional scientific-based management has focused the attention on the rational transactions that managers can control through the application of incentive systems. These approaches enable managers to extrinsically motivate employees, but fail to trigger and nurture their intrinsic motivation which basically results from people's feelings and engagement. Accordingly a creative environment aims 'to shape a space and time' in which people can be engaged with their feelings in thinking and developing new ideas that can make an impact on organisational business performance.

According to Dick Richards (1995) 'engagement occurs when [people] experience a deep sense of caring about the work, a sense that what [they] are doing is worthwhile in and for itself' (p. 31). The creation of this 'sense of caring' requires that organisations address people's emotions (Richards 1995). Although Mayo's studies of the 1930s recognised the role of work-related emotions to explain work performance (Roethlisberger and Dickson 1939), management attention throughout the twentieth century has considered emotions as a variable to be controlled for instrumental ends, rather than as a value-added dimension to be disclosed and managed (Flam 1993). A tight vision of the organisation prevailed and most of the attention to the management of emotions within organisations has been focused on emotional control (Stearns 1989, Waldron and Krone 1991). The application of modern management principles through managerial actions, such as the design of space and time, the control of information flows, the definition of formal and informal disciplinary rules, the establishment of organisational culture and values by senior staff, has been traditionally aimed at controlling emotions within organisations.

Due to their subjective, unpredictable and immeasurable nature emotions have been conventionally seen as a variable interfering with the regularity, stability and reliability of organisational system components. In other words, the loose nature of emotions has been considered as a problem rather than as a source for organisational performance. But in order to motivate employees to fully use their intelligence, the integration of the rational and the emotive reality of an organisation plays a fundamental role. A creative environment aims to shape an organisational context in which these two realities can be synergistically integrated. It can be seen as a platform in which the rational and emotive elements of an organisation are in a continuous ideal conversation so that they can be fused and nurtured by each other. The emotive dimension involves touching people's feelings and moods, and making sure they are in touch with and present to themselves. Conversely, the rational dimension refers to the set of rules and procedures that define how activities have to be carried out.

The fundamental scope of a creative environment is first and foremost to avoid overspecialisation ('silos') and/or a paralysis of thinking among employees and to spur the full engagement of human potential. Its development presupposes the recognition of the human-based nature of organisations; actually a creative environment has to be able to fully incorporate and reflect the human nature. This presupposes that creative environments can only be shaped in those organisations that are aware of and develop their living nature, and take into account the relevance and influence of people's emotions upon organisational and business activities.

Organisations as Techno-human Systems

The function of any organisation is characterised and based on vital phenomena. These include, at the same time, the tight rational dimensions of working processes and the loose emotive and inner dimensions of human experiences. These two dimensions cannot be separated unless an organisation is made into a 'machine-like system' removing the human presence. So they have to be intertwined and continuously put in conversation, though with different roles and relative importance according to the diverse situations and scope of organisational activities.

To stress the dual and inseparable twofold rational and emotive nature of organisational and business realities, the view of organisations as techno-human systems is proposed. This view is aligned with the tradition of organisation theory (Argyris 1964, Likert 1961, Pfeffer 1981) and conceives organisations as living organisms (Burns and Stalker 1961, Wheatley 1999). However, it is mainly inspired and supported by recent organisational study streams focusing on the relevance of aesthetics and emotions in organisations (Fineman 1993, Frost et al. 1985, Linstead and Höpfl 2000, Mintzberg 1985, Strati 1992, 2000a, Turner 1990). This techno-human perspective on organisations recognises that in the new business age, organisations need to manage not only their tight dimensions, i.e. the technological and rational-based elements, but increasingly they have to take into account, when organising and managing businesses, the loose dimensions in the form of aesthetic and emotive features as explaining factors of the success and excellence of organisations (Strati 1992, 2000a, Taylor and Hansen 2005). Indeed, emotions explain and contribute to the quality of the organisational value-creation mechanisms. They can act as enablers or as barriers towards business models and processes, having the capacity to moralise and demoralise, mobilise and immobilise organisational energies (Frank 1988).

Emotions affect the engagement of people and act as catalysts for important explanatory factors behind business performance, such as satisfaction, enthusiasm, flexibility, loyalty, creativity, change and innovation propensity, identity, diversity, culture, risk-taking, and so on (Flam

1993). They influence the outcomes of organisational business activities and help to explain both the failure and the success of an organisation's ability to adapt to external environmental changes or to proactively create changes. Therefore the organisational capacity of being adaptable, resilient and innovative has strong ties to the development of capabilities that are rooted in organisational emotive traits and elements. Thus, emotions contribute to explaining organisational as well as individual behaviours.

Managing Organisational Aesthetic Dimensions for Shaping Creative Environments

The challenge for managers is how to operationally handle the emotive characteristics and elements of an organisation so that they can be integrated with the traditional technical and rational-based mechanisms of organisations' processes. This can be achieved by managing the organisational aesthetic dimensions as a way to harness people's emotions with the scope of positively impacting on the organisational capacity for business performance improvements. For this reason increasingly organisations are focusing their attention on how to develop creative organisational environments exploring the application of interior design, playfulness elements, services and more generally searching for experiential activities that could engage employees. Pixar, for example, by integrating playfulness in workplaces, has traditionally paid great attention to the creation of an organisational atmosphere in which employees could be happy, inspired and energised.

The management of aesthetic dimensions can address organisational aesthetic experiences and/or properties. Organisational aesthetic experiences refer to the quality of employees' experiences within the organisation, including their well-being, the quality of their daily work activities and the engagement level in what they do. Organisational aesthetic properties characterise the aesthetic qualities of the organisation as a whole. This involves the capacity of the organisation's tangible and intangible infrastructure (from equipment and interior design to workplace culture and climate) to affect people's experiences.

In order to shape creative environments in which people can be fully engaged with their cognitive capabilities, it is important to make sure that emotions are disclosed and exploited within organisations alongside the rational dimensions. This can be achieved by promoting bisociation processes (Koestler 1964) with the scope of sparking and supporting a continuous conversation between emotions and rationality. From a practical point of view this required first of all the capacity of handling emotive dimensions so that they can be managerially integrated in the traditional tight working elements of organisations. This can be carried out by focusing the attention on the management of organisational aesthetic dimensions. In fact, aesthetics and emotions are two dimensions which are closely intertwined. Aesthetics generate feelings and feelings affect aesthetics. Aesthetics can be used to mobilise and manage emotions within and around organisations, and emotions can be put in place to better tune organisational aesthetic capabilities. By managing aesthetic dimensions within organisations managers can make sure that connections between emotions and rationality are realised. Managing aesthetic features equals to affect how people make sense of the reality around them by using their senses. For example, the integration of emotional and rational dimensions characterising the definition of a company strategy can be carried out by using visualisation techniques based on artistic drawings that allow an aesthetic representation and communication of the aims and contents of a company's strategy. In this case the traditional rational definition of the company's strategic objectives achieved through strategy planning techniques is enriched with the aesthetic features of drawings that act upon visual senses to engage employees' emotions. The drawings allow a more intuitive understanding of the company's strategy and promote people's imagination and creativity.

In order to manage organisational aesthetic dimensions and define a platform for emotions and rationality to be in conversation, artistic projects and practices can be adopted. Indeed, the managerial deployment of art forms and attitudes allows managers to handle and affect the organisation's aesthetic dimensions. Through the arts it is possible to foster people's aesthetic experiences and manipulate the aesthetic properties of an organisation's infrastructure. This can support managers to handle the organisation's emotive features and to integrate these dimensions with rational-based elements grounding the working mechanisms of business processes.

ARTS AND THE DEVELOPMENT OF ORGANISATIONAL CREATIVE ENVIRONMENTS

The arts as a cornerstone of human life represent a knowledge domain which can be used for transforming organisations, making them more suited to cope with the business challenges of the twenty-first century (Adler 2006, Austin and Devin 2003, Darsø 2004, Nissley 2010, Schiuma 2009, Taylor and Ladkin 2009). In other words, from an instrumental and utilitarian point of view, the arts represent a vehicle that can inspire managers to develop management innovation, frame new organisational and business models, and draw on new approaches and instruments to tackle continuously emergent business challenges (Schiuma 2011).

The arts have the power of influencing and creating organisational aesthetic properties and experiences (Strati 2000a, 2000b). They can be adopted as an instrument to develop people and/or to transform the organisation's infrastructure both tangibly and intangibly. Addressing people development issues, the arts can be deployed as a means to create aesthetic experiences that can affect employees' emotive dimensions with an impact on their level of engagement to the organisation's activities and life. For example, Spinach, an English marketing company, uses the arts as a means to develop and maintain an engaging and energising organisational atmosphere. The company's creative director, who is a professional artist, systematically designs and manages arts-based experiences, which can take the form of hands-on or hands-off activities, with the aim of sparking emotions and creating a positive work environment in which employees can feel positively engaged and stimulated to exercise their creativity.

On the other hand, the arts can be used as a tool for developing the organisation's infrastructure. They can be applied with the scope of affecting the aesthetic properties of the tangible and/or intangible components of an organisation. So, the arts can be deployed for designing and enriching workplaces, for communicating the culture, identity and image of the organisation, for emotional-driven design of facilities, equipment and products, and for creating impactful meaning that can influence individual and collective behaviours as well as acting as drivers for personal development. Consider those organisations that use the visual arts as a means to represent and communicate the company's values and culture. The creation of an exhibition, or even of a company's museum, can be addressed to define the company identity and recall its history.

From an operational point of view, the managerial implementation of the arts is carried out by means of arts-based initiatives (ABIs) (Schiuma 2009, 2011). An ABI is the planned managerial use of any art form or combination of art forms to address management challenges and business problems with the aim of developing employees and organisational infrastructure that positively affect the company's value-creation capacity. The underlying assumption is that the adoption of ABIs is fundamentally aimed at humanising organisations, by harnessing the emotional and experiential dynamics characterising organisational life and business activities.

Through ABIs it is possible to develop those organisational dimensions that cannot be controlled analytically and rationally, and nevertheless play a fundamental role in explaining the organisation's success and excellence. We label these elements as loose dimensions in order to distinguish them from the tight dimensions that in the form of rules, procedures and formal mechanisms regulate organisational behaviours.

The ABIs stand for approaches and tools that instrumentally use the arts to create or to affect organisations' aesthetic dimensions. In particular, ABIs can be used as instruments to shape creative environments that act as catalysers and amplifiers of human emotive abilities and can foster the development of an organisation's adaptability and continuous innovation. By adopting ABIs, organisations can employ and exploit the aesthetic properties and experiences associated to an artistic product and/or to an artistic process in order to create a frame of reference which promotes the connection of employees' technical and emotive knowledge. For example, the use of arts-based methods derived from performing arts can be used to engage employees in experiential learning processes that can help them to reflect and discover the emotions that are attached or detached from their working activities. This can support the understanding of how to be more engaged in what employees do by discovering and paying attention to features of their work activities that they really like, or simply attributing new meanings to their tasks.

The use of the arts can lead to the development of a creative environment which sparks and supports the integration and conversation between emotive and rational dimensions of an organisation. In this way, as called upon by Gary Hamel (2009), the virtues of the modern management paradigm such as stability, discipline, reliability, precision, modularisation and measurability, which constitute the tight elements of an organisation, can be synergistically integrated with emotive-based virtues such as malleability, resilience, toughness, agility, imagination, creativity, happiness and intuition, which denote the loose elements of an organisation.

In shaping creative environments the ABIs can fundamentally play a twofold role. On the one hand, they can act as a learning platform (Darsø 2004). On the other hand, they can represent a device or vector to influence organisational aesthetic dimensions (Schiuma 2009).

The perspective recognising ABIs as a learning platform considers the arts as an instrument to support individual and organisational learning mechanisms both by transferring artistic skills, which are useful in the business context, and/or by shaping an experiential organisational atmosphere, which can engage people with their emotions. The use of the arts as a learning platform is fundamentally aimed at developing human capital. This transformation is mainly based on the learning processes taking place both at the individual and at group level to nurture the development of employees. It may also have a positive impact on the internal and external organisational relationship dynamics as well as on the development of organisational and business models valuing emergent coordination, distributed wisdom, full engagement of people and distributed authority. In particular, arts-based methods are useful to spark reflections on the leadership style and culture characterising an organisation. ABIs can be applied to develop and enhance leadership skills not only at top management level but across the entire organisation. This is particularly useful in those contexts in which there is a need for distributed leadership. Using arts-based methods, employees can understand the meaning and the characteristics of leading and how to share this task with others. For example, using theatre-applied methods people can be fostered to reflect on their values, on how they interact with others, on the challenges of directing a group and sharing the responsibilities and the trust among the group's members.

The use of the arts as a device and vector is mainly related to the use of ABIs to embed aesthetic properties into tangible and intangible organisational infrastructure and products. So, for example, the arts can be used as a way to shape workplaces that can be inspiring. Offices can be artistically designed and beautified in order to spark and energise people. But the use of the arts can also be focused on managing the intangible elements of the organisational capital such as, for example, culture, values, identity and image. These dimensions can be made visible, more understandable and emotive through the use of artworks that symbolise them. For instance, the use of sculptures or visual arts can be deployed to represent metaphorically the identity of the company and its fundamental values.

The adoption of the arts either as a learning platform or as a device allows shaping creative environments, by creating a frame of reference in which rational organisational characteristics that are ingrained in the working mechanisms of today's organisations are put in conversation and integrated with the emotive features.

In the next section the case example of Elica, a world-leading Italian company in the production of kitchen hoods, is presented. Elica is using arts as a managerial instrument to support the development of the organisation as a human-centred living organism as well as a means to foster creative processes and maintain an organisational creative environment.

USING THE ARTS TO SHAPE A CREATIVE ENVIRONMENT: THE CASE OF ELICA

Elica is world leader in the design, production and commercialisation of kitchen hoods; it also designs, manufactures and sells motors for central heating boilers for domestic use. It has a market share of 17 per cent in the world and 43 per cent in Europe. With over 2300 employees, an annual output of about 16 million units of kitchen hoods and motors, a turnover in 2011 of 282 million euros and an EBITDA of 20.4 million euros, the Elica Group has ten plants: five are in Italy, one is in Poland, one in Mexico, one in Germany, one in India and one in China.

Elica has achieved a world-leading competitive position by revolutionising the traditional mature sector of kitchen hoods. In particular, the company has changed the traditional image of the kitchen cooker hood, transforming it from a simple accessory and household appliance into a design object. Elica's products are associated with an image of unique objects, with unusual shapes and incorporating innovative technologies. They combine meticulous care for the design, for the quality of material and for cutting-edge technology, which is also the result of the partnerships created with world-leading companies such as Artemide, in the lighting sector, and Whirlpool, in green and smart technologies. So the fundamental competitive value drivers of Elica's products are: the integration of high technological quality with a design-driven innovation capability, and the aesthetical dimensions combined with high functional quality.

The fundamental idea behind Elica's products is that they have to represent sources of inspiration and well-being, beautiful to look at and capable of providing the highest technological performance in order to meet customers' wants and needs. In other words, they are interpreted as an important component of the living house. In this perspective Elica's products are designed and produced on the basis of high technological and aesthetic features, making sure they embed intangible value and generate positive experiences for customers. In order to meet this challenge, Elica has understood that the development of products that can have a positive impact on people, first and foremost, is driven by an organisation which deeply embeds the features and potential of human nature. Consequently, they have developed a strong awareness about the relevance of being and operating as a human-centred living organism, paying great attention to managing organisational aesthetic dimensions and handling emotive features.

Elica attributes a fundamental centrality to people whose technical and emotive competences are considered the engine of competitive success. The declaration of the fundamental values of the company points out the relevance attributed to people in shaping the company value-creation capacity as well as highlights the importance that Elica attributes to emotions as a value driver for company performance. It is worth noting that even the language that they use to describe their values is itself emotional and aesthetic in tone and meaning, underlying the intention of sparking employees' emotions and engagement. The following values represent the strong reference point for all organisational activities: Love your customers – put passion into working for them; Use innovative thinking; Make it easy for everyone to be involved in their own work; Employ and communicate total energy; Identify new objectives and achieve them; Stay curious and never stop learning; Want to win; See change as an opportunity; and Fight to reduce costs and simplify your work. Elica, on the basis of these values, focuses great attention on the creation of an organisational atmosphere in which creativity can flourish and be nurtured.

As stated by Deborah Carè, Elica Group Brand Marketing Manager, the notion of promoting creativity is fundamentally interpreted by the organisation as the capacity of coping with the risk of the 'paralysis of thinking'. For Elica it is essential that employees do not carry out their activities in a mechanistic way without too much questioning about it. Elica strongly believes that it is fundamental to foster the development of a creative environment which encourages people to think and to engage in what they do. This is considered essential in order to foster an organisational environment capable ultimately of developing and producing products that combine and embed high technology and emotive/aesthetical features. For this reason, they have integrated in the management system the use of the arts as a managerial instrument to support the development of employees' adaptability to changes and their innovation-oriented behaviour. This integration, even if not explicitly declared as an attempt to activate bisociation processes, makes possible an ideal conversation between the emotive and rational realities of the organisation.

Elica interprets the arts as a powerful means to contaminate traditional management and technical knowledge with emotive and experiential stimulus coming from the art world. They are seen as a fundamental factor to push the organisation beyond the traditional business model and break conventional paradigms that have characterised the company in the past when it was just focused on producing standard appliance hoods.

Elica is using the arts as a strategic managerial instrument to nurture an organisation's behaviour towards imagination, innovation behaviour, problem-solving-oriented capability and creativity. Some of the main organisational issues addressed through the arts are: communication of the company's philosophy, development of productive and well-being-oriented workplaces, strengthening of ties with clients and more generally with society and territory, employees' development, promotion and communication of organisational image and reputation, enhancement of product development capacity.

From an operational point of view, Elica has launched different ABIs to shape a creative environment. In particular, identifying people and workplaces as two fundamental dimensions of the creative environment, they have developed two specific arts-based programmes as follows: the programme named 'Lifestyle' and the programme named 'E-straordinario'.

Elica's 'Lifestyle' programme aims to shape workplaces that secure well-being and productivity as well as create an atmosphere which spurs creativity and positive emotions so that new ideas can converge and be created. According to Elica, the workplaces have to be a kind of 'open porthole' on a different concept of being, of living and acting; so they have to be places for meeting and renovating the mind. The creation of engaging workplaces is achieved by adopting the arts as an instrument to shape the aesthetic properties of facilities and the organisation's culture, values, identity and, more generally, climate. Offices are artistically designed and host exhibitions both of artworks from public and private contemporary art collections, and of artistic artefacts created by employees with the support and facilitation of artists. Among the different Lifestyle initiatives it is worth mentioning Elica Contemporary. This arts-based project – initially promoted as the showroom of the company in the area of Brera in Milan, using the private arts collection of Francesco Casoli, president of the Elica Group – created an unusual mix between an art exhibition and an industrial marketing event. The art exhibition was integrated with the presentation of the products of the company. Elica's products were put next to artworks in order to point out their intrinsic 'artistic' nature. At present Elica Contemporary has been integrated within the organisation, and the artworks together with the company's products are exhibited in different spaces within the company. This has an impact on the aesthetic characteristics of the workplace, on the capacity of communicating the company's identity, highlighting its mission of creating products which aspire to be 'artworks for the living house', and on the engagement level of employees fostering their pride in the results of their work activities.

On the other hand, the E-straordinario programme is aimed at supporting employees' development. Its purpose is the creation of an aesthetic experiential learning process that can engage employees with their emotions. It works on the basis of a set of conceptual and practical arts-based seminars and workshops in which artists work on a project within the organisation and with employees. The selected artists brought into the company are asked to conceive and carry out an artwork which can engage the company's employees intellectually, emotionally and physically. The artist(s) works with a facilitator in order to make sure that the insights can be distilled from the arts-based initiatives. The artists' projects to be implemented in the organisation are selected on the basis of different criteria, particularly: experimentation, contamination of different codes, hands-on participation of employees, quality of contents, capacity of challenging established habits and behaviours, moving employees out of their comfort zone, and the use of the arts as an ethical model. An example of an arts-based project developed as part of the E-straordinario program is the 'Saiettatori'. This project has been named on the basis of Michelangelo's artwork 'I Saettatori' (The Archers), which has been used as a metaphor to explore issues related to the soft dimensions moving a community and a group of people towards success, and more specifically characterising the success of a creative process. In Michelangelo's artwork, the archers have already shot their arrows. This can be noted by observing in the drawing the tension of the archers' bodies, but they do not hold the bows. It is as if the archers are firing the arrows with their energy.

Elica's aim with this project was to help employees to reflect on the soft features grounding an artful creative process and to understand how these dimensions affect work activities. In this perspective the use of the metaphor of the archers has helped employees to reflect on the key soft characteristics affecting organisational excellence and high performance. The bows have been interpreted as an analogical symbol for the technical knowledge, while the energy and orientation towards the goal have been identified as the key soft dimensions at the basis of success.

The overall project has been developed through different stages with a different level of involvement of employees. First, focusing on the art of incision and printing, which is the basis of the artwork 'I Saiettatori', employees through hands-on participation have learned the techniques for incision and the challenges of creating an artwork. At this stage the art of incision and printing has been used as an analogical model to artfully understand the critical dimensions distinguishing a creative process. This stage has also helped employees to discover the fun and enjoyment of the creative process and reflect on the relevance of being in touch with their emotion in the work activities. Second, an exhibition of artworks of nine different artists has been arranged in the company with the aim of sparking conversations around the techniques adopted by the artists in developing their work. Then, finally, the employees have been engaged in debriefing sessions during which, with the help of an expert facilitator in human resource development, they have distilled insights and implications from the overall artful experiences related to the project. On the basis of the reflections developed as well as of the skills learned during the project, employees have been stimulated to identify the key competences distinguishing an artist, and in turn they have discussed how these competences differ from those characterising a successful creative employee in the work life. In particular, the four key competences that have been identified are: a tension for results; toughness; perseverance; and methods.

Both programmes are based on the fundamental assumption that people have a central role in organisational value-creation capacity and competitiveness. They are aimed at creating space and time, fostering the integration of the organisation's emotive and rational dimensions. By affecting people's aesthetic experiences, the arts stimulate human senses and create processes or contexts in which people's emotions arise and can be combined with rational elements grounded in the organisation's working activities. By blending the emotive reality with the traditional rational working mechanisms, Elica has been able to shape a creative environment which is producing positive impact on people's innovation behaviours and more generally on company innovation capacity. Indeed, the number of employees' potential innovation idea suggestions has increased in the last few years by an average of 10 per cent annually, new products have been developed and produced, the company is considered one of the best Italian companies to work for and, more generally, the quality of the organisational climate has improved. Although these results cannot be exclusively attributed to the management of the organisational aesthetic dimensions, this has surely played an important direct and indirect role.

Although the case example of Elica cannot be generalised, it offers important implications to identify some critical factors about the relevance of the arts for shaping a creative environment.

FINAL REMARKS

Increasingly the twenty-first-century business landscape will challenge organisations to exert more organic- and human-oriented capabilities, such as adaptability, agility, flexibility, imagination and creativity. The traditional view of the organisation as an efficient system to be steered towards planned and designed directions fails to meet these requirements. A renewed interpretation of the organisation is necessary, which recognises the centrality of people in the organisation's value-creation mechanisms. For this reason the view of the organisation as a techno-human system acquires great relevance. This perspective points out that organisations need to integrate the traditional rational-based principles with the emotive features of human life and understand that emotions play a fundamental role in organisational life and in the pursuit of business excellence.

Emotions can be considered as the loose elements in the sense that they denote all those factors of human expression that cannot be reduced to rules or procedures and in such a way controlled; rather, they need to be disclosed and channelled for contributing to the organisational value-creation mechanisms. On the other hand, rationality represents the tight organisational elements that have been traditionally addressed by scientific management to guarantee efficiency and control. Both emotions and rationality matter for the success of an organisation and in today's business context they need to be integrated. Their integration is at the heart of shaping creative environments in which people, through a process of bisociation, can develop and blend their technical and emotional knowledge. Creative environments allow people to achieve their full human potential in order to contribute to the success of organisations.

In order to shape creative environments, it is suggested that organisations manage their aesthetic dimensions. For this purpose the use of the arts is proposed as a management instrument to shape the organisation's aesthetic experiences and properties, which in turn can support handling emotive elements in organisational contexts. From a practical point of view the arts can be deployed within organisations to shape creative environments in the form of arts-based initiatives (ABIs). The case example of Elica shows how the use of ABIs can contribute to develop a creative environment.

In conclusion, the fundamental underlying assumption of this chapter is that the definition and development of creative organisational environments through the use of the arts is aimed at making organisations more human, acknowledging the relevance of the human-based nature of business. A creative environment is capable of engaging employees in their daily work activities, of inspiring executives to build igniting visions and energise people, and of making organisations more aware of the value propositions delivered to stakeholders.

QUESTIONS FOR DISCUSSION

1. What might be the challenges of integrating the arts into management systems and developing a systematic use of arts-based initiatives to shape a creative environment?
2. The adoption of the arts as a management instrument to shape creative environments can be met by some level of scepticism among managers and workforce. How would you overcome such scepticism?
3. How can we measure the benefits of deploying arts-based initiatives for shaping a creative organisational environment? What are the pitfalls of measurement in this case and how might these be addressed?
4. Might some art forms be more effective than others in shaping a creative organisational environment? Which art forms would be best suited to which organisational challenges?

ACKNOWLEDGEMENTS

I would like to thank Christopher Bilton, who has reviewed and provided useful comments to significantly enhance the clarity of this work, whose quality and contents remain entirely my responsibility. I am also very grateful to the Elica's managers, and particularly to Deborah Carè, for their willingness to share their practices on the use of arts-based programmes.

REFERENCES

Adler, N.J. (2010), 'Going beyond the dehydrated language of management: leadership insight', *Journal of Business Strategy*, **31**(4), 90–99.
Adler, N.J. (2006), 'The arts and leadership: Now that we can do anything, what will we do?', *Academy of Management Learning and Education*, **5**, 486–99.
Argyris, C. (1964), *Integrating the individual and the organisation*, New York: Wiley.
Austin, R. and L. Devin (2003), *Artful making: what managers need to know about how artists work*, New York: Prentice-Hall.
Burns, T. and G.M. Stalker (1961), *The management of innovation*, London: Tavistock.
Darsø, L. (2004), *Artful creation – learning-tales of arts-in-business*, Gylling: Narayana Press.
Fineman, S. (1985), *Social work stress and intervention*, Aldershot: Gower.
Fineman, S. (ed.) (1993), *Emotion in organisations*, London: Sage.
Flam, H. (1993), 'Fear, loyalty and greedy organisations', in Fineman S. (ed.) *Emotion in Organisations*, London: Sage, pp. 58–75.
Frank, R.H. (1988), *Passions within reason: the strategic role of the emotions*, New York: W.W. Norton.
Friedman, T.L. (2005), *The world is flat: a brief history of the 21st century*, New York: Farrar, Straus and Giroux.
Frost, P.J., L.F. Moore, M.R. Louis, C.C. Lundberg and J. Martin (1985), *Organisational culture*, London: Sage.
Hamel, G. (2000), *Leading the revolution*, Boston: Harvard Business School Press.
Hamel, G. (2007), *The future of management*, Boston: Harvard Business School Press.
Hamel, G. (2009), 'Moon shots for management', *Harvard Business Review*, **87**, 91–8.
Held, D., A. McGrew, D. Goldblatt and J. Perraton (1999), *Global transformations*, Stanford, CA: Stanford University Press.
Koestler, A. (1976[1964]), *The act of creation*, London: Hutchinson.
Likert, R. (1961), *New patterns of management*, New York: McGraw-Hill.
Linstead, S. and H. Höpfl (eds) (2000), *The aesthetics of organisation*, London: Sage Publications.
Mau, B. and The Institute Without Boundaries (2004), *Massive change*, London: Phaidon Press, Ltd.
Meredith, R. (2007), *The elephant and the dragon: the rise of India and China and what it means for all of us*, New York: Norton.
Mintzberg, H. (1985), 'The organisation as a political arena', *Journal of Management Studies*, **22**, 133–54.
Mol, M.J. and J. Birkinshaw (2008), *Giant steps in management*, London: FT Prentice-Hall.
Nissley, N. (2010), 'Arts-based learning at work: economic downturns, innovation upturns, and the eminent practicality of arts in business', *Journal of Business Strategy*, **31**(4), 8–20.
Pfeffer, J. (1981), *Power in organisations*, Marshfield, MA: Pitman.

Richards, D. (1995), *Artful work: awakening joy, meaning, and commitment in the workplace*, San Francisco: Berrett-Koehler.

Roethlisberger, F.G. and W.J. Dickson (1939), *Management and the worker*, Boston: Harvard University Press.

Schiuma, G. (2009), 'Mapping arts-based initiatives – assessing the organisational value of arts', *Arts and Business*, UK.

Schiuma, G. (2011), *The value of arts for business*, Cambridge: Cambridge University Press.

Stearns, P.N. (1989), 'Suppressing unpleasant emotions: the development of a twentieth-century America', in A.E. Barnes and P.N. Stearns (eds) *Social history and issues in human consciousness*, New York: New York University Press.

Strati, A. (1992), 'Aesthetic understanding of organisational life', *Academy of Management Review*, **17**, 568–81.

Strati, A. (2000a), 'Aesthetic theory', in H. Linstead and H. Höpfl (eds) *The aesthetics of organisation*, London: Sage Publications.

Strati, A. (2000b), *Theory and method in organisation studies*, London: Sage Publications.

Taylor, S.S. and H. Hansen (2005), 'Finding form: looking at the field of organisational aesthetics', *Journal of Management Studies*, **42**(6), 1211–31.

Taylor, S.S. and D. Ladkin (2009), 'Understanding arts-based methods in managerial development', *Academy of Management Learning and Education*, **8**, 55–69.

Turner, B. (1990), *Organisational symbolism*, Berlin: De Gruyter.

Waldron, V.R. and K.J. Krone (1991), 'The experience and expression of emotion in the workplace: a study of a corrections organisation', *Management Communication Quarterly*, **4**, 287–309.

Wheatley, M.J. (1999), *Leadership and the new science: discovering order in a chaotic world*, San Francisco: Berrett-Koehler.

PART V

AROUND THE CREATIVE CYCLE

18. Creative management in practice: bisociation with 'timely balance'

Zhichang Zhu, Chris Bilton and Stephen Cummings

Throughout this handbook, we and our contributors have highlighted the bisociative connections which lie behind creativity and its variants, and which also characterise the relationship between creativity and management. The dichotomous pairs of discovery–creation, diligent–dilettante, vision–action and loose–tight properties provide a pattern for analysing and understanding creativity and its management. But how can we now turn this understanding into action? How might the theoretical and empirical models and ideas advanced in this handbook be applied in practice? How can we turn the nouns – innovation, entrepreneurship, leadership, organisation – into verbs – innovating, 'entrepreneuring' (see Chris Steyaert's Chapter 9 for an explanation), leading and organising?

Koestler's notion of bisociation, the theoretical underpinning of the handbook, argues that the creative mind brings together two habitually disconnected frames of reference. But, interestingly, Koestler acknowledged that bisociation works differently in different settings. Scientific creativity, Koestler argued, works towards a resolution, following a dialectical process which ultimately resolves or reorders apparently contradictory phenomena. Artistic creativity, on the other hand, works towards juxtaposition – the two opposing ideas remain unresolved, a source of creative tension and mental stimulation for the recipient. Scientific bisociation ultimately works through the creative process towards a resolution, a harmonious order or balance. Artistic bisociation throws up thought-provoking problems, challenges and questions.

Probably the longest running debate in management circles has been whether management is more art or science. The closest thing to an agreement as to what the answer might be is that management has elements of both. This makes it interesting to consider how Koestler's concept of bisociation might be operationalised in a management setting. Should managers attempt to find a balance between two opposing positions, or should managers switch between opposing positions, keeping a foot in both camps? To take the example of creative leadership, should a creative leader steer a course between extremes, as in Marcus Aurelius's model of the 'virtuous' leader with which we began Part III? Or should a creative leader draw on a repertoire of styles and skills depending on the situation, batting between charismatic and transactional leadership, alternately deploying 'soft' and 'hard' skills? Marcus Aurelius's model is closer to Koestler's model of scientific creativity, adopting a stable, balanced 'middle way'. In practice, the multi-tasking, adaptive leader described by Lucy Küng or Vikki Heywood in Part III may be closer to Koestler's model of artistic creativity, juggling different apparently opposing mindsets (and risking accusations of inconsistency and contradiction).

We first proposed the idea of seeing creativity in organisational settings in terms of four bisociative elements – innovation, entrepreneurship, leadership, organisation – in a book called *Creative Strategy: Reconnecting business and innovation* (Bilton and Cummings 2010). In his review of that book, Zhichang Zhu (2010) identified a crucial omission in this argument, noting that managers need not only to understand the contradictions and paradoxes of creativity and strategy but to find a way of negotiating between them. In particular, Zhu was critical of the notion of Aristotle's 'golden mean' or 'right mean' advanced in the final section of *Creative Strategy*. Managers were being advised to find a 'balanced or middle way' between two extremes of 'loose' and 'tight' organisation. At the same time managers were encouraged to 'switch roles and relationships' and to develop an organisational culture containing 'just enough disunity for progress', and so on. But how, exactly, would one achieve this? As Zhu noted in his review, 'we would all love these "just enough" good things at "the middle way", but one wonders how to get there in the first instance . . . You can't have it both ways can you? Is [this] paradoxical thinking, or ambivalent thinking, or mystical thinking?'

Zhichang's reflections on this and other related topics led to the creation of a book called *Pragmatic Strategy: Eastern wisdom, global success*, written with Japanese knowledge management guru Ikojiro Nonaka (Nonaka and Zhu 2012). In this book, he and Ikojiro grappled with how managers can act when faced with such paradoxes, by drawing not just on Western thinkers such as Koestler and Aristotle, as we did, but on Eastern thinkers too.

Subsequently, in seeking to develop a conclusion to this handbook, we were compelled to engage Zhichang, and he very kindly agreed to work on something with us. What follows is the result of our conversations on the topic of how to actively manage the bisociative paradoxes that underlie creativity.

* * *

So, how can we now help those charged with the management of creativity to turn the insights put forward in the *Handbook of Management and Creativity* into action? And how might the theoretical and empirical models and ideas advanced in the handbook be applied in practice?

Perhaps the best place to begin to answer these questions is to outline what not to do. We do not suggest that the practical response to the bisociative paradoxes that frame the contents of this book should be any of the following:

- Going for the middle ground. (Even if we could work out where that was and how to get there, we would likely end up with a mediocre muddle, or simply exhaust energy and rhetoric in pursuit of an elusive and illusory 'best practice'.)
- Avoiding a 'deficit' or an 'excess' on either side of the bisociation. (Who would know what constitutes a deficit or excess *ex ante*?)
- Searching for the theoretical balance: 'just enough' tightness or structure and 'just enough' looseness or chaos. (Same problem: how to judge 'just enough' in real time.)
- Implementing both 'extremes'. (In practice, this would be contradictory and confusing.)
- Hopping between opposites. (This would make momentum, efficiency and a clear sense of corporate identity impossible. It would also be extremely costly, in every sense.)
- Fitting equal amounts of balanced innovation, entrepreneurship, leadership and organisation into action plans. (This does not take into account that different situations call for different mixes.)
- Laying out innovation, entrepreneurship, leadership and organisation in a processual sequence, moving through one element and then to the next. (This would be to underestimate the interconnecting, systematic nature of creativity, and undermine the potential for learning through doing and double-loop learning – or questioning and adapting practices as one sees their effects.)

These seven possible responses to a paradoxical and bisociative theory of managing creativity will not do, because they can only lead to either overly mechanistic or mysterious undertakings, and consequently refer us back to an all-knowing, all-certain 'one-best-way' of doing things: a pre-determination that goes against the nature and possibilities of human creativity.

So what should we do? Nonaka and Zhu's (2012) notion of 'timely balance', developed in the book *Pragmatic Strategy*, suggests a way forward.

Unlike the concept of the 'golden mean' (certainly modern conceptions of what this means, at any rate), *timely balance* promises no quick fix or set, programmable response. Instead, it acknowledges uncertainty, complexity, ambiguity and emergence, and encourages managers to exercise their limited but significant agency so as to act wisely in the world. And in the context of this handbook, *managing with timely balance* can facilitate real value-adding creativity, which is by definition outstanding, novel, unknown beforehand and hence unpredictable. According to Nonaka and Zhu,[1] *timely balance* can be achieved via the following five simple practices:

I.   do something, purposefully;
II. act upon practical certainties;
III. engage in gesture-response processes;
IV. learn through consequences; and
V.   build adaptive capabilities through bringing substantial diversity to bear.

And, while all of these practices could be applied holistically to each of the four elements of this handbook, we have linked them to particular parts of the underpinning diagram with which we began the handbook in Chapter 1 (see Figure 18.1), in order to build a heuristic framework as an aid for people who want to actively promote creativity in organisations.

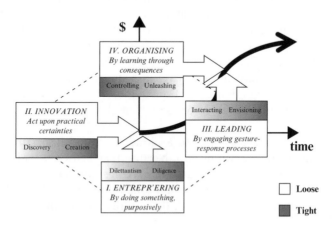

Figure 18.1   Four 'timely balance' practices toward the practical management of creativity

I. ENTREPRENEURING BY DOING SOMETHING, PURPOSEFULLY

The Chinese Taoist Zhuangzhi famously said: *Tao* is made in the walking on it. Similarly, contemporary Western strategic thinking increasingly stresses phrases such as having a 'bias for action' and 'action rationality'. In management, as in creativity, wise managers place a premium on trying something, rather than endlessly analysing a situation to discern an optimal course of action. Claude Lévi-Strauss, the French anthropologist, even coined a special word for just doing in this manner: *bricolage* – use whatever materials are at hand to construct workable solutions as problems unfold.

Deng Xiaoping provides a good example. When China embarked on its economic and political reforms, no one knew how a market economy should work in that vast, undeveloped, socialist country. To wait for a proven, correct model would have led nowhere. 'Cross the river by touching the stones' was Deng's mantra. Deng was not an all-knowing, all-powerful 'chief architect' – no one is; China's economic reform succeeded chiefly because Deng allowed 1.3 billion people to experiment and edge their way along even without knowing how things would play out.

Make sure to do something, then, but not just anything. In managing creativity this doing must be done with a creative purpose. The late strategy professor Sumantra Ghoshal distinguished 'purposeful action-taking' and 'active non-action'. While the former gets what matters done against all odds, with a clear purpose and persistent focus, the latter keeps running all the time, extremely busy, but fails to make a difference, not even knowing what is being done. Doing something purposefully is a realistic yet tough call; it demands skill, judgement and drawing on experience.

We think this approach relates well to the entrepreneurial element of creative management, combining the dilettante's adventurous, open-minded willingness to 'just do it' and the diligent, purposeful attitude needed to take a new venture forward. In particular, Zhu and Nonaka's approach here moves away from any assumption that there can be a perfect entrepreneurial opportunity or an idealised combination of entrepreneurial personality traits. Entrepreneurs make the best of things and draw on a repertoire of ideas, skills and attitudes to get the job done. In the context of timely balance, timing is all – making the most of the here and now rather than planning for the perfect moment, and recognising that the right balance of action and purpose here and now reflects the needs of a particular time and place, not a permanent recipe for success. At the very least, momentum is achieved and, even if the doing leads to short-term failures, that momentum and the active minds it engenders can help the learning and adjustment process and build resilience and future agility (see timely balance practices IV and V, above).

There are echoes here of the 'agile' creative technologists in the Happenstance project described by Bilton in Chapter 7, or Chris Steyaert's unemployed steelworkers in Chapter 9. Plunging into the world, following the mantra of 'start entreprenuering, work out the details later', takes an initial leap of faith (do *something*); Chris Steyaert describes this as the AH moment, a sensual engagement with the world around us which brings to light new possibilities. This is succeeded by focused action (do something, *purposefully*) as the entrepreneur commits to a course of action and rehearses and refines the idea (from AH to AHA). That initial entrepreneurial impulse to seize the initiative, even before the true purpose or direction has been discovered, remains purposeful. While such doing may appear random, unplanned or spontaneous from the outside, the entrepreneurial act is nevertheless framed by the entrepreneur's sense of purpose: a purpose to create value in a particular way.

Pertinently, Kate Oakley in Chapter 8 reminded us that not all entrepreneurs enjoy the independent agency needed for purposeful action-taking. For many young entrepreneurs working in the cultural and creative industries, entrepreneurial activity is no longer an act of choice; it is forced upon them, or they internalise this feeling and it churns away uncomfortably inside them. The felt risk of 'active non-action' is reflected in the cultural entrepreneur's precarious reliance on short-term and underpaid (or unpaid) work, raising the question as to whether what Kate calls 'forced entrepreneurship' can actually be classified as creative entrepreneurship. And this distinction helps up see further the importance of the unforced entrepreneurial spirit – the passion and joy in doing something despite the risks – as so crucial at the start of a creative process.

II.   BEING INNOVATIVE BY ACTING UPON PRACTICAL CERTAINTY

We began our handbook with 'innovation' rather than 'entrepreneurship'. But as Cummings et al. noted in Chapter 6, innovation still requires the entrepreneurial uplift to convert innovative ideas into sustained value-creation. Indeed, all creativity must be driven by an entrepreneurial spirit of purposeful action. Koestler defined creation as an 'act' and, while innovation may provide the raw material for creative management, entrepreneurial action (driven by purpose rather than planning) ignites it. As our diagram shows, innovation and entrepreneurship create this uplift in tandem (see the bottom left-hand corner of Figure 18.1). But a book is read in a linear way and we put innovation first in our introduction. It is useful to demonstrate here in our conclusion, in concert with Nonaka and Zhu's ideas, that entrepreneurship can just as correctly come first. But having covered the importance on entrepreneuring by doing something, purposively, we now turn to look at how innovation can be guided by acting on practical certainty.

Rejecting the quest for certainty and acknowledging that creativity cannot be managed by top–down planning and control, we do not need to accept an 'anything goes' mindset, or begin every time anew with a knowledge ground-zero. Here, the German socio-philosopher Jürgen Habermas's notion of 'practical certainty' is useful. We step onto a bridge only when we know with practical certainty that the bridge is safe, suggests Habermas. Britain will not become a desert in a week's time, Japan will not become an energy-rich country tomorrow, and Chinese firms are likely to continue using personal connections in business dealings for the foreseeable future. These are all practical certainties that we can act upon. And there are many others.

Hence, there is both uncertainty and certainty in organisational life. Such a balanced view allows us to get on with life wisely. We implicitly act on all sorts of practical certainties and only, albeit frequently, when encountering frustrations are we compelled to face uncertainty, to question what we have taken as unproblematic, and to seek alternative course of action. We need to justify knowledge claims; we need, too, to justify doubts toward such claims, the American pragmatist Charles Sanders Pierce reminded us. In this way, we can act pragmatically without falling into a paralysing scepticism. It is with such 'disciplined commonsense' that we value and act upon lessons from the experiences of ourselves and of others in order to enrich our pool of resources and hence our resourcefulness. And it is based on practical certainties that we judge what we should or should not attempt. Practical certainties particularly relevant to creativity management include good practices such as generating and reviewing real options, putting in place useful rules and getting out of the way and allowing them to work, investing in diversity, and so on.

Innovation is not only concerned with the generation *ex nihilo* of new ideas. Many of the innovations charted in this handbook build upon, extend or reconfigure existing knowledge. Previously we have identified several 'degrees' of innovation, beyond the straightforward invention of new ideas to variations in the way innovations are combined, packaged and experienced (Bilton and Cummings 2010). Others have described these variations in terms of 'soft innovation' or 'hidden innovation', acknowledging a range of practices by individuals and organisations which extend beyond and enrich the one-off generation of a novel idea.

Following Grabher (2004), Hearn and Bridgstock noted in Chapter 3 that the novel solutions generated by advertising agencies draw on an existing body of knowledge (and contacts) in the wider project ecology. The 'embedded creatives' they describe are more likely to innovate incrementally, building on practical certainties within the firm rather than operating outside it and applying their specialists skills as designers to a range of problems and issues inside the firm. In the past, this kind of incremental innovation may have been seen as a lesser form of innovation than the 'big bang' or 'out of the blue' innovation stories that often populate management books. But, according to Nonaka and Zhu's practice of acting upon practical certainties, incremental innovation is an excellent thing for the creative manager to aim for. This dovetails well with an entrepreneuring that seeks to do something rather than getting bogged down in analysis. In our experience, organisations often fail to innovate because they are looking so hard for the big out-of-the-park 'home run' that they neglect the incremental possibilities that might get them at least to 'first base'.

The notion of 'practical certainty' acknowledges that new ideas build incrementally on existing knowledge, and the practice of innovation itself builds upon some necessary building blocks. Interestingly, most of the 'practical certainties' highlighted by Nonaka and Zhu relate to 'uncertainties' – investing in diversity, experimenting and reviewing methods and practices, generating and reviewing options all require us to diversify our approaches to innovation beyond a 'golden mean' between two alternatives, and acknowledge a range and diversity of possibilities. In their chapter on the practice of film-making, Elizabeth Gulledge and her co-authors considered how improvisation and just-in-time innovation are framed by 'minimal structures' set by plans and budgets in Chapter 2. The interface between certainty and uncertainty recalls the 'mind's marshy shore' between sleeping and waking described by Koestler (1970), where dreams and realities collide. Innovation needs a context – we cannot launch into invention without some known starting points – but we also need room for doubt and uncertainty.

As a scientist and writer, Koestler recognised that substantial creativity occurred at the intersection between scientific and artistic innovation as well as within each domain. Schematically, scientific 'discovery' reveals an existing reality; artistic 'creation' makes a new one. Yet both these processes, as outlined in the introduction to this handbook, can overlap. Passive discovery is animated by active creation; creation of the new recasts pre-existing elements. So artists are inspired to create by their discoveries, and scientific discoveries must be interpreted and directed by a deliberate act of creation. Very often the management and organisational examples of innovation in this handbook combine deliberate and passive approaches, and occur between 'creative' and 'non-creative' activities.

Seeking to unravel where and how innovation occurs in our global creative economy in Chapter 5, Lim and Oyama suggested that it is the product of intersecting relationships between Eastern and Western companies, between cosmetics creators and cosmetics brands, between and across musical styles and genres. Similarly, in Chapter 4, Sundbo and Sørensen showed how models of innovation from manufacturing and service industries can be combined in the 'service lab'; the practical certainties of the R&D lab are tempered by the more responsive, adaptive approaches of user-led service innovation.

If 'do something, purposefully' captures the entrepreneurial impulse towards action, 'acting upon practical certainties' describes the innovative process which operates in tandem with that action to create lasting value. Working with the building blocks of practical knowledge, but also allowing for improvisation and doubt, innovation in this handbook is described as adaptive and multi-faceted, drawing on and extending a repertoire of knowledge and skills. Nonaka and Zhu's first two practices suggest how the apparent contradictions between certainty and doubt, between passive discovery and active creation, can be negotiated by a manager employing the concept of timely balance and can light up new pathways for creativity in any organisation.

III. LEADING BY ENGAGING IN GESTURE-RESPONSE PROCESSES

Leadership provides the next step beyond innovative exploration and entrepreneurial action, setting the framework in which creativity can be managed and supported along those new pathways. So, how do leaders employ Nonaka and Zhu's concept of timely balance to facilitate creativity where envisioning and interacting are both key?

Seen from the 'conversation of gesture-response' perspective, originated by the American pragmatist-sociologist George Herbert Mead, leaders make gestures in the form of vision statements, innovation agendas, and so on, which, to have meaning and effect, must be picked up, interpreted and acted upon by 'local agents' among the rank and file of the organisation. Local responses to leaders' gestures are usually varying and surprising, partly because of the diversity among local agents and partly because no rule or policy can cover every contingency. The diverse and surprising local responses will then be picked up as gestures from 'below' by leaders for making their own responses – issuing further gestures. The responding gestures from 'above' are seldom homogenous or consistent either due to differences among leaders as well as further unexpected contingencies.

During such ongoing 'conversation', leaders' gestures can be deliberate and forceful, but they cannot generate effective outcomes alone. In settings where creativity is important, agency is distributed through intra- as well as inter-organisational gesture-response process. No one can deny the significance of Deng's leadership, but without the creative responses from Chinese farmers, Deng's leadership would have come to nought. 3M Corporation's PostIt Notes® were not innovated by a single engineer let alone a CEO or a COO, nor through 'teamwork' or 'joint effort' in the conventional sense, but by distributed agency which made different kinds of contributions at different times and places, with different degrees of involvement and commitment. The upshot is that wise leaders not only lead, they get out of the way and let others lead as the moments come.

As noted above, the gesture-response process is comparable to the 'leading from the middle' philosophy advocated in the Leadership section of this handbook and the approach advocated in Wilson and Proctor-Thomson's Chapter 11 to develop more creativity-friendly leadership theory. In all of these instances, leadership is not the preserve of the leaders at 'the top'; others must be in on the conversation. Indeed, notions of 'distributed leadership' (especially in the arts and creative industries) and 'followership' (or 'first follower theory'), if they are taken seriously, start to shine a light on the collective nature of leadership.

For distributed leadership to operate from below, leaders at the top need to provide channels and opportunities for creative ideas, and indeed leaders, to flow upwards through the organisation and influence top-level strategy. In Chapter 13, Vikki Heywood's description of her stewardship of the Royal Shakespeare Company, alongside Michael Boyd, provided a practical model of how this might be achieved. In order for leadership gestures to be understood and acted upon, it is necessary to define a language and ethos within which gestures can be interpreted and embodied, and to trust the followers to shape the leadership agenda. Without an 'agentic response' from below, leadership from above can never be more than an empty gesture. As Wilson and Proctor-Thomson observe, 'visionary, transformative' leadership might not be the best way (and so should certainly not be the only way) to mobilise active, independent and creative followers; followers too must become 'empowered' and accorded 'agency and freedom to act' in order to take the initiative themselves.

The diversity of models and perspectives on leadership in this section of the handbook underlines a key argument throughout this handbook: there can be no perfect or 'best practice' approach to management and creativity. Leadership behaviour draws on a repertoire of signals and symbols to communicate a vision; if gestures are ignored or misinterpreted, the leader cannot blame others in the organisation, he or she must offer something different to kick-start a new conversation. And such gestures are only meaningful or effective within a context. As with Lucy Küng's analysis of Michael Eisner's leadership at Disney, outlined in Chapter 10, the repertoire must move with the times, and what works in one scenario may become counterproductive in another.

There are obvious challenges here for how leadership is taught, especially as part of the typical business school MBA curriculum. Here Richard Hall and David Grant's experiences described in Chapter 12 concur with Nonaka and Zhu's argument that educating leaders is not about the transfer of best practice theories, but about seeking to put students in situations where they must lead and then help them mature as they develop their responses. By the same token, the first task of creative leadership may be to work as a team and stimulate creativity in others. In turn, the first task of a leadership curriculum is to stimulate a variety of leadership styles and approaches, and to develop an ethos which is 'modest, measured, authentic, collective, collaborative and compassionate'.

We first proposed 'leadership from the middle' as an alternative to 'top–down leadership'. However, Zhu and Nonaka's formulation of 'gesture-response process' suggests an additional insight: that leadership is a process located in the channels between leaders and followers, drawing upon an exchange of diverse inputs and responses from both sides. The choice of styles and skills assumed by both leaders and followers will be shaped by their experience of being in the middle of events, not above or outside them.

This leads us to what we see as Nonaka and Zhu's insights related to creative organisation: that it should be an adaptive process which is shaped by experience.

IV. ORGANISING BY LEARNING THROUGH CONSEQUENCES

Despite our best efforts, often what we try does not work and attempts at innovating, entrepreneuring, leading and organising to create lasting added value may be considered to have failed. This is a humbling admission, and one that might be demoralising, unless we recognise that such failures can be pathways to success, if we learn from them. Humans are failing and learning beings. To the neurophysiologist Warren Sturgis McCulloch, 'To have proved a hypothesis false is indeed the peak of knowledge.' To the developmental psychologist Jean Piaget, knowledge (incorporating learning quickly through failure) is a 'higher form of evolution'.

Seen from such an evolutionary perspective, we act, the world resists; we construct, nature destructs; we propose, reality disposes; but during the process we gain 'robust fits' and accomplish valued novelty. As to those proposals that pass evolutionary selection and work (at that point in time, in that context), we keep them, and act upon them, until justifiable doubts rise and better alternatives emerge. Creativity is therefore not just evolution, it is humanised evolution; it is not just what emerges, it is emergence with a human touch. We act, then we learn, therefore we are.

Creative organisations, in this handbook, are organisations capable of acting, absorbing and processing a diversity of experiences, including failure, adapting and moving on. The arts organisations which 'learned to fail' through their experience of working with digital technology, described by Chris Bilton in Chapter 7, provided one such example; learning to fail and learning from failure, while described as elements of entrepreneurship, are also characteristics of a creative organisation. Giovanni Schiuma's description in Chapter 17 of organisations absorbing and learning from 'arts-based interventions' provides further examples of this. These interventions add value to the organisation by helping to develop the emotional intelligence and openness to allow employees to look in different ways, express themselves differently and develop their intrinsic motivation to create.

The key, according to Nonaka and Zhu, as with creative leadership, lies in seeing organisation as a verb rather than a noun – an active, evolving organising process, not a static organisational chart or model. Failure is necessary in order to shape organisational processes and ensure a more robust, timely fit with the changing external environment. An organisation which cannot own up to and learn from its mistakes is liable to repeat them.

The interplay between experience and action extends into networks and relationships beyond the single organisation. Especially in the creative industries, as Doris Eikhof reminds us, 'transorganisational' learning and knowledge transfer have become increasingly important. The First World War-style military analogy of the organisation as a kind of fortress, buttressing its internal structure and culture against the world, is replaced by a more fluid interaction across boundaries. Deadlines and constraints may provide necessary scaffolding and boundaries for the creative process, but these are not fixed and are a product of temporary relationships and collaborations towards a particular goal. Relatedly, it is overly simplistic to assume that 'open space' equates with creative freedom and structure with constraint. As Thanem and Värlander noted in Chapter 15, our relationship with an organisation, and the physical environment which embodies it, is more nuanced and 'tactical' than this straightforward assumption allows. Through their analogy of free running (*parkour*), they argue that rather than trying to design and construct organisations to shape creative behaviour, organisations should plan less and allow workers to 'transgress' the organisational space, finding channels through boundaries and moving between open and closed space. There are echoes here of Eikhof's transorganisational networks and of Levi-Strauss's 'bricolage', with organisational dynamics emerging from interactions and relationships between and outside organisations rather than from a single, fixed entity.

All of our contributors to the creative organisation section of the handbook advocate a mix of 'open' and 'closed' organisational spaces and practices, and blur the boundaries of the single 'stand-alone' organisation. Boundary-crossing has long been associated with creative thinking in the work of Margaret Boden, Keith Sawyer, even Edward de Bono. Oliver, Heracleous and Jacobs in Chapter 16 argued for a fluidity and pragmatism in the design and application of organisational structures and processes which in turn can shape different ways of thinking, from divergent to convergent. They relate this paradoxical combination of divergent and convergent processes and structures to 'hybrid thinking' and 'serious play', an approach capable of opening up to diverse inputs but also of focusing and integrating these elements towards a common purpose. The combination of thinking styles described in their cases of serious play and the learning gained through the experiences and outcomes of their simulations are great examples of the adaptive learning process promoted by Nonaka and Zhu in action.

V. BUILDING ADAPTIVE CAPABILITY THROUGH DIVERSITY ACROSS THE SYSTEM

So, from a practical point of view one can aim to manage the paradoxical elements underlying creativity through the first four practices of timely balance:

1. One can actively acknowledge that the entrepreneurial spirit is absolutely key to the creative organisation, do something entrepreneurial in line with an overarching purpose, rather than analysing the spirit out of things, and encourage others to do the same.
2. One can encourage innovation that builds out from already existing practical certainties, that gets the ball rolling incrementally based on previous experiences.

3.   One can see leading creativity as a conversation involving people from all parts of an organisation and seek to encourage others to lead creative initiatives where possible and open up channels where such initiatives can be discussed.
4.   And, one can seek to create an organisation where learning through different experiences, perspectives and challenges (including failure) is highly valued.

These are all useful things to do and they can realistically be done with a little confidence, skill, good judgement and support.

But the fifth practice takes us back to the heart of Zhu's critique of the bisociative model of creativity and management described at the beginning of this chapter. How are managers, practically, to sustain an organisation that encompasses seeming contradictory elements over time? Because the balance we seek for all elements of creativity will not be timely unless they adjust as the contexts shift and times change, the key to the process overall and to all the four paradoxical elements within it lies in 'adaptive capability'.

The institutional economist Douglas North argues that in an uncertain world where no one can fully know future concerns, economic perform- ance over time depends on adaptive efficiency that stems chiefly from sufficient diversity of options and resources. The same applies, we would suggest, to creativity and its management. To put it another way, for evolution to work there must be variety to select from. Enriching inputs at hand is hence the key for survival because it supplies more capability to answer to unpredictable challenges. In market economies, in order to select rather than being selected by environmental forces, firms must gen- erate internal variation, or what old-fashioned cyberneticists called 'requi- site variety'. As 3M CEO George Buckley puts it: 'in a creative company, you want to give as much variability as possible.'

All this points to increasing investment in diversity, but investing in diversity is not cost-free, hence it needs to be handled wisely. Many organisations today invest heavily in demographic, or what we might call 'surface', diversity in terms of sex, age and national origin. However, it is useful to reflect on what really adds to creative responses, and that is 'substantial' diversity: diversity in experiences, insights and mindscapes. Recruiting two young computer science graduates, one from MIT in Boston and another from Tsinghua in Beijing, you may get only limited diversity. Encourage a marketing professor from IIM in Bangalore, and a medical surgeon and a factory owner from the same suburb and ethnic background to work together, and the responses to problems and sub- sequent capability development could be eye-opening. Hence, what is important is not diversity *per se*, but the depth of diversity and, above all, purposeful interaction and recombination within and between diverse bodies. Not just one set of experiences, not just one type of process, not just one type of space.

We began this handbook by contrasting the monoculture of a group of financiers on the board of Arsenal FC with the diverse collection on the board of Bayern Munich. A creative model of human evolution and adaptation depends on variety; just as 'natural selection' proceeds through mutations and deviations, not perfect repetition, a creative model of selective adaptation requires what Chris Steyaert calls 'anomalies'. So an organisation which can encompass different perspectives and people – in innovating, in entrepreneuring, in leading and in organising – is more likely to adapt and learn and to achieve timely balance over time than one where everybody agrees.

The key criterion here, as Zhu observes, is that diversity should be 'purposeful', just like the doing something (rather than doing just anything) that represented the entrepreneuring spark. It should be geared towards achieving new combinations and relationships, not atrophying into separatism and opposition. The costs of investing in diversity are human as well as financial, and need to be weighed against the benefit of meaningful difference. Here differences in experience and expertise are more likely to yield new insights than demographic variations. A truly diverse workforce – referred to by Richard E. Caves as the 'motley crew' principle of creativity – can generate new options and allow creative management to adapt and evolve. Variation and diversity allow managers to pick different elements from the creative management system, from innovation and entrepreneurship to leadership and organisation. Diversity-driven adaptation allows us to build new purposeful combinations from these elements and apply them to the task in hand. And this fifth practice, building capability through promoting substantive diversity into each dimension of the creative process, should feed into everything.

While we are not saying that things will be as tidy and linear as Figure 18.2's attempt to represent the five timely balance practices to the creative management process, we hope that it may provide readers with a simple heuristic device that can be remembered and adapted in practice.

* * *

We have outlined five practices for promoting timely balance in creative management and the management of creativity. Unlike many of the seven possibilities we ruled out early on, here they add up to a philosophy that is not mystical but realistic, that is not merely about talking creativity but

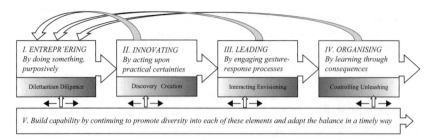

Figure 18.2   Five 'timely balance' practices toward the practical
management of creativity

actioning it. It is not a quick fix, but rather aimed at long-term systematic development and success. Where the bisociative framework developed in our introduction and used to organise this handbook might appear as a set of alternatives, extreme positions to be avoided or switched between, in this final chapter Nonaka and Zhu's model of pragmatic strategy has injected some dynamism. The blending of diverse options, the wise selection from a palette of possibilities, is above all *purposeful* – driven by the needs of the enterprise – but also *adaptive*, learning from experience rather than attempting to plan and predict every possible outcome in advance. In the design of this handbook we have tried to achieve this eclecticism, but we hope that readers also make purposeful connections between chapters and sections. The aim is always to avoid a one-sided view of management or creativity, or any single formula such as the 'golden mean' or 'just enough' tension or 'perfect balance'. Readers can judge for themselves which elements are most useful to them right now and in the future.

Management and creativity are not as straightforward as you may have expected when you began this book or as they are sometimes presented in others. But, after all, they should not be thought of as mystical or exceptional either – they are best defined through practice, by plunging into the world, trying things out, making mistakes and learning from them, to find out what works best – for you. This might entail what Van der Heijden (1996) called 'strategic conversation' – a dialogue between theory and practice, between the models and methods we have enumerated through this handbook and your own particular experiences and contexts. Through conversations and experience we can bridge between divergent perspectives and ideas and choose wisely from the options available to suit the times we are in. The role of the creative manager is to engineer and facilitate these strategic conversations, between what is theoretically possible and what is practically achievable. Creativity and management bring together apparently contradictory mindsets and processes which defy any single, definitive summary – in the end we must choose, as wisely as we can, act and adapt.

NOTE

1. For more detailed elaboration and case studies on each of these philosophies, see Nonaka and Zhu (2012).

REFERENCES

Bilton, C. and S. Cummings (2010), *Creative strategy: reconnecting business and innovation*, Chichester, UK: Wiley.

Grabher, G. (2004), 'Temporary architectures of learning: knowledge governance in project ecologies', *Organization Studies*, **25**, 1491–514.

Koestler, A. (1970), *The act of creation*, London: Hutchinson.

Nonaka, I. and Z. Zhu (2012), *Pragmatic strategy: Eastern wisdom, global success*, Cambridge: Cambridge University Press.

Van der Heijden, K.A. (1996), *Scenarios: the art of strategic conversation*, Chichester, UK: Wiley.

Zhu, Z. (2010), 'Book review: Strategy without design, complexity and organisational reality, creative strategy', *Organisation Studies* **31**(12), 1752–7.

Index

'Chris Bilton's and Stephen Cummings' *Handbook of Management and Creativity* collects some of the very best research on creativity and why and how it matters to companies and their management. It is an important addition to our understanding of the management of creativity and talented and creative people.'
    – Richard Florida, University of Toronto, Canada, New York University, USA and author, *Rise of the Creative Class*

'In many organisations creativity is so often seen as the preserve of a small number of people with "artistic temperaments" but in my experience all sorts of people have creative abilities which can be used to the benefit of a "creative" organisation. The task of a manager is to find ways of exploiting this. This *Handbook* provides the reader with insights to help them and others to promote the kind of creativity that adds real value.'
    – Greg Dyke, Chair, British Film Institute; Chair, Football Association; Chancellor, University of York, UK and Director-General of the BBC 2000–2004

'Creativity and management are often thought of as two opposite worlds. Management is dull control and creativity is exciting liberation. This exciting *Handbook* put this assumption into question. The contributors show how creativity can be managed and how creative management might be. It provides a valuable resource for anyone interested in how organizations seek to create novelty, and some of the challenges this might give rise to.'
    – André Spicer, City University London, UK

'Bilton and Cummings' *Handbook of Management and Creativity* takes two areas which we often view as diametrically opposite and brings them together in a unique and insightful manner, the core idea being that both creativity and management are essential in effective creative processes. Drawing on research from a wide range of interesting contexts including movie-making, this book will be essential reading for both students and scholars interested in examining the entwining relationship between creativity and management.'
    – Jean Clarke, Leeds University, UK

'In using the concept of "bisociation", contributors highlight ambiguities, paradoxes and contradictions in the management of creativity. Such an approach demonstrates the complexity of creative processes and the challenges in harnessing creative energies. The wide range of industries and organizations in different geographical regions presented offer insights in a global perspective. It is amazing that this *Handbook* can address the comprehensive range of issues in a coherent manner.'
    – Can-Seng Ooi, Copenhagen Business School, Denmark

'What is the relationship of creativity and innovation to management? This extensive and extremely well researched *Handbook* provides fresh insights into this crucially important question. The chapters in the *Handbook* do so with academic depth and gusto, and together provide an excellent overview of various approaches to creativity and innovation across different academic perspectives, methods and empirical contexts. The *Handbook* will form an important resource and reference for researchers, students and practitioners with an interest in creativity, innovation and entrepreneurship.'
    – Joep Cornelissen, VU University Amsterdam, The Netherlands, University of Leeds, UK and Consulting Editor, *Journal of Management Studies*